European Immigrants and American Society

A Collection of Studies and Dissertations

•

Edited by
Timothy Walch and
Edward R. Kantowicz

•

A Garland Series

EDUCATION AND GREEK IMMIGRANTS IN CHICAGO, 1892–1973

•

A Study in Ethnic Survival

•

Andrew T. Kopan

GARLAND PUBLISHING, INC. • NEW YORK & LONDON • 1990

Library of Congress Cataloging-in-Publication Data

Kopan, Andrew T.
Education and Greek immigrants in Chicago, 1892–1973:
a study in ethnic survival/ Andrew T. Kopan.
p. cm.—(European immigrants and American society)
"A Garland series"—Ser. t. p.
Thesis (Ph. D.)—University of Chicago, 1974.
Includes bibliographical references.
ISBN 0-8240-7425-4 (alk. paper)
1. Greek Americans—Illinois—Chicago—History.
2. Greek Americans—Education—Illinois—Chicago—
History. 3. Education—Illinois—Chicago—History.
4. Chicago (Ill.)—Social conditions. I. Title. II. Series.
F548.9.G7K49   1990
371.97'8930773'11—dc20   90-21602

Printed on acid-free, 250-year-life paper.
Manufactured in the United States of America

Design by
Julie Threlkeld

Dedicated to:

Tom C. Kopan (1885–1939)
Katherine Mehos Kopan (1894–1984)
Pericles A. Orphanos (1899–1978)
Tula Siaramantis Orphanos (1911–1982)

Who lived the Greek immigrant experience in America

PREFACE

Πατρός τε καί μητρός καί τῶν ἄλλων προγόνων
τιμιώτερον ἐστι καί ἀγιώτερον ἡ πατρίς.

Socrates

This ancient injunction that one's country is more honorable and
sacred than one's parents has been an ideal which Greek immigrants kept
close to their hearts. Mindful that they were descended from a glorious
nation, Greek immigrants left no effort unturned to inculcate into their American-born children lasting respect for their ethnic heritage.

Growing up Greek in the multi-ethnic city of Chicago meant continuous exposure to the various informal and formal educational agencies
established by Greek immigrants to transmit the cultural legacy. At the
same time, often it meant confrontation with other Americans concerning the
reality and validity of one's ethnic background. This study is an attempt
to better understand the Socratic ideal and its relationship to the American
social order while remaining free from the spirit of filiopiety.

During the 1960s the social climate in the United States was supportive of such an undertaking and served as an incentive for my research.
Blacks struggled for self-identity; other ethnic groups were attempting to
reaffirm their self-concept. It seemed to be an appropriate time to investigate the raison d'etre of Greek identity and its survival in America. But
writing on identity, survival, and educational adjustment of a particular
ethnic group to American life is not an end in itself; the test of any given
study is its relevance to American society as a whole. Hopefully, this research offers yet another insight into the process by which immigrants are
transformed into Americans. By investigating the forces that have impinged
upon immigrants and their progeny—some working for the narrowest kind of
"100 percent Americanism," some emanating from the nostalgic desire to
maintain their identity, and others moving toward a blending of culture without the total obliteration of any—avenues for inquiry into the complicated
process of the creation of Americans may be charted. In the educational
aspirations and adjustment of an ethnic group, such as the Greeks in Chicago, may in part, be found some of the answers to this process.

iii

This dissertation could not have been brought to completion without the assistance and cooperation of many individuals. My greatest debt of gratitude is to Professor Robert L. McCaul of the Department of Education at the University of Chicago, who, as chairman of my advisory committee, provided unfailing encouragement and support throughout the long years of research. I am deeply grateful for his critical analysis of the manuscript and his insightful counsel. I am also indebted to Professor Donald A. Erickson, formerly of the Department of Education at University of Chicago and presently at Simon Fraser University in Vancouver, Canada, and Professor Richard J. Storr, formerly of the Department of History at University of Chicago and now at York University in Toronto, Canada, for their review of the manuscript and helpful suggestions, as members of the advisory committee. Responsibility for shortcomings which remain, despite the sage counsel of my mentors, is solely mine.

Gratitude is expressed to Professor Robert J. Havighurst of the Department of Education at University of Chicago for encouraging me to pursue research in ethnicity long before the project materialized. Likewise, appreciation is expressed to Professor Andrew M. Greeley, formerly of the Department of Sociology at University of Chicago, for his advice.

Sources used were diverse and extensive, and unfortunately, restricts me in acknowledging everyone by name. To the many gracious participants--interviewees, colleagues, and reference personnel--at University of Chicago, Chicago Public Library, Chicago Historical Society, Immigrant Archives Center at University of Minnesota, New York Public Library, Greek Orthodox Archdiocese in New York, Greek Orthodox churches and communal schools, Jane Addams Memorial Collection Center, Immigrants' Service League, Library of Congress, and to many others, I am most grateful. Special appreciation is expressed to Ione A. DuVal and Bessie Spirides for use of their resource collections; and to Estelle Kanakis and George Beres for their masterful assistance in the production of the manuscript.

To my wife Alice, I am deeply indebted for her tangible and intangible services which are so essential in maintaining one's perspective amidst scholarship. Without her countless hours of steadfast work, unequivocal support, inspiration, and commitment--the completion of this dissertation could not have become a reality.

iv

TABLE OF CONTENTS

TABLE 1

GENERAL IMMIGRATION TO THE UNITED STATES, 1820-1970

Period	Number of Immigrants
1820-1830	176,473
1831-1840	640,086
1841-1850	1,702,605
1851-1860	2,940,257
1861-1870	2,660,189
1871-1880	2,812,191
1881-1890	5,246,613
1891-1900	3,687,564
1901-1910	8,795,386
1911-1920	5,735,811
1921-1930	4,107,209
1931-1940	528,431
1941-1950	1,035,039
1951-1960	2,515,479
1961-1970	3,321,677

SOURCE: U. S. Department of Commerce, Bureau of
the Census, Historical Statistics of the United States:
Colonial Times to 1957 (Washington, D. C.: Government
Printing Office, 1961), pp. 56-57; U. S. Department of
Justice, Immigration and Naturalization Service, Annual
Reports.

NOTE: Statistics for Greek immigration are presented
in chapter 1.

LIST OF TABLES

LIST OF FIGURES

CHAPTER I

THE GREEK IMMIGRANTS IN HISTORICAL PERSPECTIVE

The Old World Background

To understand the Greek immigrants who settled in Chicago beginning in the 1890s, it is necessary to know something about their land of
origin--Hellas, as the Greeks call their country. Familiarity with geographic, political, social, economic, religious, and educational conditions
of Greece will provide insight into why Greeks came to the United States
and what prompted their particular adjustment to the American milieu. Furthermore, it affords an understanding of why Greek immigrants were determined to develop informal and formal educational systems which would
provide for participation in American economic life while perpetuating ethnic
identity and survival. As will be shown in this study, a subculture evolved
which was different from that brought from Greece, yet not part of the mass
American culture. An overview of the Old World background of the Greek
immigrants follows.

Geographical Description

When considering the nature of a country in its historical framework,
it is necessary to look for a man-land relationship. Man and his activities,
whether economic, political, or social, are distributed in various patterns
over the landscape. The physical environment is a major determinant of the
direction in which a people will develop, and holds the resource base upon
which much of the economic potential of a culture depends. Therefore, the
problems faced by the inhabitants of Greece were determined by causal relationships to their physical geography.

Approximately 80 percent of Greece is mountainous, and one-fifth
of its land arable. The three thousand mile-rugged seacoast has deep ba-
sins, numerous inlets, bays, and islands--"a naked land with all the bones

1

showing." The present area of Greece, including its islands, is 50,944 square miles--slightly smaller than the state of Illinois. In 1969, Greece's population was estimated at 8,834,560. Between 1900 and 1920, the period of heaviest migration to the United States, its population was under 5,000,000, of which 3,000,000 lived in "Old, or Free Greece." With frontier expansion resulting from wars, the majority of Greeks came to live within the national state. The bringing together of these scattered Greeks of the Near East within the ring-fence of the enlarged Greek state was a reversal of the historic past. Throughout the centuries, Greeks had dispersed outside Hellas proper; therefore, moving inward toward a geographic center was a new phenomenon in Greek history.[1]

Approximately 1,500,000 Greeks have emigrated from Greece: 600,000 to the United States, 450,000 to Cyprus, 270,000 to western Europe, 100,000 to Africa, and 80,000 to Asia. In 1965, the population density of Greece was 166 per square mile compared with 52 for the United States and 60 for the world.[2] Historically, Greece's disequilibrium between population and resources has been an important factor in the continuous phenomenon of emigration.

Political Development

An understanding of the political turmoil of Greece throughout the centuries helps give some insight into political forces which influenced the

---

[1] Information about the origins and development of the Greek people may be secured from the following standard sources, which, unless otherwise noted, are in agreement upon the matters cited: A. Jardé, The Formation of the Greek People (New York: Alfred A. Knopf, 1926), pp. 55-77; Will Durant, The Story of Civilization, vol. 2: The Life of Greece (New York: Simon and Schuster, 1939), pp. 3-64; William H. McNeill, The Rise of the West: A History of the Human Community (Chicago: University of Chicago Press, 1963), pp. 188-205; and Pierre Lévêque, The Greek Adventure (Cleveland: World Publishing Co., 1968), pp. 9-86.

[2] U. S., Department of Commerce, Bureau of the Census, Statistical Abstract of the United States (Washington, D.C.: Government Printing Office, 1965), p. 910.

course of Greek culture and ethnic survival. Although Greecé claims close to a four thousand year continuous span, its documented history does not commence until 776 B.C., the date of the first Olympic games.[1] The diverse groups of Greeks were ruled by tyrants, especially during 600 to 500 B.C. Gradually, democracy evolved with constitutions, social laws, equal rights in court, and the privilege of being tried by jury. Fifth century B.C. was called the Golden Age of Pericles, Socrates, Plato, and Aristotle.

In 336 B.C., Alexander the Great became king of Macedon, and in his brief thirteen year reign united the Greek city-states, conquered Persia, Phoenicia, Palestine, Egypt, and practically the rest of the known world. However, in 46 B.C., Greece was conquered by Rome, became a Roman province, but, in turn, Hellenized the Romans. In 395 A.D., Greece became a part of the Byzantine Empire, which was saturated with Greek ideas and became the center of civilization for over one thousand years. During this expansive period, Greece was a buffer state protecting southern Europe against the eastern hordes.

With the fall of Constantinople in 1453, Greece was conquered by the Turks. This began Hellenism's dark ages of four hundred years of misrule, taxation, atrocities, massacres, and conscription of children to be raised as Mohammedan soldiers.[2] Bands of Greeks known as Klephts main-

---

[1] Historical information regarding the political development of Greece has been secured from the following standard sources: C.C. Felton, Greece, Ancient and Modern, 2 vols. (Boston: Ticknor and Fields, 1867); George Finlay, History of Greece 146 A.D.-1864 A.D., 7 vols. (Oxford: Clarendon Press, 1877); Constantine Paparrigopoulos, Epitomos historia tou Hellinikou ethnous [Abridged history of the Greek nation], 2 vols. (Athens: Demetrios Demetrakos Publishing House, 1952); Robert Byron, The Byzantine Achievement: An Historical Perspective A.D. 330-1453 (New York: Alfred A. Knopf, 1929); A. A. Vasiliev, History of the Byzantine Empire 324-1453 (Madison: University of Wisconsin Press, 1952); William Miller, A History of the Greek People, 1821-1921 (London: Methuen & Co., 1922); C. M. Woodhouse, A Short History of Modern Greece (New York: Frederick A. Praeger Publishers, 1968); Apostolos E. Vacalopoulos, Origins of the Greek Nation, 1204-1461 (New Brunswick, N. J.: Rutgers University Press, 1970); and Douglas Dakin, The Unification of Greece, 1770-1923 (New York: St. Martin's Press, 1972).

[2] For a description of the child-tribute trained to become the hated Janissaries fighting their own kin, see Felton, 2:397-98. For a scholarly account, see Speros Vryonis, Jr., "Isidore Glabas and the Turkish Devshirme," Speculum 31 (July 1956): 433-43 and his "Seljuk Gulams and Ottoman Devshirmes," Der Islam 41 (October 1965): 224-52; also see S. M. Sophocles, A History of Greece (Thessaloniki, Greece: Institute for Balkan Studies, 1961), chap. 3.

tained a semi-independent existence by hiding in mountains and raiding Turkish territory.[1] As the Turkish severity became unbearable, the Greeks revolted on various occasions. With the aid of the Great Powers, the 1821 Greek revolt succeeded. In the Peloponnesus they massacred 12,000 Turks. The Turks answered massacre with massacre. Slain in Chios were 23,000 Greeks and another 47,000 were sold into slavery.[2] In 1827, Russia, along with France and England intervened, and the Turks were defeated. Greece gained independence, but received only one-third of the territory it claimed and but one-fifth of its people in "Old Greece." Since Greece had no royal family, the Great Powers forced the new nation to accept a seventeen-year-old Bavarian prince, Otho, as king. He ruled as a German, and crushed several revolutions with the aid of foreign soldiers, thereby wounding Greek pride. In 1843, he was forced to sign a constitution providing for two governing houses. Members of the chamber were elected, but the senate was largely under the crown's control.

During the Crimean War, Greece thought it opportune to seize Turkish territory, but France and England would not permit it. In 1862, another revolution drove the king from his throne. After much hawking over the crown, Prince George of Denmark accepted kingship, and ruled until 1913. Progress and constitutional reform began in 1864. A new democratic constitution was adopted, and England ceded the Ionian Islands to Greece. In 1881, following a brief war with Turkey, Greece acquired the province of Thessaly. Disregarding the advice of foreign diplomats, it went to war again with Turkey in 1897, over Crete. The "Thirty Day War" was disastrous. Greece lost part of its territory and had to pay an indemnity of $20,000,000. Crete became

---

[1] For a cursory account, see Felton, 2:390-407, and Woodhouse, Short History of Modern Greece, pp. 99-124.

[2] A first hand account of this struggle is to be found in Samuel G. Howe, An Historical Sketch of the Greek Revolution (New York: White, Gallaher and White, 1828). A year-by-year account of the revolution is to be found in Harris J. Booras, Hellenic Independence and America's Contribution to the Cause (Rutland, Vt.: The Tuttle Co., 1934), pp. 21-152. A comprehensive view is given in C. M. Woodhouse, The Greek War of Independence in its Historical Setting (London: Hutchinson's University Library, 1952). A modern account of the war is to be found in Douglas Dakin, The Greek Struggle for Independence 1821-1833 (Berkeley: University of California Press, 1973).

autonomous, but remained under the suzerainty of the Sultan. Later, Greece took part in both Balkan wars, and gained 18,000 square miles and 1,800,000 people. After much hesitation, Greece entered World War I and gained additional territory. However, much of the new territory was lost later in a war with Turkey, with Turkey insisting on a forceful exchange of population.

Political upheavals and changes of premiers in Greece have been rapid since World War I. The king was exiled as a result of a struggle between King Constantine I and Eleutherios Venizelos, a liberal prime minister who opposed the monarchy. Constantine's son, George II, was forced to quit in 1923, and in 1925 Greece proclaimed itself a republic. In 1935, another revolution restored the monarchy and George II to the throne. During World War II, Greece was attacked by Italy, later by Germany, and after a heroic resistance, was occupied by Axis powers between 1941 and 1944. Greece emerged from the occupation only to be convulsed by a civil war. It was not until after the promulgation of the Truman Doctrine in 1947, with American economic and military aid, that Greece thwarted the Communist threat and began to recover from the ravages of war. Greece's chronic political instability continued until 1967, when a military dictatorship assumed power. It was deposed in 1974. A constitutional government has been reinstituted at this time. Currently, Greece is involved with Turkey in the struggle over Cyprus.

It must be remembered that domestic politics and controversies are an integral part of Greece's lifestyle. Political conflicts reached floodtide proportions in the late nineteenth and twentieth centuries, and served as another reason for Greeks to emigrate to America. The homeland's political dissension and division continued in America, as the Greeks developed their local ethnic communities as described in future chapters.

Social Traits

The Greeks have gone through a social development similar to other southeastern European peoples--as masters and slaves, nobles and serfs, landlords and peasants, absorbing large numbers of foreign stock, and subject being to foreign rulers. Yet, the Greek way of life differs from other Balkan peoples in ethnic origin, language, ideology, and a distinct heritage. Jaeger states that the "world-wide historical importance of the Greeks as educators was derived from their . . . awareness of the position of the individual in the community."[1] Another writer says:

> Nowhere in antiquity had the individual man a greater value, nowhere was the organization of social life, by the action of the law itself, more favorable to the full development of the individual [than in ancient Greece.][2]

One of the most noticeable traits of Greeks has been their extreme individualism. It has manifested itself in jealousy, rivalry, factiousness, and self-assertion; on its positive side, it found expression in the Periclean democracy of the rule of the many, where peoples' voices were supreme in the smallest detail of political life. An American observer of the Greco-Turkish War of 1897 wrote about Greek individualism by describing a funeral procession he witnessed:

> Men walk together on the street, but do not keep step. A Greek funeral procession presents a disorderly and individualistic appearance. The people go on foot. Each seems to be strolling on his own account. There is no fixed order of procedure. Everyone does what seems to him good. If a halt occurs in the proceeding, a debate may ensue. Three out of four of the bearers will prove to be orators. There is no person in authority. Five or six different ones are giving orders or making suggestions at the same time. The same popular trait shows itself wherever masses of people are assembled.[3]

This passion for individual liberty has made group effort difficult to achieve, and sometimes brought about catastrophic results among Chicago's Greek immigrants, as they disputed over communal issues, as shown later in this study. Their insatiable curiosity and zeal for inquiry makes them fearlessly discuss a subject which they know nothing about with one who has

---

[1]See Werner Jaeger, Paidea: The Ideals of Greek Culture, 2nd ed., vol. 1: Greece: The Mind of Athens, trans. G. Highet (New York: Oxford University Press, 1960), p. xviii.

[2]Jardé, p. xii.

[3]Benjamin I. Wheeler,"The Modern Greek as a Fighting Man," North American Review 164 (April 1897): 609.

devoted a lifetime to its study.[1] Even the illiterate peasant has a master of speech. He greets one with a direct probe, "ti neon--what's new?" and awaits an answer. This question is posed often by Greek-Americans as they meet each other in social gatherings. Urban Greeks have been avid readers of history and regard it as a recreational activity.

Sophism made Greece both great and small as a culture. Education was a question of receiving, displaying, and professing "wisdom." Many Greeks perceive themselves as potential statesmen, and their dissatisfaction with conditions results in an intense interest in politics. Also it accentuates a genuine spirit of democracy which has prohibited the development of any caste system in Greece's long and troubled history.

Although Greeks are religious and superstitious, the church never has dominated their secular lives. Formal religion means faithful adherence to dogma and sacramental practices. Unknown to Greeks in Greece are the numerous social organizations attached to religious life in the West. The church calendar listed the feastdays, which were extensive, and served as a source of social interaction. Superstitions survived, especially in the rural areas, and were incorporated in the early Christian church.

Through the ages, conceit and pride have been essential clues to Greek character. All persons not Greek were labelled barbarians. Writers have charged that a Greek's vanity is his pitfall. In contemplating the

---

[1] Information about the social traits and ethos of Greek people has been secured from standard sources, which, unless otherwise noted, are in agreement with the matters cited: Fairchild, chap. 1; Burgess, chap. 6; Henry M. Baird, Modern Greece (New York: Harper & Bros., 1856); Z. Duckett Ferriman, Home Life in Hellas: Greece and the Greeks (London: Mills & Boon, 1910), chaps. 3-4; Enestine Friedl, Vasilika: A Village in Modern Greece (New York: Holt, Rinehart & Winston, 1962); Lucy M. J. Garnett, Greece of the Hellenes (New York: Charles Scribner's Sons, 1914); Lacey, Social Heredity, passim; John Cuthbert Lawson, Modern Greek Folklore and Ancient Greek Religion: A Study in Survivals (New Hyde Park, New York: University Books, 1964); George A. Megas, Greek Calendar Customs (Athens: Press and Information Department, Prime Minister's Office, 1958); William Miller, Greek Life in Town and Country (London: G. Newnes, 1905); Rennell Rodd, The Customs and Lore of Modern Greece (London: David Scott, 1892); and Irwin T. Sanders, Rainbow in the Rock: The People of Rural Greece (Cambridge: Harvard University Press, 1962).

greatness of Greece's past, the Greek fails to perceive the gulf which separates him from it. In the beginning of the twentieth century, the Greeks were imbued with the Great Idea of recapturing Constantinople and resuscitating the Byzantine Empire. They spoke of Europe being located elsewhere. Foreigners were tolerated and liked, but lacked the essential qualities which constituted Hellenic superiority.

The average rural Greek does not overwork. His existence is interrupted often by holidays and "namesdays." Every saint has his day of celebration, and persons with the saint's name are obligated to hold an open house and feast, a practice that continues in the United States in many Greek homes. It was not uncommon to have farming, industry, and business come to a halt for village celebrations. Poverty has been a way of life for peasants and laborers, who often lived in one-room houses with dirt floors. Food is coarse, consisting chiefly of vegetables and bread. Meat is a luxury to be had on special holidays or for special guests.

Along with individualism, the Greek value system focuses upon family loyalty. Underlying all institutions of Greek society is a highly-developed sense of philotimo (individual self-esteem). It was a primary factor in regulating behavior and a source of ethical and moral standards. The word philotimo derives from the concept of honor, dignity and, in a more extended sense, social worth and rank. A person is said to have philotimo if he places matters of honor, his good name, and his social position above all other, often more profitable considerations.

In such a setting, the family is the focus of social values. A person is judged as the representative of a family, and his actions, be they honorable or dishonorable reflect upon parents, siblings, and extended kin. Despite the value placed on freedom and self-sufficiency, there is little or no virtue attached to being independent from one's family. In the villages, the punctilious regard for local traditions and customs is valued as high as family loyalty, and is expected from every member of the community, including those who had left, then returned as successful men.

Personal and collective defeat tend to be attributed to external factors such as God, fate, or nature, rather than to personal inadequacies. Criticism of oneself or of individual shortcomings of others constitutes an insult to philotimo. Dignified behavior rests upon the assertion of masculinity, social rank, and the right to be treated with equal esteem by others.

Courage, hardiness, skill, and generosity are valued male attributes. In this context, a "true" man proves his courage by meeting a challenge and seizing every opportunity to prove himself. He takes risks in a spirit of gambling, for the sake of the risk itself rather than for the material gain it may offer. Female honor is mostly associated with sexual modesty. To be regarded as respectable in such an environment, a woman has to be a virgin and a sedate wife; indiscretion draws strong disapproval.

Work represents the personal fulfillment of a function. Diligence depends upon self-discipline and free initiative. In contrast to the Calvinistic notion that through work man expiates his original sin, the Greek belief is that he loses freedom if he has to labor under the compulsion of work as a virtue. All work done under pressure, such as time limitations or the prodding of an employer, means loss of freedom.

The Greek attitude toward death is one of stoic acceptance if it occurs from natural causes, after a long life. Death is even regarded as heroic, if it follows a long struggle to remain alive. Greek folklore characterizes death as emigration from among the living, and holds that the deceased person may have melancholy reminiscences of the life he has left; death is tragic only if it occurs in young people, or when it takes a first-born male, or a young mother.

The Greek family is patriarchal, and the authority of the eldest male is recognized by all family members. Authority is vested in the father, but if the grandparents are part of the household, a grandfather is the family head. In general, a son, no matter what his age, displays respect and obedience to his father in the traditional Greek setting.

The wife is expected to carry out the wishes of the husband without questioning the motives. Her loyalty does not allow her to reveal her husband's shortcomings to anyone. The mother is quite influential in molding and sustaining the moral character of the children. She transmits the traditional social values and is a source of emotional warmth and security, whereas, the father serves as disciplinarian.

Respect for the aged is instilled at an early age. Widowed and elderly parents are expected to live with one of their children; even elderly aunts and uncles are accepted into the household. Married sons, in the strict tradition, commonly live in the same house as their parents; some form separate households. Younger siblings are expected to obey older siblings; brothers are responsible for the welfare of their sisters, including married sisters and their families.

Childlessness is regarded as a grave misfortune for which the woman is held responsible. Boys are preferred, since they continue the family name and help in agricultural tasks. Girls are less desirable, although loved, because at the time of marriage, the family loses her and the property that forms her dowry. Having a dowry is an economic necessity; otherwise, households would be difficult to maintain in a land of poverty. In order to educate or dower a child, the family may assume great debt and endure poverty.

Because of its ancient cultural traditions and economic impoverishment, the Greek family was a closely-knit unit. However, present day Greece is unlike the rural-agrarian Greece at the turn of the century. The Greek immigrants who came to the United States tried to retain the family solidarity and cultural values they had known in the homeland and made these values a pivotal part in their attempts for ethnic survival. Yet, modern social forces in Greece brought about the evolvement of a more dynamic society with new cultural patterns. This "frozen" portrayal in Greek-American communities has created amazement to those who return to the ancestral land and discover a different Greece from that of the late nineteenth and early twentieth centuries.[1]

Modern Greek culture reflects the influence of three divergent historical currents. First, that of classical antiquity as expressed in language and folklore; second, of Christianized Byzantium as manifested in centralism, conservatism, and bureaucratic organization; third, of Turkish domination, which created isolation from the West and shaped attitudes of servility.[2] Most Greeks looked upon the almost four hundred years of Turkish occupation

---

[1] For transitional changes in Greece see Herbert Stroup, "Social Changes in Greece," Sociology and Social Research 39 (1955): 387-93; H. J. Psomiades, "The Economic and Social Transformation of Modern Greece," Journal of International Affairs 19 (1965): 194-205; and Irwin T. Sanders, "Greek Society in Transition," Balkan Studies 8 (1967): 317-32.

[2] George Theotokas, "Some Reflections on the Psychology of the Modern Greek," The Link 1 (1938): 66-70.

as the primary cause for any unfavorable manifestations of contemporary Greek culture.[1] It is important to stress that the social traits of individuality, the need to excel, pride and vanity over ancestral legacy were important factors in perpetuating ethnic identity in the New World.

Economic Conditions

Historically, Greece has been known as one of the poorest countries in natural resources, though, it possesses one of the longest coastlines in the world. Most villages are within fifty miles of the sea, which explains why the early Greeks turned to navigation and commerce and encircled the Black, Adriatic, and Mediterranean seas with colonies, becoming the chief traders and merchants of the ancient world. It was natural for Greeks to emigrate to other parts of the world, since they had close affinity with the sea and a large merchant marine.

Greek industry and commerce surpassed all other medieval states during the Byzantine era. The empire's location at the junction of communications between Europe-Asia and Europe-Africa made Byzantium the center of lavish international trade. Its mercantile fleet was mistress of the seas down to the Mohammendan period. From the fifth to the twelfth centuries, the Byzantine Empire was the richest and most populous state in Christendom.[2] The collapse of the empire caused a temporary halt in Greek economic life. The merchant republics of Venice, Genoa and other Italian states, and later France and England, gained control of the Mediterranean economy.

In 1715, after the Turkish conquest of Venetian possessions in southern Greece, the Greeks were permitted to engage in commerce provided taxes were paid and recruits were given for the Turkish fleet. This enabled the

---

[1] Demosthenes Danielides, E neoelleniki koinonia kai oikonomia [Modern Greek society and economy] (Athens: G. Samaropoulos, 1934).

[2] See "The Economic Life of the Byzantine Empire" in Norman H. Baynes and H. St. L. B. Moss, Byzantium (Oxford: At the Clarendon Press, 1948), pp. 51-70; and "Economic Power" in Charles Diehl, Byzantium: Greatness and Decline, trans. Naomi Walford (New Brunswick, N. J.: Rutgers University Press, 1957), pp. 79-93. During the period of foreign domination down to the fifteenth century the cities of Greece had a prosperous middle class, far advanced of France and England. See Ferriman, p. 312.

Turks, a people without a seagoing tradition, to maintain control over vital sea routes by transforming the Aegean Islands into recruiting grounds for the Ottoman fleet.

As a result, in the eighteenth century the Greeks developed a flourishing international commerce again, a new merchant marine and an industry (metal works, yarns, dyestuffs, textiles, etc.) through individual enterprise and cooperatives of a native pattern.[1] The emergence of Russia as a major European power further enhanced their mercantilistic endeavors. Considering itself as the rightful heir of the Byzantine Empire and champion of Orthodox Christians under Turkish domination, Russia forced the Turks to permit Greek ships to ply their trade under the protection of the Russian flag. The Napoleonic wars increased further the economic wealth of Greek merchants who made huge profits by running the British blockade of French ports. When the Greek Revolution broke out in 1821, no doubt hastened by the maritime activity and contact with the West, Greece had acquired an excellent fleet of ships to do battle with the Turks.[2]

Despite modern Greece's accelerated swing toward industrialization after regaining its independence, Greece remains predominantly agricultural (over 70 percent) and must feed nine million inhabitants on a soil only one-fifth arable. Economic support comes from shipping, tourism, and foreign loan investments.[3]

---

[1]Many similarities are found between Greek practices and those of New England communities discussed by Samuel Eliot Morison in his Maritime History of Massachusetts, 1783-1860 (Boston: Houghton Mifflin Co., 1941), especially pp. 11-12,23.

[2]One Greek island Hydra, had from 86 to 158 ships between 1786 and 1806. In 1815 it had 23 ships listed with over 400 tons. By comparison, the ship Endeavor used by Captain Cook on his first voyage to Australia in 1768-71 was 370 tons and a crew of 34. See Constantine E. Michaelides, Hydra: A Greek Island Town (Chicago: University of Chicago Press, 1967), p. 12-21; and Raymond Matton, Hydra et la guerre maritime 1821-1827 (Athens: Collection de L'Institute Francais d' Athenes, 1953), passim.

[3]Maurice S. Thompson, "Notes in Social and Economic Conditions in Greece," Sociological Review 6 (July 1913): 213-21; Thomas Davidson, "The Present Condition of Greece," International Review 6 (June 1879): 597-615; K. A. Doukas, "Agrarian Reform in Greece," American Journal of Economics and Sociology 5 (1945): 79-92; George Coutsoumaris, "Possibilities of Economic Development in Greek Agriculture" (Ph.D. dissertation, University of Chicago, 1953); George K. Constantacoulos, "Economic Development of Greece in the Post War Setting" (Ph.D. dissertation, Columbia University, 1963).

During the time of heavy emigration to America, taxes in Greece were overbearing. They affected income, profits, transfer of property, inheritance, cultivated land, net profits on agricultural enterprises, crops, licenses, insurance premiums, military service exemption, education, patents, and many other matters. In brief, Greece taxed both production and consumption, thus pushing a rural exodus of Greek immigrants to the United States to earn enough money and return later to the homeland to live the "good life."

Religious Life

Christianity was wedded to Hellenism. It did not clash with the ancient culture, nor did it aim at suppressing it. The early Greek Christians made use of pagan thought and lore to help them in their spirituality. The Greek fathers of the early Christian church were important leaders and formulators of early Christian church doctrines, and by 380 A.D., Christianity was adopted as the official religion in Greece. Out of these influences the early church was born as a religion, a worship, and a theology. Christianity in Greece evolved as part of the Eastern church and came under the jurisdiction of the Ecumenical Patriarch of Constantinople. This was followed with a division of the Christian church into eastern and western sections, which resulted from the administrative separation of the Roman Empire, when the Emperor Constantine transferred the capital to the Greek city of Byzantium, renaming it Constantinople. The bishop, or patriarch, of Constantinople assumed jurisdiction of the Eastern church along with the patriarchs of Alexandria (Egypt), Antioch (Syria), and Jerusalem (Palestine); the bishop, or pope, of Rome assumed jurisdiction of the Western church as the sole patriarch in the West.

Both sections were considered part of the ancient and undivided church, and both shared the same theological beliefs. In 1054 A.D., a schism resulted over controversies involving newer beliefs and practices, and the Roman pope and Greek patriarch excommunicated each other.[1] The

---

[1] This centuries-old excommunication was lifted on 7 December 1965, by Pope Paul VI and the late Patriarch Athenagoras of Constantinople in simultaneous ceremonies. See Deno John Geanakoplos, Byzantine East and Latin West: Two Worlds of Christendom in Middle Ages and Renaissance (New York: Harper & Row, 1966), Preface.

western division became the Roman Catholic church; the eastern, the Greek Orthodox church.

As a result of early missionary activities, the Greek Orthodox church became the church of the Russians, Ukrainians, Serbians, Rumanians, Bulgarians, Albanians, Syrians, Lebanese, and other Arab groups, as well as for some Poles, Hungarians, Czechs, and Finns. Following the conquest of the Byzantine Empire by the Turks in 1453, these churches (with the exception of the Russian and Arab), remained under the jurisdiction of the Ecumenical Patriarchate. But in 1830, when Greece regained its independence, it declared itself autocephalous, and did not want to remain under the jurisdiction of the Patriarch of Constantinople, who was still subject to Turkish control.[1] As other Balkan nations gained their freedom from the Ottoman Empire, they, too, established independent churches.

Today the Eastern church consists of fourteen national churches, all sharing the same doctrines, practices, and liturgy, though differing in language. Each national church is independent, self-governing, and administered by a holy synod composed of bishops, the president of which is called a metropolitan, or patriarch. All groups acknowledge the spiritual jurisdiction of the Ecumenical Patriarchate at Constantinople (Istanbul), analogous to the papacy at Rome. The church of Greece is governed by a synod of bishops, with the archbishop of Athens as president. It is from this church that Greek emigrants began arriving in America at the turn of the century.[2]

---

[1] See Steven Runciman, The Great Church in Captivity (Cambridge: At the University Press, 1968); and Timothy Ware, Eustratios Argenti: A Study of the Greek Church under Turkish Rule (Oxford: Clarendon Press, 1964).

[2] Information about the religious affairs of Greek people has been secured from standard sources, which, unless otherwise noted, are in agreement with matters cited: Ernst Benz, The Eastern Orthodox Church: Its Thought and Life (New York: Doubleday & Co., 1963); Thomas J. Lacey, A Study of the Eastern Orthodox Church, 2nd rev. ed., (New York: Edwin S. Gorham, 1912); John Meyendorff, The Orthodox Church: Its Past and Its Role in the World Today (New York: Random House, Pantheon Books, 1962); Basil K. Stephanides, Ecclesiastiki historia [Ecclesiastical history] (Athens: Astir, 1948); Frank Gavin, Some Aspects of Contemporary Greek Orthodox Thought (Milwaukee: Morehouse Publishing Co., 1923); Timothy Ware, The Orthodox Church (Baltimore: Penguin Books, 1963); and Panagiotis Bratsiotis, The Greek Orthodox Church, trans. Joseph Blenkinsopp (Notre Dame, Ind.: University of Notre Dame Press, 1968).

Along with Christianity, another spiritual force left a deep imprint on the psychology of the Greek people. It was the memory of the longstanding Byzantine Empire. Even with the conquest of Constantinople in 1453, Mohammend II, the Turkish sultan, allowed the Ecumenical Patriarch and clergy considerable civil and spiritual powers over the Greek inhabitants. The world of Islam did not recognize any official division between religious and political authority.

Archbishops and bishops were empowered to hold civil courts to resolve matters of inheritance, family feuds, and other concerns of the Orthodox Christian community. The Greeks favored this practice since Turkish justice meant exposure of personal wealth to Turkish authorities which invited blackmail or confiscation. In effect, the church became an indispensable force of Greek tradition and culture in every facet of the communicants' lives. This is why Greek immigrants did not separate nationality from religion. To be Greek meant being an Orthodox Christian; they were inextricably interwoven.

A description of the church during the Turkish period and its initial role in the Revolution of 1821 is described by one writer as follows:

> . . . in spite of subjection to Turkish caprice, contempt, and cruelty, the Greek church showed remarkable tenacity in all internal affairs and gradually recovered a measure of independence as a result of its obstinate conservatism. Its state may be pejoratively described as stagnation; but from another point of view it was resistance to change that safe-guarded its existence in those centuries and enabled a strong national Greek church to emerge at the time of the Revolution both with the respect of the Greek revolutionaries and with an ardent devotion to the cause of national liberty. The "stagnant" Greek church was the champion of "liberty," as was none of the "advanced" churches of Western Christendom. The patriarchs, the metropolitans, the bishops, the monastic orders and the village priests, were the protectors of the oppressed nation while there was none other to protect them. In many cases it was the priest who gave the men the summons to strike for freedom; and at the monastery of Megaspelaion on . . . [25 March] 1821 it was not a philhellene from Western Europe, but Germanos, Archbishop of Patras, who raised the standards of revolt.[1]

When the Greek rebellion began, the Turkish sultan ordered the strangulation of Patriarch Gregory VII and his bishops. On Easter day, 1821, their bodies hung outside the episcopal palace at Constantinople. After Greece's

---

[1] Terrence Spencer, Fair Greece Sad Relic (London: Weidenfeld & Nicolson, 1954), p. 98. Compare the leadership of Archbishop Makarios in the independence struggle in Cyprus today with the role of the clergy in the Greek Revolution.

liberation from the Turks, the Greek constitution guaranteed religious toleration of all faiths. Over 98 percent of the people in Greece were Orthodox
Christians. The Moslem struggle had caused Greeks to feel that membership in the Greek church was evidence of patriotism and that church affiliation was similar to citizenship. If a Greek switched his church affiliation,
he would "lose" his nationality and be a traitor, or renegade. Hence, missionary and reform movements met with little success in Greece.

In the beginning of the twentieth century, the Greek church was primarily sacramental--baptizing, marrying, and burying its communicants.
Oftentimes, the village priest was as illiterate as his parishioners. He was
nominated by the people and ordained by the local bishop. Although the
priest played an essential role in the lives of Greeks, he did not enjoy social
superiority. The sacramental fees were his salary.

The Greeks were not spiritual fanatics, except over political and
religious issues affecting national or ethnic aims. The importance of religion in national survival was evidenced in Chicago, as the Greek immigrants
had as one of their first concerns the acquisition of a priest for the establishment of a church community, as will be shown in chapter 3. Greek life was
deeply imbued with religious and nationalistic feelings; the rites of the
church gave meaning and a sense of security to all strata of Greek society.

Education and Schooling

Since the Homeric Age aristeia, or the pursuit of excellence, has
been a motivating and deliberate pedagogical ideal in Greece.[1] Homer's in-

---

[1] Information concerning educational development in Greece has been
secured from the following sources, which, unless otherwise noted, are in
agreement with matters cited: Kalliniki Dendrinou Antonakaki, Greek Education (New York: Bureau of Publications, Teachers College, Columbia University, 1955); Lazarus Belelis, Kapodistrias os idritis laikis paideias en Helladi
[Capodistrias as founder of popular education in Greece] (Athens: John N.
Sederis, 1908); Kenneth J. Freeman, Schools of Hellas: An Essay on the Practice and Theory of Ancient Greek Education from 600 to 300 B.C. (London:
Macmillan & Co., 1907); Christos P. Economos, Koraes os ethnikos paidagogos [Koraes as national educator] (Athens: John N. Sederis, 1904), 2nd. ed.;
Cornelius C. Felton, The Schools of Modern Greece (n.p., 1861); H. I.
Marrou, A History of Education in Antiquity (New York: Sheed and Ward, 1956),
passim; U. S.,Office of Education, Report of the Commissioner of Education
for the Year 1896-97, "Education in Greece," by Daniel Quinn, vol. 1
(Washington, D.C.: Government Printing Office), pp. 267-346; and George

fluential documents, the Illiad and Odyssey, provided the basic education of Greek youth. These epics portrayed excellence in aristocratic chivalry, honor, and virtue. Two distinct conceptions of aristeia emerged with the growth of the city-states. The Spartan emphasized physical prowess and puritanical morality; the Athenian depicted paideia as the "sum total of all ideal perfections of mind and body--complete kalokagathia."[1] This intellectual pursuit expanded by the end of the fifth century, and produced teachers like Socrates, Plato, Aristotle, Protagoras, Isocrates, Archimedes, and Euclid.

Greece's conversion to Christianity and the establishment of the Byzantine Empire fused pagan classical education with Christian concepts. A vigorous and selective three-stage educational system was available in formal schools for intellectually competent youth in primary, secondary, and higher levels. The study of religion was prominent in the curriculum, but did not dominate secular schooling until the last two centuries of the Byzantine era. Even then, the church nurtured pagan learning that helped to keep alive Hellenistic consciousness through the long period of Turkish occupation, 1453 to 1821. Because of this nurturing, classical schools did not disappear in Greece as in the West after the fall of Rome in 476. One thousand years later, the reading of Homer was part of Byzantine Greek education. Greek children could chant the alphabet backwards and forwards along with "tongue-twisters" and "declensions" which were common exercises of Greek schools.[2]

Schooling reached a low ebb and almost disappeared in Greece after the fall of Constantinople in 1453. Teaching Greek was forbidden by Turkish authorities, but churches could remain open, if tribute was paid. Schools fell into neglect, because personal survival was a primary concern under

---

Milo Wilcox, Education in Greece (n.p., 1933). For an analysis of recent educational developments in Greece see Andreas M. Kazamias, "The Style of Educational Change in Greece," Phi Delta Kappan 43 (November 1961): 69-74; and Antonakaki, passim, as well as Wallace Graves, "Public Secondary Education in Greece," The High School Journal 45 (May 1962): 329-34.

[1]Kalokagathia relates to the quality of being a fine, graceful and good man. See Jaeger, 1: 286.

[2]Marrou, p. 455.

deplorable living conditions.[1] Since Greece ceased to exist as a political
entity, the churches and monasteries became the educational centers for the
populace. Secret schools were organized in cellars of churches, where
Greek was taught and the embers of freedom kept alive by priests who served
as teachers. One source indicates that Greeks availed themselves of
schooling, and, despite Turkish domination, the proportion of Greeks who
could read and write was as great as any European nation.[2]

These clandestine schools became the centers of hope for freedom,
and by the end of the eighteenth century, pedagogical methods began to be
studied. Adamantios Koraes, the famous Greek patriot and professor of
Greek at Sorbonne in Paris

> . . . speaks of the new notions of Pestalozzi and his reforms in the
> practice of education, and says that although he does not know whether
> Pestalozzi was improving the system of education or not, yet he thinks
> that the Greek community of Constantinople ought to send two young
> men to Europe for the purpose of studying the Pestalozzian system and
> of introducing it into the East if they found it good.[3]

These schools were permeated with patriotic literature that lifted the spirit
of liberty and culminated in the outbreak of the Greek Revolution in 1821.

Despite obstacles, harassment, and the struggle of war, public
schools were erected and operated in Greece under a community development
scheme. The demotic (primary) schools were supported by the deme (com-
mune) which were governed by local councilmen and presided over by a bishop
or priest. Later, the local school inspector and director of the regional gymnasium (secondary school) were added to the council. Funds for school
support were raised by the local councils, and this was the practice of financing schools for many years after Greece's liberation from the Turks.

At the first Greek National Assembly in 1822, constitutional rights

---

[1] Philipos Johannis, "Public Instruction in Modern Greece," American
Journal of Education 12 (1862):571-72. However, higher education was
allowed to continue as Mohammed II, conqueror of Constantinople, permitted
Patriarch Gennadius Scholarius to reestablish the patriarchal school. See
G. Chassiotis, L'Instruction publique chez les Grecs depuis la prise de
Constantinople par les Turcs, jusqu'a nos jours (Paris: Ernest Leroux, 1881),
p. 4, 34-42.

[2] See Ferriman, pp. 42, 259-60.

[3] Quinn, p. 290.

were drawn to provide free elementary education for all at the expense of the state. This was an interesting contrast with the legal status of elementary education in France, England, and the United States at that time. The followup report in 1824, suggested the formation of a tripartite system of education. The demotic (elementary) schools were to have a four-year course; the middle (secondary) schools were divided into two types--the three-year Hellenic schools, followed by the four-year gymnasia; and the university. This system remained unchanged, for the most part until 1929, when Hellenic schools were abolished and demotic schools and gymnasia were extended to six years.

The nationwide implementation of universal education in Greece had to wait until 1911. Prior to that time, turbulent conditions and lack of funds made it impossible to execute the educational plan. Elementary schools received priority and the Lancastrian system of instruction was employed because of low cost of operation. The growth of elementary education received added impetus with the election of Capodistrias as the first president of Greece in 1827. He was an advocate of elementary and middle schools, but opposed higher education because it might lead to unrest and disorder. [1] According to a Ministry of Education report in 1830, there were seventy-one elementary schools with a total enrollment of 6,121. Within a year after the success of the Greek Revolution, which cost Greece the lives of nearly half of its population, about one percent of the populace was enrolled in demotic schools. [2]

Prince Otho of Bavaria became king after the assassination of Capodistrias in 1831. He furthered the development of education, and a law was passed in 1834 establishing compulsory schooling for children between the ages of five and twelve. Parents who failed to send their children to school were fined. This law was not enforced and illiteracy remained a persistent problem. According to a United States Bureau of Education report published in 1883, the districts of Thebes and the Peloponnesus had a 90 to 95

---

[1] Quinn, pp. 296-97.

[2] In 1828, the population of independent Greece was 753,400; see Antonakaki, p. 261.

percent illiteracy. This was the time when immigrants from these areas were arriving in great numbers in America. According to Quinn, two-thirds of the population of free Greece was unable to read in 1885.[1]

The Lancastrian method of instruction was discontinued in 1842. The demotic schools modelled themselves after the French system (Guizot Law of 1833), and teachers were procured from newly-established teacher academies. These teaching academies were similar to the German schools, especially those of Bavaria. Teachers were drawn from the National University established in 1837 at Athens. Since the communes were negligent in paying teachers' salaries, the government assumed that responsibility in 1856. Education was made a function of the state under the supervision of the Ministry of Public Instruction, which regulated secondary and higher education. Elementary schools, with some guidance from the ministry, remained under the control of local communes.

This was the general educational background of Greeks who emigrated to America at the turn of the century. The vast majority had a minimum amount of schooling. Those immigrants who came to the United States after the 1930s--especially following World War II--had a higher level of schooling, made possible by Greece's enforcement of the compulsory school law and the upgrading of school facilities. In 1928, illiteracy was 23 percent for the male population and 57 percent for females.[2] By 1966, illiteracy had dropped to 17 percent for women and 8 percent for men. It was estimated that 98 percent of those of starting school age attended school.[3] Table 2 shows the decline of illiteracy by sex and age based on various census returns.

------

[1] See U.S., Office of Education, Education in Italy and Greece (Washington, D.C.: Government Printing Office, 1883), p. 7; and Quinn, p. 341.

[2] Antonakaki, p. 24.

[3] See "Education in Greece," Reference Papers, no. 201 (September 1966), Foreign Press Division, Ministry of Prime Minister, Athens, p. 1.

TABLE 2

ILLITERACY IN GREECE BY SEX AND AGE GROUPS
IN 1907, 1928, AND 1951

Age	M a l e s			F e m a l e s		
Groups	1907	1928	1951	1907	1928	1951
10-14	26.5	10.5	5.8	68.3	28.3	10.9
15-19	34.6	18.4	8.5	73.0	42.2	16.3
20-24	38.3	16.3	6.0	76.6	47.2	13.7
25-29	39.2	15.8	5.5	80.8	54.9	16.9
30-39	41.4	20.7	8.0	84.2	64.8	31.6
40-49	46.6	29.9	12.0	87.8	74.4	48.7
50-59	50.3	35.7	15.0	89.7	79.8	62.0
60 +	56.1	47.5	29.5	92.6	86.3	75.9

SOURCE: Vasilios G. Valaoras, "The Stand of Science and Education in Greece," Hellenic Review 2 (November 1960): 16.

It is discernable from this table that in 1907, the peak year of Greek immigration to the United States of young males between the ages of ten and twenty-four, the illiteracy rate averaged 33.1 percent, one of the highest of all immigrant groups. By comparison, the same age group of young males arriving in this country under the Displaced Persons Act of 1951, had an average illiteracy rate of 13.6 percent, a distinct improvement over the 1907 rate. It is obvious that schooling in Greece had been updated.

Indicative of further school improvement in Greece have been new educational reform laws of 1959 and 1964, which have the gymnasia divided into two levels: the gymnasium contains the first three-year secondary cycle without examinations; the lyceum has the second three-year cycle opened to those passing entrance examinations. The former is concerned with general education; the latter is diversified with eight types (i.e., classical, practical, technical, etc.) which reflect the country's newer social and economic needs. In addition, compulsory schooling has been extended three years, ages, six to fifteen.[1]

---

[1] See Ephimeris tis kyberniseos tou basileiou tis Hellados [Government newspaper of the kingdom of Greece], No. 182 (Athens: 24 October 1964); and Salomon Wald, Individual Demand for Higher Education in Greece (Paris: Organization for Economic Cooperation and Development, 1966).

Language loomed as a problem in the schools of Greece, because of the two Greek dialects. The high literary Greek (katharevousa, or purist form, based on classical Greek) is the official language of the state government and church. The low, or demotic (popular), Greek is the vernacular used by the press. Generally, the former was the language of schools, while the latter was the spoken language. The language issue has been one of the most important school concerns for Greek people. Demoticism was associated with communism between 1910 and 1930. The problem has lessened since the Papandreou reforms of 1964, when demotic became the official language for elementary schools and the purist form for secondary schools.[1]

In the early immigration movement to Chicago, the language problem was complicated, because the uneducated could not understand high Greek; the educated understood both the purist and vernacular. Hence, the use of Greek language in the first Greek schools in Chicago became a painful issue between the supporters of the "ancient," classical Greek and those of the "modern," demotic Greek language. As future chapters will illustrate, the language issue was a significant school concern tied to the desire to perpetuate ethnic survival among Greek immigrants in the New World. Because laymen participated in local school councils in Greece, they were accustomed to the idea of lay participation in school matters, which helps to explain their involvement in establishing communal schools in Chicago.

The Phenomenon of Greek Emigration

Throughout the history of the Greek people, emigration--the leaving of one's homeland--has been a distinct Hellenic phenomenon. The reason is to be found in the geography of Greece and in the nature of the people. Poor land, overpopulation, and the urge for adventure and economic gain led the Greeks to remote parts of the world. Since ancient times their main highway was the sea, and they became a mercantile people engaged in world commerce.

The boldness and extent of Greek travel are suggested by the belief that as early as 2,000 B.C., Greeks had sailed to the British Isles and that

---

[1] Antonakaki, p. 261; and Quinn, pp. 341-43.

Pythias, a Greek navigator, had reached England, Ireland, and Iceland.[1]
By the seventh century B.C., they had established colonies throughout the
Mediterranean and Black seas. At the height of Greek civilization during the
fifth century, Greek colonies extended from the Pyrenees to the Caucasus
and from southern Russia to northern Africa. The conquests of Alexander the
Great in the fourth century further extended Greek colonization, especially
toward the East, and brought about the Hellenistic Age. In 146 B.C., Greek
emigration ceased for a time with the conquest of Greece by Rome.

The next Greek migratory resurgence occurred during the Byzantium
era, when Greeks came into contact with the Far East via the far-flung trade
routes. Upon the collapse of the Byzantine Empire in 1453 Greek emigration
was rekindled. The first to emigrate to Italy and then to other Western nations were Greek scholars. This emigration of scholars contributed to the
rebirth of Greek letters during the Renaissance.[2] Later, in order to escape
the Turkish oppression, Greeks emigrated individually and collectively in
large numbers to Russia, Austria-Hungary, Italy, Egypt, and other parts of
the Levant. Smaller numbers landed in Spain, France, Holland, Belgium, and
England.

Emigration ceased once more after Greece regained its freedom in
1821, and Greeks became imbued with the "Great Idea" of liberating all enslaved Greeks under Ottoman control. The irredentist policy brought Greece
and Turkey into conflict several times, and a century later, resulted in the
disastrous Greek defeat while trying to free some 1,500,000 countrymen in
1922.

A treaty for the compulsory exchange of nationals between Greece
and Turkey in 1923 formalized the exodus of Greeks from Asia Minor and pro-

---

[1] Vilhjalmer Stefansson, Iceland, the First American Republic (New
York: Doubleday, Doran & Co., 1945), pp. xv and xvii.

[2] For an account of the flight of Greek scholars see Deno John
Geanakoplos, Greek Scholars in Venice: Studies in the Dissemination of
Greek Learning from Byzantium to Western Europe (Cambridge: Harvard Uni-
versity Press, 1962) and his Byzantine East and Latin West. See also Kenneth
Setton, "The Byzantine Background of the Italian Renaissance," Proceedings
of the American Philosophical Society 100 (February 1956): 1-78.

vided Greece with an acute problem of population assimilation. It had to absorb into its national life a sudden influx of 26 percent more people, two-thirds of whom were totally destitute. Greece became frightfully congested, while parts of Turkey were underpopulated. By 1930, with help from the League of Nations and the United States, Greece was able to tackle this difficulty.[1] In the course of time, migrations of Greek seamen took them to Asia, Africa, Europe, and North and South America.

Forerunners of the "New" Immigration

Voyagers to America

Greek names, or people with "greco" and "griego" attached to their names, appeared in America throughout colonial times. They were men without a country--adventurers, merchants, seafarers. Webster defines "gringo" as a corruption of the Spanish "griego" used disparagingly by Spanish for the numerous Greeks in Spanish expeditions to the New World. Later, it was used by the indigenous population to imply a "foreigner."

The first authoritative reference to a Greek in the New World is mentioned by Cabeza de Vaca. A Greek called Don Teodoro served in the expedition of Panfilo de Narvaez which explored the Gulf of Mexico in 1528. While on a land mission, Teodoro was captured by Indians and lived among them in the area that is now Mobile, Alabama. DeSoto learned about his death when he explored the central Mississippi area during 1538-42.[2]

In 1660, a Captain Thomas Grecian, who was in command of an English ship, settled with his family in Boston. Other Greeks probably were in that city, since the British crown authorized two Greeks, John Dye and

---

[1] Edward Hale Bierstadt, The Great Betrayal (New York: Robert McBride & Co., 1924); F. A. Rose, C. L. Fry, and E. Sibley, The Near East and American Philanthropy (New York: Columbia University, 1929); and Harold B. Allen, Come Over into Macedonia: The Story of a Ten-Year Adventure in Uplifting a War-Torn People (New Brunswick, N.J.: Rutgers University Press, 1943).

[2] The Journey of Alvar Núñez Cabeza de Vaca and His Companions, from Florida to the Pacific 1528-1536 trans. F. Bandelier (New York: A. S. Barnes & Co., 1905), pp. 38, 46-47; and Edward Gaylord Bourne ed., Narratives of the Career of Hernando de Soto, 2 vols. trans. Buckingham Smith (New York: A. S. Barnes & Co., 1904) 2: 17, 122-23.

John Dervish, to travel from there to Holland in 1689 for commercial reasons.[1]
During the colonial period, the best known Greek in America was John
Paradise, who lived in Williamsburg. He was a friend of Thomas Jefferson
and first introduced Jefferson to Adamantios Koraes, the intellectual father
of the Greek Revolution, who resided in Paris.[2]

Historical accounts of Spanish expeditions to the New World make
numerous references to Greeks sailing with Cortez, Pizarro, Coronado, and
Magellan; others with Sir Francis Drake and Thomas Cavendish. One of the
better known sailors accompanying the Spanish expeditions was John Phocas,
who was known by his Hispanized name, Juan de Fuca. He spent forty years
exploring the West Indies, and in 1592, while in the employ of the Regent of
Mexico, he discovered the straits between Washington and Vancouver Island
which now bear his name.[3]

In the Pacific Northwest, an entrepreneur specializing in furs,
Eustrate Delarof, who had migrated from Greece to Moscow, became director
of the Russian-American (Fur) Company in 1783, and subsequently served as
the first Russian governor of Alaska until 1791.[4] At the southeastern end of
the continent, in 1767, a mass migration of Greeks landed in Florida. They
were on eight ships carrying nearly 1,500 Greeks, Italians, and Minorcans.
This was the largest importation of white inhabitants ever brought to America
at one time--larger than the colonization of Jamestown in 1607, and Plymouth
in 1620. The Scottish entrepreneur, Dr. Andrew Turnbull, had secured a royal

---

[1] Chicago Daily News, 22 April 1924.

[2] New York Times, 1 September 1957. For the life of this versatile
Greek in England and the colonies see Leslie Stephen and Sidney Lee eds.,
The Dictionary of National Biography vol. 15, pp. 200-201; William and Mary
College Quarterly 6 (1898); 58-59; and The Virginia Magazine of History and
Biography 12 (1914): p. 271.

[3] See Hubert and George R. Stewart, Names on the Land (Boston:
Houghton Mifflin Co., 1958), pp. 174-78; Malafouris, pp. 26-32; C.J. Lampos,
"The Story of the Greek Explorer Juan de Fuca," Athene 8 (1947): 7-10; and
John Metaxas, "The Story of John Phocas: Explorer of America," Athene 9
(1949): 3-8, 44.

[4] Hubert Howe Bancroft, The History of Alaska 1730-1885 (San Francisco: A. L. Bancroft & Co., 1886), pp. 271-72, 314-21; and Clarence Leroy
Andrews, The Story of Alaska (Caldwell, Idaho: Caxton Printers, 1938),
pp. 42, 47-48.

grant from the King of England to establish a plantation in Florida. His colony was named New Smyrna in honor of the birthplace of Turnbull's wife, a Greek woman from Smyrna. Eleven years later, after many deaths and harsh privation, the Greeks escaped the ill-fated commercial venture and moved up the coast to Saint Augustine, where they became Hispanized following the departure of the English in 1783.[1]

Around 1790, the first "Greek" school in America was organized in Saint Augustine. The edifice which housed the school still survives as "the oldest wooden school building and the first coeducational school in the United States." Today, it is preserved as a historical shrine and is commercially operated. Records show the school operated from 1790 to 1934, with Juan Gianopoli (John Giannopoulos) as the first teacher. This writer's attempt to determine the language of instruction was unsuccessful. One researcher (Beeson) contacted said he believed the language was Catalan, the Spanish dialect of Minorca.[2] In this writer's estimation, it was more likely a combination of Greek and Catalan. Oddly, a receipt for tuition dated 1821, and signed by Gianopoli, was in English. In that year, Florida became part of the United States and the influx of new settlers probably made English the dominant language.

---

[1] For an excellent account of this little known episode in American colonial history, see E. P. Panagopoulos, New Smyrna: An Eighteenth Century Greek Odyssey (Gainesville, Florida: University of Florida Press, 1966). A somewhat biased account written by a descendant of Turnbull, Carita Doggett Corse, Dr. Andrew Turnbull and the New Smyrna Colony of Florida (Saint Petersburg, Florida: Great Outdoors Publishing Co., 1967), is also useful. Contemporary testimony of this colonization is to be found in the Virginia Gazette of 29 September and 6 October 1768. For added perspective see James Grant Forbes, Sketches, Historical and Topographical of the Floridas (New York: C. S. Van Winkle, 1821), pp. 19-20; M. E. Eschavannes, Histoire de Corinthe relation des principaux énénements de la Morée (Paris: Just Rouvier, 1854), pp. 160-61; and William W. Dewhurst, The History of Saint Augustine, Florida (New York: George P. Putnam Sons, 1881), chap. 15.

[2] Interview with Kenneth H. Beeson, Jr. at Saint Augustine Historical Society (Florida), 23 July 1968. See also Kenneth H. Beeson, Jr., "New Smyrna Colony " (Master's thesis, University of Florida, 1959); Seraphim G. Canoutas, Hellenism in America (New York: Cosmos Publishing Co., 1918), pp. 50-53; and Orthodox Observer 31 (February 1965): 37-38.

During the American War of Independence, Demetrios Ypsilanti, a scion of a mercantile Greek family, outfitted a small ship and with a band of Greeks sailed to fight in the war. Some sources claim that his group participated in the Battle of Monmouth, New Jersey, in 1778, under the command of General Lee.[1]

During the first two decades of the nineteenth century Greek ship owners plied the Atlantic to the Antilles to share in profitable trade. Evidence indicates that trade flourished between Turkish-occupied Greece and the new American nation. Figs, currants, almonds, carpets, etc., were exported. A diplomatic report shows a Greek sea captain returned to Greece from the United States in 1805, with a cargo of molasses, rum, and coffee, which he sold at great profit.[2] In order to protect this trade and uphold the freedom of the seas, the United States went to war with the Barbary pirates in the early part of that century. After 1821, the Greek trading ships were commandeered to fight the naval war against the Turks in the Greek Revolution.

Despite these early Greek forerunners to America by way of explorations, expeditions, and trade, American knowledge of the country of Greece and its people was scant. Greece had disappeared as a political entity in 1453, and the absence of a national structure and its isolation from the West contributed to the loss of Greek identity. Only in academia were there flickers of knowledge of ancient and Byzantine Greece.

Hellenic revival

The nineteenth century was one of revolt throughout the Western world. The search for national independence and unity was putting an end to empires. One revolt, however--that of the Greek Revolution--stirred support and sympathy among Americans, and Hellenism's revival pervaded architecture, the arts, and democratic principles in the United States.[3] Names such

---

[1] Canoutas, pp. 58-59; and Booras, pp. 157-58.

[2] Canoutas, pp. 59-60.

[3] For the influence of the Greek War of Independence on American architecture and literature between 1820 and 1860 see: Talbot Hamlin, Greek Revival Architecture in America (New York: Dover Publications, 1944); and Marios B. Raizis and Alexander Papas, Greek Revolution and the American Muse (Thessaloniki, Greece: Institute for Balkan Studies, 1972).

as Athens, Troy, Ithaca, Ypsilanti were given to new towns as an American tribute to Greek heroism. This wave of philhellenic sentiment swept America and Europe; passionate orations, large sums of money and other aid, philanthropic activity, and public opinion all merged for the cause of Greek liberty.[1]

Dr. Samuel Gridley Howe of Boston was among those Americans who went to Greece and participated in its struggle. He was in charge of the American relief supplies to Greece. Colonel Jonathan P. Miller of Vermont, Lieutenant-General George Jarvis and William G. Washington (a relative of George Washington) fought on the Greek battlefield, the latter two dying there.[2] As a result of the eleemosynary work of Americans in Greece, Greek refugees and individuals appeared on the American scene.

It is generally recognized that the Greek Revolution of 1821 was an event of world significance, because it was the first successful national struggle (the third successful revolution after the American and French) during a period of reaction after the Napoleonic wars. It led the way for liberation of other peoples in the Old and New Worlds. During the revolution, Koraes, a leading Greek intellectual and precursor of the struggle for Greek independence, turned to Jefferson for advice and technical help to organize democratically the new Greek state.[3]

In Congress, Daniel Webster and Henry Clay championed the Greek cause with stirring oratory and urged an inquiry to ascertain whether the

---

[1] For an account of the "Greek fever" that swept America at the time see Stephen A. Larabee, Hellas Observed: The American Experience of Greece 1775-1865 (New York: New York University Press, 1952), chaps. 3-7; William St. Clair, That Greece Might Still Be Free: the Philhellenes In The War of Independence (New York: Oxford University Press, 1972); Edward M. Earle, "American Interest in the Greek Cause, 1821-1827," American Historical Review 33 (October 1927): 44-63; Booras, pt. 1; and Myrtle A. Cline, American Attitude Toward the Greek War of Independence 1821-1828 (Atlanta, Georgia: Higgins-McArthur Co., 1930).

[2] Howe wrote a personal account of the Revolution. See Howe, passim and Larabee, chaps. 4-5.

[3] Stephen George Chaconas, Adamantios Korais: A Study in Greek Nationalism (New York: Columbia University Press, 1942), pp. 130-32; for the full text of the correspondence with Jefferson see David M. Robinson, America in Greece: A Traditional Policy (New York: Anatolia Press, 1948), pp. 36-42. An abridged version in the original French is to be found in Chaconas, "The Jefferson-Korais correspondence," Journal of Modern History 14 (March 1942): 64-70.

situation warranted American recognition of Greece as an independent nation.
President James Monroe, in his annual message to Congress on 3 December
1822, expressed the American sentiment:

> The mention of Greece fills the mind with the most exalted sentiments,
> and arouses in our bosoms the best feelings of which our nature is sus-
> ceptible. Superior skill and refinements in the arts, heroic gallantry in
> action, disinterested patriotism, enthusiastic zeal, and devotion in
> favor of public liberty are associated with our recollection of ancient
> Greece. That such a country should have been overwhelmed and so long
> hidden, as it were, from the world under a gloomy despotism, has been
> a cause of unceasing and deep regret to generous minds for ages past.
> It was natural, therefore, that the reappearance of these people in their
> original character, contending in favor of their liberties, should produce
> that great excitement and sympathy in their favor which have been so
> signally displayed throughout the United States. A strong hope is enter-
> tained that these people will receive their independence and resume their
> equal station among the nations of the earth.[1]

United States recognition of Greece as an independent state precipitated much debate in Congress. The government was committed to certain
traditional foreign policies and was wedded to nonintervention in political
affairs in Europe and modern Greece. Due to the insistence of the Secretary
of State, John Quincy Adams, the American government observed strict neu-
trality. This reaction was formally expressed by the promulgation of the
Monroe Doctrine. There was fear that the European powers might construe
American recognition of beleaguered Greece as United States interference.
Nonetheless, President Monroe made a second declaration on behalf of Greece
during his famous Monroe Doctrine message to Congress on 2 December 1823.[2]

During the closing years of the war and shortly thereafter, numerous
Greek youth, victims of war, were brought to America by sympathetic Americans serving in Greece. In 1823 alone, some forty orphans came with Quaker
missionaries. Adopted by American families, many became well-educated
and served in positions of responsibility. Some returned to Greece to assist
in its recovery from the ravages of war. Some of the foremost individuals

---

[1] For the full text of the message see Annals of Congress, 1789-1824,
42 vols. (Washington, D.C.: Government Printing Office, 1834-56), vol. 40:
12-19.

[2] Annals of Congress, vol. 41: 13ff. For the development of the
Monroe Doctrine see W. C. Ford, "Genesis of the Monroe Doctrine," Massachusetts Historical Society Proceedings 15 (1902): 373-437; and Dexter Perkins,
Hands Off: A History of the Monroe Doctrine (Boston: Little, Brown & Co.,
1948).

who remained in America included Michael Anagnos, who married the daughter of the eminent philhellene, Samuel G. Howe, and who became director of Boston's famed Perkins Institute for the Blind in 1876, until his death in 1906,[1] and Lucas Miltiades Miller, who eventually settled in Oshkosh, Wisconsin, and served in the Mexican War and in the Fifty-second Congress of the United States--the first person of Greek descent to be so elected.[2]

Others include Evangelos A. Sophocles, professor of Greek at Harvard for forty-one years (1842-1883) and compiler of several Greek lexicons,[3] and Alexander Dimitry (actually born in New Orleans, a son of an early Greek immigrant), who became a newspaper editor and the first state superintendent of public instruction in Louisiana from 1847 to 1851.[4] Also, during the Civil War there was a captain George Musalas Colvocoressis USN, a graduate of West Point and commander of U.S.S. Saratoga. His son, Rear Admiral George P. Colvocoressis (born in Connecticut in 1847) served forty-eight years in the United States Navy and was Admiral Dewey's executive officer on his flagship during the Battle of Manila.[5] Another example was an acting surgeon for the Army during the Civil War, John Zachos, later sought to rehabilitate Negro slaves who had been freed, and spent the later years of his

---

[1] Anagnos was brought to America by Howe in 1867, when the latter had gone to Greece on behalf of the Cretan insurrection. See Burgess, pp. 208-25; Booras, pp. 197-99.

[2] Canoutas, pp. 86-88; Burgess, pp. 196-97; Booras, pp. 195-96; and Chicago Daily Journal, 22 April 1924.

[3] See Handlin, "The European Scholar as a Teacher," in his Immigration as a Factor in American History, pp. 119-24. His portrait still is on display in Harvard's Widener Library.

[4] Rodney Cline, Builders of Louisiana Education (Baton Rouge: Louisiana State University Press, 1963), pp. 1-4. For a history of the Dimitry family see Stanley C. Arthur and George Kernion, Old Families of Louisiana (New Orleans: Harmanson Publisher, 1931), pp. 401-5.

[5] Burgess, pp. 190-96; Canoutas, pp. 91-92; Booras, pp. 193-97. For a listing of Greek immigrants in the Union Navy, see George P. Perros, "Officers of Greek Descent in the Union Navy, 1861-1865," Athene 24 (Autumn 1963): 12-14ff.

life as curator of Cooper Union in New York.[1]

These are some forerunners of the Greek mass immigration that followed in 1882. The factors that brought these early settlers to America, for the most part, were different from those motivating their countrymen who arrived later. The historical events of the Greek voyagers and the Hellenic revival are indicative of the extent of the phenomenon of Greek emigration to the New World.

The Greek "New" Immigration

In tracing the flow of Greeks to the United States, five waves of emigration are discernable, peaking during the years of 1890, 1897, 1907, 1922, and 1956. The causes were diverse:

1. Around 1890, the Greeks from the Peloponnesus and the Greek Islands emigrated primarily for economic reasons.

2. The abortive 1897 war with Turkey was coupled with the agricultural crisis and Greece's inability to feed its growing population.

3. The travel agents' propaganda of golden opportunities awakened the Odyssean spirit of adventure for islanders and peasant farmers in the 1907 period. Further enticement was the emergence of the United States as an industrial power, following the Spanish American War; this meant getting a job.

4. The expulsion of Greeks from Asia Minor by the Turks in 1922, and the ensuing Greek military debacle sent another wave of Greek refugees to the United States. Unlike previous groups, many of these refugees came with their families, determined to make the New World their permanent home.

5. After World War II, the immigration quota restrictions became relaxed temporarily. The new arrivals were victims of the German occupation of Greece, the Greek civil war, and earthquakes that ravaged Greece during the postwar period. When possible, these people came with their families; otherwise, individuals subsequently brought family members under a special congressional act.

---

[1] Burgess, pp. 197-201.

Beginnings

The New World offered its bounty to the curious, brave, and oppressed peoples of other nations. During the decade of the 1890s the most conspicuous development in American immigration was the shift in national and geographic origins of immigrants. The English, Germans, Irish, and Scandinavians were replaced by Italians, Slavs, Jews, Greeks, and others from s outhern and eastern Europe. These different kinds of people were part of the "new" immigration to the United States.[1]

Prior to 1890 the prospects of Greeks coming to America appeared slim. The professional classes had ties with London, Vienna, Paris, and Berlin. In their opinion, the United States was a surviving outpost for the poverty-stricken, adventurers, wealth seekers, and "failures." It was considered the land of the Irish, Germans, Italians, Chinese, Negroes, and other unassimilated ethnic groups. Emigrating Greeks preferred Egypt, Rumania, Russia, Italy, and other European lands close to home. Except for the 8,515 Greeks who lived officially in the United States at the turn of the century, Greece had failed to discover the New World.

However, once the immigration to America began, hopefuls from all parts of the Kingdom of Greece and "unredeemed parts" in the Ottoman Empire joined the exodus. The Peloponesians departed in sizable numbers, coming from the oldest, poorest, and least educated section of Greece. The provinces of Laconia and Arcadia emigrated first; soon they were joined by villagers from other sections of mainland Greece, Thessaly, the Dodecanese, Turkey, the isles in the eastern Aegean Sea, and Asia Minor.

The Peloponnese departure was massive because of the drop in the price of currants, their main money crop, and the freeing of men from military service after the shortlived 1897 war between Greece and Turkey. Crop failures, poor soil conditions, floods, earthquakes, oppressive taxation and frequent government upheavals forced many to look elsewhere for the land of opportunity.

Many Greek immigrants were teenagers and young adult men. At an early age, they were taught to accept adult responsibilities. Most came with

---

[1] Peter Roberts, The New Immigration: A Study of the Industrial and Social Life of Southeastern Europeans in America (New York: Macmillan Co., 1912), p. vii.

the idea of making enough money to provide for their parents, sisters, and brothers. They were able to bear leaving home because of the vision of returning there as soon as sufficient sums of money had been saved.

Greece was economically sick after four hundred years of Turkish occupation. There was a mournful, disheartening cry of hunger, and Greece's ability to recover appeared marginal because of limited resources and industries. About one-fifth of the terrain was arable, capital was scarce, and interest rates were as high as 30 percent. The unknown land, United States, sounded like a mythical, miracle nation of wealth. Greek youth heard "get rich quick" stories:

> Why remain to struggle for a piece of bread without any security for the future, without honor and independence? Why not open your eyes and see the good that awaits you; harden your heart and seek your fortune abroad, where so many of your countrymen already have made theirs. Why linger? To protect your parents? Today or tomorrow, whether their children are here or abroad, they will close their eyes forever. It will be better for you to leave home and send a little money to provide for them in their advancing years. Or are you willing to cultivate the barren lands with the ploughshare and dig in the fields? Have you seen how much progress you have made thus far? [1]

The economic image of the United States varied among the prospective immigrants. Naive villagers believed the streets in America were paved with gold. [2] The less gullible dreamed of being a Greek Astor, Vanderbilt, or Rockefeller. Others expected to have small businesses that would help them become economically independent.

Communications from the New World magnified the glamour of a soft life. Steamship brokers and moneylenders gave a touch of realism with their pictures of transatlantic ships displayed in village stores and coffeehouses. The clarion call to leave Greece touched the remote areas with false and irresponsible job-success stories. Oftentimes the moneylender was a former immigrant who returned to persuade others to follow his good fortune. Usually the creditor offered to lend money at a high interest rate and accepted the prop-

---

[1] Emmanuel S. Lykoudes, E metanastai [The immigrants], as quoted in Theodore Saloutos, They Remember America: The Story of the Repatriated Greek Americans (Berkeley: University of California Press, 1956), p. 3.

[2] A charming account is given by Mary Vardoulakis, Gold in the Streets (New York: Dodd, Mead & Co., 1945).

erty mortgage as security. This practice proved to be lucrative for the
lender.

The prospective immigrant was easy prey for the labor agent who
used exploitative practices. The agent loosely promised a job working with
a relative or acquaintance or on railroad construction, and furnished a steamship ticket. Even more vicious was the practice of lending money to parents
of destitute youth for their transportation and extracting from the father a
promise that his son would work for a definite period in return. This became
known as the notorious padrone system, patterned after that of the Italian
immigrants.[1]

All stories that filtered to the homeland were not golden. People
had spoken of hardship, illness, prejudice, and loneliness. But this did not
dim the enthusiasm of those who contemplated emigration. One narration
about the magic attraction of America reads:

> It was the land of dreams, and gold, and opportunity. To our imagina-
> tions it was carpeted with golden fleeces. Every girl dreamed of a great
> love coming from America to take her back to luxury and adventure. Our
> favorite game was called "The Americana." We marked out a space to
> represent houses and established the girls in these as the wives and
> sweethearts; half the boys remained with the girls and the rest disappeared
> from sight. Then there would be a war-cry, "America," and the second
> group of boys would come charging up the hill. The defenders would cry
> out in alarm, "The Americans" and would rush out to the defense. But the
> women would desert to the Americans, and the game was over. The game
> was founded on facts, for the American suitors did have the best chance
> with the girls.[2]

The constant stream of chain letters which Fairchild calls "chain
migration" resulted in further enthusiasm for the New World. It heightened
the desire to leave for more promising shores. An immigrant wrote to his
former employer:

> Here people work hard and regularly, and rest only on Sundays, but we
> fare well. Today, the day I write is Sunday. I have taken my bath, I
> have had my milk, and I will pass the day happily. When did I know life

---

[1] An accurate description of the padrone system among Greek immigrants is portrayed by Fairchild, pp. 172-81.

[2] Grace E. Marshall, Eternal Greece (Rochester, New York: DuBois
Press, 1938), p. 74.

with such order in Greece? If you wish master, you will do well to come, and I'll send you the cost of passage.[1]

Women played a minor role in emigration because of the widespread conviction that the departed men eventually would return home. Hence, Greece became a nation of surplus women, children, and old people. When the heavy male outflow widened the disparity, courageous Greek women were induced to emigrate too. They heard that men went begging for wives of their own nationality and religion in America. The crushing burden of the dowry system and male shortage made them think of America as a matrimonial and economic salvation.[2]

Greeks who resided in the Ottoman Empire and Asia Minor similarly grew weary of poverty and intermittent wars, and welcomed emigration to America as an avenue of escape. Up to 1908, Christians were exempt from the Turkish army by paying a tax each year. Draft-age Greeks escaped military conscription by secretly fleeing to America without passports. One who left in 1911 recalls that "droves left for America, but it was illegal to do so. I deserted from the Turkish army, because I didn't want to kill Greeks."[3] Additional Greeks fled shortly before 1912, because of the threat of a major conflict involving Greece, Bulgaria, and Turkey.

Quantitative data of Greek emigration and immigration

In essence, the migratory profile consisted of the "push" of economic hardship in Greece and the "pull" of economic opportunity in the country of destination. The exact number of Greeks who came to the United States probably will not be known. The failure of the Greek government to keep accurate

---

[1] A survey on the sources and means of Greek immigration is found in Fairchild, pp. 83-105; Burgess, pp. 15-24.

[2] An accurate description of the dowry system is to be found in Rodd, p. 92; also in Garnett, p. 214. For emigration of females see ibid., p. 133, 392. Available figures show that of the 186,016 Greeks in the United States by 1911, some 170,775 (94.5 percent) were males and 9,883 (5.5 percent) were females.

[3] Interview with George Drossos, Chicago, 17 November 1967; also accounts, during 1967-68, from other Greek-Americans from Turkey.

records and the difficulties of defining a "Greek" account for most of the confusion.

The Greek definition of a Greek has been broader than that of an American. Authorities in Greece held that a person always retained his nationality. If his father was Greek, he also was a Greek, regardless of where he was born or where he lived. Greeks in various countries of the Levant considered themselves Greeks, not Turks, Egyptians, or Syrians. The picture was confused further because Greeks counted as their "own" many persons whom America regarded as nationals of Turkey, Italy, and Rumania.[1]

These conflicting standards produced conflicting estimates. The Greek figures showed the entrance of Greeks to the United States as substantially larger than the figures released by American immigration authorities. The leading Greek-American daily, Atlantis, divided them into two categories: those from "free" Greece and those from "enslaved" Greece.[2] On 30 June 1908 the newspaper estimated about 150,000 of the former and 75,000 of the latter resided in the United States. Immigrants from enslaved Greece included those from Turkey, Asia Minor, Aegean Islands, Rumania, and Bulgaria. Another 25,000 were believed to have arrived from Crete, Egypt, Cyprus, and nearby places.

The quantitative discrepancies are evidenced by the compilation of two different tables by students of Greek immigration. A graduate of Johns Hopkins University claims in his study that about one-tenth (over 460,000) of Greece's total population emigrated to America from 1901 to 1930.[3] The peak year was 1907, when 36,580 immigrants arrived. The second largest year was 1914, after the Balkan wars, with 35,832 persons, and the third top year

---

[1] See U.S., Department of State, Papers Relating to the Foreign Relations of the United States (Washington D. C.: Government Printing Office, 1861-) 3 (1928): 25-26; 1 (1929): 458.

[2] Atlantis, 14 January 1909.

[3] As quoted in M. J. Politis, "Greek American," in Francis J. Brown and Joseph S. Roucek, One America: The History, Contributions, and Present Problems of Our Racial and National Minorities, rev. ed. (New York: Prentice-Hall, 1945), p. 245.

was 1922, after the Asia Minor catastrophe, with 28,502. From 1820 to 1934, the total emigration was 488,824. As will be noted from table 3, Valaoras based his figures on the total number of Greeks who emigrated to the United States from Greece and from Turkey, Egypt, Italy, Rumania, and other countries.

Another study, compiled by the editor of the Ethnikos Kyrix (National Herald), a leading Greek daily newspaper, and covering the same period as the Valaoras study (1821-1934), arrived at the figure of 422,246 as the total number of Greek immigrants to the United States for the period under discussion, a difference of 66,578 from the total in the previous study.[1] But the latter study bases its figures on immigration from Greece proper (the Kingdom of Greece), and does not include Greeks who entered the United States from other parts of the world. Presumably then, the 66,578 came from outside of politically defined borders of the Greek state. Table 3 shows a comparison of the two studies.

TABLE 3

COMPARISON OF DATA FOR GREEK IMMIGRATION
FROM TWO SOURCES, 1821-1934

Year	Emigration of Greeks to the U.S. (Data by Valaoras)	Immigration from Greece to the U.S. (Data by Marketos)
1821-1830. . . .	20	20
1831-1840 . . .	49	49
1841-1850 . . .	16	16
1851-1860 . . .	31	31
1861-1870 . . .	72	72
1871-1880 . . .	210	210
1881-1890 . . .	2,308	2,308
1891-1900 . . .	15,979	15,979
1901-1910 . . .	173,513	167,519
1911-1920 . . .	196,119	184,201
1921-1930 . . .	91,369	51,084
1931-1934 . . .	9,138	757
Total for 1821-1934	488,824	422,246

SOURCE: Brown and Roucek, p. 647.

[1] Ibid., p.245.

This factor is depicted more explicitly by the tabulation in table 4, which come from the official figures of the United States Immigration Department. They show that in one decade (1900-1910), nearly 20 percent (33,370) of Greek immigrants emigrated from elsewhere than the independent Kingdom of Greece. The vast majority probably came from Turkish-occupied, or "unredeemed," Greece. Yet, on the census rolls they were often listed as Turks from Turkey. According to one source, between 1900 and 1924, only 5 percent of the people entering the United States from Turkey were Turks; 27 percent were Greeks, 25 percent Syrians, and 18 percent Armenians.[1]

TABLE 4

GREEK IMMIGRATION FOR 10 YEARS,
SHOWING PROPORTION OF GREEKS
FROM GREECE PROPER (1900-1910)

	Total No. of Greeks	From Kingdom of Greece
1900	3,773	3,771
1901	5,919	5,910
1902	8,115	8,104
1903	14,376	14,090
1904	12,625	12,515
1905	12,144	10,515
1906	23,127	19,489
1907	46,283	36,580
1908	28,808	21,489
1909	20,262	14,059
1910	39,135	26,675
Total	214,567	173,197

SOURCE: Lacey, Social Heredity, pp. 43-44.

---

[1] Hannibal G. Duncan, Immigration and Assimilation (New York: D. C. Heath & Co., 1933), p. 508.

A further illustration is presented on table 5 which shows the foreign-born Greek population in the United States by country of origin, in addition to Greece. In 1920, of the 174,658 foreign-born Greeks in the nation, 6,382 were not from Greece. Likewise, in 1930, of 189,066 Greeks in America, a total of 19,420 did not emigrate from Greece. The sharp rise of Greek immigrants from European and Asiatic Turkey in 1930 reflects, no doubt, the expulsion of the Greeks from that country after the 1922 military disaster of the Greeks in Asia Minor.

TABLE 5

FOREIGN-BORN GREEK POPULATION IN UNITED STATES
BY COUNTRY OF ORIGIN, 1920 AND 1930

Country of Origin	Number	
	1930	1920
Greece	169,646	168,276
Asiatic Turkey	11,499	1,451
Italy	1,493	135
Albania	1,094	187
European Turkey	744	2,034
Yugoslavia	682	194
Africa	379	197
Austria	309	634
Bulgaria.	288	134
Other Countries	2,932	1,416
Total	189,066	174,658

SOURCE: Brown and Roucek, p. 647.

The difference in estimates of "Greek immigration" as compared to "immigration from Greece" and the diverse definitions as to what constitutes a Greek have been all-pervasive in the literature. As shown, the terms "enslaved Greece," "Greece proper," "unredeemed parts," and "Greek diaspora" have led to subjective estimates of the total number of Greeks in the United States.

However, the official summary figures of United States Greek immigration, according to a decennial breakdown with Greece as the country of last permanent residence, is shown in table 6. It can be discerned from this table that mass immigration lasted from approximately 1890 to 1930, with the most intense period from 1900 to 1920. The peak year was 1907, when 36,404 persons were recorded as immigrants from Greece. The actual total in that year was 46,283, but 9,879 came from Turkey and other countries and were not listed as immigrants from Greece. According to the United States Commissioner-General of Immigration, the Greek immigration rate for 1907 was about 7 per 1,000 population for all Greeks, and 14 per 1,000 for Greece, the highest rate for any country. The sharp drop of immigrants starting in the 1920s reflects the restrictive covenants of the Immigration Quota Act in 1925. The total immigration from Greece for the 150-year period from 1821 to 1970, is 573,148. It will be noted from the table that a new "mass" immigration from Greece has developed since the relaxation of immigration quotas. In the last two decades--1951-1970--133,677 immigrants from Greece entered the United States.

Characteristics of Greek immigration

An important characteristic of Greek immigration to the United States was the heavy male proportion of immigrants. Very few females crossed the ocean; their small percentage increased significantly only after 1923. This percentage continued to rise as the unmarried Greek immigrants brought wives from Greece. From 1896 to 1900, only 4 women arrived for every 100 men coming to the United States. Five women for every 100 men was the proportion for the decade 1901 to 1910, and 16 for every 100 men was that for 1911 to 1920. The figure jumped to 67 for every 100 men for the period from 1921 to 1924, and by the 1930s, the figure leveled to 35 women for every 100 men.[1] It was not until after World War II that women equaled and sometimes exceeded men in the renewed Greek immigration that followed the postwar period.

It is this feeble representation of Greek women in the United States

---

[1] Brown and Roucek, p. 247.

TABLE 6

IMMIGRATION FROM GREECE BY DECADES
1821-1970

Decade	Number
1821-1830.	20
1831-1840.	49
1841-1850.	16
1851-1860.	31
1861-1870.	72
1871-1880.	210
1881-1890.	2,038
1891-1900.	15,979
1901-1910.	167,579
1911-1920.	184,201
1921-1930.	51,084
1931-1940.	9,119
1941-1950.	8,973
1951-1960.	47,708
1961-1970.	85,969

Total for 150 years 573,148

SOURCE: U.S. Department of Justice,
Annual Report of the Immigration and Natural-
ization Service (Washington, D.C.: Govern-
ment Printing Office, 1965), pp. 47-49; U.S.
Department of Commerce, Bureau of the
Census, Statistical Abstract of the United
States, 1972 (Washington, D.C.: Govern-
ment Printing Office, 1972),p. 92.

that made so precarious the permanence of Greek male immigrants in the new
country during the early years of Greek immigration and hindered considerably their assimilation in the host country. It can be argued, however, that
the lack of Greek women resulted in a high rate of intermarriage and, therefore, accelerated assimilation. And while various sources hint at the considerable rate of intermarriage among early Greek male immigrants, there is
ample evidence that most waited to return to Greece to bring a bride from their
village.

One of the outstanding characteristics of Greek immigration, especially in the first three decades of the twentieth century, has been its impermanence. The Greeks were, for the most part, unwilling to make their home in the United States.[1] The almost exclusive male Greek immigrant population was expected to work in the new land and send regular remittances home to parents and/or siblings. After they had earned money, and after family debts had been paid off, or after dowries had been completed in Greece, they were expected to return and settle in their own native villages.

Many immigrants who had retained close ties with the homeland through correspondence, ethnic Greek press, church, and various Greek organizations felt the pangs of nostalgia. The homeland was seen as the idealistic place of peaceful life, and with the passing of time, many of the undesirable aspects of life in Greece were forgotten. Their bitterness toward the hard lonely life in America was reinforced by the nationalistic feelings aroused in the several war adventures of Greece, and many immigrants crossed the ocean to return again to the familiar soil of their birth.

According to United States government statistics, between 1908 and 1923, the number of immigrants from Greece totaled 366,454. Of these, 168,847, or about 46 percent, returned to Greece.[2] By 1931, some 197,000, or about 40 percent of Greek immigrants to America between 1908 and 1931, were repatriated.[3] These figures do not, however, indicate the number of foreign-born Greeks who finally remained in the United States. Many of those who left for their homeland returned again, or went to Greece only to visit, fight in a war, bring relatives, or simply get married and bring over their wives.[4]

---

[1] G. Abbott, "A Study of the Greeks," p. 380.

[2] Duncan, p. 200.

[3] Saloutos, They Remember America, p. 30. Many of those who were repatriated to Greece returned to the United States, some because of unsuitable conditions in Greece; others to earn additional funds. Indeed, many made several voyages to the homeland before settling permanently in America.

[4] Helen H. Balk, "Economic Contributions of the Greeks to the United States, " Economic Geography 19 (1943): 273.

The Greek Stock in the United States

The foreign-born population of the United States has been vanishing rapidly in recent years, and the closing of the gates after 1924, signified the passing of the early generations and the increase of the native-born population. Table 7 presents the distribution of the Greek ethnic stock in the United States for 1850 to 1970. It distinguishes between the "first generation" (those born in Greece) and "second generation" (native-born of Greek or mixed parentage). From table 7, it can be perceived that from 1900 to 1910, the Greek element increased by over 1,000 percent. The year 1920 has the highest proportion of Greek-born (first generation) population; 1940 was the year when the native-born (second generation) and foreign-born were equal.

TABLE 7

GREEK STOCK IN THE UNITED STATES, 1850-1970

Year	Total	1st Gen.	2nd Gen.
1850	. . . . .	86	. . . . .
1860	. . . . .	328	. . . . .
1870	. . . . .	390	. . . . .
1880	. . . . .	776	. . . . .
1890	. . . . .	1,887	. . . . .
1900	. . . . .	8,515	. . . . .
1910	111,249	101,264	9,985
1920	228,055	175,976	52,083
1930	303,751	174,526	129,225
1940	326,672	163,252	163,420
1950	364,318	169,083	195,235
1960	377,973	158,894	219,079
1970	434,571	178,282	256,289

SOURCE: U.S. Department of Commerce, Bureau of the Census, Immigrants and their Children, 1920, by Niles Carpenter (Washington, D.C.: Government Printing Office, 1927), pp. 78-79; 1940 Census, Nativity and Parentage of the White Population, table 2, p. 10; 1950 Census, vol. 4, Special Reports, table 13, p. 75; 1960 Census, United States Summary, Detailed Characteristics, table 162, p. 366; 1970 Census, United States Summary, General Social and Economic Characteristics, Final Report PC(1)-C1 (1972, table 70, p. 363.

By 1970, the native born second generation exceeded the foreign-born first generation by approximately 78,000 persons. Interestingly, the ratio of increase between the native-born and foreign-born Greek-Americans was almost two to one, 37,210 persons of Greek or mixed parentage born in the United States between 1960 and 1970, compared to 19,388 who immigrated from Greece. Table 8 shows the percentage increase in the Greek-born population of the United States between 1860 and 1920, considered the period of heavy Greek immigration in the United States.

TABLE 8

PERCENT INCREASE IN GREEK-BORN POPULATION
FOR THE UNITED STATES, 1860-1920

Decade	Percent
1860-1870	18.9
1870-1880	99.0
1880-1890	143.0
1890-1900	351.2
1900-1910	1,089.5
1910-1920	73.7

SOURCE: Carpenter, pp. 80-81.

Notable in table 8 is the percentage for the period between 1900 and 1910, which is higher than those other foreign-born groups in the same period.

Despite this, persons from Greece constitute a very small percentage of the total foreign-born stock in the United States. In 1900, they comprised only 0.1 percent of the total ethnic stock, as compared to 1.2 percent in 1930, and 1.3 percent in 1970.[1] At the same time, native Americans of Greek ancestry increased from 0.2 percent in 1920 to 0.7 percent in 1940, and 0.9 percent in 1960, which is still a negligible proportion of the total population of foreign

---

[1] U.S., Department of Commerce, Bureau of Census, 1940 Census of the Population, vol. 2, Characteristics of the Population, pt. 1, U.S. Summary, table 15, p. 43; 1950 Census of the Population, vol. 4, Special Reports, pt. 3, chap. A, Nativity and Parentage, table 12, p. 71; 1970 Census of the Population, General Social and Economic Characteristics, Final Report PC(1)-C1, U.S. Summary, table 70, p. 363.

or mixed parentage.[1]

The changes in the population of Greek immigrants and the coming of a new generation, i.e., the children of Greek immigrants, can be shown in table 9, which presents the ratio of the first to second generation for the period between 1920 and 1960.

TABLE 9

RATIO OF FIRST TO SECOND GENERATION, NATIVE-BORN
OF GREEK OR MIXED PARENTAGE PER 100 GREEK-BORN
1920-1960

Year	Ratio
1920	30
1930	74
1940	100
1950	115
1960	138

SOURCE: Hutchinson, p. 14; U.S. Department of Commerce, Bureau of the Census, 1940 Census, Nativity and Parentage of the White Population, table 2 p. 10; 1950 Census, vol. 4, Special Reports, table 13, p. 75; 1960 Census, U.S. Summary, table 162, p. 366.

From table 9 and also from other information introduced in this study, it can be concluded that the decade ending in 1940, can be considered the important turning point in the demographic history of the Greek ethnic group--the year when the native, second generation began to outnumber the foreign-born, first generation.

Demographic discussions concerning Greek immigrants and Greek stock in the United States are further complicated by the general practice of the United States Census Bureau of tabulating only the first and second generations of immigrant groups, often lumping these together in an aggregate "foreign-stock" category. Third and subsequent generations in the United States are included as "native-born of native parents." Consequently, there

---

[1]U.S., Department of Commerce, Bureau of the Census, 1920 Census of the Population, vol. 2, Population, p. 899; 1940 Census of the Population, Nativity and Parentage of the White Population, pp. 9, 21; 1960 Census of the Population, U.S. Summary, table 162, p. 366.

are no hard data available with reference to third generation "ethnic groups." In spite of this, the present study will attempt to show that the third generation Greek stock is very much part of the Greek ethnic group, due to the informal and formal educational arrangements which sought to perpetuate the ethnic subculture and provide for survival of the Greek ethnic collectivity. The data in this dissertation should help show whether or not the census takers are premature in their implicit assumption that the third generation is already assimilated into the "native stock."

Lacking hard data relative to the size of third generation "Greeks" in the United States, their number must be estimated. By using two different criteria, we are able to arrive at an approximate figure. The first criterion is the fertility rate. According to the United States census, the fertility rate of women in America was 2.1 in 1930.[1] Applying this rate to half of the 129,225 persons of the second generation shown in table 7, (unlike the first generation which was predominantly male, the second generation had a normal sex ratio between males and females), the third generational offspring would be 135,686. Adding this figure to the 434,571 first and second generations listed as Greek stock in the 1970 census (see table 7), we arrive at a three-generational total of 570,257.

Using a second criterion, that of birth rate, we arrive at a higher figure. According to the census, the crude birth rate in 1930, was 21.3 per thousand.[2] In that year, there were 129,225 children of Greek immigrants in America. If we apply the 21.3 birth rate per 1,000 to these individuals who are now middle-aged, their offspring would total 275,249 persons to constitute the third generation. Adding this figure to the 434,571 persons of Greek stock in 1970, produces a grand total of 709,820 persons of Greek ancestry in the United States.

Thus, using these two criteria, the range of the three-generational Greek stock population in the United States is projected from 570,257 to 709,820. Both figures are conservative, as they do not include those born after 1930, who also produced children. An approximate estimate would then

---

[1] World Almanac and Book of Facts (New York: World New York Telegram, 1933), p. 331.

[2] Statistical Abstract of the United States 1971 (Washington, D.C.: Bureau of the Census, 1971), p. 48.

be about 750,000 or perhaps 800,000; still fewer than the 1,000,000 to 1,875,000 usually claimed for persons of Greek descent in the United States.[1]

Policy and Prejudice

As mentioned in chapter 1, the Greeks were part of the "new" immigration from southeastern Europe that entered the country in great numbers after the 1880s. In addition to their "normal" difficulties of adjustment, the distrust of other ethnic groups, and the general hostility and discrimination encountered in the American milieu, the Greek immigrants' problems were compounded in the years before World War I. Native Americans, already somewhat suspicious of the unassimilated aliens in their midst, perhaps were somewhat startled and chagrined to witness the spectacle of fully-armed Greek regiments practicing in several fields in Chicago and then leaving to fight for Greece in the Balkan wars. An estimated 57,000 immigrants returned to Greece from the United States for this conflict.[2]

The native populace expressed concern about the influx of the "alien horde" represented by the "new" immigration, who infected American life with their foreign loyalties and ethnic activities. The mushrooming pressure for more rapid assimilation perhaps found its clearest and most outspoken expression in Theodore Roosevelt's speech to the Knights of Columbus in New York on 12 October 1915:

> No man can be a good citizen if he is not at least in the process of learning to speak the language of his fellow-citizens. And an alien who remains here without learning to speak English for more than a certain number of years should at the end of that time be treated as having refused to take the preliminary steps necessary to complete Americanization and should be deported. But there should be no denial or limitation of the alien's opportunity to work, to own property, and to take advantage of his civic opportunities. . . . . If we leave the immigrant to be helped by representatives of foreign governments, by foreign societies,' by a press and institutions conducted in a foreign language and in the interest of foreign governments, and if we permit the immigrants to exist

---

[1] For examples of estimates of Greeks in the United States, see among others, _Argonaut_ I (1959): 166; George Vournas, "Greeks in America." _Congressional Record_, Proceedings and Debates of the 86th Congress, 2nd sess., vol.106, p. A137; _Statistical Abstract of the United States_, 1971, p. 42.

[2] Lacey, _Social Heredity_, p. 13.

as alien groups, each group sundered from the rest of the citizens of the country, we shall store up for ourselves bitter trouble in the future.[1]

A number of organizations and institutions set out to work toward a quick assimilation of foreigners. It was conceived that the first step toward assimilation would be the learning of the English language by the immigrants. The Educational Alliance of New York, the YMCA, the American International College, and other institutions, societies, and committees provided the newcomers with courses in English and on a variety of subjects in several languages. Many societies, in their eagerness to assimilate the immigrant, hammered the concept that they must forget, as soon as possible, about their past, their language, their culture, and their customs.

The extreme nationalism of the Greeks, their inconsistent attitudes, their illiteracy due to their peasant background, and the impatience of Americans for a fast assimilation made the American attitude toward the Greeks more inflexible. The mere fact that Greeks were immigrants was not in their favor: they felt even more handicapped because of their southern European origin and their relatively late arrival in the United States. Prejudices and discrimination were mostly from competition with other immigrant groups, but there also were cases of riots and mob action against Greeks led by native Americans. In general, however, discrimination against them did not take any organized form.[2] America was the land of "gold-paved streets," the land of "milk and honey." But for many of the Greek immigrants, who experienced resentment by older immigrant groups, America was also the land of inhuman indifference, of ceaseless and back-breaking work, and of people hostile to different customs and traditions.[3]

As indicated in chapter 1, between 1914 and 1924, American immigration policy changed decisively. The changing attitude toward immigrants was

---

[1] Cited in Philip Davis, Immigration and Americanization (Boston: Ginn & Co., 1920), p. 655.

[2] For certain manifestations of prejudice and discrimination against the Greeks in the United States, see Theodore Constant, "Racial Prejudice and the Greek Stock in the United States," Athene 5 (1944): 8-11.

[3] Helen Zeese Papanikolas, "Toil and Rage in a New Land: The Greek Immigrants in Utah," Utah Historical Quarterly 38 (Spring 1970): 100-203.

due to a combination of events. First of all, there were the fears and appre-
hensions aroused by the various ethnic groups whose countries of origin opposed the United States in international conflict. On the other hand, the
great waves of immigrants imperiled the standards set by the labor organizations and created fears of lowering the standard of living, creating pauperism
and crime. A new policy of restriction began developing; its underlying
assumption was the basic superiority of the "older" over the "newer" immigrants.

The heightened nativistic movements affected the Greeks in two ways.
One was a frustration-aggression which developed from the feelings of infer-
iority and the striving for a higher status within the American society. This
resulted in the fast discarding of the ethnic culture by some for a speedier
identification with the dominant culture. In contrast, ethnic ideology increased in many Greeks, and the feeling of superiority, derived from the
glory of their ethnic past, developed a sense of exalted Hellenism. As
Wheeler observed at the turn of the century, "No motive appeals more
strongly to the modern Greek than the desire to be worthy of those he believes to be his ancestors . . . "[1] It was this latter, intense feeling which
led to the determination of Greek immigrants to perpetuate their culture at all
costs and to provide whatever educational agencies necessary to insure the
survival of Hellenism in the New World.

Summary

In this chapter, a brief description of the Old World background of
Greek immigrants was presented to acquaint the reader with the environmental
factors which conditioned and influenced the attitudes and lifestyle of these
immigrants in the New World. A physical description of Greece portrayed its
political, social, economic, religious, and educational conditions in the historical context which molded the Greek immigrant and gave reason for his emigration to the United States. The impetus to emigrate was traced briefly to
illustrate that emigration has been an age-old Greek phenomenon. It was
shown that prior to the advent of the "new" immigration of the 1890s,numerous
Greeks had arrived in the New World in a variety of ways and capacities. The

[1]Wheeler, p. 609.

chapter concludes with an attempt to determine the number of Greek immigrants who came as part of the "new" immigration and the extent of the present Greek stock in the United States. It now remains for the next chapter to discuss the nature of this Greek immigration with particular reference to its settlement in Chicago, the locale of this study.

CHAPTER II

THE SETTLEMENT OF GREEKS IN CHICAGO

In the previous chapter, an overview was presented of the social
structure, cultural forces, and ethos of Greek people from ancient times to
the period of mass emigration to America. This chapter portrays their struggle
and adjustment for ethnic survival when they arrived in Chicago. It also
highlights the "Greek way of life" and the basic institutions that were paramount in the lives of Greek immigrants.

Greek Communal System

Institutions as primary forms of a social order that structure the activities and relationships of members and groups build up into complex patterns
which are relatively stable and persistent and which also define their network
of values.[1] The family, church, school, voluntary associations, language
factor and immigrant press--all intertwined in helping Greeks to cope with
the demands of physical and social existence and give meaning to life. They
were the bedrocks for fulfilling the most basic needs and wants for individual
and collective ethnic survival.

The nature of ethnic groups has been delineated in varied ways. Max
Weber states that

> . . . in colonies, the attachment to the colonists' homeland survives
> despite considerable mixing with the inhabitants of the colonial land
> and despite profound changes in the tradition and hereditary type as
> well.[2]

---

[1] For a survey of major institutions in the Greek community of Chicago
see Constance Bikos, "Greek Institutions in Chicago" (Master's thesis,
Roosevelt University, 1966).

[2] Max Weber, "Ethnic Groups," in Talcott Parsons et al eds., Theories
of Society (New York: The Free Press of Glencoe, 1961), 2: 305-8.

He further says that the sense of an ethnic community is determined by such diverse factors as sharing the same language and specific culture; sharing distinctive social traits and "political memory" with old communities; objective or subjective belief in consanguinity and style of economic life; and the unceasing strength of kinship groups and other communal relationships pervasive between the old and new community.[1] Therefore, these were universal elements of ethnic affinity.

According to Toennies, the ethnic group appears to be a subtype of the Gemeinschaft, which is formed by the transposition of characteristics from primary face-to-face groups to those of the secondary group. Once the ethnic group has reached a certain maturity, the ideology may change without affecting its identity.[2]

Weber's definition is supplemented by Francis' six factors in attempting to determine the nature of the ethnic group.[3] They include: (1) culture, which is usually regarded as a fundamental factor, (2) social interrelationship, since all social relations presuppose contacts and communication; hence, a common language, (3) racial affinity, where endogamous marriages are the rule and marriage outside the group is taboo, (4) physical and mental traits which may be based on heredity and common descent and which influence the social behavior of the group, (5) space factor, since human beings are spatial entities, and (6) time factor, giving the group a feeling of solidarity that has been achieved mutually over a period of time, obliterating the possibility of having belonged to another ethnic group.

Expansion, fission, and new combinations are the stages of development of new ethnic groups in America, according to Francis. For him, the factors of religion and language seem to be the most essential forces in the formation or revival of ethnic groups.[4] As will be seen in this and future chapters, these two factors were important motivating forces in the Greek

---

[1] Ibid.

[2] Ferdinand Toennies, "Gemeinschaft and Gesellschaft" in Parsons et al., 2: 191-201.

[3] E. K. Francis, "The Nature of the Ethnic Group," American Journal of Sociology 52 (1946-47): 393-400.

[4] Ibid., p. 398.

community.

Louis Wirth classifies ethnic or minority groups into four types--
pluralistic, assimilationist, seccessionist, and militant.[1] The first two
types are relevant here. A pluralistic minority is one which seeks toleration
for differences on the part of the dominant group. A pluralistic minority will
generally discourage intermarriage and intimate social intercourse with the
dominant group, while the assimilationist minority puts no such obstacle in
its members' paths. Instead, the latter looks upon the crossing of stocks
and blending of cultures as wholesome end products.[2]

It was this type of "melting pot" idea that encouraged the belief that
thirty-eight million immigrants would be absorbed and blended into a new
American culture at the turn of the century. Investigation shows that the
"melting pot" failed to "melt."[3] In his earlier work, Glazer elaborated on
the evolving American society as follows:

> What has changed in America primarily is the sense of homogeneity that
> is a natural part of most great cultures . . . which has been replaced
> by a pervasive sense of heterogeneity. A hundred years ago, there were
> three American subcultures, New England, the South and the West. All
> three shared a good deal in common. Today, there are scores. There is
> the life of the big cities, of the urban Negroes and the rural Negroes,
> of the Jews, and the Italians, of the midwestern farmers, of the city
> middle classes and the self-conscious intellectuals . . . so the immi-
> grant groups have changed American culture: within this changed culture,
> they, as well as the long-settled groups of English, Irish, and Germans,
> are now quite at home.[4]

When ethnic communities persist beyond the early immigrant stages,
they contain individuals with varying degrees of acculturation, according to
Broom and Kitsuse. The organizations and institutions of the ethnic group
change, and some take on the essential characteristics of the larger society.
Broom and Kitsuse designate them as parallel ethnic institutions that can be
significant in acculturation in at least three respects:

> they ameliorate the stresses of interethnic situations and provide
> contexts of acculturation under relatively permissive conditions;

---

[1]Louis Wirth, "The Problem of Minority Groups," in Parsons et al.,
2: 309-15.

[2]Ibid., pp. 312-13.

[3]Glazer and Moynihan, pp. 310-15.

[4]Nathan Glazer, "The Integration of American Immigrants," Law and
Contemporary Problems 21 (Spring 1956): 256-83.

they provide criteria of acculturation for the less acculturated and more isolated members of the ethnic group;

they legitimize the status system of the ethnic community in which we can expect to find transplanted important aspects of the stratification criteria of the dominant society.[1]

The myriad defintions for ethnic groups suggest the conscious or unconscious inclination for such groups to want "my kind of people" and perpetuate ethnic identity and survival. These preferred associates for the intimate aspects of life provide identification in the midst of an impersonal metropolis.

Chicago During the Progressive Era

Chicago's Greek immigrants were among the alien groups who were caught up in the great progressive and reform movements that swept the nation in the latter part of the nineteenth and the first decades of the twentieth centuries. They arrived in large numbers during the height of the Populist movement in the 1890s, and built their communal institutions during the muckraking period, 1900 to 1914. These two movements took place during the rapid and turbulent transitional era when conditions switched from agrarian to modern urban life. Without being cognizant of the social and political reform movements swirling about them, the Greek immigrants found themselves participating in the nation's industrialization and urbanization.

The millions who poured into the United States from southern and eastern Europe discovered that

. . . America was no longer in a come-one, come-all mood. Many of the older settlers, feeling crowded and cornered, had little welcome for any newcomer, and every prejudice in the American collection was roused by immigrants who were predominantly impoverished and unskilled, short and dark in appearance, Catholic or Jewish in religion. Rapidly the national speech was acquiring phrases that carried as much sneer and hiss as any in the language--"wop" and "dago" for the Italian, "bohunk" for the Hungarian, "grease-ball" for the Greek, and "kike" for the Jew.[2]

Out of the clash between the needs of the immigrants and the sentiments of the natives emerged two different systems of political ethics. One,

---

[1]Leonard Broom and John Kitsuse, "The Validation of Acculturation: A Condition to Ethnic Assimilation," American Anthropologist 57 (February 1955): 45.

[2]Eric F. Goldman, Rendezvous with Destiny: A History of Modern American Reform (New York: Random House, Vintage Books, 1956), pp. 29-30.

founded upon the indigenous Yankee-Protestant political traditions and middle-class life, assumed and demanded the constant, disinterested activity of the citizen in public affairs; the other, founded upon the European background, was unfamiliar with independent political action, although aware of hierarchy and authority, and placed strong personal obligations and loyalties above allegiance to abstract codes of law or morals. Thus, the Progressive era was influenced by the conflict between these two codes, "elaborated on one side by the highly moral leaders of the Protestant social reform and on the other by the bosses, political professionals, and immigrant masses.[1]

The conflict between these two systems of political ethics found the immigrants subjected to a vast naturalization and Americanization effort. The Yankee Protestant traditionalists argued that only by acquainting the immigrants with the English language and civic instruction could they become true Americans and place the civic good above personal needs and aspirations.[2]

General Demographic Conditions

At the turn of the century Chicago experienced extraordinary growth and became a microcosm of the broader nation.[3] Industrialization, urbaniza-

---

[1] Richard Hofstadter, The Age of Reform (New York: Random House, Vintage Books, 1955), pp. 8-9. Standard texts on social aspects of the reform movement in the United States for this period are Frederick Lewis Allen, Only Yesterday (New York: Harper and Row, 1931); and Dwight Lowell Dumond, America in Our Time, 1896-1946 (New York: Henry Holt & Co., 1947).

[2] An insightful look at the social relationship between industrial growth and immigrants with reference to Americanization is to be found in Gerd Korman, Industrialization, Immigrants and Americanizers (Madison: State Historical Society of Wisconsin, 1967). The chapter on "The Fabric of Society" in her History of Chicago,Bessie Louise Pierce provides a survey of immigrant groups in Chicago during the period 1871-93, as they struggled through the transition from loyalties to the old country to acceptance of the new; see Bessie L. Pierce, History of Chicago, 3 vols. (New York: Alfred A. Knopf, 1937-57), vol. 3.

[3] Arthur Meier Schlesinger, The Rise of the City, 1878-1908 (New York: Macmillan Co., 1933), pp. 64-66. Standard works on the growth of American cities are Blake McKelvey, The Urbanization of America, 1860-1915 (New Brunswick, N.J.: Rutgers University Press, 1963); Constance McLaughlin Green, American Cities in the Growth of the Nation (New York, Harper and Row, 1965); and Barbara Habenstreit, The Making of Urban America (New York: Julian Messner, 1970).

tion, and later, Americanization were dominant influences.[1]

As shown in table 10, the population of the city increased at the rate of more than 500,000 each decade from 1880 to 1920, a span of time when Greek immigration to Chicago was heaviest.

TABLE 10

GROWTH OF CHICAGO'S POPULATION, 1870-1970

Year	Population	Absolute Growth in Decade	Percent Increase
1870 . . .	298,977	189,717	173.6
1880 . . .	503,185	204,208	68.3
1890 . . .	1,099,850	596,665	118.6
1900 . . .	1,698,575	598,725	54.4
1910 . . .	2,185,283	486,718	28.7
1920 . . .	2,701,705	516,422	23.6
1930 . . .	3,376,438	674,733	25.0
1940 . . .	3,396,808	20,370	0.6
1950 . . .	3,620,962	224,154	6.6
1960 . . .	3,550,404	- 70,558	. . .
1970 . . .	3,366,957	-183,447	. . .

SOURCE: Compiled from Hauser and Kitagawa, Fact Book for Chicago 1950, table A, p. 2; and U. S. Department of Commerce, Bureau of the Census, 1970 Census: General Social and Economic Characteristics, United States Summary, Final Report PC(1)-C1 (Washington, D.C.: Government Printing Office, 1972), table 28, p. 116.

The city's spectacular growth diminished by 1940, as a result of the Immigration Quota acts in the 1920s and the Depression of the 1930s. By 1950, an increase began again, probably due to the immigration of blacks and the early effects of the Displaced Persons Act. The 1960 and 1970 censuses

---

[1] Frances Kellor, "Americanization by Industry," Immigrants in America Reviews (April 1916), cited in Hyphenated Americans, 1914-1924 of Makers of America series, 7: 30-33. Kellor advocated that industry should take the lead in Americanizing immigrants.

show a decrease, reflecting a population shift of middle-class families to the suburbs.

The Thirteenth Federal Census of 1910 revealed that a total of thirty-six nationalities represented the city's ethnic groups.[1] The proportion of foreign-born persons in the total white population of Chicago was considerably larger than that of the United States. In 1920, only 14.5 percent of the white population in the nation was foreign-born, while the Chicago rate was double--29.8 percent (incorrectly listed as 28.4 percent by Jeter).[2] As seen in table 11, Chicago's proportion of about two-thirds native-born and one-third foreign-born remained fairly constant from 1890 to 1920. In the decades 1920-1940, because of war and federal immigration restrictions, the foreign-born population dropped from 29.8 percent to 19.8 percent. As of 1920, however, only about one-fourth of Chicago's residents were of native parentage; three-fourths of the white inhabitants were either of foreign birth or of foreign or mixed parentage.[3] This composition did not begin to change until after World War II, the foreign-born residents dropping from 19.8 percent in 1940, to 14.5 percent in 1950, and to a low of 9.7 percent in 1960, but rising again up to 11.1 percent in 1970, reflecting renewed emigration to the city (see table 11).

Chicago had become the terminal point of opportunity for immigrants who were attracted by its growing industries. The city became a patchwork quilt of diverse ethnic groups whose commonalities were poverty and a determination to get ahead. Despite the immigration restrictions of the 1920s, Chicago continued to be one of the most ethnic cities in the United States. A comparison with other major cities with large ethnic populations during 1960 (see table 12), shows that Chicago ranked third in the number of people of foreign stock residing in the metropolitan area. Roughly one-third (2,015,562) of the total population consisted of first or second generation foreign stock. According to the 1970 census, 11.1 percent was foreign-born and 18.6 percent was second generation (see tables 11 and 15).

---

[1] G. Abbott, Immigrant and Community, pp. 221-22.

[2] Helen R. Jeter, Trends of Population in the Region of Chicago (Chicago: University of Chicago Press, 1927), p. 35.

[3] Ibid., p. 20.

TABLE 11

COMPARISON OF TOTAL POPULATION, FOREIGN-BORN AND GREEK FOREIGN-BORN CITY OF CHICAGO 1890-1970

	1890	1900	1910	1920	1930	1940	1950	1960	1970
Total Population	1,099,850	1,698,575	2,185,283	2,701,705	3,376,438	3,396,808	3,620,962	3,550,404	3,362,947
Foreign-born White	449,628	585,420	781,217	805,482	855,777	672,705	526,058	438,392	373,919
Percent Foreign-born (white)	40.9	34.5	35.7	29.8	25.3	19.8	14.5	9.7	11.1
Greek	245	1,493	6,564	11,546	14,815	13,972	13,011	NA	15,816
Greek Percent of Foreign-born	.05	.25	.84	1.4	1.7	2.1	2.5	NA	4.2

NA = not available

SOURCE: Compiled from Hauser and Kitagawa, Fact Book for Chicago 1950, pp. 2, 291; U.S. Department of Commerce, Bureau of the Census, 1970 Census: General Social and Economic Characteristics, Illinois (Washington, D.C.: Government Printing Office, 1972), table 40, p. 325. Data for Greek foreign-born compiled from U.S. Census.

TABLE 12

FOREIGN STOCK IN FIVE MAJOR CITIES, 1960

City	Population	Total Percent Foreign-born	Percent 1st Gen.	Percent 2nd Gen.
New York	10,695,963	45.8	17.4	28.4
Chicago	6,220,913	32.4	9.7	22.7
Detroit	3,764,131	30.1	9.7	20.4
Boston	2,590,040	41.8	12.4	29.4
Pittsburgh	2,406,301	28.8	6.5	22.3

SOURCE: U.S. Department of Commerce, Bureau of Census, 1960 Census: General Social and Economic Characteristics, United States Summary, table 141, pp. 292-93.

The current extent of Chicago's ethnic composition is shown in table 13. Major nationality groups are listed according to the 1960 and 1970 census figures, indicating changes that have taken place in the ethnic population of the city.

Greek Population and Distribution

The number of foreign-born Greeks in Chicago from 1880 to 1970 is indicated in table 11. These figures represent actual immigrants, and give no indication of how many remained in the city. Since the Greeks had a high repatriation rate, it is safe to assume that many returned to Greece. Those that remained permanently in Chicago became the pioneers of the Greek community and progenitors of the second and third generations that make up the bulk of the city's Hellenic population.

These figures show how diminutive the Greek element was in the city's total population. Greek immigrants constituted only 1.4 percent of the total foreign-born white population in Chicago during 1920; 1.7 percent in 1930; 2.1 percent in 1940; 2.5 percent in 1950; and jumped to 4.2 percent in 1970. The Greek immigrant population rose from an insignificant .05 percent of Chicago's total foreign-born population in 1890 to 4.2 percent in 1970. This rise took place during an eighty-year span when the city's total foreign-born white population decreased drastically from a high of 40.9 percent in 1890,

TABLE 13

COUNTRY OF ORIGIN OF FOREIGN STOCK (FIRST AND SECOND GENERATION)
FOR MAJOR NATIONALITY GROUPS: CITY OF CHICAGO, 1960-1970

National Origin	1960	1970	1960-1970 Change Number	Percent
Poland	258,657	191,955	- 66,702	- 25.8
Italy	134,963	97,742	- 37,221	- 27.6
Germany	161,567	99,413	- 62,154	- 38.5
U.S.S.R.	96,626	64,179	- 32,447	- 33.6
Ireland	85,120	56,412	- 28,708	- 33.7
Czechoslovakia	50,003	30,492	- 19,511	- 39.0
Sweden	51,537	26,988	- 24,549	- 47.6
United Kingdom	52,039	30,101	- 21,938	- 42.2
Lithuania	47,634	31,629	- 16,005	- 33.6
Austria	41,664	28,524	- 13,140	- 31.5
Yugoslavia	31,958	28,738	- 3,220	- 10.1
Hungary	24,240	16,143	- 8,097	- 33.4
Greece	25,120	27,990	+ 2,870	+ 11.4
Mexico	44,686	82,097	+ 37,411	+ 83.7
Puerto Rico	32,371	78,963	+ 46,592	+143.9
All Countries*	1,277,341	1,000,982	-276,359	- 21.6
Negro Population	812,637	1,102,620	+289,983	+ 35.7
Total Population	3,550,404	3,366,957	-183,447	- 5.2

SOURCE: Pierre de Vise and Ruth Ramirez, Shifts in
Chicago's Ethnic Communities, 1960-1970 (Chicago Regional Hospital Study, 1973), p. 16. (Mimeographed.)

*Puerto Ricans are not included in foreign stock totals.

to a low of 11.1 percent in 1970. Likewise, table 14 shows that the percentage of the Greek stock (foreign-born and native-born) rose from 1.2 percent in 1930 to 2.8 percent in 1970. This happened despite the fact that the total foreign white stock in Chicago decreased from 2,193,516 to 1,000,982. A factor to be taken into consideration is the influx of new arrivals who emigrated to Chicago during the postwar period and the fact that the total percentage of foreign white stock was halved between 1930 and 1970. Accordingly, by 1970, Greek immigrants in Chicago constituted 4.2 percent of all foreign-born whites in the city, and together with their American-born children, comprised 2.8 percent of the total foreign white stock.

TABLE 14

COMPARISON OF TOTAL GREEK FOREIGN STOCK
IN CHICAGO, 1930 AND 1970

	1930	1970
Total Population	3,376,438	3,362,947
Total Foreign White Stock	2,193,516	1,000,982
Percentage of Foreign White Stock . . .	65.0	29.7
Greek or of Greek ancestry	26,384	27,990
Percentage of Foreign White Stock . . .	1.2	2.8

SOURCE: Compiled from Evelyn M. Kitagawa and Karl E. Taeuber, Local Community Fact Book: Chicago Metropolitan Area, 1960 (Chicago University of Chicago, 1963), p. 293; U.S. Department of Commerce, Bureau of the Census, 1970 Census, General Social and Economic Characteristics, Illinois (Washington, D.C.: Government Printing Office, 1972), table 81, p. 382.

Quantitatively, the number of Greeks was sufficiently large to permit the formation of a viable subcultural community. From this ethnic community a large number of children, in relation to the size of the community, enrolled in Chicago public schools, a lesser amount in the communal day schools, though practically all became exposed to some form of ethnic schooling, as explained in chapter 5.

As depicted in table 15, the number of American-born children of Greek immigrants in 1930 was 11,569, and they comprised only 0.9 percent of the total native-born Americans of foreign or mixed parentage. In 1970, the figure was 12,174 (this figure does not include those who, by this time, were living in the suburbs): 3.3 percent of all native-Americans of foreign stock.

TABLE 15

COMPARISON OF NATIVE-WHITES OF FOREIGN OR MIXED PARENTAGE
WITH NATIVE-BORN OF GREEK OR MIXED PARENTAGE
CHICAGO, 1930 AND 1970

	1930	1970
Total Population	3,376,438	3,362,947
Total Native-born White		
Foreign, or Mixed Parentage .	1,337,739	373,919
Percentage	39.0	18.6
Greece	11,569	12,174
Percentage	0.9	3.3

SOURCE: Compiled from Kitagawa and Taeuber, p. 292; U.S. Department of Commerce, Bureau of the Census, 1970 Census: General Social and Economic Characteristics, United States Summary (Washington, D.C.: Government Printing Office, 1972), table 144, p. 474.

According to the United States census, in 1960, there were 25,120 persons of Greek stock in Chicago (foreign-born and native-born). This made them the fourteenth largest ethnic group in the city. In 1970, the figure was 27,990 for both generations, an 11.4 percent increase for the decade, placing them thirteenth among the largest ethnic groups in Chicago (see table 13). These figures do not include third generation "Greeks," since the United States census defines foreign stock as only those of foreign-birth or children of foreign-born. This excludes grandchildren of immigrants. Since 11,569 of the 26,334 ethnic Greeks living in Chicago in 1930 were native-born or second generation (see table 15), and assuming that these 11,569 married and had 2.1 children (1930 fertility rate),[1] there would have been produced approximately 24,295 children of the third generation. But this presumes that they all married outside of their ethnic group. Obviously, this was not generally the case, since endogamy was still an important feature of Greek life,

[1] World Almanac and Book of Facts 1933, p. 331.

though many did marry outside of their group. Assuming, therefore, that these 11,569 married one another, their offspring would total 12,148, patently a conservative figure.

For the sake of argument, therefore, if the third generation figure of 12,148 is added to the 27,990 of the first and second generation Greek stock listed in the 1970 census, it can be stated that the conservative estimate of the "Greek" population of Chicago is 40,138. But this amount does not include those who married outside of their ethnic group, nor those residing in the suburbs, though it would be assumed that many of those moving to the suburbs would be members of the third generation included in the figures above.

A study of table 16 makes apparent the shift of Greek stock to the suburbs. It will be noted that Chicago's total Greek stock increased between 1960 and 1970 by only 2,870 persons, while the Chicago metropolitan area (CSMSA--does not include suburbia) increased during the same period by 10,469. Suprisingly, 6,209 of these were foreign-born, while 4,260 were native-born, suggesting a higher upward mobility of the first generation over the second generation. Thus, in 1960, of 34,000 foreign-stock Greeks in the metropolitan area, 25,120 lived in Chicago and 9,425 in the suburban fringe. By comparison, in 1970, of 45,014 living in the metropolitan area, 27,990 resided in Chicago and 17,024 in the suburbs, a shift of nearly 10,000 for the decade.

Accordingly, if the 12,148 persons of the third generation were added to the 45,014 first and second generation Greek stock residing in the Chicago metropolitan area in 1970, a total three-generational figure of 57,162 can be arrived at. Using the second criterion--the 21.3 per thousand birthrate in 1930--and multiplying this figure with 11,569 (second generation), we arrive at a third generation total of 24,642. Adding this total to the 27,990 Greek stock (first and second generation 1970 census), we get a grand total of 52,632. A more realistic figure would be to add 24,642 (third generation) to 45,014 (first and second generation) for a total of 69,656 Greek stock residing in metropolitan Chicago. Consequently, on the basis of these two criteria, the range of the three-generational Greek stock population is projected from 57,162 to 69,656.

But even this is a conservative estimate for it does not allow for

TABLE 16

COMPARISON OF GREEK FOREIGN STOCK IN STATE OF ILLINOIS, CHICAGO
STANDARD METROPOLITAN STATISTICAL AREA (CSMSA)
AND CITY OF CHICAGO FOR 1960 AND 1970

	Total Foreign Stock	Foreign Born	Native Born of Foreign or Mixed Parentage
1960			
Illinois	38,846	16,660	21,186
CSMSA	34,545	14,995	19,550
Chicago	25,120	NA	NA
1970			
Illinois	48,669	22,308	26,361
CSMSA	45,014	21,204	23,810
Chicago	27,990	15,816	12,174

NA = Not Available

SOURCE: U.S. Department of Commerce, Bureau of the Census,
Census of Population: 1960, vol. 1, Characteristics of the Population,
pt. 15, Illinois (Washington, D.C.: Government Printing Office, 1961),
table 99, p. 475; 1970 Census: General Social and Economic Characteristics, United States Summary (Washington, D.C.: Government Printing
Office, 1972), table 144, p. 474.

second generation children born after 1930, or for the offspring of mixed marriages, nor for those of the fourth generation who would be, for the most part,
under the age of 10. Nonetheless, there are probably fewer than 75,000 persons of Greek descent in metropolitan Chicago. This figure represents
approximately 10 percent of all persons of Greek stock in the United States
over a three-generational span. It is considerably less than the 125,000 to
250,000 which the Greek press and community leaders claim for the Greek
community of Chicago. But from its initial stages until recently, it has been
the largest Greek community in the United States and the first to respond to
the need for educational adjustment and ethnic survival.

As shown in table 11, the census figures for 1900, reveal that there

were 1,493 Greeks in Chicago. A profile of the population dispersion before
1900, indicated that in the early 1890s, the first Greek shops were found at
Clark and Kinzie Streets, just north of the Loop. It was here that the city's
first "Greektown" was located, with the first organized church at Union and
Randolph Streets and later at 60 West Kinzie Street.[1]

By 1895, the Greek immigrants began to move to the near West Side.
A newspaper account observes:

> The better class of Greeks is to be found on South Water Street, while
> the poorer class is sandwiched in the settlements of Italians, Syrians,
> and Slavonians [sic] on the West Side. West Polk Street from the
> river to Blue Island Avenue is thickly populated with Greeks.[2]

A later newspaper account gives a further delineation of the Greek settle-
ment by indicating three areas of concentration: Fifth Avenue (Wells) and
Sherman Street between Van Buren and Twelfth Street; the North Side at
Kingsbury, Kinzie, and Illinois Streets; and "the vicinity of Tilden Avenue,
Taylor Street and Center Avenue on the West Side."[3]

The Greek population of Chicago grew rapidly at the beginning of
this century. In 1904, there were reportedly 7,500 Greeks; in 1909, about
15,000, of whom 12,000 came and went according to their work in the city
or on the railroad lines in states further West.[4]

As the Greeks became more numerous, they invaded the Italian section, gradually displacing the Italians from the area. The district surrounded
by Halsted, Harrison, Blue Island, and Polk Streets was known as the
"Delta" and was just north and west of the famed Hull House and the present

---

[1]Greek Press (Chicago), 6 January 1935.

[2]Chicago Tribune, 7 April 1895.

[3]Chicago Tribune, 15 February 1897.

[4]Fairchild, p. 123. These figures do not concur with those of Grace
Abbott in her sociological study of Greeks in Chicago. She cites that, according to the school census of 1908, there were 4,218 Greeks in Chicago,
of whom 3,521 were foreign-born and 697 American-born. She does add,
however, that the Greeks claim four or five times as many, for "undoubtedly
during the winter the colony is very much larger"due to the school census
being taken in May after the "gang" workers on the railroad had gone out for
the summer, "so that a great many of those who make Chicago their home
during the winter months were not counted." See G. Abbott, "Study of the
Greeks," pp. 379-80.

location of the University of Illinois Chicago Circle Campus. It became Chicago's famous "Greektown"--the oldest, largest, and most important settlement of Greeks in the United States.[1] By 1930, this area had a foreign and native-born population of 10,000 to 15,000 Greeks.

The first permanent Greek community comprised of church and school was organized in the Delta. In this transplanted part of Greece emerged the first Greek language newspapers, offices of benevolent, fraternal and social organizations, and new businesses which soon surpassed those on Lake Street. According to Fairchild, the district became more typically Greek than some sections of Athens. Practically all

. . . stores bear signs in both Greek and English, coffee-houses flourish on every corner, in the dark little grocery stores one sees black olives, dried ink-fish, tomato paste, and all the queer, nameless roots and condiments which are so familiar in Greece. On every hand one hears the Greek language, and the boys in the streets and on the vacant lots play, with equal zest, Greek games and baseball. It is a self-sufficient colony, and provision is made to supply all the wants of the Greek immigrant in as near as possible the Greek way. Restaurants, coffee-houses, barber-shops, grocery stores and saloons are all patterned after the Greek type, and Greek doctors, lawyers, editors, and every variety of agent are to be found in abundance.[2]

While the Delta was to remain the largest concentration of Greek immigrants in Chicago, by no means was it the only one. A second concentration of Greek newcomers developed on the South Side. After 1904, Greek shops and stores appeared in the Woodlawn district, mainly along Sixty-third Street between Wentworth and Cottage Grove. Subsequently, a second church community was organized with the assistance of a dissident group from the original Delta community. It became known as the church and school of Saints Constantine and Helen, and a building was erected in 1909

---

[1] Ibid.

[2] Fairchild, pp. 123-24. For a colorful description of Chicago's Greektown at Halsted and Harrison Streets see Edward A. Steiner, On the Trail of the Immigrant (New York: Fleming H. RevellCo., 1906), pp. 282-91; Theano P. Margaris, Chroniko tou Halsted street [Chronicle of Halsted street] (Athens: G. Phexis, 1962) and her Etchings of Chicago (Athens: n.p. 1967); Jimis Brooklis [K. T. Argoe], To spiti tou metanasti [The house of the immigrant] (Chicago: Institute for Greek-American Historical Studies, 1967); also, G. Abbott, Immigrant Community, pp. 243-44.

at Sixty-first and Michigan Avenue.[1]

Similarly, Greek immigrants began to move to the North Side, some coming from the first area of settlement at Clark and Kinzie Streets. A third church and school community was organized and erected independently at LaSalle and Oak Streets in 1910 and dedicated to the Annunciation of the Virgin Mary. Gradually, as Greek immigrants dispersed to other parts of the city, additional church communities were organized. By 1930 Greek immigrants had organized eleven formal communities in Chicago. Today persons of Greek descent are dispersed throughout the metropolitan area and clustered around seventeen Greek Orthodox parish churches, six of which are located in the suburbs. Each parish church represents a _koinotis_ (community) named after the church's patron saint. The nucleus of such a _koinotis_ is the church, which serves as a multi-functional center for religious, educational, social, and cultural activities.

The church is an ecological concept for Greek Orthodox Christians. If asked where one lives, he is more likely to use the name of the church as a place of reference. Generally, church parishes in the central city tend to be oriented toward recent immigrants coming after World War II. Parishes toward the northern, western, and southern outskirts of the city tend to be oriented toward first and second generation Greek stock. Suburban parishes are all postwar phenomena representing the movement of second and third generations to the suburbs. Figure 1 on page 96 shows the location of the original church communities, their subsequent relocation, and the location of the newly-organized church communities in the suburbs.

General Living Conditions

The foreign population influx made it necessary for Chicago to increase housing, sanitation, transportation, and other municipal services. The Great Fire of 1871 had destroyed the entire central city. The primary urgency was to rebuild. Additional impetus was provided by the Columbian Exposition of 1893. Enterprising men became attracted to new opportunities

---

[1] For a detailed history of this community see James Steve Counelis and Andrew T. Kopan, "Chicago--Bastion of Orthodoxy: The Story of Saints Constantine and Helen," _Athene_ 16 (Summer 1955): 17-31.

68

Figure 1. Greek Orthodox Church Communities of Chicago and Suburbs (1892–1973)

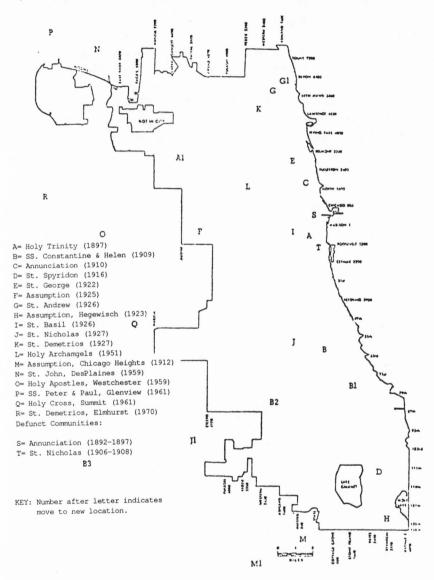

A= Holy Trinity (1897)
B= SS. Constantine & Helen (1909)
C= Annunciation (1910)
D= St. Spyridon (1916)
E= St. George (1922)
F= Assumption (1925)
G= St. Andrew (1926)
H= Assumption, Hegewisch (1923)
I= St. Basil (1926)
J= St. Nicholas (1927)
K= St. Demetrios (1927)
L= Holy Archamgels (1951)
M= Assumption, Chicago Heights (1912)
N= St. John, DesPlaines (1959)
O= Holy Apostles, Westchester (1959)
P= SS. Peter & Paul, Glenview (1961)
Q= Holy Cross, Summit (1961)
R= St. Demetrios, Elmhurst (1970)
Defunct Communities:

S= Annunciation (1892–1897)
T= St. Nicholas (1906–1908)

KEY: Number after letter indicates
     move to new location.

and worked closely with the "gray wolves"--Chicago's City Council alder-men.[1] Collaborations between Chicago's upper echelon and the corrupt politicians so infuriated a visiting English editor, William T. Stead, that he spent several months documenting the collusion, hopeful of arousing the citizenry of Chicago to action.[2] His revelations helped evolve a new civic conscience that launched the first Chicago reform movement of any importance, the Civic Federation.[3]

Stead was appalled not only by the corrupt city government, but by the plight of the working man and the indifference of the city to its poor. The thousands of desolate immigrants were the locus of the so-called "sweating system" of the clothing trade, which was centered in the area around Hull House. Other immigrants worked at menial tasks in the city's stockyards and factories under appalling working conditions.[4]

It was such offensive working conditions and the financial panic of 1893 that, in part, contributed to the Haymarket Riot of 1886, and the Pullman strike of 1894.[5] The fact that these occurrences were led primarily by

---

[1] For a colorful description of the "boodling" practice whereby Chicago's officials were bribed by industrialists for franchises and the corrupt nature of the city's government see Lloyd Wendt and Herman Kogan, Bosses in Lusty Chicago (Bloomington, Ind.: Indiana University Press, 1967), passim; and Ray Ginger, Altgeld's America, 1890-1905 (New York: Funk & Wagnalls Co., 1958; reprint ed., Chicago: Quadrangle Paperbacks, 1965), chap. 4.

[2] William T. Stead, If Christ Came to Chicago (London: Review of Reviews, 1894).

[3] Wendt and Kogan, p. 92.

[4] For a description of conditions in one Chicago industry see Mary E. McDowell, "A Quarter of a Century in the Stockyard District," in Clyde C. Walton, ed., An Illinois Reader (DeKalb, Ill.: Northern Illinois University Press, 1970, pp. 336-51. In 1910 the Dillingham Commission reported that in the twenty-one industries it studied, 57.9 percent of the laborers were foreign-born, two-thirds of them from countries in southeastern Europe; see also Jones, p. 218.

[5] Harvey Wish, "Governor Altgeld Pardons the Anarchists," Journal of Illinois State Historical Society 31 (December 1938): 162-72; idem, "The Pullman Strike: A Study in Industrial Warfare," Journal of Illinois State Historical Society 32 (September 1939): 288-312. For a portrayal of these troubled times in Chicago see idem, "The Administration of Governor John Peter Altgeld of Illinois, 1893-1897" (Ph.D. dissertation, Northwestern University, 1936).

immigrant leaders who had become spokesmen for the oppressed workers increased the hostility of native Chicagoans against immigrants.

Living conditions for the wage earners, native and foreign-born, were equally deplorable and demoralizing. One of the worst slums in the nation was the Nineteenth Ward where Hull House stood and where eventually most of the Greek immigrants settled. One summer during the gala Columbian Exposition, a social worker from Hull House, Florence Kelley, was directed to survey living and working conditions in a mile square area.[1] The investigation found the diseased underbelly of Chicago's growth, out of whose muck rose the White City at Jackson Park. Profit as the single-minded pursuit had overshadowed decency in housing, employment, or health care. The way to make money was to build factories, warehouses, and streetcar lines rather than homes and parks.

Capital and labor power of Chicago were devoted to productivity. Newly-arrived wage earners clustered around the factories like calves around a mother cow. The shacks near the factories were placed on wheels and hauled away; a solid tenement of three or four stories went up with no light and often no plumbing. Still more workers came and the small yards behind the tenements became sites for more shacks, until no empty space was left.

In this squalid area where the working poor lived, the death rate from typhoid, caused by the city's contaminated water supply, was twice that of New York or Boston.[2] The family was hardly a distinct unit in such an atmosphere. It was common for several families to share a kitchen and apartment together. The ward had many residences that were not occupied by families and were candidly reported in the census as brothels, or "sporting houses," where prostitutes listed their incomes as varying from five to fifty dollars a week. This was the notorious levee district, just east of Hull House between Harrison and Polk, Clark and Dearborn Streets, and along the Chicago River. It was run mainly by the Lords of the Levee--aldermen "Hinky Dink" Kenna and "Bathhouse John" Coughlin--and it was the un-

---

[1] Hull-House Maps and Papers (New York: Thomas Y. Crowell & Co., 1895).

[2] See Ginger, p. 24.

doing of many immigrants who frequented the area in the pursuit of pleasure.[1]

The splendor of the exposition was starkly contrasted with the insensitive setting of destitution, council-boodling, squalor of the working sections, gambling,and vice. This bleakness motivated Stead, the perceptive Englishman, to refer to Chicago as the "cloaca maxima," i.e., the greatest sewer--one of the most conglomerate of all cosmopolitan cities! He wrote:

> It is impossible to describe Chicago as a whole. It is a congeries of different nationalities, a compost of men and women of all manner of languages. It is a city of millionaires and of paupers; a great camp of soldiers of industry, rallying around the standard of the merchant princes in the campaign against poverty. This vast and heterogeneous community, which has been collected together from all quarters of the known world, knows only one common bond. Its members came here to make money. They are staying here to make money. The quest of the almighty dollar is their Holy Grail. From afar the name and fame of Chicago have gone abroad to the poor and the distressed and the adventurous of all nations, and they have flocked and are still flocking to the place where a few men make millions and where all men can get food.[2]

Furthermore, according to Stead, if Christ were to come to Chicago He would find that many citizens had forgotten the existence of any moral law apart from that which was embodied in the state or municipal legislatures. If it was legal, it was right. Nor would He find churches receptive to the plight of the poor. Most probably, He would go first to the machines of the Democratic and Republican parties--the politicians. Despite their ulterior motives, it was they who alleviated the suffering of Chicago's immigrants and the poor. It was they who were doing the work that the churches ought to have been doing.[3]

Greek Living Conditions

The enormous number of male emigrants between the ages of fourteen and forty-five who arrived alone in the city fostered living conditions that were unlike immigrant groups who came with families. For these boys and

---

[1]Wendt and Kogan, pp. 80-81, 282-86, 295-302.

[2]Stead, p. 110.

[3]Ibid., pp. 54-55, 86, 264-65.

men, the only alternative to the lodging house, where most other families settled initially, was collective housekeeping in communal clusters. The mode of living was simple. From five to twenty-five men shared an apartment or house, and each paid between $1.50 to $2.50 a month.[1] Sometimes, one of the men acted as "boss" and became responsible for the operation of the household. Occasionally, if the "boss" manager was married or had sisters living with him, they would undertake the household tasks. On other occasions, the men hired a cook for a dollar per month from each tenant or ate at restaurants and coffeehouses.

A survey made in 1909 of the occupation of 965 Greek men in Chicago revealed a correlation between lifestyle and occupation. Approximately 71 percent of the laborers and 84 percent of the peddlers lived in non-family groups, while 65 percent of the owners of ice-cream parlors and 75 percent of the restaurant keepers lived in family groups.

Since many Greek men entered the peddling trade initially, they lived above the barns in which their horses were housed. Such a housing arrangement accentuated unsanitary conditions and the need for health care and contributed to a high rate of illness.[2] A city social welfare agency had become concerned after receiving reports of large numbers of "very young boys" who were exploited and lived in unsatisfactory situations involving

---

[1] Edith Abbott, Immigration: Select Documents and Case Records (Chicago: University of Chicago Press, 1924), pp. 529-31. A survey showed that the average rent paid per person was $1.74 per month. It appears that Greeks paid higher rent for their accommodations.

Greeks ($2.75)	North Italians ($1.91)
Swedes ($2.60)	Slovaks ($1.37)
Hebrews ($2.55)	Poles ($1.34)
Russians ($2.33)	Slavenians [sic] ($1.29)

As quoted in Florence J. Chaney, "The Social and Educational Protection of the Immigrant Girl in Chicago " (Master's thesis, University of Chicago, 1912), p. 7.

[2] Fairchild, pp. 198-200; and G. Abbott, "Study of Greeks," pp. 389-91. Despite these conditions Fairchild observed "that in the matter of living conditions the Greeks are more cleanly [sic] and in general more respectable than the Italians." Abbott observed that "even in non-family groups, the houses are often well kept and the food well prepared by the men themselves."

sanitation and morals.[1] The lifestyle changed with the arrival of Greek women and the establishment of households. To be sure, single men who worked as peddlers continued to live in non-family collective housing. However, those who married and who had accumulated enough money moved into apartments or houses. In order to augment the family income, lodgers sometimes were welcomed.

The non-family groups lived most often on the northern and western fringes of the downtown area. With the establishment of families, there was a movement toward the Halsted and Harrison district which was occupied heavily by Italians, who had succeeded the Germans and the Irish.[2] They inhabited the area immediately north and east of Hull House, Polk and Halsted Streets, thus forcing the Italians to retreat south and east of Hull House. This location was considered one of the poorest, most crowded sections of Chicago.[3] It became the largest Greek community in the United States by 1914. A survey of housing conditions made that year described the newly-entrenched Greeks as

> . . . a sturdy people, swarthy, well built, often handsome, . . . Keenly intelligent, shrewd, a little inclined to be clannish and to be suspicious of other nationalities, they have easily made a place for themselves in business, and have settled in the better-class tenements on the more important streets of the district. Blue Island Avenue . . . is the main thoroughfare of the colony. Its sidewalks are for blocks lined with stores which bear upon their windows Greek characters. Here are the offices of the Greek newspapers, bookstores, groceries, labor agencies, saloons, coffeehouses, and poolrooms. In the directory of the large office building at the corner of Blue Island Avenue and Harrison Street are the names of many Greek dentists, physicians, and

---

[1] League for the Protection of Immigrants [later changed to Immigrants' Protective League], _Annual Report, 1909-1910_, p. 32. The League considered organizing clubs and classes for the Greek boys and men in order to protect the younger and weaker members of the group.

[2] An interesting study of this sociological phenomenon is Paul F. Cressey, "The Succession of Cultural Groups in the City of Chicago" (Ph.D. dissertation, University of Chicago, 1930).

[3] _Hull House Maps and Papers_, p. 3. A vivid portrayal of this section of the city that was shared also by Jews is found in Louis Wirth, _The Ghetto_ (Chicago: University of Chicago Press, Phoenix Books, 1956), pp. 195-201.

businessmen. As it is on Blue Island Avenue, so it is on Halsted Street, from Harrison Street south to Polk Street--everywhere Greek words, both written and spoken, and Greek faces.[1]

The Hull House survey included the Italians on Taylor Street and the Russian Jews on Maxwell Street. The density was 265 people per acre, totalling 10,125 residents. Of these 57 percent (5,748)were adults with families; about 30 percent (3,067) were children; the remaining 1,310 were adult lodgers, the floating element of the population.[2] The two-story frame cottages contained from two to four small apartments; Greeks and Italians paid a higher median rent than other groups, but some were willing to pay for better facilities.[3]

Mobility accelerated among the Greeks after World War I, as they climbed on the socio-economic ladder. During the 1920s, new Greek communities organized with church and school on the North, West and South Sides of Chicago. These second areas of settlement were not as concentrated as those in the central city. With the exception of the Austin and Ravenswood communities, most Greeks lived interspersed with other citizens who had reached middle-class status. Further acceleration of this dispersal trend took place when second and third generation Greek-Americans moved to the outer fringes of the city. As shown in figure 1, after World War II, many shifted to the suburbs, where schools and churches were organized to serve their social and religious needs.

Greek Social Structure

As stated earlier, Greek immigrants were products primarily of an agrarian environment. A local newspaper described them as ". . . mostly

---

[1] Natalie Walker, "Chicago Housing Conditions. X Greek and Italians in the Neighborhood of Hull House," American Journal of Sociology 21 (November 1915): p. 286.

[2] This "floating population" consisted mostly of Greek non-family groups of males, who got most of the blame for high rents and crowded, unsanitary ways of living. Ibid., p. 289.

[3] Interview with Thomas Chakinis, Chicago, 23 May 1968. See Mary S. Economidou, E Hellenes tis Amerikis opos tous eida [The Greeks in America as I saw them] (New York: D.C. Divry, 1916), pp. 236-39.

of the poorest and most illiterate class."[1] Early immigration records, as shown in table 17, give the percentage of Greek immigrants who could neither read nor write.

TABLE 17

ILLITERACY OF GREEK IMMIGRANTS, 1900-1908

Year	Read But Not Write	Neither Read Nor Write	Percent Illiterate	Percent Males
1900 . . .	2	578	15.3	96.6
1901 . . .	3	1,398	23.6	97.2
1902 . . .	5	2,224	27.4	96.8
1903 . . .	5	3,653	25.4	95.9
1904 . . .	16	2,821	22.4	95.4
1905 . . .	10	2,665	21.9	96.3
1906 . . .	12	5,256	22.7	96.4
1907 . . .	19	13,883	30.0	93.6
1908 . . .	3	7,951	27.6	93.7

SOURCE: Reports of Commissioner-General of Immigration as quoted in Fairchild, Greek Immigration, p. 255.

The average Greek illiteracy for the period 1900-1908, was approximately 27 percent. For this same period, other nationalities had an illiteracy rate as follows: Germans, 4.2; Hebrews, 19.4; North Italians, 10.4; South Italians, 49.7; Scandinavians, 0.4.[2] In 1910, 24 percent were unable to read or write; by 1920, the illiteracy rate had dropped to 3.2 percent. This dramatic change probably was due to the compulsory education laws that were beginning to be enforced in Greece.[3]

---

[1] Chicago Tribune, 7 April 1895.

[2] Fairchild, p. 115.

[3] U.S., Department of Labor, Bureau of Immigration, Annual Report of the Commissioner-General of Immigration, 1910 (Washington, D.C.: Government Printing Office, 1910), table 8, pp. 20-21; Annual Report of the Commissioner-General of Immigration, 1920, table 7, pp. 95-97.

Fairchild states that in 1909 there were 15,000 Greeks in Chicago, of which 700 to 800 were women and approximately 200 were children.[1] Such a disproportionate overabundance of men gave an unusual character to the Greek colony, and resulted in a community in which men either lived by themselves, or in communal groups.

In fact, the Abbott study considers this factor the cause of so much "immorality" among the Greeks.

> The men who are here alone must live together in large groups without the restraining influences which come with normal family relationships. Certainly, this would account for much of the immorality with which the Greek men have been charged. There is little doubt that in this respect they are worse off than at home, due probably to the demoralizing effect which living in a city's congested district, where invitations to vice are on every side and where there is no counter-claim or attraction of a home, always has on men and women.[2]

In comparing the nationalities in regard to criminality, Fairchild found that the German was addicted to crimes against property, the Irish and Scotch to drunkenness, the Italian to violence, the French and Polish to chastity, the Greeks to violations of corporation ordinances and the sanitary code.[3]

A preponderance of men in early Greek immigration is compared with those of other ethnic groups for 1907, the peak year of Greek immigration. Only 1,636 of the 46,283 admitted were women. From these and similar figures, it is apparent that, with the exception of the southern Slavs, the proportion of males among Greek immigrants far exceeded all other ethnic groups. The vast majority emigrated for economic reasons, the main exception being those who fled conscription into the Turkish army after 1908.

------

[1]Fairchild, p. 125. Indicative of the paucity of female Greek immigrants is the following statistical information. From 1 July 1910 to 30 June 1915, only 7,516 Greek women entered the United States, 4,894 of whom were between the ages of 14 to 21; 2,622 between 22 to 29. The total number of female immigrants of the same age bracket was 525,200. See Report of Commissioner-General of Immigration as quoted in G. Abbott, Immigrant and Community, p. 156.

[2]G. Abbott, "Study of the Greeks," p. 384.

[3]As cited in Lacey, Social Heredity, p. 52.

TABLE 18

PERCENT OF MALE IMMIGRANTS
IN UNITED STATES, 1907

Germans	60.4
Hebrews	53.9
Italians (north)	79.4
Italians (south)	78.7
Scandinavians	63.9
Greeks	96.0
Slavs	97.2

SOURCE: Report of the Commissioner-General of Immigration as
quoted in Fairchild, pp. 112-13.

As late as the 1930s, the ratio between men to women was almost
three to one. The 1930 census reveals 129,101 Greek-born men in the United
States compared to only 45,425 Greek-born women. By 1940, the men had
dropped to 117,324 (perhaps indicative of the repatriation period), while the
number of women remained constant at 45,928. One inference is that many
Greek immigrants married non-Greek women or American-born daughters of
earlier Greek arrivals.[1]

With arrival of Greek women, the family as a basic social unit reassumed its traditional status of being patriarchal, patrilineal, and patri-
local. As the Greek men became adjusted to social and economic conditions
here, and as a result of the forces of acculturation, they sent for their wives
to join them in the new land; others contacted their home village for the importation of willing females. Many returned to their villages and married the
girls of their choice, with or without a dowry, and brought them back to the
United States. An important factor for Greek emigration was the need for
fathers and brothers to amass funds for dowries to marry off daughters and
sisters. Abbott states:

---

[1] Abstract of the Sixteenth Census of the United States (Washington,
D.C.: Government Printing Office, 1940), table 14, p. 42.

The Greek boy has been taught to believe that he must support his sister, provide her with a liberal marriage portion, and care for her after her husband's death, if she is left without means. The result of this training is that "the sacred tradition that brothers must see their sisters settled in life before they themselves marry" has become well established.[1]

This tradition of fulfilling their filial role accounted for many men marrying late in life, and, with minor variations, this practice continued until the outset of World War II. Concomittantly, the males were mature and economically more stable, thus, strengthening the home. The Abbott study discloses that the Greek women made good housewives, and maintained clean and comfortable homes.[2]

For the early immigrants, the role expectations were similar to those in Greece. There was a freezing of the Old World culture in the family social system, with the father governing the overall activities of the household. Marriage was perceived as lofty and sacred, one of seven sacraments of the Greek Orthodox church.[3] Motherhood and being a "good wife" were the woman's primary function. She was the spiritual head, responsible for the religious training of the offspring.

The children were considered related to the paternal family and mode of life. They were to be seen, not heard. In theory, the eldest son was expected to be at his father's side to see that the commands were respected. He served as a counselor and guide for younger brothers and sisters. The sons were not required to follow in their father's footsteps; opportunity dictated this. Education was sensed as holding the key to economic and social success. For the "uprooted" parent who had to work the hard way, schooling was a worthy investment that paid off. Quite often, the young men worked for the parents or relatives at an early age in order to help meet the family's financial needs. Respect for the aged was one manifestation of the Greek patriarchal society, and caring for the aged was assumed to be a re-

---

[1] G. Abbott, "Study of the Greeks," pp. 387-88.

[2] Ibid., p. 389; Lacey, Social Heredity, p. 54.

[3] Warner and Srole, Social Systems, pp. 102-55. See Panos Bardis, "Main Features of the Greek Family During the Early Twentieth Century," Alpha Kappa Deltan 26 (1956): 17-21.

sponsibility of children.

A greater degree of rigidity was exercised on girls. Although schooling for girls was not frowned upon, the educational goals were subordinate
to the demands placed on a woman to uphold the subculture's basic institution, the family. Essentially, the primary concern of the closely-regulated
family was to preserve and transmit the language, faith, and traditions; to
deviate from this norm would create a family crisis.[1]

Adjusting to the American way of life was a difficult task faced by
Greek immigrant families. The men needed to learn sufficient English to
earn a living and graft the social and cultural life of the Old World to the
New. Thus, the family faced an uphill struggle in attempting to learn to
speak English and, simultaneously, to instill in children an appreciation for
the Greek language and heritage.

The Greek immigrant had foresight in recognizing the need for an
avenue of communication. He knew that his children could learn English in
public schools, but who would teach them Greek? It was a matter of necessity as much as one of culture. Here was an immigrant parent with little or
no formal schooling, worrying and fearful lest his children reach adulthood
ignorant of the native tongue. Yet, he was harassed by American patriotic
groups, the American press, and other critics, reminding him of his obligation to speak English and "forget" Greek, since he lived in a new land. In
facing this dilemma, Greek parents opted for the transmission of the Greek
language through educational arrangements made for their children. They
urged the establishment of Greek schools. Families living in small towns
moved to Chicago so that their children could attend Greek schools.[2]

As shown elsewhere in this study, attitudes of parents changed with
the passage of time and the rise of the second generation. Acculturation
brought about a gradual attitudinal shift and a growing realization of the un-
likelihood of returning to the mother country. During the 1920s and 1930s,
increased value was placed on professionalism, as noted in the founding of
the Hellenic Professional Society in 1924. Prestigious personages in the

---

[1] See Theodore Saloutos, The Greeks in the United States (Cambridge:
Harvard University Press, 1964), pp. 310-25; Xenides, pp. 91-96; and Lacey,
Social Heredity, passim.

[2] Interview with Katherine Mahos and Bessie Christoplis, Chicago,
5 May 1968.

Greek community were featured in the ethnic press:

> The Greek Press is continually given the privilege of publishing the accomplishment of the Greek men and women in colleges and universities. The large number of university graduates among the Greeks each year is a good indication of the upward trend of our people.[1]

Social activities of the early Greek community included celebrations of life-cycle events of individuals. The entire community often participated in baptisms, namesdays, marriages, and church holidays.

One of the most ubiquitous signs of the Greek settlement is the kaffeneion (coffeehouse). It is a distinctively Hellenic institution which was introduced at Cambridge, England, by a Cretan named Konopios as early as 1652. Several references to "Grecian coffeehouses" have appeared in English works.[2] Lacey considers the coffeehouse an illustration of the social heredity of the Greeks, who from the days of Homer have been abstemious.

In Chicago, every Greek community had its share of coffeehouses. They played a vital role, serving the Greek as the beer garden served the German. The coffeehouse was the foremost social center for Greek men. Women did not frequent it. It was the place to conduct business, get jobs, learn the news of the day, exchange gossip, play cards, and read church and school announcements. It also served as a recreation center. So popular was the coffeehouse that it rivaled the church as a viable community center.[3] Oftentimes the local Greek priest would visit the coffeehouse in order to discuss with the men urgent community concerns.

Warner and Srole considered the coffeehouse the highest development of an informal association in the Greek community.[4] Writers have portrayed the coffeehouse in various ways. In the words of one writer:

> At any hour, day and night, you will find groups of men sitting around small tables, sipping black coffee, smoking cigarettes, and arguing

---

[1] Greek Press (Chicago), 31 August 1933.

[2] Burgess, p. 37.

[3] In 1908 Chicago's Greektown had twenty-two coffeehouses. Fairchild, p. 128.

[4] Warner and Srole, pp. 260-61.

vehemently. Here and there on the walls is a framed chromo depicting some battle scene, for the people are steeped in race history and love to dream of the glorious past of Hellas and its even greater future. They are possessed with the "Great Idea," the vision of a Greek empire which shall reproduce the Byzantine era in extent and power.[1]

In the words of another writer:

> The coffeehouse was a community social center to which the men retired after working hours and on Saturdays and Sundays. Here they sipped cups of thick black Turkish coffee, lazily drew on narghiles, played cards, or engaged in animated political discussion. Here congregated gesticulating Greeks of all kinds: railroad workers, factory hands, shopkeepers, professional men, the unemployed, labor agitators, amateur philosophers, community gossips, cardsharks, and amused spectators.[2]

In essence, the Greek coffeehouse linked the Greek community to its homeland. Its importance in the educational adjustment of the early Greek immigrants is best understood when it is perceived as an informal, but potent, community center. Unlike organizations that met weekly or monthly, the coffeehouse had a daily clientele who found it a refuge in which they could learn ways to adapt to their new surroundings. It antidated the establishment of formal groups such as the church and voluntary societies. Plans for these institutions were formulated at the coffeehouses. As the immigrant became oriented to American life and when he established his family, gained new friends, increased his language skills, and gained economic proficiency, the coffeehouse declined in importance as his learning center.

Acculturation of the Greeks depended largely on how well they coped with their new surroundings and their willingness to adapt to American ways. Some conformity occurred in order to move ahead economically. However, the shift from a rural and patriarchal structure to a more democratic and individualized arrangement produced conflict and disorganization that was more pronounced in the second generation Greek family. Perhaps the Greek family can be visualized in terms of a continuum--ranging from an unacculturated Old World type to a varied, acculturated, urbanized "Greek-American" form. This shifting pendulum might be analyzed by characterizing Greek

---

[1]Lacey, Social Heredity, pp. 51-52. Other contemporary descriptions are to be found in some of the Greek language newspapers such as Saloniki (Chicago), 18 September 1915, and Greek Press (Chicago), 9 April 1930.

[2]Saloutos, Greeks in United States, p. 79.

family life in America as the Old World peasant group which existed at the time of the heaviest period of migration and which can be placed at the unacculturated end of the continuum; the second generation Greek family, which was much like the first at the beginning of contact with American culture, but continues to change so that it occupies a position somewhere between the two extremes; and the third generation, which represents a mixture of the first generation and the American contemporary urban family.

Striking similarity is found in a study of Italians made by Campisi, who identifies three stages in the persistent and continuous process of acculturation.[1] His suggested pattern, transposed to that of the Greek immigrant family, can be described as follows:

Initial stage. It is characterized by the first generation living a highly integrated family life as in the Old World. The demands of the American community are not seriously felt in the insulated Greek colony, and the children are too young to effectively articulate their newly acquired needs and desires. The family is stabilized by the strong drive to return to Greece.

Conflict stage. In this period, the first-generation family experiences its greatest change and is slowly alienated from its Old World foundations. There is conflict between two ways of life--American and Greek--resulting in conflicting roles and values between parents and children. The family is affected by the societal forces of external pressure. The family patterns, already weakened, now begin to change visibly: the father's role diminishes in importance, the children acquire unheard of independence, etc. When the offspring find the demands of courtship and marital conformity too difficult to obey in the Greek subculture, they marry outside of the ethnic group.[2]

---

[1] Paul J. Campisi, "Ethnic Family Patterns: The Italian Family in the United States," American Journal of Sociology 53 (January 1948): 443-46. Other works that show similar conflicts between the Old World and American-born generations are Irvin L. Child, Italian or American? The Second Generation in Conflict (New Haven: Yale University Press, 1943); and Herbert J. Gans The Urban Villagers (New York: Free Press of Glencoe, 1962), pp. 17-41.

[2] See for example, Evangeline Mistaras, "A Study of First and Second Generation Greek Out-Marriages in Chicago" (Master's thesis, University of Chicago, 1950).

Accommodation stage. This begins when the offspring reach adulthood, marry, and establish households of their own. Factors which operate to bring about a new stability in the family are: the permanence of living in America; the adult age of the offspring; the dependency of parents on offspring as informants, interpreters, guides, and translators of the American world; recognition that social and economic success can come to the offspring as they become more like "old Americans"; and the gradual understanding by the children that successful interaction with the American world is possible by accepting marginal roles. Hence, complete denial of the Old World family is unnecessary.[1]

In short, the opposing demands of the Old World and New World created disharmony and posed continual threats to the newly-arrived. Parents feared that their children would depart from the Orthodox church, prefer English to Greek, and marry persons outside the ethnic community. These threats to parental status and control led parents to stringently enforce the traditional Greek behavior modes. Few other nationality groups were so cohesively organized within the larger American society.[2] Endogamy was an important example of their structural unity, and for many decades Greeks had a low percentage of marriages outside their ethnic group.[3]

---

[1] See also George Psathas, "Ethnicity, Social Class, and Adolescent Independence from Parental Control," American Sociological Review 22 (1957): 415-23; Park, "Human Migration and the Marginal Man," pp. 881-93; and Samuel Koenig, "Second and Third Generation Americans," in Brown and Roucek, pp. 471-85.

[2] Mayonne Stycos, "Community Cohesion Among the Greeks of Bridgetown," in Arnold M. and Caroline B. Rose, eds., Minority Problems (New York: Harper and Row, 1964), pp. 253-58. See also Brown and Roucek, pp. 242-57; and Burgess, pp. 52-86. For a description of symbolism and its relationship to Greek practices, see Phyllis Pease Chock, "Greek-American Ethnicity" (Ph.D. dissertation, University of Chicago, 1969).

[3] Interview with Director, the Rev. George Roussos, Department of Registry, Greek Orthodox Archdiocese, New York City, 17 March 1972. The subject of matrimony among Greeks can be found also in "Research in Intermarriage: A Survey of Accomplishments and Prospects," American Journal of Sociology 57(1951): 249-55; August B. Hollingshead, "Cultural Factors in the Selection of Marriage Mates," American Sociological Review 15 (1950): 619-27; and John L. Thomas, "The Factor of Religion in the Selection of Marriage Mates," American Sociological Review 16 (1951): 487-91.

Origins of the Church Community

The significance of the institution of the Greek Orthodox church within the structural cohesiveness of the Greek community in Chicago is paramount. Along with the family, it was and is the enduring force in keeping the Greek ethnic group together. A leading theologian stated that "church and society are one in their essential nature: for the substance of culture is religion and the form of religion is culture.[1]

Further clarification of terminology is necessary to describe the structure of what is called the Greek community. The organized community was known as koinotis, (congregation) opposed to paroikia (colony). The latter was a term applied to any group of Greek immigrants in a given locality; the former, a specialized term designating a regularly organized community centered on a church organization and usually called "The Orthodox Greek Community."[2]

All Greek immigrants were considered members of the koinotis (community) until later, when a church dues system was begun. A general assembly was called for the entire membership to elect a board of trustees (symboulion) which would govern the affairs of the community by electing officers headed by a president. The actions of this self-governing board served as a barometer of community opinion. They disputed over priestly qualifications and role expectations, educational concerns, teachers and board members, political affiliations and rival leaders, use of church funds for projects, community policies, the use of the English language, and kindred concerns.

The Great Fire of 1871 was a milestone in the history of Chicago's Greek settlement. A large number of Greeks emigrated to help rebuild the demolished city and get a chance to escape poverty in Greece, with the hope of returning with "riches."

---

[1] Paul Tillich from "The Interpretation of History," in the Chicago Tribune, 5 July 1970.

[2] The distinction is made by Canoutas, pp. 162-63 (footnote), and Burgess, pp. 52-53.

Prior to 1871, only a few Greeks had come to Chicago.[1] The first to set foot were several pioneer traders who came to Fort Dearborn from New Orleans by way of the Mississippi and Chicago Rivers around the 1840s. They returned to their homeland with glowing tales of the Midwest and came back with relatives. One was Captain Nicholas Peppas who arrived in 1857 and lived on Kinzie Street for over fifty years. Another was Constantine Mitchell, who was taken prisoner by the Union Army during the Civil War and brought to Chicago.

An accelerated pace of Greek immigration occurred after the Chicago Fire, when Christ Chakonas, known as the "Columbus of Sparta," persuaded relatives and compatriots from Sparta to emigrate to Chicago. They procured construction jobs or became fruit peddlers or merchants along Lake Street and other downtown streets. News of their "success" reached the homeland, and a new wave of Greeks arrived to seek their fortunes. This time, people from the neighboring villages in the province of Laconia joined the emigration movement, and by 1882 the Greek settlement was a community of several hundred people who resided in the vicinity of Clark and Kinzie Streets on the near North Side. Soon Chicago became the largest Greek settlement in the United States, with a distinctive Peloponnesian composition of mostly men from the provinces of Laconia and Arcadia.

The first Greek woman in Chicago has been reported to be Mrs. Peter Pooley, who, in 1885, organized the Greco-Slavonic Society for the purpose of forming a common house of worship.[2] However, the zig-zag jurisdictional controversies of the church created monumental problems for the Greek community. The Greek immigrants were members of the Church of Greece, while American jurisdiction was under the Patriarchate of Constantinople by canon law. The Greeks ignored these lines of authority and petitioned to the Holy

---

[1] In an 1839 Chicago directory containing 1,600 names is found an entry of the name Grannis, most likely a Greek. See The Chicago Herald, 10 May 1887. Other early arrivals were John Margaritis and Constantine Masters (Pargianos) who became one of Chicago's foremost tailors. "Uncle" Thomas Combiths' son, Frank, born in 1869, supposedly is the first Greek child to be born in Chicago.

[2] See the Greek Star (Chicago), 9 April 1937, and the Chicago Herald and Examiner (undated newspaper clipping in scrapbook of Mrs. Bessie Spirides--possibly 1938); Chicago Tribune, 15 and 21 February 1897; and Chicago Daily Journal, 22 April 1924.

Synod of Greece for their first priest in 1892.[1] A formal church community, the Annunciation, was established.[2] The first resident pastor, the Reverend Peter Phiambolis, officiated at the northeast corner of Randolph and Union Streets in a rented upper level warehouse near the produce market where most Greeks worked. On 25 March 1893 the church was consecrated by the first Greek hierarch to visit the United States, Bishop Dionysius Lattas of Zante. He had come to represent the Church of Greece at the World Congress of Religions at the Columbian Exposition. Later, the Annunciation Church community, in cooperation with the Lycurgus Society, rented a Masonic hall at Clark and Kinzie Streets. At the new location Russian Orthodox Bishop Nicholas officiated along with several newly-arrived priests.[3]

The contemporary American press described religious services in this early church as follows:

> Greek service is said at a church on the second floor of an unpretentious building in Kinzie near Clark Street. Here come regularly 3,000 members of the Greek colony of Chicago to hear bearded Father Phiambolis clad in canonical robes. The mass is said in the Greek tongue like it has been sung in Greece for nearly 2,000 years. It is, for the time being, a part of ancient Greece, transplanted and set down in the heart of a busy, bustling community, where the rattle of wagon wheels and the clang of street car bells break in with striking rudeness on the holy intonation of the priest. To the casual visitor who knows the Greeks in a business way and is conversant with their quickness in adapting themselves to American methods and manners, the impression thus given is a forceful one.[4]

---

[1]Canoutas, pp. 184-86; Chicago Herald and Examiner, 2 May 1938; and Burgess, p. 54. For an interesting account of the pioneer priest see Ariadne Thompson, The Octagonal Heart (Indianapolis: Bobbs-Merrill Co., 1956).

[2]This was the first organized immigrant Greek church in the United States. The church formed in New Orleans in 1864, was established by Greek merchants to serve their families and crew who were in port. It became an immigrant church much later, when the merchants liquidated their commercial interests and the church was absorbed by newcomers. It is interesting to know that the parish minutes were kept in English until 1908. See Zoustis, pp. 43-51, and Canoutas, pp. 160-62. The New York parish organized shortly after the one in Chicago in 1892.

[3]Saloniki Greek Press (Chicago), 12 December 1931.

[4]Chicago Tribune, 21 February 1897.

The newly-located church became the scene of tension and discord. One account claims that a few influential Spartans of the Lycurgus Society wanted to place a tax on "certain Halsted Street Greeks," namely the Arcadians, who were beginning to settle there in greater numbers. The feud brought about a split in the organized community, forcing the Arcadians to organize their own association, Tegea, followed by a parish of their own. In 1897, they purchased a former Episcopal church at 1101 South Johnson Street (later named Peoria Street), and obtained an Arcadian priest. The new parish, Holy Trinity Church, became the focal point of a new Greektown on the near West Side.[1]

For practical purposes, during this early period of Greek migration, the churches were placed under the spiritual jurisdiction of the Russian Orthodox bishop at San Francisco. The Russians were the first to introduce Orthodoxy into the United States and had the only resident bishop.[2] For the Greeks, such dependency meant humiliation. They were proud, nationalistic, and owed allegiance to a state church.[3]

Meanwhile, the Patriarchate officially transferred the jurisdiction of its immigrant churches to the Church of Greece in 1908 for composite reasons. Numerous editorials in Greek language newspapers demanded the establish-

---

[1] Holy Trinity Church, Forty Years of Greek Life in Chicago, 1897-1937 (Chicago: Aristotle Damianos, 1937), pp. 19-22. Great consternation arose among Arcadian Greeks over the purchase of a permanent church edifice. Many felt that their stay in America was temporary and a rented hall would suffice. Ibid., pp. 43-44. For interesting accounts of the organization of other Greek communities in America see Robert James Theodoratus, "The Influence of the Homeland on the Social Organization of a Greek Community in America" (Ph. D. dissertation, University of Washington, 1961); Helen Halley, "A Historical Functional Approach to the Study of the Greek Community of Tarpon Springs" (Ph. D. dissertation, Columbia University, 1953); and Helen Weinberger, "A Study of the Assimilation of Foreign-born Greeks in Cincinnati, Ohio" (Master's thesis, University of Cincinnati, 1942).

[2] On 24 September 1794, eight Russian Orthodox monks landed on Kodiak Island. In succeeding years, thousands of Aleuts were baptized, and in 1824, the mission was run by John Veniaminov, who translated the Gospel in Aleutian, created schools, and constructed Aleutian grammar. When, in 1867, Alaska was sold to the U.S., a separate diocese was created with the episcopal residence in San Francisco and later in New York. A detailed missionary account appears in the Encyclopedia Britannica, 1955 ed., s.v. "Orthodox Eastern Church," by Matthew Spinka.

[3] Burgess, p. 54; and Saloniki Greek Press (Chicago), 12 December 1931.

ment of an American diocese, but no action was taken other than special assignments of Greek bishops to visit and return to the homeland. This situation paralleled somewhat that of the colonial Anglican church which, prior to the revolution, was forced to fend for itself due to the lack of a resident bishop.

The outbreak of the Russian Bolshevik Revolution and the Greek Venizelist-Royalist dispute altered radically the Greek church development in this country. Deprived of canonical direction between 1917 and 1923, the Russian diocese in America disintegrated. In 1922, the Patriarchate of Constantinople reassumed control of American Orthodox churches to remove them from the political factionalism and sectionalism that had intensified in the communities. Along with this jurisdictional change came the formation of the Archdiocese of North and South America, and Chicago received its first bishop in 1923 when the area was made a diocese.

Unfortunately, the fierce turmoil persisted within the newly-formed archdiocese, with two political factions--Venizelist and Royalist--each establishing its own hierarchy and parishes.[1] Finally in 1930 with the nomination of Athenagoras as archbishop for the United States the wounds and schism were healed gradually.

The erratic action of the church community during this period created modifications in the statutes describing the archdiocese as being "Hellenic" and composed of churches using Greek as the liturgical language. All other Orthodox Christians were formally excluded.[2]

It is important to remember for the purpose of this study that Hellenism and Greek Orthodoxy intertwined to keep the immigrant attached to the mother country, nourished his patriotic appetite and helped him preserve the

---

[1]A list of "canonical" and "uncanonical" clergymen based on the political division engendered by the royalist-liberal controversy is to be found in the Monthly Illustrated National Herald 11 (April 1925): 299-301. In Chicago, three of the four Greek churches were Royalist. In 1924, a national meeting was called by the Royalist churches to force the Greek government to rescind the Patriarchal Tome of 1922, and again place the American churches under Greece. See E en eti 1924 en Sikago laiko-kleriko syneleusis [The Chicago laity-clergy conference in the year 1924], pp. 8-11. Printed minutes of proceedings in possession of writer.

[2]Orthodoxy 1964 (Athens: Brotherhood of Theologians ZOE, 1964), pp. 350-54.

faith and language of his parents. Absence from and fear of never returning to his ancestral home and the thought of losing his ethnicity and of dying in a strange land caused him for a time to embrace his religion with a fervor unknown to him in Greece.

This compelling aggressiveness characterized the organization of the Greek community. The koinotis (community) assumed a vital communal character, because of its permanency and function. It was a constant influence on and focal point for spiritual needs and instruction in the Greek language and a trustworthy barometer of the temper, mood, and opinions of the congregation. The affairs of the koinotis were in the hands of an elected symboulion (board of trustees) rather than the priest, and this practice persisted despite the innumerable inbroglios which resulted.[1]

The symboulion managed finances of the church and school, including the salaries of the priest and teachers. This lay control, along democratic lines, hired and fired personnel. After 1922, the koinotis remained singularly autonomous in its internal affairs, and had control of the communal property and parish policy. The clerical hierarchy had only spiritual jurisdiction over religious matters and assignment of clergy to the koinotis.[2]

Membership was given to all baptized Orthodox Christians, but only those who paid dues had voting privileges. Immigrants could not understand why it was necessary to support the church in America by membership fees and contributions. The separation of church and state in this country was difficult to comprehend, because all baptized persons were automatically church members in Greece. Furthermore, only men could be members, and until World War II, women could not vote in parish affairs or serve on the parish council.

The clergy were trained in ecclesiastical colleges in Greece or territories considered Greek. The early priests sent to Chicago were highly-

---

[1] The symboulion of the Association of the Community of Holy Trinity Church, the first Chicago koinotis, was often at odds with the parish. On several occasions, it became involved in court litigations. See Gregory A. Papailiou v. Demetrios Manousos et al., 108 Illinois Appellate Court 272 (1903.)

[2] For a description of the democratic organization of the Greek church as koinotis, see Warner and Srole, pp. 176-92.

educated and dedicated. They exerted leadership in organizing the parish,
voluntary, philanthropic, and mutual aid societies, and parish schools, and
often assumed the teaching functions.[1] However, other clergy came without official credentials. As opportunists, they seized the chance to establish rival parishes in order to secure a job. Also, there came clerics from
the Greek districts of the Ottoman Empire who kept their parishioners in a
perpetual state of nationalistic excitement by accusing them of being remiss
in their patriotic mission.[2]

The role of the priest was not regarded as separate from the community. He was, by special training and ordination, an ambassador of the
sacred church as well as a mortal by nature and existence. The priestly
character was thus described:

> As although [the Greeks] may sometimes despise the man for his lack
> of education or his worldly-mindedness, they nevertheless respect
> the priest and treat him with the proper marks of courtesy, as doffing
> their hats, or rising when he enters the room.[3]

Because of the deep-rooted democratic tradition, the priest had no
formal control; he had considerable informal influence, if he cared to exercise it. And some exercised it extensively! These "empire builders" led
the uphill battle for the promotion of ethnic education. Often they faced
direct confrontation with the koinotis, which resented control of communal
schools by clergy. The leaders were anticlericalists who found such clerical involvement incompatible with the immigrants' experiences in Greece.

An example of this stance appeared in an editorial at the time the
Greek community was debating the establishment of a communal school.

> With our Greek schools in America springing up like mushrooms
> beside Greek churches, the Greeks in Chicago and elsewhere are
> warned to bear in mind the futile efforts of the church in the past to
> dominate public instruction. History tells us that the church for many
> centuries took to itself the role of guardian of the entire education of
> youth. In Spain, Italy, Austria, Greece, and other countries where the
> church exercised such influence and its superstitions flourished un-
> checked, the result was an increase in those dubious theories which are
> the precursors of sciolism [superficial learning]. This happened simply

---

[1] Ibid.

[2] Canoutas, pp. 326, 228, 330; and Economidou, pp. 151-63.

[3] Burgess, p. 108.

because the complete education of youth was left in the hands of the church, or rather the church succeeded in dominating the education of youth.

Under so superstitious an education, ignorance, antagonism to science, and intolerable nonsense reached such heights that history records no other characteristic products of this theocratic education than religious dogmas, letters of blood, and the resigned submission of the populace.

The real educational system, under which the human mind expands cosmologically, and by which false theories and superstitions are routed, is to be found here in America. And we Greeks of America, for our own interest, the interest of coming generations, the interest of our adopted country, and the interest of the church itself must accept this great American educational system which is free from any ecclesiastical domination. Church is an imperative necessity for a nation, but school is the nation's whole life, and public schools which are free from theocracy are the real bulwarks of the country. Let us profit by the pitfalls into which others have fallen and maintain freedom of education if we wish to produce good, useful, broad-minded citizens whose knowledge and enlightenment will promote and protect the welfare of the church.[1]

A Greek was born into his religion and nationality. It was unthinkable to be anything else. Yet, evangelical groups succeeded in making inroads in converting Greeks away from the Orthodox faith.[2] Strong opposition set in, with Greeks blaming the chaotic conditions on quarreling parish councils and partisan clergy failing to minister to the needy and distressed. Others had little sympathy for "traitors" who embraced a strange faith. In their patriotic estimation a man who renounced the Greek Orthodox church was no Greek.[3]

All of these vexing problems--dissension within church communities, unqualified priests, evangelism--underscored the long-recognized need for a workable central authority. They awaited a bishop who could function with a stern hand, but none came because of the difficult political conditions in Greece.[4] The Greek church communities floundered on their own.

---

[1] Greek Star (Chicago), 21 October 1904 (Chicago Foreign Language Press Survey, WPA Project, 1942).

[2] Greek Star (Chicago), 26 February 1909; and Saloniki (Chicago), 19 June and 17 July 1915.

[3] Greek Star (Chicago), 5 March 1909; and Saloniki (Chicago), 10, 15, 17 July 1916.

[4] Theodore N. Constant, "The Religion of the Hellenes," Athene 6 (March 1945): 12; and Atlantis (New York), 12 July and 17 December 1908.

Conditions in Chicago from 1914 to 1917 revealed the degree of low prestige of clergy and local ecclesiastical administrations held by the koinotis (community). The Greek press continued its attack on so-called greedy, grasping priests who, in league with conscienceless members of parish councils, trampled on the dignity of the church and integrity of the communities. Lengthy court trials, criminal waste, and extravagant use of church funds for litigation and fees became a disgrace.[1] Cleric commercialism became a journalistic theme. Priests were accused of neglecting pastoral duties in order to officiate at sacramental events for lucrative fees.[2] Additional complaints involved their failure to adjust and relate to new surroundings, furnish relevant educational programs, and meet basic concerns of parishioners.[3]

Frequent pleas were voiced for unifying the parishes of Chicago. In the autumn of 1915, the United Greek Parishes of Chicago announced formation of a committee designed to bring order out of confusion. It was comprised of local priests, council presidents, and representatives, and called for a thorough auditing of financial records, public listing of debts, purchase of a communal cemetery, maintenance of a consolidated school, establishment of a high school with dormitories for all Greek students in the United States, creation of special funds for the needy, and the building of a hospital.[4]

The ambitious plan for unification went unheeded. This was due, in part, to the existing factionalism and feud over the Venizelist-Royalist political issue. As stated earlier, the church communities found themselves in a degrading and hopeless controversy from which they could not extricate themselves. The formation of a diocesan structure in 1923, attempted to effect a union of the Greek communities, but the damage had been done, and

---

[1] Saloniki (Chicago), 18 February 1914 and 13 November 1915.

[2] Saloniki (Chicago), 4 December 1915 and 15 December 1917; and Loxias (Chicago), 4 March 1911.

[3] Saloniki (Chicago), 4 December 1915.

[4] Saloniki (Chicago), 16 October 1915.

they were unable to unite into an organized entity.[1] Consequently, each community attacked its concerns independently, a practice which continues into the 1970s.

By studying the role of the Greek ethnic church in its social context, one can glean its profound impact on the lives of communicants. The church subsystem is the repository of the sacred values and national attitudes of the original society. Since these are assertive aspects of the ethnic personality, it was inevitable that the first formally organized structure of the Greek community should be the church.[2] And, since religion and nationality were inextricably interwoven, it was natural that the next institution established would be the ethnic communal school which would teach the precepts of Hellenism, as will be shown in chapter 5.

Economic Status

In view of the Greek immigrants' peasant background, it is noteworthy that he should have business acumen of such skill and resourcefulness.[3] Few had ventured beyond their native villages or had contact with other ethnic groups. They arrived in the New World with no liquid capital or experience in the world of work in which they were to become so conspicuous.[4]

Employment for the unskilled Greek immigrant was found in textile mills and shoe factories of New England; in diverse industries in New York, Philadelphia, and Chicago. Labor agents persuaded many to work on rail-

---

[1]Two communities, Annunciation and Saint Demetrios, managed to unite into a consolidated community in 1942.

[2]For detailed accounts of the role of the church in the Greek community see Warner and Srole, pp. 156-219; Saloutos, Greeks in the United States, pp. 118-37; Burgess, pp. 87-122; Lacey, Social Heredity, pp. 37-39; and Stycos in Rose and Rose eds., pp. 255-56.

[3]Peter Jensen Hill, "The Economic Impact of Immigration into the United States " (Ph.D. dissertation, University of Chicago, 1970). See also Thomas Brinley, "The Positive Contribution by Immigrants: The Economic Aspect," in United States Economic History, Harry Scheiber ed., (New York: Alfred A. Knopf, 1964), p. 397.

[4]Saloniki (Chicago), 7 September 1918.

road and waterfront construction jobs in Utah, Nevada, Oregon, and Washington. Many newcomers underwent mental and physical suffering, and as soon as possible, ventured into business on their own. [1]

Business appealed to the Greek immigrants for diverse reasons in addition to the desire to be "one's own boss." Some, desiring wealth and status so that they could return to their native villages and flaunt their success before their detractors, believed this was the surest way to economic success, and certainly preferable to working for others for wages. Wherever one turned, the admonition was to work hard, save, invest, succeed, become independent. [2] In short, unknowingly perhaps, the Greeks were practicing the "Protestant ethic" of hard work and success.

As stated in chapter 2, marked individualism was one of the inherent traits of Greek immigrants. An early writer commented on the dominant characteristics of the Greek Zeitgeist:

> We noted as characteristic of ancient Hellas an extreme individual freedom. The same individualism is as marked today as in ancient times. Jealousy, rivalry, restiveness, factiousness, self-assertion, inherent in the national character. [3]

These traits had a profound impact upon their business successes and economic failures. They were, for the most part, unable or unwilling to work cooperatively and harmoniously with one another. In time, through exposure, interaction, and acculturation with the dominant American culture, there appeared a modification of these traits.

In their early years in Chicago, the Greek immigrants became peddlers. It was not long before the Greek peddlers achieved a large share of the banana and fruit business, gaining control from the Italians, and began moving into the wholesale business. The Chicago Tribune wrote:

> . . . the Greeks have almost run the Italians out of the fruit business in Chicago not only in a small retail way, but as wholesalers as well, for the big wholesale fruit houses on South Water Street are nearly all

---

[1] See Julius Drachsler, Democracy and Assimilation: The Blending of Immigrant Heritages in America (New York: Macmillan Co., 1920), p. 177.

[2] Greek Star (Chicago), 19 January 1906.

[3] Lacey, Social Heredity, p. 27.

owned by men from the isles of burning Sappho. As a result, there is a bitter feud between these two races, as deeply seated as the enmity that engendered the Graeco-Roman wars.[1]

Two years later, the same newspaper described the proclivity for Greek immigrants toward economic independence by stating " . . . true Greek will not work at hard manual labor like digging sewers, carrying the hod, or building railways. He is either an artisan or a merchant, generally the latter."[2]

The successful Greek fruit and vegetable peddlers were confronted with numerous problems. One was the neighborhood merchant who resented their competition. In 1904, the Grocers' Association accused the peddlers of being the parasites of the trade, and asked the city council to prohibit them from selling in alleys and streets, or else impose a heavy tax. The struggle between grocers and peddlers was fierce. In some cases, it was a Greek grocer versus a Greek peddler. The peddlers, by insisting they rendered a public service to the housewives who preferred produce that was cheap and fresh, won a temporary victory which encouraged them to organize a fruit and vegetable dealers' association to ward off future attacks from grocers.[3]

The peddlers also suffered from the effects of graft-ridden law enforcement agencies. Often they were intimidated and forced to pay small fees to dishonest policemen. Their ignorance of the law, passive attitude, or lack of necessary funds to acquire a license often invited unscrupulous police officers to threaten them with prosecution for the violation of a municipal ordinance.[4]

Because of alleged violations of city ordinances, Greeks were arrested in large numbers. The Abbott study indicates that in 1908 alone there were 1,157 Greek arrests, of which 891 were for a city ordinance.

---

[1] Chicago Tribune, 7 April 1895.

[2] Chicago Tribune, 21 February 1897.

[3] Greek Star (Chicago), 1 and 22 April 1904.

[4] Greek Star (Chicago), 25 September 1908; and interviews with Pericles Orphanos, George Damolaris, et al., 21 May 1968.

Based on the Greek population in the 1908 school census, it stated that twenty-seven out of every hundred Greeks in Chicago had violated the law; whereas, for the rest of the city's populace it was only four per hundred. The Abbott study suggests that these figures were unfair because there probably were three to four times more Greeks in Chicago than revealed in the 1908 census.[1]

In 1909, when the City of Chicago attempted to raise the peddlers' license fee from $25 to $200 a year, the anger of the Greeks and other nationality groups was aroused. The Greeks had special reason to believe that this legislation was aimed at them, because of their firm grasp on the peddling business. These legal maneuvers made clear to them the need to become American citizens and reinforce their protests through the power of the vote.[2]

Other ventures undertaken by the Greek immigrants met with similar obstacles and discrimination. The restaurant business, which became a major economic enterprise for them, began with the selling of "red hots" and "hot tamales" from push-carts and lunch-wagons scattered throughout the city. Then under the administration of Mayor Carter H. Harrison II, the city-county, responding to pressure from native restauranteurs who feared the Greek competition, passed an ordinance prohibiting the sale of food on the streets.[3] At first, the Greek merchants organized to fight the ordinance, but finally agreed to abandon their street vehicles. All those who could scrape together enough money, oftentimes by mortgaging the homestead in the old country, rented stores and opened restaurants. Their apparent success aroused increased resentment by rivals, Americans who opposed foreigners, and an unsympathetic press.

Eventually, the Greek restaurant owners organized to defend their growing trade against the anti-foreignism of native businessmen. The Greek Restaurant Keepers' Association was formed, but factionalism among the Greeks made the association almost impotent.[4] Nonetheless, the Greek

---

[1] See G. Abbott, "Study of the Greeks," pp. 382-84.

[2] Loxias (Chicago), 12 February and 4 June 1910.

[3] Chicago Herald and Examiner, 6 November 1927.

[4] Loxias (Chicago), 21 May and 15 October 1910.

immigrants began to realize that they could compete with Americans, and their restaurants became an important part of the Chicago commercial establishment.

Similarly, Greek merchants entered the shoe shine and repair, florist, confectionery, ice cream, and hotel businesses. Beginning meagerly with small stands, they expanded their respective industries, and, in some cases, became pioneers in the field. In fact, the first soda fountain was established in a Greek ice cream parlor, and the first sundae reputedly was invented by Greeks in Chicago. Fairchild predicted that if immigration from Greece were to continue at the current rate, the candy, soda, and perhaps the fruit businesses of the country would be a Greek monopoly after twenty years.[1]

By the 1920s, Greek immigrants were among the foremost restaurant owners, ice cream manufacturers, florists, fruit and vegetable operators, and confectionery merchants in Chicago. A metropolitan newspaper asserted:

> Chicago Greeks operate more than 10,000 stores--500 of them in the loop--an aggregate monthly rental that exceeds $2,500,000. These stores, it is estimated, do a business of more than $2,000,000 a day.[2]

The attitude of the Greek immigrant community toward their success was expressed in 1907, in an editorial in a Chicago Greek language newspaper, the Greek Star:

> The Greek with his active mind and his American-acquired scope of operations, enhanced by the greatness of the American spirit, has flooded America with confectionaries, restaurants, flower shops, fruit stores, commission houses, shoe repair shops, shoe shine stands, grocery stores and many other businesses. . . . And this handful of Greeks in America have made themselves known to the whole country as a progressive element in the United States, and have made themselves a locomotive power pushing Mother Greece . . . The phenomenal superiority of the American-Greeks over all Greeks, according to our reasoning, is attributed to the spirit of America which the Greek immigrant to America has accepted, adopted, and injected into his being.[3]

---

[1] Fairchild, p. 171. At one time, Chicago had as many as one thousand Greek-owned candy stores. It still remains the Greek-American center of the candy industry. In 1947, an estimated 350 to 400 shops and eight to ten candy manufacturers were located in the city. See Greek Star (Chicago), 15 June 1906; and Malafouris, p. 274.

[2] Chicago Herald and Examiner, 6 November 1927.

[3] Greek Star (Chicago), 8 June 1907. For the Horatio Alger stories see Monthly Illustrated National Herald 11 (April 1925): pp. 333-53.

Despite obstacles, many climbed the socio-economic ladder, and by 1919,
it was estimated that 10,000 of the 18,000 men owned their establishments.[1]

Later, the Greeks moved into the coffee and fur businesses, real
estate, and entertainment field. They gained holdings in the movie industry,
and became operators of theater chains and ballrooms, such as the famed
Aragon and Trianon. Another indication of their economic progress is reflected in the large sums of remittances they sent back to the homeland. As
dutiful sons, they lived abstemiously and frugally, usually saving half of
the profits. They sent sizable portions back home to pay off mortgages and
family debts, buy real estate, and provide dowries for unmarried sisters or
relatives. Between 1903 and 1908, these remittances amounted to approximately $5 million annually--an average of $50 per capita. According to
American consular officials in Greece, it was the highest average remittance
of any ethnic group surveyed.[2] Between 1919 and 1928, they averaged $52
million annually, the peak being $121 million in 1920.[3] Not until 1963, was
this amount surpassed with a figure of $126 million.[4] These remittances
formed one of the chief invisible imports of Greece.

The role of Greek women in the labor force was another story. For
the most part, rigid tradition forbade their entrance into the labor market,
especially after marriage. If they worked, it was usually in industries with
the Polish, Bohemian, Russian, and Italian females. It was frowned upon to
be a domestic. With some exceptions, domestic work was done by Swedish,
Norwegian, Irish, German, Canadian, and Scotch women.[5] Only five of 246

---

[1] Greek Star (Chicago), 14 November 1919.

[2] Other ethnic groups contributed per capita as follows: Germans,
$4.05; English and Irish, $7.14; Italians, $30; Slavs, $28.10; Russians,
$14.80. As quoted in Fairchild, pp. 191-92.

[3] Eliot Grinnell Mears, Greece Today: The Aftermath of the Refugee
Impact (Stanford, Calif.: Stanford University Press, 1929), pp. 195-97.

[4] This was due to the resurgence of Greek immigration following the
Displaced Persons Act of 1948. See E. N. Botsas, "Emigration and Capital
Formation: The Case of Greece," Balkan Studies 10 (1969): 127-34.

[5] Chaney, p. 31.

Greek women and girls over fifteen years of age were gainfully employed in the Abbott investigation. Because the Greek male considered it a disgrace to have a wife or a sister working outside the home, many families suffered economically.[1] This "sacred tradition" was part of the Greek immigrant's cultural baggage inherited from his agrarian background.

That the Greek immigrant finally achieved status as an enterprising entrepreneur was revealed in 1952, at the hearings of the Truman Commission on Immigration and Naturalization. Argument in favor of liberalizing the quota for emigrants from Greece stated that the contemporary professional commercial and intellectual prominence of the Greek was "impressive." The Greeks who had come to America and "carved successful niches in the business and professional worlds. They were on their way to a new status . . . the immigrant of yesteryear had established sobriety, industry, and integrity."[2]

The economic wealth of Greek immigrants helped reinforce their ethnic pride, and many gave financial assistance to Greek communities for ethnic schooling. Successful businessmen provided leadership by becoming members of church boards of trustees and school boards.

Political Orientation

> The Greeks are the most politically obsessed
> people on earth. Paradoxically, this may be
> part of the reason why they have not made a
> success of politics.[3]

This apt modern description of the political temperament of the Greeks is indicative of their passionate absorption in politics. The very term "politics" is Greek, and a citizen of the Greek polis was expected to be concerned with the affairs of his city-state.

---

[1] G. Abbott, "Study of the Greeks," p. 388.

[2] U.S., Congress, House of Representatives, 82nd Cong., 2nd sess., Hearings before the President's Commission on Immigration and Naturalization (Washington, D.C.: Government Printing Office, 1952), pp. 216-18, 431-33, 536-37

[3] Kenneth Young, The Greek Passion: A Study in People and Politics (London: J. M. Dent & Sons, 1969), p. 473.

Unlike other ethnic groups, Greek immigrants came to America for
economic opportunity rather than to escape from political or religious persecution. They were different from the Germans who came here after 1848, or
the Poles who fled after the failure of the Insurrection of 1830, or the Slavic
groups and Jews who fled the persecution of Austria-Hungary and the Russian
pogroms in the closing years of the nineteenth century. There was no hostility or bitterness for the Greek, because he was in accord with the politics
and religion of the fatherland. This accounts for the reason why some 40
percent (197,000) returned to their homeland between 1908 and 1931.

Patriotism was one of the most prominent characteristics of the
Greek immigrants and it was often expressed in exceedingly boastful terms.

> They were always ready to tell you of the superiority of the Greek sol-
> dier over any other, and the men who had been to college in Greece
> speak of American schools and American scholarship with almost German
> contempt. A small Greek boy was sure that he won the affection of his
> Irish school-teacher by showing her pictures of "the Athens." Most of
> them feel it is their duty to spread the fame of their noble race wherever
> possible.[1]

The patriotism of Greek immigrants was shown vividly when thousands returned to Greece to fight against the Turks--cheerfully, eagerly, and at great
personal sacrifice. Five-hundred Greeks left Chicago and crossed the
Atlantic to fight for their native land in the ill-fated War of 1897. During the
Balkan War of 1912, some five-thousand Chicago Greeks volunteered and
helped to bring victory over Turkey to the Greek army.[2]

Their uncompromising patriotism contributed to the undermining of
unity among them. Always responsive to political events and movements in
the homeland, the Greeks in America hopelessly became divided over the
Royalist-Venizelist dispute, which plagued Greece for over two decades.

The dispute erupted after the successful Balkan wars in which Greece
doubled her territory, and was led by a modern Greek statesman, Eleutherios
Venizelos, leader of the Liberal Party. He advocated the entry of Greece on

---

[1] G. Abbott, "Study of the Greeks," p. 385.

[2] Chicago Herald and Examiner, 5 November 1927. The intense Greek
patriotism is described in the Chicago Tribune, 18 February 1897: ". . . at
a meeting held at the Kinzie Street Greek Church . . . a row ensued because
three of the six [Greek] societies wanted to wait until the Greco-Turkish war
becomes official, before raising a regiment. Bellicose Greeks did not want
to wait. Lights had to be put out to prevent a free fight."

the side of the Allies in World War I, hopeful of fulfilling the "Great Idea" of having a ruscitated Byzantine Empire with Constantinople as its capital. The opponents were the monarchists who sought to keep Greece neutral and were led by King Constantine, who was married to the Kaiser's sister. The ensuing conflict was marked by assassinations, coup d' etats, revolutions, counter-revolutions, and military executions, and reached its climax in 1922, with the military catastrophe in Asia Minor. Actually, the conflict did not abate until 1936, when the monarchy was restored under the Metaxas dictatorship.

The factional political controversy between the Venizelists and the Royalists caused serious repercussions in the lives of the Greek-American populace, as shown elsewhere in this study. Division over the issue was reflected in the two most influential Greek daily newspapers in the United States. The Atlantis championed the cause of the Royalists; the National Herald that of the Venizelists.[1] There was hardly any Greek language newspaper or periodical that did not declare its position, and Chicago became an important distributing center for political propaganda.

The most devastating effect manifested itself in the Greek church. The issue was argued passionately, leading to divisions which disrupted seriously the normal life of the parishes and eventually led to a schism within the church.[2] The appointment of a bishop for the Chicago diocese by King Constantine, temporal head of the church, led to a court injunction against the bishop by the Venizelist faction, prohibiting him from occupying his cathedral.[3]

Similar incidents throughout the urban Greek colonies in the United States induced the Ecumenical Patriarchate at Constantinople, the spiritual head of the Greek Orthodox church, to withdraw the church in America from the jurisdiction of the Church of Greece and place it under his own jurisdiction.[4] Healing the strife and establishing the leadership of a new archbishop

---

[1] Peter J. Sarres, Historia ton Hellinon en Ameriki [History of the Greeks in America] (New York: Anatolia Press, 1941), pp. 93-94.

[2] Germanos Polyzoides, Ekkliastiki historia [Ecclesiastical history] (New York: D. C. Divry Press, 1939), pp. 119-25.

[3] New York Times, 14 August 1921.

[4] Polyzoides, p. 120; and Zoustis, pp. 149-57.

sent by the Ecumenical Patriarch took time and effort.[1]

The effects of the division within the Greek community were felt in schooling endeavors and aspirations. Above all, the educational philosophy was scrutinized and challenged. The Royalist faction tended to be culturally conservative, concerned with the preservation of the Greek language and the blockage of assimilation. The Venizelists were more liberal in attempting to provide for social adjustment and acculturation of the Greeks to American life. Indicative of acculturative forces at work was the indifference of the Greek community to the military coup that overtook Greece in 1967, as contrasted with the Venizelist-Royalist feud of the 1920s and 1930s.

His intense individualism and traditional passion for politics led the Greek to community factionalism and sectionalism, as indicated by the topika somateia (hometown associations). Over ten church congregations emerged, some developed on the geographical origins of their members in the native country.

In the early years, the immigrant's main concern was to accumulate money and return to the homeland, so he did not get involved in or concerned with American politics. However, with the erosion of Hellenic sentiment over the Venizelist-Royalist feud, many Greeks in Chicago began taking their citizenship papers. By 1940, 59.4 percent of all foreign-born Greeks in the United States were naturalized, compared with 44.7 percent in 1930, and 16.8 percent in 1920. Of twenty-four ethnic groups surveyed, the Greeks ranked last in 1930 in length of residence and acquisition of citizenship. This bears out their initial reluctance to acquire American citizenship because of their pending return to Greece.[2]

The acquisition of American citizenship, however, was complicated by the fact that the Greek government refused to recognize the status of

---

[1] New York Times, 2 July and 14 August 1930. This special emissary was Archbishop Athenagoras, later Patriarch Athenagoras, who during his eighteen years in this country healed the schism and brought an end to political factionalism within the church.

[2] Brown and Roucek, p. 657.

the naturalized American citizen who had emigrated from Greece. Theoretically, no Greek immigrants could become naturalized without the consent of the Greek government.[1] Despite several United States attempts to negotiate a treaty of naturalization with Greece, none materialized. Consequently, the United States State Department warned all naturalized Greeks against returning to Greece unless they were naturalized before 5 January 1914. Naturalizations prior to that date were not questioned by Greece.[2]

The continued insistence upon subjecting Greek-Americans to military conscription upon returning to Greece, along with the anxiety, delay, and loss of money provoked the immigrants. Numerous Greek-American societies and individuals asked the State Department for help. State officials found it extraordinary that Greece preferred to penalize its people rather than encourage a social and economic bond which would be advantageous to her.[3] Politically, as far as the mother country was concerned, the Greek immigrants in America had been abandoned.

Aside from their desire to return to the homeland, the Greeks in Chicago engendered additional hostility as nativism developed against "new" immigrants from southern and eastern Europe.[4] The United Order of Deputies was one of the strongest nativist groups and was ". . . the most powerful secret society which exists in America at the present time, and its object was to prevent anyone having anything in politics or anywhere else that was

[1] U.S., Department of State, Papers Relating to the Foreign Relations of United States, 1921 (Washington, D.C.: Government Printing Office, 1922), 2: 176.

[2] Ibid., 1928, 1: 497-98; 1929, 1: 458-59.

[3] Ibid., 1928, 3: 25-27. Today the situation has vastly improved with reference to exemption from military service, but the issue remains basically the same. Naturalized Greek-Americans and American-born of Greek parentage are considered by Greece to be Greek citizens. Hence, they 'enjoy' dual citizenship. To date, the United States has not concluded a naturalization treaty with Greece. See Illustrated Monthly National Herald, 11: 266; and Stephen G. Xydis, "Diplomatic Relations between the United States and Greece, 1868-1878," Balkan Studies 5 (1964): 47-62.

[4] Jane Addams reported how "the Greeks are filled with amazed rage when their very name is flung at them as an opprobious epithet." See Twenty Years at Hull-House (New York: Macmillan Co., 1910; New York: Signet Classics, 1961), p. 183.

not born on American soil."[1] While the objectives of this organization were aimed at all immigrants, the small Greek colony in Chicago seemed to be a special target, possibly because it showed business proclivity.[2]

The settling of the Greeks in the old Nineteenth Ward on the near West Side exposed them to corrupt political forces. Although small in numbers, they became part of the city's political machine, and their experiences with "bossism" were not dissimilar to those of other ethnic groups in the area.[3] An example of this practice was evident on 6 November 1910, when an Irish-American politician addressed the newly-formed Archaian League. The group was perhaps one of the earliest political voluntary associations organized by the Greek immigrants concerned with American politics in Chicago. It is probable that its organization was brought about by city-hall politicians who were interested in organizing the arriving Greek immigrants into an ethnic voting block. The speaker informed the assembled Greeks how the early Irish immigrants were discriminated against, much as the Greeks were, until they organized themselves and secured political power. This could also be the case for the Greeks:

> You Greeks can do the same. You have behind you the sentiment and traditions of ages; all you lack for success is organization and united effort . . .
> There has been formed in Chicago an organization called the Archaian League. Its purpose is to promote American citizenship among the people of Hellenic descent and to enforce and protect the rights of such citizens. Join this league, and get your friends to join! Its officers will see that you become naturalized, that your citizenship papers are issued to you, that you are registered as voters . . . [4]

The records are silent as to the outcome of this early attempt to organize politically the Greek immigrants in Chicago.

---

[1]Stead, p. 41.

[2]Interviews with John L. Manta, 2 October 1967 and Nikitas Nomikos, 8 July 1967.

[3]See Humbert S. Nelli, "John Powers and the Italians: Politics in a Chicago Ward, 1896-1921," Journal of American History 57 (June 1970): 67-84; and Greek Directory of Chicago and Vicinity, 1921-1922 (Chicago: Nickolson Bros., 1921), p. 26.

[4]Chicago Foreign Language Press Survey, WPA Project, 1942.

After World War I, it became apparent to a growing number of Greek-Americans that political organizations for the promotion of foreign interests could no longer be tolerated. They had to "feel thoroughly American," but belonging to a native American organization could prove ineffective due to the language barrier.[1] In 1925, the Greek political activists made an abortive attempt to organize the National League of Greek Voters. Overtures were made to the Republican leaders, suggesting that they would function forcefully in presidential elections with state and branch units throughout the country.[2] Again, factionalism among the Greeks made these efforts shortlived.

However, local political clubs mushroomed, and Chicago became an important political center of Greek Republican and Democratic groups. They attempted to resolve the difficult problem of adjustment for Greek-Americans in American politics.[3] Estimates of Greek voters varied. One study placed them at twenty-five thousand.[4] Another had Greek shopkeepers in Illinois at twenty thousand and the voters in excess of fifty thousand.[5]

In time, the Greek Democrats caught up with the Republicans in organizational ability. A delegation representing the Alfred E. Smith for President Greek-American Political Club met Smith at the Congress Hotel in 1928, and pledged support of 80 percent of the Greek-American vote in eight midwestern states.[6] The drift toward the Democrats in city elections was unmistakable. During 1931 the political groups in Chicago united in support of Anton Cermak for Mayor. The Greek language newspapers, Kathemerini (Daily), Hellenikos Astir (Greek Star), Democrat, and Saloniki, joined forces

---

[1] American Hellenic Review (Chicago), 20 June 1925.

[2] Ibid., 21 November 1925.

[3] A Greek Republican Club of Cook County and a Greek Liberal Democratic Club of Chicago were in operation during 1921. See Greek Directory of Chicago, pp. 21, 428.

[4] Chicago Daily Journal, 31 December 1926.

[5] Chicago Daily News, 25 March 1926.

[6] Saloniki (Chicago), 29 November 1924; and 27 October 1928.

to make the press unanimous for Cermak. <u>Kathemerini</u> advised its readers:

> Greeks--if you are the descendants of the ancient Greeks and Pericles, the original author of the democratic form of government, you must go to the polls on April 7, raise your voices, and clean up the City Hall of Chicago.[1]

In Chicago, the Greek-American political organizations reorganized for the 1932 presidential election to be in line with regular party structure. A representative was assigned to cooperate with the Democratic ward committeemen. In this manner, Greeks could obtain recognition from political leaders instead of being ignored, as had been the practice in the past.[2]

It was not long before Americans of Greek ancestry were appointed to minor municipal positions by the Democratic Party.[3] Also the Greek-American Citizens League of Metropolitan Chicago in 1936 endorsed Greek candidates for various offices. After World War II, with the maturation of the second generation and through growing prosperity and the efficient though quarrelsome political organization, the Greek-American became somewhat influential in Chicago politics.

Having become primarily supporters of the Democratic Party, Greeks won elections to municipal judgeships, the state legislature, and State Office of Public Instruction, among others. The majority of the candidates were American-born children of Greek immigrants, and practically all were products of Greek schools in the city. Factionalism among the Greeks had abated and had become restructured along party lines. The majority of Chicago's Greeks aligned with the immigrant <u>Greek Press</u> newspaper as Democrats. A vociferous minority remained loyal Republicans, and used the organ of the <u>Greek Star</u> for support.[4]

---

[1] <u>Kathemerini</u> (Chicago), 2 and 6 April 1931.

[2] <u>Proodos</u> (Chicago), 5 and 12 October 1932.

[3] <u>Athene</u> 25 (Summer 1964): 50.

[4] For a general treatment of ethnic influence on politics in Chicago, see Arthur W. Thurner, "The Impact of Ethnic Groups on the Democratic Party in Chicago 1920-1928" (Ph.D. dissertation, University of Chicago, 1966); and John M. Allswang, "The Political Behavior of Chicago's Ethnic Groups, 1918-1932" (Ph.D. dissertation, University of Pittsburgh, 1967). For the story of the realignment of ethnic political loyalties see Samuel Lubell, <u>The Future of American Politics</u> (New York: Harper & Bros., 1952).

A shift in political affiliation occurred as Greeks left the areas of first residency and moved to affluent sectors of Chicago and suburbs. Still, many of the first and second generation Greek-Americans remained somewhat loyal to the Democratic Party. Today the small Greek-American community is considered to be "wealthy and politically active."[1] The Greek's traditional keen interest in political affairs has been rekindled within the broader American milieu.

In reviewing the political orientation of Greeks, the intense factionalism caused by the Royalist-Venizelist controversy had serious repercussions in all aspects of Greek life, as shown throughout this study, and especially on school objectives and curriculum. As their political activism transferred to American issues, the Greek immigrants found that their involvement provided an avenue for acculturation and linkage between the American and Greek cultures.

Communications Media

The Language Factor

The Greek immigrants considered their language a binding force in contributing to their structural unity within the Greek community. Despite their paucity of formal schooling, they were intensely concerned in learning more about their nearly four thousand years of continuous history and linguistic accomplishments.[2] They recognized the fact that Greek stood as the oldest living spoken language in Europe and that it was an essential aspect of the Greek way of life.[3] In fact, to ethnocentric Greeks the Greek tongue

---

[1] Chicago Daily News, 26 August 1970.

[2] Cedric H. Whitman, The Vitality of the Greek Language and Its Importance Today (New York: Greek Archdiocese, 1954), p. 6. W. Lloyd Warner and Paul S. Lunt, The Status System of a Modern Community, "Yankee City Series," vol. 2 (New Haven: Yale University Press, 1942), p. 87.

[3] Burgess, p. 3. "The recorded history of Greeks now can be traced . . . around 1400 B.C. Although Greek paganism eventually yielded to Christianity, the Greek language has survived as a written language on the same soil for at least 3,350 years (and probably much longer as a spoken language) . . . The fact remains that they alone [along with the Hebrews] have preserved across the millennia an unbroken awareness of their past, and an attachment to their ancient land and language." See Cyrus H. Gordon,

made possible the achievements of their people. Twentieth century Greeks felt kinship with Homer and Plato and with the Byzantine accomplishment. Nor could they forget that the New Testament and the theology of the early Christian church were written in Greek. Another link with the ancients was the church's liturgical language, which had remained unchanged through the centuries.

Perpetuation of the Greek language became a prime concern of the early Greek immigrants, and they demanded that their children learn the language that "gave light to the world." The intensity of this feeling manifested itself everytime a new Greek community was established. After establishing the church, the Greek school was given top priority. Every facet of the community, from voluntary associations to the Greek language press, was used to promote formal and informal schooling for language preservation. The preoccupation of learning the parental tongue probably accounts for the fact that the vast majority of children knew Greek as their first language until the 1930s.[1]

The spoken Greek by second and third generation children was not classic nor pure Greek. They and their parents borrowed commonly--used English terms and, after Hellenizing them, made them part of the popular "Greek" language spoken by the Greek immigrants in America.[2] In the formal Greek schools, language maintenance was complicated further by the dicho-

---

The Common Background of Greek and Hebrew Civilization (New York: W. W. Norton & Co., 1965), p. 32.

[1] A sociological study of three generations of Greeks residing in San Antonio, Texas, revealed that 100 percent of the families interviewed spoke Greek. See Helen Capanidou Lauquier, "Culture Change among Three Generations of Greeks," American Catholic Sociological Review 22 (1961):224.

[2] For this phenomenon, see Soteris S. Lontos, "American-Greek," American Speech 1 (1926): 307-10; Lowry Nelson, "Speaking of Tongues," American Journal of Sociology 54 (1948): 202-10; James A. Macris, "An Analysis of English Loan-words in New York City Greek" (Ph.D. dissertation, Columbia University, 1955); and especially Paul D. Seaman, "Modern Greek and American English in Contact: A Socio-linguistic Investigation of Greek-American Bilingualism in Chicago" (Ph.D. dissertation, Indiana University, 1965).

omy of purified versus popular dialect. The well-educated leaned toward the ancient form, while the moderns supported the vernacular (demotic) form. During the days of heavy Greek immigration to the United States, the language question caused considerable polarity, and even today it is a subject of contention in literary circles.[1] As will be shown in chapter 5, the issue in the Greek schools was usually resolved with the demotic (vernacular) employed in the first four grades and the purified (kathareuousa) in the upper grades.

The tenacious effort of the Greek community to preserve and perpetuate the Greek language was under attack following World War II. The maturation of the native-born generations and the growing identification with America, along with the gradual disappearance of the original Greek immigrants, precipitated a shift in ethnic values. No longer was the transmittal of the Greek language deemed of prime importance (though it continued to retain its cultural importance). Rather, the perpetuation of the religious heritage for succeeding generations came to be considered of greater value. The attack on language maintenance was due, in part, to identification with Greek chauvinism, which some American-born found objectionable. As will be discussed in later chapters, the Greek communities became divided into the cultural conservatives who wished to continue the teaching of Greek, and the assimilatives who emphasized the importance of preserving the religious heritage within the framework of a Hellenic cultural legacy.

The role of language in the Greek community, and especially in its religious life, continues to be controversial. The pros and cons appear in newspapers and periodicals, and orators give their views over the Greek-sponsored radio and television media. In one church periodical of the Assumption Church, there appeared two articles presenting differing points of view. A college student stated his case for the English language in the Greek Orthodox church:

> The vast majority of the younger people, with little if any knowledge of Greek, do nothing more than "sit and stare" in Church . . . Whenever Greek young people meet, the topic of English in the Church comes under discussion, and although in most cases, there is not yet open rebellion among the youth, there is a gradually increasing lack of interest

---

[1] For a view of this language issue, see "Perspective of Greece: An Atlantic Supplement," Atlantic 195 (1955): 143.

that can generate into full-blown dissension in the years to come.[1]
A rebuttal on the subject of English in the Church was given by the local
pastor:

> The language question should be put in the right perspective. The use
> of Latin has not prevented the Roman Church from producing saints and
> keeping its millions of members . . . There is no greater number of
> youth in the Protestant Churches where worship has been simplified and
> the language is more modern than in ours . . . the language is a
> means and not an end. What other language is more subservient to the
> cause of Christianity and of Orthodoxy than Hellenistic and Patristic
> Greek? . . . Greek stands for us not as a national language. Eccle-
> siastical Greek is spoken by no one today. It stands as a traditional
> means of communication among all Christians, . . . it is rooted within
> the New Testament itself.[2]

The language issue within the Greek community in Chicago and the
nation reached its pinnacle in 1970, when the highest legislative authority of
the Church, the Twentieth Biennial Ecclesiastical Congress, succumbed to
its American-born communicants and decreed the permissive introduction of
English in the Divine Liturgy. In reality, this decree had been practiced by
anticipation in communities where most church members did not understand
the Greek language. However, the decree opened a Pandora's box of forceful protests by ethnocentrists and cultural conservatives who got the Ecumenical Patriarchate in Istanbul to invalidate the decree. Charges and counter-
charges have appeared both in American and Greek newspapers, radio programs
and television programs in Chicago. One American-born columnist stated:

> Inevitably, the way the Greek Archdiocese has handled the situation in
> the press releases and at the Congress, and the way tremendous opposi-
> tion to English has grown in this country, way out of proportion to what
> it should be, will show that we are on the brink of disaster. We may
> very well be set back many decades by this upsurge of Greek nationalism
> on the part of those who are from Greece . . . Greek is still necessary
> where the majority of the parishioners speak Greek . . . But by the
> same reasoning . . . Are the children of the first immigrants to be re-
> jected because of the newcomers? . . . The furtheraway we get from
> the immigrant progenitors, the less Greek will be learned.[3]

---

[1] Clifford Argue, "A Case for English," Community Life 8 (Spring 1962):
16.

[2] The Rev. T. N. Thalassinos, "Comments," Community Life 8 (Spring
1962): 17.

[3] Greek Press (Chicago), 5 August 1970.

Another writer in a Greek-American newspaper said:

> . . . an English-speaking Orthodox Church in America can be just as
> Greek, if not more so in terms of the historical universality, catholi-
> city, and comprehensiveness of the Greek ideal. . . . A Hellenism
> that lacks compassion for man is no Hellenism at all . . . it is simply
> a counterfeit Hellenism that serves only to hide self-interest and a
> secular spirit among its proponents.[1]

Today the language topic is very much alive among members of the Greek
communities. Again this issue is polarizing some communities in Chicago.

Greek Immigrant Press

The Greek immigrant press offered a most valuable contribution to
the gradual process of integration into the mainstream of American life of the
early immigrants. The press, unlike the communal schools, developed with
comparative ease.[2] The mortality of many papers was caused by mismanage-
ment and financial shortages. Those that survived proved to be essential
links in nurturing a sense of identity and survival in an alien surrounding.
The press aided the immigrant in his educational adjustment by giving information on local and homeland activities.[3] Indeed, the stories of the home
villages and provinces led to endless debates over Greek politics. According to Burgess, in 1913 about 90 percent read the newspapers in their native
tongue, and this, along with their religion, kept the Greeks clannish.[4]

The first Greek newspaper in America was the Neos Kosmos (New
World) published in Boston in 1892, followed by another weekly, the Atlantis
in New York City in 1894, which became a daily in 1905. Another daily, the

---

[1] Greek Press (Chicago), 16 December 1970.

[2] Fairchild maintains that the Greeks probably published more newspapers than any other nationality in proportion to their total population; see
Greek Immigration, p. 209. Also see Canoutas, pp. 230-34; Malafouris, pp.
227-48; and Saloutos, Greeks in the United States, pp. 88-95.

[3] According to Park, although the foreign press was a carrier of ethnicity, it was also a means of assimilation ". . . under the terms of its existence, the press is apt to aid rather than prevent the drift toward the
American community." Robert E. Park, The Immigrant Press and its Control
(New York: Harper & Bros., 1922), p. 79.

[4] Burgess, p. 12.

Ethnikos Kyrix (National Herald), appeared in New York in 1915.

In Chicago, the Hellas (Greece) was the first weekly newspaper published, lasting from 1902 to 1912. In 1904, appeared another weekly, Hellenikos Astir (Greek Star). Along with the Atlantis and National Herald in New York, the Greek Star continues to be one of the oldest Greek language newspapers in publication.[1] Numerous other newspapers appeared in the early days, such as: Athena (from 1905 to 1912); Loxias (The Blade, 1907-1919); Thessaloniki founded in 1913, and merged with the Greek Press (1929) in 1934, and which continues to be published weekly under the latter name; Anexatitos (Independent, 1914-1919), and others of shorter duration.

From 1921 to 1926, the Greek community was able to support three dailies--Kathemerini (The Daily), Tachydromos (Express), and Embros (Forward). The latter was the official organ of the Greek Workers' Union of America, headquartered in Chicago. But the high costs of publishing and re-duced subscriptions caused, in part, by the turmoil and partisanship brought about by political conditions in Greece, forced them to become weeklies and eventually to cease. In addition, several newspapers, similar to trade jour-nals, were published which catered to restaurant owners and confectioners, the two largest business endeavors in which the Greek immigrants were en-gaged. Several satirical papers--Sanida (Sounding Board, 1905), Kambana (Bell, 1931), and Spitha (Spark, 1934), received popular support, appealing perhaps to the individualistic and iconoclastic nature of Greeks. Another newspaper, the Scholikon Pneuma (School Spirit), probably was the only edu-cational newspaper of its kind, published monthly beginning in 1926, by the students of Chicago's oldest educational institution--Socrates School.

Chicago's Greek community had one of the finest newspapers in the English language, the American-Hellenic World, founded in 1922, first as a weekly then as a bimonthly. It was edited by Demetrios Michalaros, Chicago's foremost Greek intellectual who, as a marginal ethnic, educated at an American university, sought to preserve what was best in Greek culture

---

[1]The Atlantis (New York), ceased publication in 1973, after seventy-nine years, due to labor trouble with publishing unions. Its effects were sold at public auction.

within an American framework.[1] The avowed purpose of the <u>American Hellenic World</u> was to strengthen the Hellenic ties of Greek immigrants in their adopted land. Its policy held:

> . . . those people descended from Greece and other Hellenic lands, constituted one of the most virile, progressive and law-abiding elements in our otherwise heterogeneous and polyglot immigrant population.[2]

It denied emphatically:

> . . . the so-called Mediterranean races were in any way inferior to the Northern races or unsusceptible to conversion to the ideals which primarily are the prerequisites of the Anglo-Saxon mentality.[3]

In addition to the variety of newspapers published, Chicago was also the center for the publication of Greek periodicals. One of the first, <u>Diaplasis ton Ephebon</u> (The Molding of Youth), was a monthly illustrated which appeared in 1912, and was the official organ of the League for the Molding of Greek Youth which was organized in 1908, at Holy Trinity Church to provide educational, athletic, and para-military training for thousands of young Greek immigrant boys and men in Chicago. One of the most impressive periodicals was <u>Nea Zoe</u> (New Era), which was published from 1920 to 1924, and which concerned itself with the serious problems of Greek immigrant adjustment in the New World. Another journal, <u>Synchroni Skepsi</u> (Contemporary Thought), published between 1927 and 1929, was the only philological or literary publication of its kind in America, and had great appeal for the Greek intelligentsia. Other journals were <u>Proodos</u> (Progress), <u>Hestia</u> (Hearth), and <u>Panorama</u>, which were read by the Greek intellectuals. A periodical that attempted to inform non-Greeks about Greek community activities and serve

---

[1]Michalaros learned English at Anatolia College in his native Smyrna, and secured a B.A. degree from Boston College prior to coming to Chicago in 1922. He was a poet and playwright and had published several volumes of poems and plays which were produced in Chicago. He was an advocate of Americanization and Hellenization, arguing that a good American had to be first a good Greek. Interview with Mrs. Ellie Michalaros, 28 November 1967. See also <u>Hull House Yearbook, 42nd Year, 1930-31</u>, pp. 23-24; and Nicholas Rozakos, "O Hellenoamerikanikos poetis, Demetrios Michalaros" [The Greek-American poet, Demetrios Michalaros], <u>Argonaut</u> 2 (New York 1963): 339-42.

[2]<u>American Hellenic World</u> (Chicago), 28 March 1925.

[3]Ibid.

as a link between immigrant Greeks and their new homeland was the Greek
Review, published in English between 1923 and 1926, by Michalaros and
associates.

Later, the enterprising Michalaros edited one of the most successful periodicals in the Greek community--Athene, which he subtitled "The
American Magazine of Hellenic Thought." A quarterly published entirely in
English for over a quarter of a century (1941-1967), the journal had much
appeal to the American-born generations with its well-written articles (many
by major non-Greek writers) on the different historical epochs of Greece,
with translations of ancient and modern Greek poems, book reviews on Greek
themes, and timely articles on important happenings in the Greek community.
For the first time, in this writer's opinion, Chicago's Greek immigrant progeny was exposed to intelligently written articles concerning Greek topics
without the usual hortatory and chauvinistic rhetoric that usually accompanied
them. The magazine received broad support from the city's Greek populace
and from Greek merchants whose advertising helped finance it. In due time,
it gained subscribers from all parts of the nation. Its national significance
was recognized when major public and university libraries in the United
States and abroad ordered subscriptions for their resource centers. Unfortunately, the death of the editor in 1967, ended this most successful publishing endeavor of Chicago's Greek community.

An attempt to expand on the type of Greek journal published by
Michalaros was made in 1963, with the appearance of the first volume of Greek
Heritage. Published by Christopher G. Janus, a wealthy Greek Chicago
stockbroker, and edited by another Greek-American, Kimon Friar, a translator
of the works of Nikos Kazantzakis, this "American Quarterly of Greek Culture,"
as it was subtitled, was aimed beyond the Greek community to national American clientele. It sought to capitalize on the renewed interest in Greek culture as part of cultural pluralism revival permeating the United States.
Consequently, this publishing enterprise had the broad support of American
classicists and intellectuals. In his message to the readers the editor stated:

We wish . . . in this periodical to emphasize the still living heritage
of the Greek way of life, and in no chauvinistic sense, for it has long
since passed national boundaries and become the environment of modern
man. We wish to present this heritage in all its historical variety and
to relate it consciously to modern man clearer, more vital, more ready
for his delight and instruction. We wish to bring before him the great

documents of Greece in all her history from ancient through modern
times, revitalized in the idiom of our day, that he might come to know
how modern and relevant Greek thought has always been and still is.
The tongue may be Greek to many of our readers, but never the thoughts
and ideals it embodies. The Greek heritage is everyone's heritage.[1]

The message was not lost upon young Greek-Americans. Here was a
hardcover, sophisticated magazine on a national level that was extolling the
very things that immigrant parents and Greek schools have been supporting
consistently. Here were articles on the glory of ancient Greece, the great
achievements of the Greek mind in science, the arts, and eloquence. Here
were reproduced in brilliant color the magnificent religious icons of the
Byzantine era. Here were the exploits of heroes of the Greek Revolution of
1821, in their fight for freedom against the Turks. Here were stories of the
Greek immigrant experience in America written by a rising Greek-American
novelist, Harry Mark Petrakis, himself a product of the Greek schools. The
magazine, published for five years before it succumbed to high costs, contributed to the reinforcement of the Greek culture legacy among the Chicago
descendants of Greek immigrants.

Along with cultural and intellectual journals came numerous religious
periodicals. One of the better known monthlies was the Threskevtikos Echo
(Religious Echo) which was published continuously from 1918 to 1928. Another
monthly, Phoni tis Orthodoxias (Voice of Orthodoxy), was edited until 1934,
by George Alexander, the organizer and moving spirit of the Greek Orthodox
Sunday school movement in Chicago, as described in chapter 5. Religious
periodicals also were published by parishes in the Greek language. Many
still are being published, but primarily in English.

In addition to newspapers and periodicals, Greek printing firms were
publishing Greek books, the work of local Greek intellectuals and educators.
Most had a limited circulation. One of the first to be published, in 1908, was
E Hellines en Ameriki (The Greeks in America) by Spyros Kotakis, the editor
of the newspaper Loxias. It was probably the first book describing the epic
of Greek emigration to the United States. Also in 1908, the first Calendar
and Directory of Greeks in Illinois was published, and in 1922, the first Greek-
American Commercial Directory was printed. Numerous books on poetry by

---

[1]Greek Heritage 1 (Winter 1963): 102.

local poets and national poets of Greece were printed. An exception were the Sonnets of an Immigrant, printed in English by Demetrios Michalaros in 1930, with a preface by Jane Addams. Greek priests authored some religious publications and educational treatises used in Greek schools.

The Greek community of Chicago was well-served by the immigrant press. During the period under discussion, some twenty-five newspapers, perhaps twelve to fifteen periodicals, and an unknown number of books published in Chicago supplied the communication needs of the immigrants in politics, culture, religion, patriotism, business, and education. No other Greek community in the United States had such an array of publications.[1] It is little wonder that Chicago's Greek community became the model and envy of other Greek centers in the New World.

In short, the Greek immigrant press, in its many variations, was an "institution" in its own right, guiding the adjustment of immigrants and opening new perspectives in comprehending the American milieu. More important, it served as a repository of the Greek legacy by supporting in every way possible the preservation and perpetuation of the cultural heritage, whether by formal or informal means, despite the many vicissitudes that confronted it through the years. It served to pass this legacy on to offspring of Greek immigrants, albeit, in a modified form. This, then, was the function of the Greek immigrant press in the adjustment and ethnic survival of Greeks in Chicago.

Along with the ethnic press, the language factor was the tenacious binding that united Greek people. In the words of Talcott Parsons, "human social systems are universally dependent on linguistic symbolization and communication."[2] Lloyd Warner adds, "Language, that system of defined and meaningful verbal forms which is the medium of social relations, is the absolute necessity of a social system."[3] For Greeks, the Greek language continues to be an integral part of their total culture and plays an ongoing role in ethnic identity, as shown by their efforts in behalf of language maintenance.

[1]See Malafouris, pp. 227-48.

[2]Talcott Parsons et al., p. 971.

[3]Warner and Srole, p. 220.

Voluntary Associations

In the Greek community, formal organizations appeared as early as the informal ones like the coffeehouse. Despite their factionalism, the Greeks were quicker than most other immigrants, with the possible exception of the Jews, to develop enterprising community organizations to meet utilitarian needs.[1] The long period of persecution by the Turks had forced them to gain expertise with self-help organizations in the absence of a civil government. The formation of voluntary associations was as much a part of community life as the establishment of churches and Greek language schools. They helped the immigrants in their educational adjustment and ethnic survival, as illustrated by their wide range of activities: mutual aid, charity, and humanitarianism. These groups came into existence before many members knew how to speak English.

Finding themselves in an alien culture, Greek immigrants sought out those who spoke the native language and who had similar concerns. This need facilitated the formation of voluntary associations. The first groups formed, like the Greco-Slavonic Brotherhood in 1885, and the Lycurgus Society in 1892, were concerned with establishing a church to meet the religious needs of the growing Greek community. Once this task had been accomplished, the majority of newer voluntary groups became mutual aid societies. Others were the topika somateia (local "hometown" clubs) consisting of persons who came from the same village or province. These, in turn, were followed by business organizations, fraternal groups, and professional and literary societies.

By 1897, the Greeks of Chicago had six flourishing voluntary associations to serve a variety of purposes.[2] According to a Greek Guide published by Canoutas in 1903, they had grown to one hundred societies--benevolent and fraternal groups. Less than half a century later, the Greek

---

[1] Bernard C. Rosen, "Race, Ethnicity and the Achievement Syndrome," American Sociological Review 24 (February 1959): 47-60.

[2] In addition to the Lycurgus Society, there were the Spartan, Tegea, Arcadia, Laconia, and Greek Benevolent Society. Chicago Tribune, 16 February 1897.

immigrants of Chicago had established over two hundred such voluntary associations.[1] Initially, these self-help and benevolent groups served as
"decompression chambers," helping immigrants cope with a new environment.
Park and Burgess state: ". . . it is the immigrants who have maintained in
this country their simple village religious and mutual aid organizations who
have been able to withstand the shock of the new environment."[2]

In 1907, a national organization was formed under the name of the
Pan Hellenic Union to further the nationalistic aspirations of a "Greater
Greece."[3] Many local societies (topika somateia) affiliated with the Pan
Hellenic Union and focused on building roads, schools, churches, and public works in Greece, along with providing for health care and medical needs
of their local members.[4] Their strength was evidenced by the large sums of
money continually remitted to the home village, which formed a chief invisible import of Greece and reflected the intent of the Greek immigrants to
return to their homeland.[5]

The Greek immigrants demonstrated a mania for the forming of these
local topika somateia, and every village and parish in Greece had counterpart "sons" in Chicago. The purpose of these local or regional societies
was to bring together immigrants who were from a particular part of a province
of Greece, provide assistance for that region, and perpetuate the cultural
traditions of that particular locality. The majority of these organizations,
at least in the beginning, were composed of fifteen to thirty people and
governed by a council of twelve to fifteen. Gold tassels and buttons adorned
the officers' uniforms on every public occasion. Banners, flags, and organ-

---

[1] For an analysis of Greeks as joiners of formal organizations, see
Constantine A. Yeracaris, "A Study of the Voluntary Associations of the
Greek Immigrants of Chicago from 1890 to 1948, with Special Emphasis on
World War II and Post War Period " (Master's thesis, University of Chicago,
September 1950).

[2] Robert E. Park and E. W. Burgess, The City (Chicago: University
of Chicago Press, 1925), pp. 120-21.

[3] Kathemerini (Chicago), 18 April 1929.

[4] Brown and Roucek, p. 52.

[5] Supra., p. 126.

ization seals were essential equipment for these societies. Onlookers undoubtedly found it difficult to understand this zeal for societies, especially
since the members were poor and had to deny themselves the basic comforts
to pay dues and raise money to aid their villages. In establishing such societies, the Greeks furnished a meeting place for old acquaintances and led
to the formation of new friendships, status, entertainment, political activities, and cultural events which contributed to the overall effort for their
ethnic survival. In time, they joined other formal Greek organizations to
support the educational efforts of the Greek community in perpetuating the
ethno-religious heritage among the American-born offspring.[1]

Eventually, these *topika somateia* united to form nationwide federa-
tions of societies from the same provinces of Greece. In this manner, the
Pan Arcadian Federation (those from villages in the province of Arcadia), the
Pan Laconian, Pan Epirotan, Pan Cretan, Pan Messenian, and other "Pan"
groups evolved, and Chicago became the national headquarters for many.
These federations continued to collect monies for public projects in Greece
which benefited the entire province or district rather than individual villages.[2]
And while their emphasis remained on providing aid to the homeland, they increasingly became involved in ethnic and language maintenance activities
among the American-born children.

Following the Great Depression of the 1930s, these *topika somateia*
gradually declined. The pace quickened again after World War II to help
the war-ridden areas in Greece. However, they soon became mere vehicles
for personal aggrandisement. Native-born Greek children rarely joined the
topika somateia upon reaching adulthood, despite organized attempts to re-
cruit them. They did not know the village of their parents, nor did they
share the nostalgic dream to resettle in Greece. Instead, they preferred to
look upon Greece as another cultural entity.[3]

Despite the demise of many of these organizations, they contributed
much by way of their activities toward the ethnic survival of Greek immi-

---

[1] See *Saloniki* (Chicago), 5 and 26 December 1914.

[2] *Greek Press* (Chicago), 18 December 1929.

[3] Yeracaris, pp. 47-49, 97-99.

grants in Chicago. Their constant campaign to raise funds for projects in Greece, their strong intention of returning to the homeland, the sponsorship of language maintenance programs, and their aid to Greek schools helped keep alive the flames of ethnic survival, even though these organizational activities were viewed by many of the younger American-born generation as chauvinistic.

Hull House

In addition to topika somateia organizations, the Chicago Greeks formed a plethora of mutual aid and burial societies, business and trade groups, professional, religious, and educational organizations, athletic, theatrical, and musical associations. Many organized under the protective concern of Hull House and the benevolent influence of Jane Addams, who had an immeasurable impact upon their lives. In commenting on these types of societies, Park states:

> These organizations are not, in fact, pure heritages, but the products of the immigrants' efforts to adapt their heritage to American conditions. The immigrant, therefore, comes to a society of his own people, and this non-native American society is the matrix which gives him his first impression. The character of this society . . . is the primary influence in determining the desire and capacity of the immigrant to participate in American life.[1]

The Hull House Theater, the first of its kind in the nation, was inaugurated in December 1899, with a presentation of the classical Greek tragedy "The Return of Odysseus." The actors were Greek immigrants who attracted wide attention in the city. It was the first public recognition of the Greek immigrants in Chicago. This play, which was presented again at the Studebaker Hall in May 1900, was unique in that it was the first time an ancient Greek tragedy was acted out by actual Greeks rather than American college students. Hull House imported a person from Boston expressly to train the Greeks for the occasion. Indicative of the wide attention it received is the sympathetic account written by Lorado Taft:

> The thought which came over and over again into every mind was: These are the real sons of Hellas chanting the songs of their ancestors, enacting the life of thousands of years ago. There is a background for you! How noble it made these fruit merchants for the nonce; what distinction

---

[1] Park, Old World Traits, p. 121.

it gave them! They seemed to feel that they had come into their own.
They were set right at last in our eyes . . . The sons of princes,
they had known their heritage all the time; it was our ignorance which
had belittled them. And they had waited.

The feeling which these humbly proud fellow-citizens of ours put
into the play was at the same time their tribute to a noble ancestry and
a plea for respect. Those who saw them on that stage will never think
of them again in quite the same way as before . . .[1]

The success of "The Return of Odysseus" prompted the Greek community to work on another theatrical production. Under the tutelage of Miss
Addams the "Ajax" of Sophocles was presented in December 1903, in six
performances at the Hull House Auditorium. As in the production four years
earlier, it was presented in the original Greek with all actors and performers
in the chorus being young Greek men who had recently emigrated to Chicago,
some of whom had performed in the previous production. As stated in a Hull
House publication of the period:

For many reasons "The Ajax of Sophocles" was chosen as suitable to be
given by native Greeks on the Hull House stage. . . . A large part
of the work is that of the chorus, the music for whose laments and re-
joicing was written by Mrs. Willys Peck Kent of New York for the special occasion. . . . When invited by Miss Addams to give a Greek
tragedy at Hull House, Miss Barrows studied nearly a year in the best
libraries of the country, for there was no other source of suggestion.
"Ajax" having never been played in this country, and but once on an
English stage, in Cambridge many years ago.[2]

The special attention given by Jane Addams to the Greek immigrants
and her espousal of Greek culture as indicated by these activities and many
others that she sponsored, quickly endeared her to the Greek community as
a patroness of Hellenic arts and ideals. It did much to help solidify ethnic
solidarity and pride among the Greek immigrants of Chicago.

The Greeks had more and larger clubs than other ethnic groups using
Hull House.[3] In fact, they began to think of it as their own institution,
often trying to keep other ethnic groups from using the facilities.[4] A regular
participant in the activities of Hull House in the early days remembers

---

[1] Chicago Record, 13 December 1899.

[2] Hull House Bulletin 6 (1903-04): 18.

[3] Hull House Yearbook, 1 January 1916, p. 33.

[4] G. Abbott, "Study of the Greeks," p. 385.

the philhellenic attitude of Jane Addams that gave the Greeks impetus to center around Hull House.[1]

Numerous clubs for men and women met regularly at Hull House.[2] On Sunday evenings a large male social club attracted an average of four hundred people weekly to provide entertainment for lonely men. A Greek-American athletic club had exclusive use of a room for its trophies as well as use of the gymnasium on Sunday mornings. Many began to engage in amateur wrestling and won national and regional titles for Hull House.[3]

Interestingly, the gymnasium was used by the Greeks for military training in preparation for the Balkan wars.[4] Even boards of trustees from church parishes used the Hull House facilities. No less important were the numerous educational activities that served as 'springboards' for subsequent educational designs by the Greeks. They availed themselves of every opportunity to attend night classes to study the English language, learn music, dancing, and handicrafts and hear lectures on various topics. The staff made a concerted effort to accommodate the Greeks, since they were the most immediate neighbors of the settlement house.[5]

Hull House, located on Polk Street, was in the approximate center of Chicago's great immigrant colonies. Immediately adjoining it to the north

---

[1] Dr. S. N. Soter, "Jane Addams, the Hull House, and the Early Greek Immigrant," Greek Star (Chicago), 25 November 1964, p. 3.

[2] Addams, Twenty Years, pp. 268-69. Also see Hull House Yearbook, 1 January 1916, p. 37. Additional Greek tragedies, never performed in this country, were presented in the original Greek by these immigrants. See Hull House Bulletin 6 (Mid-winter 1903-04): 18. Hull House Yearbook, 1 September 1906-7, p. 36; and 1930-31, p. 29.

[3] Ibid., 1 January 1913, pp. 23, 26-27; 1 January 1921, pp. 9-10.

[4] An impressive ceremony was held at Bowen Hall of Hull House, where two hundred young men were blessed by a Greek priest prior to their departure for Greece. Subsequently, the Greek government presented Jane Addams with the Order of the Phoenix for her "help" in training young immigrants for the Greek army. Later, the award hindered her peace efforts, much to her chagrin. See Hull House Yearbook, 1 January 1913, p. 23; and Forty Years of Greek Life, p. 57; also Addams, Twenty Years, pp. 304-5.

[5] Hull House Bulletin 6 (Autumn 1904): 23-24.

was the Greek community; immediately to the south was the Italian colony,
followed by the Jewish, German, Polish, Russian, and Bohemian areas.[1]

The Greeks complained constantly about the hostility and discrimination they encountered from the native American population. The Hull House
Bulletin lists the following grievance:

In the last five years, since Greeks have been coming in large numbers
to Chicago, they found that Americans made no distinction between
them and other more ignorant immigrants from southern Europe. As the
modern Greek is devoted to his own country and race, the Greek immigrant bitterly resents the criticism of his manners and habits in America
by Americans who he believes, disregard his historical background and
tradition.[2]

Hence, Greek leaders arranged with Miss Addams to host a meeting "in
which Americans should speak in English of the glorious history of Greece,
and the Greek speakers should tell their countrymen in their native tongue
some of the duties and requirements of their adopted country."[3] This first
of a series of sessions was held on 3 January 1904, with a capacity crowd
who viewed a cultural program, listened to speeches by Jane Addams, Professor Paul Shorey--classicist from the University of Chicago--and Mayor
Dunne of Chicago, who received a standing ovation. Miss Addams describes
the event as follows:

As the mayor of Chicago was seated upon the right hand of the dignified
senior priest of the Greek Church and they were greeted alternately in
the national hymns of America and Greece, one felt a curious sense of
the possibility of transplanting to new and crude Chicago some of the
traditions of Athens itself, so deeply cherished in the hearts of this
group of citizens.[4]

Due to Jane Addams' ceaseless dedication, Hull House became the
spiritual and cultural hearth of the Greek immigrants--their veritable second

---

[1] A detailed description of social conditions on Halsted Street is to
be found in Addams, Twenty Years, pp. 80-83; see also Jane Addams, "Social
Settlements in Illinois," in Walton, pp. 324-25, 333-34.

[2] Hull House Bulletin 6 (Autumn 1904): 23-24.

[3] Ibid.

[4] Addams, Twenty Years, p. 184.

home. A young arrival who aspired to become a poet wrote:

> We had problems and Jane Addams was always there to straighten them
> out for us. She was like a mother to us; she was our protector and our
> advisor. It was a great alliance based on nobility and understanding.
> What's more, Jane Addams admired Greek culture, and felt that the
> modern Greeks who had come here to make America their home, pos-
> sessed many of the virtues of their ancestors.
> I used to go to Hull House quite often. One day I showed Jane
> Addams some of my poetry, some verses I had published here and there.
> She became interested. She was always ready to give advice and I
> learned to appreciate her judgment. And when in 1930 my sonnets were
> about to be published, under the title "Sonnets of An Immigrant," she
> wrote the foreword to the book . . . [1]

In 1930, in recognition of her meritorious work on behalf of the Greek immigrants, she was awarded a medallion by the Greek Consul of Chicago.[2]

The Greek immigrants' apogee at Hull House was reached on 12 February 1911. On that day, while visiting the world-famed settlement, former
President Theodore Roosevelt was informed that the young men in the gymnasium were Greeks. Seizing this opportunity, the President addressed the
assembled immigrants and stated that they, unlike other ethnic groups who
were expected to abandon old-world loyalties and look toward a new life in
America, were exempt because of their own illustrious history.[3]

Those who had an intimate association with Hull House, when interviewed described it as epitomizing humaneness toward fellowman--a lone
outpost of succor in a bewildering metropolis. The "soul" of Hull House is
recollected in this example:

> I remember the red brick Hull House well. My mother used to press
> three pennies in my hand and send my sister and me two blocks to the
> House, where we were showered, cleaned, and sent to an "open air"
> room to dry off. Later, we spent our three pennies for a bowl of lentil
> soup, a bologna sandwich, and a glass of milk.[4]

[1] Demetrios Michalaros, "1960: Jane Addams Centennial," Athene 21
(Autumn 1960): 3.

[2] Greek Star (Chicago), 23 May 1930; and 25 November 1964.

[3] Forty Years of Greek Life, pp. 55-56, and Malafouris, p. 141.

[4] Constantine D. Orphan, "Goodbye Greektown," Inland The Magazine of the Middle West (Spring 1963), p. 20.

It is small wonder that upon the death of Jane Addams in 1935, a Chicago Greek newspaper editorialized:

> Her death has stirred in us memories that go back . . . to those days when in the buoyancy of our youth we would walk into Hull House as though we walked into our own house, there in absolute freedom to enjoy the House, not in its physical aspects but in that nurturing warmth that animated everything and all . . . there sound in our ears the soft words and sentences of the women of the House, the only soft and kind words we immigrant boys heard in those days . . . for we of foreign birth have lost our best friend and the only one who understood us.[1]

In short, the arrival of Greek immigrants during the 1890s and 1900s coincided with one of the most colorful eras of Chicago's multi-faceted history. And it was amidst such surroundings that they found their "home-away-from-home" at Hull House, and thus were assisted in coping with problems of economic sufficiency, socialization, and educational adjustment.

National Groups

Greek immigrant participation in ethnic organizations mediated their cultural adjustment to American life. Their experiences with voluntary groups, within and outside Hull House, made the Greek community one of the most structured ethnic groups in the city.

Two of the most viable national organizations that developed were the American Hellenic Progressive and Educational Association (AHEPA) in 1922, at Atlanta, Georgia, in response to anti-foreign agitation of the revived Ku Klux Klan in the South, and the Greek American Progressive Association (GAPA) in 1923, at East Pittsburgh, Pennsylvania, as a reaction to AHEPA.

Soon local chapters formed. In Chicago, the first AHEPA unit was Chapter Forty-six started in 1924, followed by Woodlawn Ninety-three, in 1926. The former served the original Greektown and West and South Sides; the latter served the South Side. Simultaneously, GAPA chapters organized, but were never as numerous or as potent as those of AHEPA. Nonetheless, GAPA became more instrumental in aiding established Greek language schools and in maintaining the cultural heritage.[2]

---

[1] As quoted in James Weber Linn, Jane Addams: A Biography (New York: D. Appleton-Century Co., 1935), p. 111.

[2] This was also true of AHEPA during its early history. Clippings from American and Greek newspapers in the scrapbooks of Mrs. Bessie

Perhaps these two organizations best exemplify the conflicting views on Americanization during the 1920s and 1930s. The clue to each group's orientation is found in the first word of its official name. AHEPA espoused a doctrine of Americanization, assimilation, and adaptation. GAPA looked upon the assimilative nature of AHEPA as threatening and unwise for the future of the Greek language and church. It became culturally conservative, giving preference to "Greek" over "American," even though both groups exerted energies to adjust to American society.

AHEPA assumed the trappings of an American structure. For membership, applicants had to be United States citizens or eligible to become one. They had to be Caucasians and believers in the divinity of Christ.[1] After a lengthy furor and perhaps due to the Americanization movement, the English language was adopted for all official matters of the fraternal order.

It appears that AHEPA was influenced by the rituals of the Masonic and other fraternal orders and formed along their lines with secret rituals and auxiliaries like the Daughters of Penelope for senior women, Sons of Pericles for males under twenty-one, and the Maids of Athens for young women. AHEPA abandoned its super assimilative role when the auxiliaries organized, and began to blend the positive features of Hellenism with Americanism.[2]

Despite the fact that AHEPA undertook the Americanization of Greek immigrants on a national scale and claimed to be an American organization, its raison d'etre was decidedly Greek. Its establishment in 1922 illustrates the manner in which self-conscious ethnic group activity was shaped by the situation it had to meet. Amidst the alien-baiting following World War I and

---

Spirides indicate that the Hellas chapter of the Daughters of Penelope (an auxiliary of AHEPA) raised thousands of dollars for Greek schools by holding a series of cultural events in the 1930s and early 1940s. For an up-to-date version of how the AHEPA "family" of organizations operate in Chicago, see Chicago Tribune, 16 November 1969. For a definitive account, see George J. Leber, The History of the Order of AHEPA, 1922-1972 (Washington, D.C.: Published by the Fraternity, 1972) on the occasion of its fiftieth anniversary.

[1] The Ahepan 2 (September 1929): 3; Kimon A. Doukas, "The Story of Ahepa," Athene 11 (Summer 1950): 39-43.

[2] See American Hellenic World (Chicago), 13 July 1928.

the Ku Klux Klan activism, AHEPA formed for the specific purpose of establishing Greek prestige in the American community. Its program was to fete
every distinguished person from Greece or of Greek origin, being sure to
invite press and important persons to lend maximum publicity and dignity.
It organized expeditions of bachelors to Greece, saw that the expedition was
pictured in the rotogravure section of the New York Times and other hometown
newspapers, that it was received and feted by the prime minister or king in
Greece and reports carried in the American press, and that those who brought
back wives from Greece got their pictures in the papers when they returned
home. AHEPA made a policy of holding its affairs, wherever possible, in the
best hotels; of giving banquets for outstanding political figures; of picking
up and answering all references that tended to slur Greeks. In this respect,
it was the Greek national consciousness and the attempt to win a favorable
consideration for it in America which concerned AHEPA--a situation largely
brought about by American conditions and antipathy to foreign groups.

    This purpose was reflected in the public announcements of its early
leaders. In speaking of the thinking of the founders of AHEPA, one supreme
president of the fraternity stated:

> They realized that the great need of our people was to found an organi-
> zation not for the purpose of impressing upon them the grandeur of their
> history and the glory of their language--things which they very well
> know and appreciate--but for the purpose of impressing upon the Ameri-
> can people the worth of the Greeks as constructive and useful citizens
> of this Republic.
> They realized that if Greek prestige was to be elevated, that such
> elevation must come through an organization which breathes of the at-
> mosphere and speaks the language of the land.
> And so, fully realizing these great principles, they founded an
> American non-sectarian, non-political organization for men of Hellenic
> extraction, and called it AHEPA.[1]

    The Greek men of Chicago who joined the ranks of AHEPA in the 1920s,
did so because they espoused the organization's belief, and in a short time,
the Chicago chapter became one of the most active in the order. In 1925, it
hosted the association's third national convention. The pride of these AHEPA
members is reflected in the following caption taken from a Chicago newspaper:

> The chapter has had the honor of being host to over two hundred delegates
> from various chapters, who assembled in Chicago for the Third Annual

---

[1] The Ahepan 1 (1928): 12.

convention of the order. The convention was held at the Drake Hotel and lasted for five days, during which time several public events were given with various prominent citizens from Chicago present. It may be stated that the Hellenes in the United States have been the first and only element that has taken upon itself to teach the true and sound principles of Americanism among its members, instead of waiting for the American government to accomplish the truly great task of educating foreign elements in this country.[1]

During the ensuing years, the AHEPA chapters in Chicago implemented their program of Americanization and Greek adjustment into American society, despite opposition to its principles by GAPA and other conservative groups. AHEPA members, at least those in Chicago, were also concerned with the fate of the Greek language and Hellenic tradition. Therefore, they sponsored parallel activities to Americanize the Chicago Greek immigrant and promote Greek studies and financial assistance for the city's Greek schools.[2] Indeed, the order had to explain its position repeatedly to Greek immigrants, stating that its program of Americanization, the use of the English language, and its assertion of being nonpolitical and nonsectarian should not be construed as heretical, but rather as a facility for Greek adjustment and survival in the United States without losing the cultural heritage. A local chapter officer commented on the compatibility between Hellenism and Americanism by stating in 1926:

> There are ignorant extremists among us who insist that the immigrant of today, to become a real American, must forget entirely and absolutely the land of his birth, and must wipe his memory clean of all the cherished recollections that cluster around his native land. Such views cause the more reasonable elements of our society to wonder what would we have in this country today if such had been the case with the earliest to the latest arrivals to America from foreign lands. Certainly, we could not have had the Americanism of today. Americanism is the result not of utter forgetfulness, but of vivid memories. We have become the fortunate heirs of the good things of all the ages. The men and women who left their native lands preserved and brought with them only those things worth preserving. And of those things Americanism was born.[3]

Nonetheless, AHEPA continued to be accused of seeking to eradicate the Greek language and of "downgrading the Greek school." The fact was,

---

[1]Chicago Daily Journal, 31 December 1925.

[2]Interview with William J. Russis, Chicago, 31 July 1971.

[3]Leber, p. 194.

however, that while the order insisted on the sole use of the English lang
uage in its proceedings and functions, chapters in Chicago gave full sup
and assistance to the enlargement and maintenance of local Greek school
where the sons and daughters of members learned the Greek language eitl
in day or afternoon schools. The order's auxiliaries sponsored programs
tinuously to raise funds for these schools and, in many instances, gave
direct financial support to Greek schools.[1] The official view of AHEPA o
this matter was perhaps best expressed by the remarks of its supreme pre
dent, George E. Phillies, who said in 1929:

> Much has been written and said these days concerning our attitude
> towards the Mother language. Once more, and in the most categori
> manner, we are declaring that writings tending to show that we are
> lectful or antagonistic to our Mother language, either in practice, f
> or form, are completely unfounded. Our avowed policy has been to
> teach the Greek language to those who need it and the English langu
> to those who need it.[2]

Again in 1932, the association's magazine, The AHEPA, emphasi
the importance of the Greek language by editorializing:

> If you have any respect for your noble ancestry, any love for your
> adopted country, you will make it a matter of prime concern to your-
> selves that the language and history of Ancient Greece be not forgot
> This you may do, first by providing in your parochial schools, a
> you are now doing, for instruction in Greek . . . But this is not
> enough. You are required to encourage the youth of this land, whet.
> of Greek descent or otherwise, to the study of Greek language and l
> ature . . . Only your persistent efforts can save this, your adopt
> country . . . from the loss of that which has proved so beneficial to the
> great men of the past. . . . If you do not do this, you are not wor
> of their name. You should not be permitted to call them your father:
> By neglecting these matters you disinherit yourselves.[3]

The history of AHEPA clearly shows that it was concerned with tl
retention of the Hellenic heritage in the New World despite its accusers.
After World War II, when AHEPA's task of Americanizing the Greek immig
had been achieved, it turned its attention to the need for perpetuating th
Hellenic heritage among the native-born offspring of the immigrants. An

---

[1] Greek Press (Chicago), 10 February 1932; Greek Star (Chicago),
2 April 1929; and The Ahepan 22 (January-February 1948): 15.

[2] Leber, p. 241.

[3] The AHEPA Magazine 6 (March 1932): 28.

torial in its official journal in 1948, is indicative of this shift in the emphasis of the order which came into major focus in the postwar years. The editorial, in part, reads:

> . . . AHEPA is undergoing a most striking evolution which almost re-
> verses its entire scope--mainly from that of the Americanization of
> Greek immigrants, which purpose we can proudly say that AHEPA has
> successfully fulfilled, to that of the maintenance of a Hellenic cultural
> and religious conscience among the American-born Hellenes. In other
> words, from Americanization to Hellenization. Hellenization not by any
> means in the sense of nationalism or ethnical or racial discrimination,
> but the maintenance of a heritage of ideals and culture which is a con-
> tributing factor to the richness of American culture.[1]

In contrast to AHEPA, the Greek American Progressive Association,
or GAPA, as it became known, espoused openly and with much fanfare the
preservation of the Greek church, language, and traditions. Membership was
restricted to those belonging to the Greek Orthodox church, and the Greek
language was used in all official functions. Its prime purpose was the support of Greek schools, and the Chicago chapters of GAPA took upon themselves the responsibility of providing financial aid to the Greek community
schools. Faced with the fact that there was no training institution for Greek
teachers in America at the time, GAPA underwrote a program of sending American-born Greek women to Greece for training at teacher colleges. They then
returned and taught in Greek schools in the United States.[2]

The organization objected to what it considered an unintelligent program of conformity preached by AHEPA, one that jeopardized the future of the
Greek language and church. The battle was joined with critics who charged
AHEPA with downgrading the Greek church and schools as well as general
de-Hellenization.[3] Ahepans and Gapans formed ranks, and Chicago became
a veritable battleground. Despite their conflicting philosophies, both organizations provided valuable support for Greek institutions that was crucial
during the 1920s and 1930s.

Both were products of Greek-American efforts to adjust to American

---

[1] The Ahepan 22 (May-June 1948): 4.

[2] Orthodox Observer 2 (13 September 1936): p.11.

[3] American Hellenic World (Chicago), 2 April 1927.

society. Both provided positive programs of action for the perpetuation of the Hellenic heritage in spite of their avowedly different approach. Both accepted in common the belief that their members were in the United States to remain permanently (in contradiction of nonmember Greek immigrants), but they differed over the emphasis that was to be placed on matters Greek. Perhaps the most notable argument in defense of GAPA is that members refused to be placed into the strait jacket of conformity by going along with the trend against foreignism. This courageous group waged a relentless, if ineffective, campaign to retain its cultural heritage at a time when many others were discarding theirs.

Despite its gradual demise, brought about, in part, by the immigration restrictions of the 1920s and the erosion of Hellenic sentiments during the 1930s, GAPA continued to remain a culturally conservative group. While some native-born Greek-Americans joined its ranks, its membership, at least in Chicago, was comprised of immigrant first-generation Greeks who kept alive the ideals of their legacy. As late as 1966, the association presented to the University of Chicago $100 thousand (out of a projected one million dollars) for the establishment of scholarships for students of Greek ancestry.[1] The Chicago contingents did not cease to provide financial emoluments to the Greek schools of the city.[2]

Currently, this organization is enjoying a revival of long dormant chapters in Chicago.[3] The revitalization of GAPA is due probably to the influx of new Greek immigrants in Chicago after World War II. Once again, voices are being raised for the preservation of the Greek heritage, not unlike those that were raised by the founders of GAPA fifty years ago.

Both AHEPA and GAPA were prestigious national organizations that served as vehicles in helping Greek immigrants adjust to the new environment. AHEPA played a more acculturative role in interacting with the larger American society; GAPA focused primarily on the need for the preservation of the Hellenic legacy. In any event, both voluntary associations helped to

---

[1] Athene 27 (Autumn 1955): 44.

[2] Greek Press (Chicago), 29 January 1963; and 8 December 1967.

[3] See Greek Star (Chicago), 19 July 1973.

ɔp another cohesive bond toward ethnic identity.

Regional and Local Groups

Less controversial were the regional and local organizations estab-
l by Greek immigrants to promote the retention of the ethnic subculture
eal with American socialization. Three types can be distinguished:
ɔse established for the maintenance and perpetuation of the church and
:eek religious way of life, (2) those organized for mutual aid and be-
ent purposes, and (3) various intellectual and professional societies
ɂ purpose was the preservation and continuation of Greek culture and
nic tradition in America. There also were types such as American
n, Masonic, and other assimilative groups. Yeracaris records fourteen
ent types in his 1950 study (see table 19), but most can be subsumed
the three groupings mentioned.

The first type, established for religious reinforcement, was com-
l of adult bible groups, altar boys guilds, choir, and youth groups.
f the earliest religious associations was the Knights of Saint Constan-
ne Great, dedicated to the same principles as GAPA and founded in
go in 1926 or 1927. Named after the first ruler to embrace Christianity,
lights of Saint Constantine aimed to further the spiritual and moral needs
people by preserving and protecting the tenets of Greek Orthodoxy in
ca. The knights professed special concern over the plight of the second
ation and the general indifference of many parents over the spiritual up-
ng of their children. Membership was open to Orthodox Greek-American
le ritual and the meetings were conducted in Greek. The knights, despit
avowed religious purposes, denied having any official ties with the
church. Religious instruction classes were established in the Greek
age at churches and rented rooms after school hours and in evenings
xpectations were expressed that they would assume Pan American dimen-
with chapters planned for all major cities.[1] However, their goals did
aterialize and after a short while, they disbanded.

Another voluntary association which sought to provide religious in-
ion for immigrants and their children was the Orthodox Christian Educa-

---

[1] American Hellenic World (Chicago), 30 April 1927; Atlantis (New
, 2 September 1927.

TABLE 19

NUMBER AND MEMBERSHIP OF 200 VOLUNTARY ORGANIZATIONS OF THE GREEK COMMUNITY OF CHICAGO BY SEX REQUIREMENT AND 14 TYPES 31 DECEMBER 1948

	Number of Organizations					Membership				
	All		By Sex Requirement			All		By Sex Requirement		
	Number	Per Cent	Male	Female	Mixed	Number	Percent	Male	Female	Mixed
AHEPA	28	14.0	19	9	...	3,352	14.8	2,768	594	...
Auxiliaries	12	...	3	9	...	829	...	235	594	...
Main	16	...	16	...	...	2,523	...	2,523	...	...
GADA	6	3.0	2	4	...	295	1.3	170	125	...
Social	12	6.0	4	5	3	556	2.5	220	160	176
Cultural Affiliated with the Church	24	12.0	...	14	10	2,202	9.7	...	1,171	1,031
Youth Serving	10	...	...	...	10	1,031	...	...	...	1,031
Educational	10	...	...	10	...	850	...	...	850	...
Philoptochos	4	...	...	4	...	321	...	...	321	...
Professional	3	1.5	1	1	1	230	1.0	60	150	20
IWO	2	1.0	1	...	1	200	0.9	180	...	20
Religious	10	5.0	10	...	...	5,377	23.8	5,377	...	...
Beneficiary	87	43.5	54	25	8	8,418	37.2	5,858	1,728	832
Philanthropic for the Native Land	20	10.0	9	6	5	1,492	6.6	710	417	365
Philanthropic for U.S. and Greece	6	3.0	...	6	...	275	1.2	...	275	...
National Liberation	1	0.5	1	...	1	180	0.8	180	...	...
Phalanx of Greek Veterans	1	0.5	...	...	...	50	0.2	...	...	50
American Legion *	...	...	...	...	...	...	...	...	...	...
Masons*	...	...	...	...	...	...	...	...	...	...
Total	200	100.0	101	70	29	22,627	100.0	15,513	4,620	2,491

SOURCE: Adapted from Yeracaris, p. 13.   *Were not included in the tabulation.

tion Society, founded in Chicago in 1930. The work of this group in providing educational facilities for religious training as well as instruction in the Greek language is described in chapter 5.

Perhaps one of the most influential organizations for young people of the second generation, especially for girls, was the church choir in the 1920s. Female choir members did not exist in Greece, where only young boys were permitted to sing in church services. Greek tradition prohibited women from participating actively in church services. This tradition stemmed from Saint Paul's injunction that women were to keep silent in church. In Greece, as well as during the early days of Greek immigration to the United States, women were restricted to the genakoniti (women's section in balcony of church). Later in America, the custom developed for men to be seated on the right side in church, women on the left. Only recently has this latter custom been disappearing.

The first women's church choir in Chicago reputedly was organized at Saint Constantine Church in 1925. Immediately, it provoked a reaction and was considered a scandalous innovation, but the idea caught on, and within a few years most of Chicago's church communities had organized female choirs. Later, organ music was adopted to accompany the choir. This atypical practice for Orthodox churches was conceived by many as an attempt to Protestantize the faith.

The choirs grew in membership, and became important social and educational agencies for young girls and women. Meeting once or twice weekly under the direction of the priest or choirmaster, they learned church hymns in Greek which were sung on Sundays and religious holidays. This informal arrangement provided them with a deeper knowledge of religion and reinforced their training in the Greek language.

The choirs were also a social outlet for girls, since Greek custom did not permit them to leave home for social engagements unchaperoned. Therefore, choirs became reservoirs of eligible women for matrimony, and often the parish priest performed the role of a marriage broker, since he knew the girls personally and could vouch for them to prospective bridegrooms. This practice was responsible for many marriages during the 1920s and 1930s.

By the 1940s and 1950s, choirs became attractive social organizations for both girls and boys, most of the latter joining them upon completing their sojourn in the altar boy guilds. Parents liked this arrangement, as it afforded opportunities for young adults to become acquainted without the necessity of going outside the Greek community for social contacts. Eventually, the choirs were organized formally on a city-wide scale with conferences, workshops, and social events. They have become an integral part of church worship, and continue to function as educational agencies transmitting the ethnic and religious heritage to succeeding generations.

Paralleling the organization of young girls in the church was the organization of young boys. The Orthodox church always has employed the services of young boys to assist the priests and deacons in their ecclesiastical functions. These acolytes were often in service at ages five or six and remained until they reached the traditional "age of reason," twelve or thirteen. Many parents considered it an honor to have a son serve God in the church.

As Greek families expanded after World War I, a veritable flood of young boys became available for church service. These were organized into altar boy guilds, some for senior groups up to age sixteen. These guilds became important informal educational agencies through their weekly Sunday participation at worship services and their required attendance at classes on the church and religion. Classes were held in Greek, which reinforced their skills in Greek training.

The altar boy guilds, as social agencies, provided a protective environment where young boys engaged in sports, outings, picnics, and other events without the need to mingle with "non-Greek" boys. This was an important attribute of guild affiliation which parents liked, because it kept their young sons within the ethnic fold. Evidence of the success of the altar boys program is indicated by the large numbers who entered the priesthood due to the early influence of serving the church. The presence of such groups for young Greek boys probably accounts for the fact that American-type organizations such as the Boy Scouts did not gain early entry in the Greek community. The altar boy guilds continue to serve as important voluntary associations in the church community.

Another religious association with ethnic undertones was the organization of the young people of high school and post high school age. The first such group in Chicago was the Hellenic Orthodox Youth (HOY) organized in 1939, by an American-born priest at the Assumption community. Another under a slightly different name was established at Saint Constantine community in 1941. Both ostensibly were organized for religious purposes, but had as part of their objectives the transmission of the ethnic legacy to the maturing young generations. But with the intervention of World War II and the departure of many young men for the armed forces, the attempt to organize the youth into a viable organization came to an end.

The idea did not die, however. Following the war, returning veterans organized a Hellenic Progressive Association to organize the Greek community of Chicago into a more cooperative and efficient entity. A series of meetings resulted in the decision to unite the city's Greek communities into one organic whole and to establish a city-wide youth group. The former proposal failed to materialize, but the latter resulted in the establishment of the Orthodox Youth Organization (OY) in 1946, which became an aggressive movement with chapters in every Chicago Greek community.

The "O.Y. of Chicago," as it became known, suggested to the Greek Archdiocese in New York City that similar groups be organized in all Greek communities throughout the nation. At the biennial conclave of the archdiocese at Saint Louis in 1950, it was decreed that a national youth organization comprised of two sections, one for youth of fourteen to eighteen and another for young people over eighteen, be organized on a national scale. [1] By 1951, the senior group was inaugurated in Chicago with heavy media promotion under the name of the Greek Orthodox Youth of America (GOYA). [2] Subsequently, the junior youth was organized by the Archdiocese Youth Office, and the national youth organization as envisioned at Saint Louis became a reality.

Like the choir and altar boy groups, the organized youth groups served similar educational and social functions. Religious education programs and conferences, retreats, and workshops were sponsored for the youth. Unlike prewar times, the language used was English. Members of the postwar generation displayed antagonism toward the constant use of Greek and

[1] Greek Orthodox Archdiocese of North and South America, Proceedings of the Tenth Clergy-Laity Congress (New York: Greek Orthodox Archdiocese, 1950), pp. 54-56.

[2] Greek Orthodox Archdiocese of North and South America, Official Minutes of the Proceedings of the National Youth Conference of the Greek Orthodox Church in America (Chicago: n.p., 1951), pp. 4-21.

argued that the time had come for the Greek church to make use of the English language in its mission, a stance which brought about an admonishment from the archbishop.[1]

Despite GOYA's insistence upon the use of English, it did not object to the perpetuation of the Greek cultural heritage, as long as it was devoid of nationalistic overtones. It also promoted the involvement of young people in the religious life and affairs of Chicago's Greek community. In another way, it became a viable social outlet for young people, affording them the first opportunity to be together in mixed company unchaperoned. Perhaps this is one factor which led to its great popularity among the young. The formation of this formal youth group is indicative of the acculturative process and emerging theory that suggests that American ethnic groups are evolving along religious lines rather than specific "ethnic" lines.[2]

According to the Yeracaris survey of Greek voluntary associations in Chicago (see table 19), the religious organization in this first category of local groups made up 17 percent of all Greek voluntary organizations in Chicago during 1948, but contained 33.5 percent of voluntary association members in the city. And while these religious groups were permeated with Greek ethnic values, they are indicative of the importance placed by Greek immigrants on their religious heritage.

The second type of voluntary associations was the group comprised of mutual aid and benevolent societies. The mutual aid societies were among the first to be organized and, as indicated earlier, Chicago had six such groups by 1897. These societies were made necessary by the need for funds during emergencies. Most of them were burial societies. In 1948, Yeracaris counted eighty-seven beneficiary organizations which made up almost half (43.5 percent) of all voluntary associations in Chicago, with 37.2 percent of all Greek associational membership in Chicago (see table 19). Many were affiliated with the various topika somateia (hometown) associations mentioned previously.

The second category within this group was the benevolent or chari-

---

[1] Chicago Daily News, 29 May 1959.

[2] See Glazer and Moynihan, pp. 310-15.

table societies. The first ones were formed at Hull House, and gradually spread to every Greek community in the city. Comprised mostly of women, these groups attended to the needs of the poor and indigent, as their name, philoptochos, suggested. In the early 1930s, many became affiliated with the national philoptochos association under the aegis of the archdiocese.

The mutual aid and benevolent societies were in themselves educational and social agencies, and served to facilitate the adjustment of Greek immigrants to American society and at the same time attempted to perpetuate the ethnic heritage through a variety of social and cultural programs. The former consisted of programs to acquaint members with the new environment, and the latter were often fund-raising programs for the Greek language schools.

The third type of local voluntary associations was the intellectual and professional societies whose purpose was the preservation and retention of the Greek subculture and the strengthening of Greek immigrants in the professions. Young immigrant students at the University of Chicago formed one of the earliest groups in 1918. It was called the Plato Hellenic Student Association, and membership was open to all Greek students enrolled in any university in the city.[1] Although small in size, it was active in sponsoring intellectual programs, making financial loans to needy students, and publishing a collegiate journal in Greek and English, The Platonite.[2]

In 1925, college graduates organized the Hellenic Professional Society of Illinois, destined to become one of the leading Greek professional groups in the nation.[3] In due time, the Greek community boasted several active professional groups: the Hellenic Bar Association, the Hellenic Medical Society of Chicago, the Hellenic-American Dental Association, and the Hellenic Council on Education. In addition, intellectual groups such as the Greek Women's University Club, Young Ladies Hellenic Philomusical Society, Hellenic Cultural Circle, the Institute for Greek-American Historical Studies,

---

[1] Interview with Dimitri Parry, Chicago, 1 July 1971, a founder and past president of the student group.

[2] The Platonite 2 (February 1926): 2-3.

[3] Interview with Dr. S. N. Soter, Chicago, 12 October 1967, a founder and still active member of the group.

and Hellenic Philatelic Society, among others, engaged in sponsoring a plethora of cultural programs in Greek and English. Unlike other Greek voluntary associations, they had a selective membership and were respected for their educational attainment.

A different category of voluntary associations which did not fit into the three types described included the business associations organized by Greek florists, confectioners, restauranteurs, furriers, etc., mentioned in another section of this chapter. These groups, along with Greek labor organizations promoted their occupational interests within the American labor organizations. Similarly, the Greek political clubs affiliated with the Democratic and Republican parties, as described elsewhere in this study.

It can be said that Greek voluntary associations were adaptable and had an undetermined life span. These permissive groupings gave an opportunity to retain or reject Greek ways. As Handlin observed:

. . . when men felt no compulsion to deny their origins and were free to make choices without penalties, they formed friendships and marriage, worshipped and read, within a pattern of life molded by their antecedents."[1]

The topika somateia (hometown) associations, which were mostly of the beneficiary type, began to disappear in the late 1930s, due to the erosion of Hellenic sentiment and the reluctance of the native-born children of immigrants to join such groups with which they would not identify. Another contributing factor was that Greek immigrants were participating more fully in the economic life of the American community, as evidenced by the fact that they were buying life insurance which replaced the need for membership in mutual aid societies. Yet, following World War II, many of the same associations were revived, due to the arrival of new Greek immigrants. Yeracaris makes reference to the fluidity of such organizations in his 1948 study, when he states that the largest number of organizations ceased to exist during the span of twenty years (1928-1948); yet 40 percent of all Greek voluntary associations were established during the decade of the 1940s compared to only 13.4 percent established during the first thirty years (1890-1920) of the organized Greek community, and only 27.5 percent were established during the 1930s.[2] Altogether, 240 Greek voluntary associations were organized in the

---

[1] Oscar Handlin, The American People in the Twentieth Century (Cambridge: Harvard University Press, 1954), p. 231.
[2] Yeracaris, pp. 12, 27.

fifty-nine year period of 1890-1948.[1] At the present time, the Greeks of
Chicago are reported to have some 285 voluntary associations, making them
one of the most structural ethnic groups in the city "promoting Greek education and ideals among the immigrants and their descendants."[2]

In short, the role and influence of the various Greek organizations--
national, regional and local--on the process of ethnic retention and acculturation vary with each particular group. However, each voluntary association in its own way helped in the adjustment of Greek immigrants. These
groups helped them in their transition from a simple rural life to that of a
complex urban environment.[3] It gave the immigrants time to adjust and at
the same time familiarized their offspring with the mores of the Greek culture.
Also, membership in these organizations offered the newcomers an opportunity
to come together in shared experiences, a means of reaffirming their Hellenic
ties and traditions.

By having formally organized associations, Greeks capitalized on
ethnic collectivity; social positions and standards of conduct were determined by membership in designated organizations. These organizations
guided the immigrants in solving a host of problems. In trying to reach the
second generation, however, these groups modified their stance and made
accommodations for cultural ambivalence that often became major concerns.

Summary

As was noted in this chapter, an ethnic community develops its own
way of life around whatever institution holds greatest promise of keeping the

---

[1] Ibid.

[2] Interview with Dr. Kostis T. Argoe, Chicago, 21 July 1971.

[3] A study of the Greek community of Boston makes an analysis of the
importance of formal organizations as the crucial agencies in the transformation of character from peasants to citizens of a modern state. The point is
made that voluntary associations of ethnic groups, and especially those of
the Greeks, have been successful in bringing about changes in the personality desired by the larger society as contrasted to the authoritarian structures imported by the immigrants. See Mary Bosworth Treudley, "Formal
Organizations and the Americanization Process with Special Reference to the
Greeks of Boston," American Sociological Review 14 (February 1949): 44-53.

community together. For early Greek immigrants, the church community transformed into such a central institution in the New World. It served important center where Greeks clustered together and where important ele of the older culture were preserved. This was natural, since they had c from a culture in which religion and nationalism were intertwined as one

The Greeks emigrating to the United States were part of the imm tion movement in the beginning of the twentieth century, and their prese excited much comment over whether the foreign-born could ever become ful American citizens. In trying to cope with and adjust to an unfamilia environment, the Greek immigrants were assisted significantly by volun associations such as those at Hull House and the <u>topika somateia</u>. In t acculturative forces brought about modifications, but did not destroy the determination for ethnic identity and survival. Even with acculturation, Greeks, individually and collectively, sought fellowship in traditional 1 and conformity to their past. Collectively, the various voluntary assoc tions were a reservoir of ethnic reinforcement and provided moral and fin cial support to ethnic schooling.

Because there was a disproportionate ratio of men to women, fa life in the Greek colony was different from other ethnic groups that had with families and had planned to remain in America. For Greeks, the gc were different. The path of economic opportunity had led them to Chica earn sufficient sums of money and return to Greece, where they had strc nationalistic identification. However, with erosion by time and circums ces, the likelihood of their return to their homeland diminished.

As shown throughout the chapter, the Greeks were not neutral o issues concerning family, church, language, politics, legacy, and ecor proficiency. Their zeal for the perpetuation of the Greek way of life is flected in their history of settlement in Chicago. This zeal permeated t activities relating to educational arrangements, as will be discussed in chapter 5. The next chapter focuses directly on the role of the public s in Greek adjustment.

CHAPTER III

THE PUBLIC SCHOOL IN GREEK ADJUSTMENT

General School Conditions

The city of Chicago in the 1890s provided the setting for what has been called the "golden age in American education."[1] It was a city of immigrant contrasts in a turbulent decade of ferment. It was a place of wealth and power along with a poor and unassimilated mass whose labor ran the industrial city. Into this warp and woof were interwoven the influences of leaders such as Jane Addams, Francis Wayland Parker, William Rainey Harper, John Dewey, Julia Lathrop, and Florence Kelley.

Even before 1890, Chicago was America's educational storm center. From the time he arrived in the city in 1883 to his death in 1902, Francis Wayland Parker was the focal figure of bitter educational clashes. After creating considerable controversy as superintendent of schools in Quincy and assistant superintendent in Boston, Massachusetts, he became principal of Cook County Normal School. Public school critics emerged, citizens' school committees organized and Hull House provided the platform for the airing of controversial issues and views.[2]

In an exposé of Chicago schools, Joseph M. Rice rated them inferior to those of New York City and Philadelphia. The principal cause was the teacher's "lack of professional strength." He reported that very few were normal school graduates, most had no professional training and many had not

---

[1] Franklin Parker, "A Golden Age in American Education: Chicago in the 1890s," School and Society 89 (25 March 1961): p. 146 ff.

[2] See Robert E. Tostberg, "Educational Ferment in Chicago, 1883-1904" (Ph.D. dissertation, University of Wisconsin, 1961). For a discussion of the controversies concerning the Chicago Board of Education and its policies--vis-a-vis politics--during this period see John M. Beck, "Chicago Newspapers and the Public Schools, 1890-1920" (Ph.D. dissertation, University of Chicago, 1953).

completed high school. Consequently, instruction was "antiquated, absurd
. . . and unscientific." Albert Lane, the Chicago superintendent of schools,
whom Rice considered an able educator, must have long remembered Rice's
account of a teacher who admonished her students, "Don't stop to think, but
tell me what you know."[1] It is little wonder that newspapers called for immediate investigation of teaching conditions in the city.[2]

Chicago's greatest challenge became the education of its immigrants. The large influx of aliens coupled with the political hassle in the
Chicago Board of Education over organization, authority, and quality of
schools taxed the city's ability to cope with schooling problems. During
1895-96 over 80,000 of 213,825 pupils in the Chicago public schools were
foreign-born.[3] The majority spoke little or no English and understood even
less about American institutions. The problem of accommodating this immigrant group was compounded by the lack of: (1) physical facilities, (2) labor
laws for all classes of work, (3) ungraded classes, or "truant" schools,

---

[1] Joseph M. Rice, "The Public Schools of Chicago and Saint Paul,"
The Forum 15 (March-August 1893): 200-215.

[2] Chicago Tribune, 20 and 26 April 1893. An ad hoc citizens' school
committee of prominent Chicagoans including Jane Addams and Marshall
Field was organized for the investigation of schools in the wake of Rice's
expose. See also Robert L. McCaul, "Dewey's Chicago," School Review 47
(Summer 1959): 269.

[3] Hannah B. Clark, The Public Schools of Chicago (Chicago: University of Chicago Press, 1897), p. 100. For the early years of Chicago public
schools see also Shepherd Johnston, "Historical Sketches of the Public
School System of Chicago," Twenty-fifth Annual Report of the Chicago Board
of Education for the Year Ending December 31, 1879 (Chicago: Clark and
Edwards, 1880); Department of Public Education, City of Chicago, Forty-third
Annual Report Year Ending June 25, 1897. Superintendent Albert Lane's report
contains a recapitulation of sixty years (1837-1897) of school statistics and
enrollment. For the later years see John T. McManis, Ella Flagg Young and
a Half Century of Chicago Schools (Chicago: A. C. McClurg, 1916); and
George S. Counts, School and Society in Chicago (New York: Harcourt, Brace
& Co., 1928). For the more recent period see Mary J. Herrick, The Chicago
Schools: A Social and Political History (Beverly Hills, Calif.: Sage Publications, 1971).

:ate aid for their support as immigrants, and (5) enforced compulsory
ation laws.[1]

The 1895 city census revealed that large numbers of both immigrant
ionimmigrant children were not attending school. Chicago's school age
lation was 451,597, of which 68,883 were enrolled in parochial and
te schools and 213,825 in public schools. Of the 168,889 pupils not in
ɔl, over 12,000 under age 16 were known to be gainfully employed.
ly 7,000 between the ages of 7 and 14 were out of school despite labor
forbidding work in factories and shops under 14 and the state compul-
law requiring four months of school attendance during the year.[2] At
:ime, nearly one-third of the city's school age children were not in
ɔl.

Later, the State of Illinois Federal Decennial Census of 1910 estab-
d that the total number of people of school age (6 to 20 years old) in
ɔis was 1,615,914. Of these, 1,025,053, or 63.4 percent, were attend-
chool.[3] The attendance profile of schools in Chicago was lower than
tate. Of 594,012 people between the ages of 6 and 20, only 349,637,
.8 percent, attended school.[4]

The census further revealed pertinent information concerning the
ago school age population (594,012) between the ages of 6 and 20 as
n in table 20.

---

[1]While the first compulsory school attendance law was enacted in
it was not until 1897 that the State of Illinois adopted a law that was
ptable and enforceable. See Peter P. DeBoer, "A History of the Early
ɔulsory School Attendance Legislation in the State of Illinois" (Ph.D.
:rtation, University of Chicago, 1967).

[2]Clark, p. 99.

[3]U.S., Department of Commerce, Bureau of the Census, Abstract
ɘ Thirteenth Census of the United States (Washington, D.C.: Govern-
ent Printing Office, 1913), table 13, p. 227.

[4]Ibid., table 16, p. 231.

The data show that a little more than one-third of those born abroad were attending school in Chicago in 1910. Interestingly, there was a similarity of percentage attendance of the native and foreign or mixed parentage.

TABLE 20

SCHOOL ATTENDANCE IN CHICAGO: AGES SIX TO TWENTY, 1910

PARENTAL DESCRIPTION	NUMBER OF CHILDREN	SCHOOL ATTENDANCE
Native parentage	129,847	87,524 (67.4%)
Foreign or mixed parentage	368,343	224,172 (60.9)
Foreign-born whites	88,414	33,005 (37.3)

SOURCE: U.S. Department of Commerce, Bureau of the Census, Abstract of the Thirteenth Census of the United States (Washington, D.C.: Government Printing Office, 1913), table 13, p. 227.

The same census provided another attendance profile of those children between the ages of 6 and 14:

TABLE 21

SCHOOL ATTENDANCE IN CHICAGO:
CHILDREN SIX TO FOURTEEN
1910

PARENTAL DESCRIPTION	NUMBER OF CHILDREN	SCHOOL ATTENDANCE
Native parentage	79,064	70,540 (89.2%)
Foreign or mixed parentage	219,774	193,994 (88.3)
Foreign-born whites	34,078	28,760 (84.4)
Total Number of Children	332,916	293,294 (88.0)

SOURCE: U.S. Department of Commerce, Bureau of the Census, Abstract of the Thirteenth Census of the United States (Washington, D.C.: Government Printing Office, 1913), table 17, p. 232.

It is apparent from these figures that foreign-born children were only 3.6 percent below the city's average of 88.0 percent for children between 6 and 14 years of age in school attendance.

The data refute the oft-made contention that nearly 50 percent of Chicago's school age children were not in school during the early part of this century and that the percentage was even higher for children of immigrants. With reference to Greek immigrant children the inference can be made that they, too, were for the most part attending school--either the public school or one of the two communal Greek day schools that had been established by 1910.

Indeed, statistics for literacy and school attendance in the federal census of 1910 suggest that immigrant families showed as much or more zeal for education as those in which parents were native Americans.[1] Apparently, behind the immigrants' concern for learning were three interlocking motives:

> The one most explicit in their literature and also most deeply rooted in Old World experience was simply the desire to earn a better living and, if possible, to gain both riches and fame. The second, and the one which seems to have been most prominent in religious congregations in America was the need to shape a structure of family and communal life that would fit the requirements of mobile and urban existence. The other was specifically ethnic: the quest of a definition of national identity that would fulfill the sense of duty to their homeland or to their people . . . and still not contradict their new allegiance to America.[2]

The experience of the Immigrants' Protective League confirms these findings. It had a cooperative program with immigration officials at Ellis Island to forward names of all school age children destined for Chicago. School officials had follow-up activity to see whether these children were enrolled in schools, and found very few who were not in attendance. The league report concluded that the "statement very often made that immigrant parents are eager to have their children take advantage of our educational opportunities" was true.[3]

---

[1] Timothy L. Smith, "Immigrant Social Aspirations and American Education, 1880-1930," American Quarterly (Fall 1969), p. 523.

[2] Ibid., p. 525.

[3] Annual Report 1911-1912 (Immigrants' Protective League), pp. 15-16.

However, a decade earlier Superintendent Lane surmised that at
least 70 percent of those children in school never entered the fifth grade and
that the average length of their schooling was approximately three years. An
indication of the poor holding power of public schools during the 1895-96
term is shown in the daily attendance average of 165,640; enrollees were
213,825.[1] This was not a new problem concomitant with the influx of southeastern European immigrants alone. Even in 1871, when most city immigrants
were from northwestern Europe, only 16 percent of school age children with
foreign-born parents were in school; yet, half of the city's population was
foreign-born.[2]

The compulsory education law of the time did not apply to mercantile
establishments or bootblacks, newsboys, messengers, peddlers, and kindred
jobs in which numerous immigrant children, especially Greeks, were employed.[3] These variables in the education law along with the discretionary
law enforcement by the Chicago Board of Education accounted for the absence
from school of nearly one-third of Chicago's school-age children by the turn
of the century.

The problem of educating immigrant children was not confined to
Chicago. The Dillingham Commission, appointed in 1907 by Congress to
study the effects of immigration on American life, reported that in the public
schools of the nation's thirty-seven largest cities during 1909, 57.8 percent
of the pupils enrolled were of foreign parentage.

In seven of the largest cities, including Chicago, "two out of every
three school children were the sons and daughters of immigrants." Only 32.7
percent of Chicago's children were of native-born fathers, while 67.3 percent

---

[1] Clark, pp. 98-100. In 1908-9 the Dillingham Commission found a
considerable improvement in the average daily attendance--231,850 out of
235,452 enrolled in Chicago public schools. United States Immigration Commission: The Children of Immigrants in Schools, vol. 30, Reports of the Immigration Commission (Washington, D.C.: Government Printing Office, 1911),
p. 543.

[2] Herrick, p. 62.

[3] For the plight of Chicago school children and the evils of child labor
during this period see John Spargo, The Bitter Cry of the Children (Chicago:
Quadrangle Paperbacks, 1968), passim.

were offspring of foreign-born fathers.[1] This was one of the highest ratios
in the nation. The commission report confirmed that during the first two decades of the present century the most crucial problem facing the nation was
the education of immigrant children.

Nativism in American history complicated the educational problem,
because the immigrant was viewed as a threat to the social order. By 1900,
America had become a land of strangers. Approximately half of the population was foreign-born, and in Chicago only 21 percent were native-born. The
city's 1910 census showed over a quarter of a million people over ten years
of age unable to speak English.[2] The real threat was felt when the flow of
immigration shifted from northern to southern Europe.[3] The southern Europeans, which included Greeks, were an acute danger to American mores.
Therefore, these "strangers in the land" had to be Americanized to protect
the "American way" of life.[4]

This was conceived as the task of the public schools. The literature
of the period reflected the aim of the broader culture to homogenize the children of southern European immigrants to Americanism.[5] The very statement
of this goal raised many more problems than it solved, since there was little

---

[1]Abstract of the Report on the Children of Immigrants in Schools,
pp. 18-19.

[2]Sixth Annual Report 1915, (Immigrants'Protective League), p. 6.

[3]For example, during the following decades, the percent of the total
immigrant population which came from southern Europe increased as follows:
1881-91=18.3%; 1891-1901=51.9%; 1901-10=70.8%; see Samuel Elliot Morison
and Henry Steele Commager, The Growth of the American Republic, vol. 2
(New York: Oxford University Press, 1956), p. 177.

[4]For an account of the nativist reaction against southern Europeans
see Higham. An account on the attempt to Americanize the immigrant is to
be found in Hartmann.

[5]Foremost among these were Frank V. Thompson, Schooling of the
Immigrant (New York: Harper & Bros., 1920); and Herbert Adophus Miller, The
School and the Immigrant (Cleveland: Survey Committee of the Cleveland
Foundation, 1916). Both books suggested innovations in the education of
immigrant children. Also indicative of this literature was the ten-volume
Americanization Studies prepared under the direction of Allen T. Burns (1920-
24) republished as Americanization Studies: The Acculturation of Immigrant
Groups into American Society, William S. Bernard, ed. (Montclair, N.J.:
Patterson Smith, 1972).

agreement as to what Americanization meant. Professor Ellwood P. Cubberley of Stanford University, for example, was an eloquent spokesman for the view that to Americanize was to Anglicize. The southern and eastern Europeans, Cubberley declared, were essentially different from the immigrants who preceded them:

> Illiterate, docile, lacking in self-reliance and initiative and not possessing the Anglo-Teutonic conceptions of law, order, and government, their coming has served to dilute tremendously our national stock, and to corrupt our civic life.[1]

The first task of education, he concluded, was to break up the ghettos,

> . . . to assimilate and amalgamate these people as part of our American race, and to implant in their children, so far as it can be done, the Anglo-Saxon conception of righteousness, law and order, and popular government, and to awaken in them a reverence for our democratic institutions and for those things in our national life which we as a people hold to be of abiding worth.[2]

To Americanize, in this view, was to divest the immigrant of his ethnic character and to inculcate the dominant Anglo-Saxon morality. Americanization meant taking on the ways and beliefs of those who felt they embodied the true, historic America, the America worth preserving. "What kind of American consciousness can grow in the atmosphere of sauerkraut and Limberger cheese?" asked a representative of the Daughters of the American Revolution. Or, what can you expect of the Americanism of the man whose breath always reeks of garlic?"[3] There was no room in the United States for "hyphenated Americans."

Hence, surface changes did not suffice. The schools had to embark upon a new program to bring about the indoctrination of immigrant children to the correct way of American life. A classroom with children speaking a half-dozen different languages inevitably altered the schoolroom atmosphere. The

---

[1] Ellwood P. Cubberley, Changing Conceptions of Education (Boston: Houghton Mifflin Co., 1909), pp. 15-16. See also Cubberley's Public Education in the United States (Boston: Houghton Mifflin Co., 1919), pp. 485-89.

[2] Ibid., Changing Conceptions.

[3] Edward Hale Bierstadt, Aspects of Americanization (Cincinnati: Robert M. McBride & Co., 1922), pp. 114-15.

impact of the immigrants has been suggested in a hypothesis which maintains:

> that any society which accepts within its boundaries members of other societies or culture, and which attempts to put them on a common basis of understanding and activity, will itself change radically in the process.[1]

The problem went far beyond language; each subculture implied a unique heritage as well as varying attitudes toward schooling. Incorporated in the school syllabus were new activities on etiquette--manners, cleanliness dress, getting along with one another, and other day-to-day problems in life adjustment.[2] While valiant attempts were made by teachers to meet the pupils' pressing needs, there was no lessening in the concern to have them Americanized. Typical of those concerned was Ella Flagg Young who served as superintendent of schools of Chicago from 1909 to 1915. She focused on "the child" instead of teaching methods and was outspoken in her thoughts for children of immigrants, of the tenements and of the streets, who made up 67 percent of the pupils in Chicago schools in 1909. As former principal of Skinner School she had firsthand contact with immigrant children. The school was located near the Greek Delta. Miss Young's philosophy was based on the belief that public schools must be for the poor and the rich, native and immigrant, all faiths and races--all meeting on a common ground.[3] Serving on the Child Labor Committee of the Illinois State Federation of Labor, she was deeply concerned that 30 percent of those applying for a work certificate

---

[1]See Thomas, p. 253.

[2]An insightful account of this role of the public school can be found in David B. Tyack, "Becoming an American: The Education of the Immigrant," in his Turning Points in American Educational History (Boston: Ginn & Co., 1967), pp. 228-34. Also see Mary Antin, The Promised Land (Boston: Houghton Mifflin Co., 1912), chap. 10; Edward Bok, The Americanization of Edward Bok (New York: Charles Scribner's Sons, 1922); pp. 2-4; Angelo Patri A Schoolmaster of the Great City (New York: Macmillan Co., 1917); Jacob Riis, The Children of the Poor (New York: Charles Scribner's Sons, 1892), chap. 11, 12; and W. H. Maxwell, "Stories from the Lives of Real Teachers," The World's Work 18 (1909): 11877-80; and Leonard Covello, The Heart is the Teacher (New York: McGraw-Hill Book Co., 1958), pp. 24-25.

[3]Ella Flagg Young, Isolation in the School (Chicago: University of Chicago Press, 1901), pp. 3, 22, 47.

were foreign-born.[1] During her tenure as superintendent more than half of the evening school enrollment of 38,000 were immigrants learning English and studying for naturalization papers.[2]

Miss Young extolled the public schools in 1909 as being the "greatest unifying agent extant in this land, whose people represent all European peoples." She maintained that

. . . so potent has been the public school in creating a sentiment favorable to oneness, to Americanism that sectional antagonism based on racial [ethnic] characteristics maintained in their original forms is unknown. In childhood, millions of America's citizens have learned something of the fundamentals in the unity of the human race. The comradeship in experience developed by the democratic spirit pervading the methods in instruction and discipline, is a more positive factor in the sympathetic appreciation existing between members of different religious and social organizations than the associations in private or denominational schools can ever be.

It is the free public school that has made the child of foreign parentage strive to take on the habits of dress, speech, and thought that would identify him with the people whose ancestors were merged into this social and political society at an earlier date than were his.[3]

Evidence of the implementation of Miss Young's philosophy was manifested in 1906 when, as principal of the Chicago Normal School, she recommended to Superintendent Cooley that the Yale School be discontinued as a practice school for the Normal School. She based her recommendation on criticisms of principals of schools with large membership of foreign children indicating that the training program at the Normal School was not geared to meeting the needs of a system of schools as cosmopolitan as Chicago's with its large immigrant population. Up to that time, the experience of students in teaching was limited to work with American-born children from English-speaking homes who composed the student body of the Yale School. The Chicago Board of Education approved of her recommendation and designated the Harrison School, with its large foreign population located in a deteriorating residential and manufacturing area of the city, as the new practice school.[4]

---

[1] Sixty-first Annual Report of the Chicago Board of Education, 1915, p. 185.

[2] Herrick, p. 116.

[3] E. F. Young, pp. 91-92.

[4] Fifty-fourth Annual Report of the Board of Education, 1908 (Chicago), p. 224.

That the public schools of Chicago should be concerned with the large ethnic population was stated explicitly by an educational commission appointed by Mayor Carter H. Harrison in 1898. Investigating the schools and recommending changes to keep up with the growing metropolis, the commission under the chairmanship of William Rainey Harper stated in 1900 that the

> . . . essential purpose of the American school system is to form American citizens, and all proper means should be employed to make of all the children in our public schools, particularly those of foreign descent, men and women whose hearts are centered in our life.[1]

The commission recommended the establishment of ungraded rooms to meet these diverse needs, and it further enjoined the Board of Education to bear in mind that

> . . . a large part of our children are of foreign extraction, and that about 94 percent of them leave the public school at thirteen or fourteen years--that is, they do not go beyond the primary and grammar grades. An astonishingly large proportion do not get above the fifth and sixth grades. How to make the most of these few years of school life is the important question.[2]

Despite these exhortations, the Chicago public schools and those throughout the nation did not make adequate provision for the education of the immigrant child. In her sociological survey of Chicago schools, Clark points out: "One may search the records in vain to find any explicit reference to these [immigrant] conditions," and laments the lack of "any recognition of the need for special adaptation of the system to the foreign clientage." Aside from the teaching of American history and the celebration of historic anniversaries and heroic events, there "is no special adaptation of the work of the schools to foreigners."[3]

In actuality, no formal and persistent arrangements for teaching English to non-English speaking children materialized, nor was there an attempt to sensitize school personnel to ethnicity as is in vogue today. Indeed, the charge was made that far more effective techniques for learning

---

[1] *Report of the Educational Commission of the City of Chicago* (Chicago: University of Chicago Press, 1900), p. 131.

[2] Ibid., pp. 156, 175.

[3] Clark, pp. 109-10.

English were employed by our territorial possessions of Puerto Rico and the Philipines than by public schools of New York, Pittsburgh, Chicago, or Cleveland. Miss Abbott said that the least that could be done would be to use "in behalf of our immigrant population the methods developed in the schools we have established for the Filipino and the Puerto Rican [sic] children.[1]

Teaching a new language is far different from methods utilized in teaching subject matter to pupils in their own tongue.[2] Consequently, American public schools were crowded with "retarded" children who were below grade level for their age. In an effort to determine the causes of retardation, Ayres conducted a detailed study of 20,000 pupils' records in fifteen Manhattan schools. He alleged that the courses of study were geared to the unduly bright child and not to the average or slow learner. Hence, the curriculum would be especially difficult for the immigrant child.[3]

Children struggling with the new language and with poor nutrition compounded the "backward" labeling by educators. An illustration is made of Jimmie, a child of educated parents in Chicago:

> This little Greek of eleven years has reached the second grade only. Of nine children he is the only one living. Both father and mother (the father Greek, the mother French) are educated people, speaking and reading several languages. . . . the father had been ill . . . and the family was in a state of abject poverty, the mother having sold every salable article for food for herself and the boy . . . they lived in a basement tenement of five rooms, three of which were dark; for these rooms they paid twelve dollars a month.
> This boy, Jimmie, is very backward in his school work, for which undoubtedly poverty and insufficient food are partly responsible. He does not, however, give the impression at home of being a stupid child for he is very fond of playing with a little tool-chest and will work all

---

[1] G. Abbott, Immigrant and Community, p. 224.

[2] In 1901 the Cleveland, Ohio school system recognized the necessity of special provisions for teaching English to immigrant children by having special "steamer classes" before placement in regular grades. H. Miller, pp. 73-74. Later, Los Angeles developed a unique program of adapting for local needs of immigrant communities. See Davis, Immigration and Americanization, pp. 457-58.

[3] Leonard P. Ayres, Laggards in Our Schools (New York: Russell Sage Foundation, 1909), p. 5.

day long making things with his saw and hammer. This ability he has no opportunity of utilizing in school and there he ranks as a backward child.[1]

The investigation by Hull House in 1906 found the need for ungraded rooms in the public schools, because there were large numbers of children who were below their grades, and helping them was most difficult, even with conscientious teachers. The public school system appeared to ignore another charge made by first generation immigrant parents who stated that the system was driving a wedge between them and their children. Jane Addams went so far as to indict the schools on this count. With her perceptive insight she charged that the

. . . public school too often separates the child from his parents and widens that old gulf between fathers and sons which is never so cruel and so wide as it is between the immigrants who came to this country and their children who have gone to the public school and feel that they have learned it all. The parents are thereafter subjected to certain judgment, the judgment of the young which is always harsh and in this instance founded upon the most superficial standard of Americanism.[2]

Even the cultivation of patriotism in the public schools had its drawbacks. Grace Abbott states that in our

. . . zeal to teach patriotism we are often teaching disrespect for the history and the traditions that the ancestors of the immigrant parents had their part in making. This often means disrespect for the parent himself.[3]

These charges and fears were commonly acknowledged by Greek immigrant parents. They worried over the acculturative function of the public school alienating their offspring from the Hellenic heritage. Furthermore, the loosening of subcultural bonds would make adjustment difficult upon their return to the homeland. In order to avoid such a calamity, the Greek immigrants of Chicago were among the first of their ethnic group in the nation to establish communal ethnic schools.

And it was at Hull House where the first expressions of cultural pluralism arose amidst an existing mood of coercion toward "instant Americanism."

---

[1] Gertrude Howe Britton, An Intensive Study of the Causes of Truancy in Eight Chicago Public Schools including a Home Investigation of Eight Hundred Truant Children (Chicago: Chicago Board of Education, 1906), p. 29.

[2] Jane Addams, "The Public School and the Immigrant Child," National Education Association Addresses and Proceedings 46 (1908): 99-102.

[3] G. Abbott, Immigrant and Community, pp. 226-27.

Jane Addams argued for ethnic traditions and cultures to enhance and enrich formal school experiences.[1] She set up a "labor museum" to exhibit old-world crafts and trades as a means of displaying "inherited resources" of parents and grandparents to their offspring. Miss Addams believed that this museum would be in keeping with Dewey's definition of education as "continuing reconstruction of experience."[2] The spirit of cultural pluralism permeated the social and educational programs held at Hull House.

One of the few schoolmen who agreed with Jane Addams' pluralistic theory was John Dewey. In ringing terms before the National Education Association he declared his faith in the efficacy of cultural pluralism:

> I find that many who talk the loudest about the need of a supreme and unified Americanism of spirit really mean some special code or tradition to which they happen to be attached. They have some pet tradition which they would impose upon all . . . no matter how loudly any one proclaims his Americanism if he assumes that any one racial strain, any one component culture is to furnish a pattern to which all strains and cultures . . . are to conform, he is a traitor to an American nationalism.[3]

Despite the sentiments of Addams and Dewey, the concept of cultural consciousness did not have many subscribers. The schools continued to destroy the subcultures of immigrant children with the indoctrination of the "melting pot" theory, which was as old as the Republic. A naturalized New Yorker, Jean de Crevecoeur, exemplified this spirit when he wrote in 1782:

> I could point out to you a family whose grandfather was an Englishman, whose wife was Dutch, whose son married a French woman and whose present four sons have now four wives of different nations. He is an American, who leaving behind all his ancient prejudices and manners, received new ones from the new mode of life he has embraced . . .
> Here individuals of all nations are melting into a new race of men . . .[4]

---

[1] Addams, "The Public School and the Immigrant Child," pp. 99-102.

[2] Addams, Twenty Years, pp. 171-78.

[3] John Dewey, "Nationalizing Education," Addresses and Proceedings of the National Education Association 54 (1916): 184-85.

[4] Hector Saint Jean Crevecoeur, "American Farmer," in Oscar Handlin, ed., This Was America (New York: Harper Torchbooks, 1964), p. 39.

It was an idea close to the heart of the American self-image, and it gained profound significance a century later in a play by Israel Zangwill, The Melting Pot.

A lone dissenter to this concept, Horace Kallen, fought this idea and the restrictionist movement which culminated in the National Origins Act of 1924. Kallen's plea for cultural pluralism, espoused earlier by Addams and Dewey, remained a cry in the wilderness until the more recent civil rights movement, which is altering greatly public schools today.[1]

The arrival of the Greek immigrants on the Chicago scene, like that of so many other immigrant groups, coincided with the Progressive Movement in American education. Paralleling the broader movement in American society, local leaders sought to eliminate corruption in civic affairs. It was believed that the power of the "corrupt urban political machines which seemed to feed upon the saloon, the slum and the immigrant vote" could be broken.[2] All institutions traditionally relied upon in educating the young--the family, the church, the apprenticeship system, the public school--seemed inadequate. A campaign was prompted by social workers and educators to protect the classes most deeply affected by the social disorganization of a modern complex society--the Negro, the indigent child, and the immigrant. The problems faced by the first few generations of immigrant children prompted experimentation in education, and this contributed heavily to national concerns about progressive reform in both school and society, concerns which have dominated American social ideals throughout the twentieth century. A plethora of legislation resulted, such as factory and child labor laws, juvenile protection and sanitation laws. Around 1910, amidst these concerns emerged a "new education" which combined three elements: vocational training, or "education for life," child-centered school, and social reform.[3]

---

[1] For a detailed analysis of the cultural pluralism doctrine see Kallen, Culture and Democracy, and his "Democracy Versus the Melting Pot: A Study of American Nationality," The Nation, pt. 1, 2 (18 and 25 February 1915).

[2] For excellent accounts of this movement see Lawrence A. Cremin, "The Progressive Movement in American Education: A Perspective," Harvard Educational Review 27 (Fall 1957): 251-70; and Timothy L. Smith, "The Progressive Movement in American Education, 1880-1900," Harvard Educational Review 31 (Spring 1961): 168-93.

[3] Ibid., Smith, p. 171.

These educational changes were aimed at equipping and brightening the pupils' future toward a useful and upward mobile life. In Horace Mann's words, the public schools were "the great equalizer of the conditions of men, " facilitating the poor and disadvantaged into the mainstream of American economic and social life. Initially, the feeling was that the public schools had performed their task admirably. However, recent research on American schooling discounts the efficacy of public schools in coping with the mass of children's needs in the twentieth century. American public schools did not provide the golden millenium.[1] A recent critic charged:

> From 1890, at least, the schools failed to perform according to their own as well as the popular definition of their role. In virtually every study undertaken since that of Chicago schools in 1898, more children have failed in school than have succeeded, both in an absolute and in relative numbers. The educators who collaborated in the Chicago study found an exceedingly high incidence of poor school performance. They were quick to look to foreign births as an explanation, but immigrants spawned Americans and still, with each passing decade no more than 60 percent of Chicago's public school pupils were recorded at "normal age" (grade level); or "retarded" (three to five years behind). In Boston, Chicago, Detroit, Philadelphia, Pittsburgh, New York and Minneapolis failure rates were so high that in no one of these systems did the so-called normal groups exceed 60 percent, while in several instances it fell even lower--to 49 percent in Pittsburgh and to 35 percent in Minneapolis.[2]

Greer points out that school failure was not limited to those immigrants from southern and eastern Europe alone. The 1920 census revealed that even the favored English and Welsh migrants found half of their people in unskilled labor occupations. And Americans of English stock had 40 percent working in coal mines and cotton factories. The pattern of school failure was perennially uniform among all these groups.

American schools, furthermore, had taken over the curriculum and the instructional methods of European schools which had been developed to in-

---

[1] For the collapse of the progressive education movement see Lawrence A. Cremin, The Transformation of the Schools: Progressivism in American Education, 1876-1957 (New York: Albert A. Knopf, 1961), pt. 2.

[2] Colin Greer, "Public Schools: The Myth of the Melting Pot, " Saturday Review 52 (15 November 1969): 84-85; see also his Cobweb, Attitudes: Essays on Educational and Cultural Mythology (New York: Teachers College Press, Columbia University, 1970) chap. 1, and his later work, The Great School Legend: A Revisionist Interpretation of American Public Education (New York: Basic Books, 1972).

struct mainly the upper class; they made little attempt to understand the special needs of their new immigrant students. All the adjustment was expected to be on the student's part. Leonard Covello, the first Italian-American to become principal of a New York City school, describes vividly his schooling around the turn of the century, when immigrant pupils were made to feel ashamed of their parents. Typical were views of New York's superintendent of schools, W. H. Maxwell, during the early part of the century: that immigrant parents were "ignorant, prejudiced and highly excitable people." Thus, in their refusal to meet immigrant culture half-way and to adjust the schools to the children as well as the children to the schools, teachers and administrators, as the historian Michael Katz writes, "all said to the child and parent from the immigrant and working class, 'You are vicious, immoral, shortsighted, and thoroughly wrong about most things. We are right; we shall show you the truth'."[1] There were exceptions, of course. Silberman mentions the Japanese-Americans, the Greeks, and the eastern European Jews, in particular--for them the public schools did serve as the critical means for upward mobility, but this was because their ethnic cultures placed a heavy premium on individual achievement.

However, for most immigrant groups, (the Irish, Italians, Poles and the other Slavs, the groups that comprised the bulk of the immigration of the middle and late nineteenth and early twentieth centuries), education was not an important means of mobility.[2] Frequently mobility was achieved by sacrificing the education of the younger generation. Immigrants who were mostly unskilled laborers often depended on their children's earnings. But this mobility was generally short-lived, as fathers had difficulty transmitting their relative prosperity to uneducated sons, who had to begin as laborers at the bottom, as their fathers had done.[3] In this respect, Christopher Jencks

---

[1]As quoted in Charles E. Silberman, Crisis in the Classroom: The Remaking of American Education (New York: Random House, Vintage Books, 1970), p. 58.

[2]Ibid., p. 54.

[3]This is the premise Christopher Jencks takes in his treatise on poverty in America; see Inequality: A Reassessment of the Effect of Family and Schooling in America (New York: Basic Books, 1972).

recently asserted "that schools serve primarily as selection and certification agencies, whose job is to measure and label people, and only secondarily as socialization agencies, whose job is to change people."[1] This, he contends, has had a polarizing effect in American schooling.

Moreover, another recent critic has charged, public schools were not only Protestant, but also Anglo-Saxon. No attempt was made to help pupils identify with the language and culture of their parents.

> World literature was hardly touched. Italian students were not introduced to Dante, Boccaccio, Manzoni . . . . French students were not encouraged to assume a special relation to . . . Claudel, Baudelaire, Pascal, Montaigne. What books by Czechs, Slovaks, Poles, and Roumanians [sic] have been translated into the curricula for students of Slavic background? Education in America has not been conceived as a search into historical roots. It has been conceived as indoctrination into superculture.[2]

Quite correctly, Drachsler defined the function of the public school in 1921 as the ". . . leveling of all cultural differences among its pupils and the sending forth of a uniform product with the unmistakable stamp of the dominant civilization upon them."[3]

This perceptive view in 1921 about the role of the public school is receiving considerable support today in the work of contemporary critics such as Michael Katz, Colin Greer and Joel Spring, who have fostered a revisionist history of American education. Their research suggests that the school has not brought about equalization, but instead helped to perpetuate differences, or did little to reduce them.

> They argue that the schools serve the favored few and do not help the poor. They hold that our educational system is harmful to children and that the oppressiveness of the system is neither accidental nor an unforeseen consequence of once noble reform, but that, rather, it reflects the values of a bureaucratic, inegalitarian society.[4]

---

[1] Ibid., p. 135.

[2] Michael Novak, The Rise of the Unmeltable Ethnics (New York: Macmillan Co., 1971), pp. 140-41.

[3] Julius Drachsler, "The Cultural Contribution of the Immigrant and a Policy of Incorporation," Social Work 48 (1921): 491.

[4] Andrew T. Kopan and Herbert J. Walberg, eds., Rethinking Educational Equality (Berkeley, Calif.: McCutchan Publishing Corp., 1974), p. viii. For an analysis and critique of the work of revisionist historians see Marvin Lazerson, "Revisionism and American Educational History," Harvard Educational Review 43 (May 1973): 269-83.

This may account for why, instead of being concerned with the serious deficiencies of the public schools with reference to immigrant needs, educators were wrapped up in the promulgation of compulsory education laws and the expansion of school attendance rather than individualizing instruction systematically. Yet, interest in reaching immigrant pupils all but disappeared after the immigration curtailment in the 1920s. The 1930 United States census indicated that over 14 million were foreign-born and over 26 million were persons of foreign or mixed parentage. This means that over 40 million or almost one-third of the nation's population, was composed of first and second generation immigrant stock--a number greater than ever before in American history.

In spite of such astonishing large numbers of immigrants, there was a "lack of adequate appreciation of the nature of the problems by the very people who were in considerable measure guiding the destinies of the immigrant."[1] A poll of six hundred American-born children of foreign parents in grades five to eight revealed that only 15 percent considered themselves fully Americanized; less than 10 percent denied the existence of conflicts between New and Old World standards.[2]

The immigrant pupil recognized his unique problems not simply because of his foreign birth or ethnic subculture, but also by hostility faced in the broader milieu. His transition from a primary to a secondary society made for harsh adjustment in a world of industrialization. This shift from rural to urban life was a significant and difficult change. Coming from an

> . . . isolated homogeneous small village community, where life is warm, personal, and intimate, and where he lives in a world having little specialization, few machines, little reliance on individual initiative and only a minimum of private property. . . . he finds himself in a vast cosmopolitan center, swarming with strangers whose contacts with him are impersonal, casual and abstract; he is called upon to live in a world where labor is highly specialized, machines dominating industry, and where the wage system and money economy control his contacts with others. Countless persons bred in rural districts, though not immigrants

---

[1] Pauline V. Young, "Social Problems in the Education of the Immigrant Child," American Sociological Review 1 (June 1936): 419.

[2] Ibid.

have failed to make the adjustment to these conditions. 'The marvel is that so many immigrants, with their added handicaps, have succeeded.[1]

In summary, the public schools did not address themselves fully to the educational adjustment of immigrant children whether they were from one country or another. Although they helped these children in assimilating into the American mainstream, they were far from being "the great equalizer." The task of educating all youngsters was limited to theory and lip service. The lower classes, the immigrants, the so-called disadvantaged, floundered in an alien educational setting. And as Cremin has pointed out, the "commoness" of the common school was greatly exaggerated, for it has always been essentially a middle class and upper middle class institution.[2] Indeed, as pointed out by Cremin and Coleman, informal educational alternatives-- the playground, the gang, the factory, the union, the political machines, and the very openness of the American occupational structure--served as catalysts and agents of mobility and Americanization, successfully integrating European immigrants in spite of the schools.[3]

Nativity of Children in Chicago Public Schools

A paucity of specific information concerning ethnic composition is evidenced in the official documents of the Chicago Board of Education with reference to Chicago Greek immigrants in the day schools. Data are complicated further by contradictions between city and federal records. Nonetheless, generalized conclusions have been derived from records, newspapers, and testimonies that offer insight into the role of the public school in accommodating and acculturating Greek immigrant children.

---

[1]Ibid., p. 420.

[2]Silberman, p. 54.

[3]Cremin, "Progressive Movement," and James S. Coleman, "Social and Cultural Integration and Educational Policy," in Herbert J. Walberg and Andrew T. Kopan eds., Rethinking Urban Education (San Francisco: Jossey-Bass, 1972), p. 131.

Apparently the first ethnic census of Chicago schools was taken during the 1859-60 school term. It listed simply the birthplace of pupils as enumerated in table 22.

TABLE 22

NATIVITY OF PUPILS IN CHICAGO PUBLIC SCHOOLS
1859-60

Birthplace	Number	Percent
United States	9,844	69.2
Germany	1,390	11.2
England	853	6.0
Ireland	741	5.2
Canada	425	2.9
Scotland	193	1.4
Sweden	157	1.1
Norway	128	.9
All others	277	2.1
Total	14,008	100.0

SOURCE: Sixth Annual Report, Board of Education Year Ending February 1, 1860 (Chicago), p. 38.

Italy was the only southern European country listed in the "all other" category with a total of ten pupils. It is assumed that no Greek child was in attendance, since none is mentioned in the census.

The population of Chicago in 1859 was 95,000. Of the 14,008 children enrolled in public schools, 9,844, or 70 percent, were American-born. Examination reveals that 2,152, or 15 percent, were born in countries in which English was not the spoken language. However, there is no indication in school records that any provisions to learn English were made for these children or their parents. The birthplace of the American-born children in school at that time is of interest. School records too rarely preserve such data as shown in the Sixth Annual Report, table 23.

One can glean from the data a profile of mobility that helped to build the large midwestern metropolis. The native Americans had come from the eastern and north Atlantic states. The foreign groups were mostly from north-western Europe.

TABLE 23

BIRTHPLACE OF AMERICAN-BORN CHILDREN
IN CHICAGO PUBLIC SCHOOLS
1859-60

Chicago	3,906	Maine	83
Illinois (not Chicago)	758	Indiana	80
New York	2,504	New Hampshire	56
Massachusetts	472	Maryland	53
Ohio	381	Virginia	39
Pennsylvania	301	Rhode Island	38
Michigan	267	Iowa	25
Wisconsin	246	Louisiana	21
Connecticut	160	Mississippi	21
New Jersey	100	Delaware	16
Missouri	91	District of Columbia	11
Kentucky	84	Tennessee	10
Vermont	84	Others	37
		Total	9,844

SOURCE: Sixth Annual Report, Board of Education Year Ending February 1, 1860 (Chicago), p. 38.

As discussed in chapter 3 Chicago was one of America's most ethnic cities. During the period from 1880 to 1920 the makeup of Chicago's foreign population was distributed as reflected on table 24. The public schools' composition was indicative of the admixture of ethnic groups. The German and Scandinavian people had the larger portion of the non-English speaking groups and the percentage of foreign-born fell slowly after 1890. However, by the turn of the century a significant number emigrated from southeastern

countries. Those immigrants from Austria-Hungary were principally Bohemians
and other Slavic groups. The Greeks were one of the smallest of all groups.

TABLE 24

NUMBER OF FOREIGN-BORN PERSONS AND
ETHNIC GROUPS IN CHICAGO
1880-1920

	1880	1890	1900	1910	1920
German	75,205	161,039	170,738	182,281	112,288
Scandinavian	25,289	71,954	81,012	98,705	90,312
Austro-Hungarian . .	1,656	. . .	16,761	155,997	116,682
Russian-Jewish . . .	921	. . .	24,178	121,786	122,595
Polish	8,546	. . .	59,713	. . .	137,611
Italian	1,357	5,685	16,008	45,169	59,215
Greek	27	245	1,493	6,564	11,546
Others *	94,888	317,446	218,701	165,715	138,309
Percent Foreign-born .	40.7	41.0	34.5	35.0	30.0

SOURCE: Compiled from data in Population Facts for Planning
Chicago (Chicago: Chicago Planning Commission, 1942), p. 14; Ernest W.
Burgess and Charles Newcomb Census Data of the City of Chicago 1920
(Chicago: University of Chicago Press, 1931), p. 21.

* This number includes English-speaking immigrants.

But as observed in chapter 3 and as shown in this study, Greek immigrants were able to establish a viable subcultural community in Chicago,
complete with educational institutions, despite their limited number. It was
from this ethnic community that a large number of children, in relation to the
size of the community, would be enrolled in the public schools of the city.
There were nearly 12,000 children born of Greek or mixed parentage in
Chicago by 1930 (see table 15 in chapter 3). Assuming, on the basis of
available enrollment figures, that of this number approximately 3,000 attended
the communal Greek day schools for their elementary schooling from 1910 to
1930, it can be projected that some 9,000 attended Chicago public schools.
This, of course, does not include Greek school age children born abroad
who, upon arriving in Chicago were frequently enrolled in the public schools,

dropping out after completing the primary grades.

Greek Children in Chicago Public Schools

During the period of investigation the chief source for determining
the ethnic composition of Chicago's school children was the biennial school
census. It was required by Illinois school law in order to determine the
distribution of the common school fund "in proportion to the number of persons in each county under the age of twenty-one as ascertained from the
next preceding state or federal census."[1] In Chicago, the census was taken
biennially and, according to law, in addition called for the

> . . . enumeration of the number of persons under 21 years of age mak-
> ing a separate enumeration of those above the age of 12 who are unable
> to read and write and the cause of the neglect to educate them.[2]

The law did not specify other information. However, the Chicago
school census around 1890 began to list country of birth, population by
wards, births and deaths, occupations and occasionally the enumeration of
the adult population. This census has become a veritable treasure trove of
statistical information for Chicago.[3] A confusing but important distinction,
however, is that the school census gave not only the pupil enrollment, but
included the number of persons of school age--under twenty-one--residing
in the city.

---

[1] Edith Abbott and Sophonisba P. Breckinridge, Truancy and Non-
Attendance in the Chicago Schools (Chicago: University of Chicago Press,
1917), p. 212.

[2] Proceedings of the Board of Education, July 14, 1909 to July 29,
1910 (Chicago), p. 561. After 1910, the school census program was placed
under the direction of the Superintendent of Compulsory Education.

[3] At the time, this additional information was considered irrelevant
and wasteful, and could be sacrificed to a more detailed presentation of
facts regarding non-attendance; see E. Abbott and Breckinridge, pp. 219-20.

The number of Greeks in Chicago between 1894 to 1914 has been compiled from the school census and is exhibited on table 25.

TABLE 25

NUMBER OF GREEKS IN CHICAGO AS SHOWN BY SCHOOL CENSUS
1894 TO 1914

Year	Foreign-born	Native-born	Total
1894	. . .	. . .	786+
1896	564	150	714+
1898	1,186	458	1,644+
1900 . . . .) 1902 . . . .) 1904 . . . .) 1906 . . . .)	Census not broken down by ethnic groups		
1908	3,521	697	4,218+
1910	369	780	1,149#
1912	295	1,153	1,448#
1914	6,954	1,667	8,621+

SOURCE: Compiled from Annual Reports of the Chicago Board of Education.

+ = all ages, adult and minor

= only minors under age 21

The first official listing of Greeks appears in the 1894 data in which the total Greek population of all ages residing in Chicago was 796.[1] The

---

[1]The school census generally was taken during the months of May, June, or July. By this time, most Greek laborers who worked on the railroads had left for the summer so that a great many of those who made Chicago their home during the winter or who came back between jobs in the summer were not counted. See G. Abbott, "Study of the Greeks," p. 380. Likewise, the school census was known to be "unreliable" as evidenced by an internal examination of figures. For examples, see E. Abbott and Breckinridge, pp. 217-19. The first mention in school records of persons born in the Near East and attending school during 1864-65 appears in the Eleventh Annual Report which shows two pupils born in Turkey. The following year's report reveals one pupil enrolled; in 1866-67, again two persons born in Turkey are listed. (In all probability, these students were from the unredeemed territory of Greece occupied by Turkey because several Greeks were known to

1896 census offers more sophisticated information, listing residents according to city wards in three categories: (1) American-born, (2) American-born with one parent American-born, and (3) foreign-born. The Greeks are specified as 147 American-born; three American-born with one parent American-born; and 564 foreign-born. These figures totaled 714 Greeks in thirty-four wards.[1] The subsequent censuses from 1898 to 1908 indicated similarly the Greeks of all ages residing in Chicago.

Interestingly, the 1908 school census shows a dispersion from Greektown's 19th Ward to large numbers in the 17th and 18th Wards, southward to the 33rd Ward, and northward to the 20th, 21st and 22nd Wards. These shifts presaged the establishment of two additional koinotites, or organized communities--on the South Side in 1909 and the near North Side in 1910. Even with these scattered dispersals, the 19th and 1st Wards continued to retain the largest Greek populace.[2]

In accordance with school law, the 1910 school census was the first to limit data to minors under the age of twenty-one. It seems that this decision was made to avoid duplication of efforts with the Thirteenth Decennial Federal Census of that same year. The figures were smaller for Greeks, because only those under age twenty-one were counted. The net figure showed a total of 1,149 youngsters, although it cannot be determined how many were under fourteen. Since more than two-thirds (780) were American-born and approximately one-third (369) were foreign born, it can be surmised that the majority of the Greek pupils were under fourteen.

---

have resided in Chicago during the 1860s.) Sixteenth Annual Report of Board of Education for Year Ending July 1, 1870 (Chicago), p. 173.

[1]The largest concentration of Greeks (171) was in the Greek Delta area, Nineteenth Ward. However, evidence from the school census and census tracts of Chicago indicate that Greeks were scattered in practically all of the wards almost from the very beginning. This would seem to refute the commonly held belief that Greeks lived in the Greektown area only. The obverse seems to be true--the majority of Greek immigrants did not live in the Halsted-Harrison-Blue Island triangle. See school census and Ernest W. Burgess and Charles Newcomb eds., Census Data of the City of Chicago, 1930 (Chicago: University of Chicago Press, 1933), passim.

[2]Proceedings of the Board of Education, City of Chicago, July 1, 1908 to July 7, 1909, p. 153.

Again, in the 1912 census, only those under twenty-one were calcu-
lated. It showed Greek pupils as 1,448 with an American-born count of
1,153 and only 295 foreign-born. This data correlates with the data of Greek
women who arrived from the homeland and the emergence of the Greek family
unit. The 1914 census reverted back to an enumeration of the entire city population. Thus, the total Greek population is listed as 8,621, of which 6,954
were foreign-born and 1,667 were American-born.[1]

Another source for Greek enrollment in Chicago schools is the Reports
of the Immigration Commission. In 1908, the United States Immigration Commission undertook a comprehensive survey to determine differences, if any,
between school attendance and school advancement of children of different
nationalities. The report for Chicago indicated that there were 193 Greek
children in all grades but third year high school. The small number of Greek
children is shown in table 26.

TABLE 26

GREEK CHILDREN ENROLLED IN CHICAGO PUBLIC SCHOOLS, 1908

	Kinder-garten	Elementary Grades									High School					Un-gra-ded	Grand Total
		1	2	3	4	5	6	7	8	Total	1	2	3	4	Total		
Male	3	29	21	25	16	9	6	2	3	111	1	-	1	-	2	23	139
Female	3	8	15	9	9	4	1	3	1	50	-	-	-	1	1	-	54
TOTAL	6	37	36	34	25	13	7	5	4	161	1	-	1	1	3	23	193

SOURCE: Compiled from The Children of Immigrants in Schools,
vol. 2, table 2, p. 565.

The results of this study show a heavy concentration of pupils in
grades one to four. The grand total includes those students over twenty
years of age. To a degree, the pattern of enrollment of Greek children follows that of the general school population. For both, the diminution is more
rapid after the fifth grade; the eighth grade is less than one-half as large as

[1]The conflicting data are once again revealed here. While the 1914
census shows 8,621 Greeks in Chicago, Fairchild made an intensive study
of the Greek community in 1910 and lists the Greek population at about 15,000;
see Greek Immigration, p. 125.

the sixth grade. The general school populace shows the eighth grade as slightly more than a third as large as the first grade; whereas, for Greek children, the eighth grade is only about one-tenth as large as the first grade. Table 27 shows the age distribution of Greek children in Chicago schools in 1908.

TABLE 27

GREEK CHILDREN IN CHICAGO SCHOOLS, 1908
BY SEX, AGE, AND GRADE

Grade	Age	4	5	6	7	8	9	10	11	12	13	14	15	16	17	18	19	20	Total	
K	Boys	1	2																3	
	Girls		3																3	
1	Boys		1	8	5	3	2	1	1	5	2		1						29	
	Girls			5	3														8	
2	Boys			2	7	1	5		2	1		2		1					21	
	Girls			1	5	2	4	2	1										15	
3	Boys						4		1	5	2	5	1	4	2		1		25	
	Girls						4		2	3									9	
4	Boys						3	4		3	2	3			1				16	
	Girls						3		3	1	2								9	
5	Boys							2		2	1	4							9	
	Girls								1	3									4	
6	Boys								1	2	1	1	1						6	
	Girls								1										1	
7	Boys						1			1									2	
	Girls								1	2									3	
8	Boys									1		1	1						3	
	Girls												1						1	167
High School																				
1	Boys															1			1	
	Girls																		0	
2	Boys																		0	
	Girls																		0	
3	Boys													1					1	
	Girls																		0	
4	Boys																		0	
	Girls															1			1	3
Ungraded																				
	Boys															3	1	19	23	
	Girls																		0	23
TOTAL		1	6	14	15	12	21	15	12	30	11	14	7	5	4	4	3	19		193

SOURCE: Compiled from The Children of Immigrants in Schools, vol 2, table 3, pp. 569-615.

The high proportion of Greek children in the primary grades was contrasted with their infinitesimal numbers in high school. The commission warned that no inferences should be made by varying proportions of ethnic groups in different grades, because of the differences in residency in the United States. It was to be expected that the nationalities of the more recent immigration would show the largest number of children in the lower grades, while a larger number of children of earlier immigrants would be in the higher grades. Moreover, it was common for the schools to place immigrants who could not speak English in the primary grades until they acquired familiarity with the new language. The supposition employed by the schools was that more time was spent on reading and language arts in the lower grades and this would help the foreign child learn English more readily. Whether a child had formal schooling in his native land or whether his chronological age for placement varied were not factors taken into consideration. One informant who attended both the Dore and Skinner Schools described his experience as follows:

> Immigrant children in public schools were always a problem because when the children went to public schools they did not know the English language, which surprised all the American teachers. The teachers did not know where to place them, and despite their age they were usually placed in the first grade.[1]

The testimonies of Greeks interviewed indicated that this prevailing practice resulted in embarrassment, disillusionment, and dropping out of school. Those interviewed complained about the juvenile lessons and irrelevant textbook materials, the inadequate furniture and equipment, and the condescending attitude of the teachers. To wit:

> I was fourteen years old when I came to Chicago. I wanted to learn how to speak and write English. But when I went to the Dore School, they put me in the first grade. All we did there was read first grade books about "See boy run" over and over again. I got tired reading these books so I left school.[2]

Another lamented:

> I really wanted to learn, but I was put into a room with little children and the desk was too small for me; my legs were out in the aisles.

---

[1] Interview with Dimitri Parry, Chicago, 1 July 1971.

[2] Interview with Thomas Chakinis, River Forest, Illinois, 23 May 1968.

> When I tried to read the children laughed at me. I could not say the
> words well. I was embarrassed, so I quit and went to work.[1]

Still another:

> Our room had quite a few Greek boys and naturally we talked in Greek.
> But the American teacher didn't like it and scolded us. She said we had
> to forget everything Greek and become Americans. But how could we
> forget our homeland? We wanted to be both, Americans and Greeks,
> and when we told her about it, she did not like it.[2]

Placing overage immigrant children in the primary grades with the associated
ills mentioned in the above testimonies probably, in part, accounted for the
high rate of drop-out among Greek immigrants.

The range of overage Greek pupils in the public schools increased
through the fifth year and decreased to the eighth year as shown on table 27.
A considerable drop in enrollment is evidenced after age thirteen. Furthermore, promotion of immigrant children to the next grade was not automatic.
The average promotion rate for the city schools during 1909-10 was 86.6 percent. Yet, at the four schools in which Greek pupils formed significant
majorities (Scammon, Jones, Dante,and Dore), the promotion rate was considerably lower, as shown on table 28. These four schools showed an
average of 69.8, a 16.3 percentage differential from the city promotion rate.
Likewise, the average city promotion rate for the 1910-11 term was 85.7 percent. The rate for the four schools mentioned was 72 percent. Individually,
only the Dore School had a higher rate than the city's average.

It is presumptious to infer that the promotion rates at these schools
were low because of the large Greek population in these schools. In interviews with former students, they claimed that the opposite was true; their
presence increased the promotion curve. It was the "other" ethnic groups
that accounted for the low promotion figure. This statement was made with
characteristic Greek pride by several persons interviewed who attended the
Scammon and Dore Schools at the time. One woman claimed: "We Greeks
were good students . . . the teacher never had to scold us. It was the
other nationalities that had to be scolded, as we always had our work done."[3]

---

[1] Interview with George Damolaris, Chicago, 15 August 1968.

[2] Interview with Pericles Orphanos, River Forest, Ill., 7 September
1968.

[3] Interview with Mrs. Alexandra Poulos, Chicago, 19 September 1969.

Another, an elderly gentleman, stated: "The Greek boys and girls at the Dore School were always praised by the teacher. We worked hard even if it meant going without sleep to get our homework done."[1]

TABLE 28

PERCENTAGE OF ATTENDANCE AND PROMOTION
IN CHICAGO PUBLIC SCHOOLS ATTENDED BY
LARGE NUMBERS OF GREEK CHILDREN
1909-11

School	Location	1909-10 Attendance	1909-10 Promotion	1910-11 Attendance	1910-11 Promotion
Dante	DesPlaines & Ewing	94.3	82.1	95.3	78.5
Dore	Harrison & Halsted	93.1	70.6	91.9	86.8
Jirka	17th & Loomis	97.6	95.1	95.1	90.6
Jones	Plymouth & Harrison	91.7	67.6	91.5	56.3
Marquette	Wood & Harrison	. . .	. . .	91.3	80.0
Pullman	113th & Morse	93.8	89.1	. . .	. . .
Scammon	Morgan & Monroe	92.6	59.2	92.2	66.5
Walsh	20th & Peoria	93.9	89.1	93.5	93.5
	City Average	94.0	86.1	95.8	85.7

SOURCE: Compiled from the Fifty-Sixth and Fifty-Seventh Annual Reports, Chicago Board of Education, pp. 143, 163.

Still another commented: "The teacher always called upon the Greek students to recite their lessons first, because we were always ready. Our parents saw to that."[2] The likely truth is that the Greek children were in the same predicament as their immigrant peers and collectively accounted for the low promotion rates at these schools.

A closer look at the attendance figures of two schools which had large Greek and foreign enrollments also shows the prevailing pattern of

[1] Interview with Constantine Papoulias, Chicago, 10 September 1969.

[2] Interview with John T. Pappas, Chicago, 21 August 1968.

Greek immigrants refusing to send their daughters to school. Of 426 foreign students enrolled at the Scammon School, 410 were boys and only 16 were girls; similarly, at Washington School, 808 were males and 43 were females.[1] Several reasons undoubtedly account for the small number of females attending public schools. An obvious one was the smaller number of Greek girls emigrating to the United States. As shown in a previous part of this study, Greek immigration was primarily a male phenomenon--the highest ratio of all ethnic groups coming to America. Very few Greek women had arrived to the United States by 1915. Another reason, related to the first one, was the paucity of Greek families, since most Greek male immigrants were unmarried.

Among the few Greek girls living in Chicago around 1910, still fewer were permitted to attend school. The Old World belief of Greeks was that schooling would be a waste for girls since they would marry, often at a young age. The following interview is an example of this belief:

> My sister and I were brought over by my father to be married, because there were so many Greek men in this country and, since brides were in demand, no dowry would be expected from our father. But when I arrived in America, I wanted to go to school to learn . . . I wanted so much to learn about America and to speak English. But my father would not hear of it. What good would it do to know English when I would be returning to Greece with my "American" Greek husband. So I was promptly married off, but I did not return to Greece, and if it was not for the fact that I took it upon myself to attend Americanization classes after I married, I would not be able to speak and write the little English I know.[2]

Those Greek young women that were permitted to attend school oftentimes absented themselves when illness struck at home or their labor was needed there; hence, for the most part, their school attendance was irregular. One respondent, in speaking of her poor school attendance, stated:

> My mother encouraged me to go to school, but it was against my father's wishes. But I did get to attend Scammon School. I remember the very kind teacher there who was always encouraging us to attend school. But I didn't stay long. I was always needed at home to help out with the cooking and washing and then I got sick after a few months and had to stay home.[3]

---

[1] Fifty-fourth Annual Report of the Board of Education for the Year Ending June 30, 1908 (Chicago), p. 236.

[2] Interview with Mrs. Katherine Mehos, Chicago, 5 May 1968.

[3] Interview with Mrs. Catherine Orfanos, Chicago, 3 August 1969.

It is probable that it was not until the middle 1930s that a general policy of universal school attendance for girls from Greek homes began to prevail in the Greek community of Chicago. By that time, most Greek families had made the decision to stay in the United States. Since a girl was to be a permanent resident, it was important that she be schooled as other American girls. This decision was probably influenced by the broader American milieu in which the Greek family lived and the school truant laws which insisted that all boys and girls of school age be in school.

In the Dore, Scammon and Jones Schools, Greek children sometimes comprised the largest ethnic group. As early as 1904, according to an early Chicago Greek newspaper, such was the case at Jones and Scammon Schools, the latter having 243 Greeks enrolled out of 723 students.[1] Greek pupils also formed a significant part of the enrollment of the Jirka, Marquette, Pullman and Walsh Schools, as listed in table 28. In addition, a number of Greek students were to be found at Washington School (Grand and Morgan), Polk Street School (Polk near Union), Vedder Street School (Vedder and Halsted Skinner School (Jackson at Aberdeen), King School (Harrison near Western), and Haven School (16th and Wabash). While no figures are available, this suggests that there was a sizeable enrollment of Greek students in the Chicago public schools during this period.

Yet, the Immigration Commission's survey made in 1908 found only 193 Greek pupils enrolled in the public schools. Contrasting this small number with the 4,218 Greek immigrants of all ages recorded in the 1908 Chicago school census (the same year that the commission made its investigation) would suggest a large adult composition of the Greek populace. However, the 1908 school census lists 697 persons as being American-born. It is probably safe to assume that most of these were minors, the vast majority perhaps under fourteen. Presupposing, however, that only half were of legal school age, this would leave 349 children unaccounted for. During the same year, the Greek community opened its first communal school with an initial enrollment of approximately 30 students. This would still leave 319 Greek children not attending any type of formal school. If this is true, it is an indication of the lax enforcement of the state's compulsory education law,

---

[1] Greek Star (Chicago), 18 March 1904.

which meant that most of these children, at least the older ones, were not in school.

Under the law, pupils who were fourteen and had completed the fifth grade or its equivalent could apply for a school certificate which would permit them to be gainfully employed. At sixteen they could leave school regardless of grade level. Very few Greek children, however, made formal application for a school certificate to enter employment as shown in table 29. Indeed, if our assumptions are correct, this would mean that out of 319 Greek children of school age not in school during the 1908-9 academic term, only eleven boys had applied and received a work certificate. Either the law was not enforced rigidly, or the Greeks were ignorant of, or indifferent to the law.

TABLE 29

GREEK CHILDREN RECEIVING AGE AND SCHOOL
CERTIFICATES IN CHICAGO UNDER
CHILD LABOR LAW, 1903-9

Year	Males	Females	Total
1903-4	6	2	8
1904-5	2	0	2
1905-6	3	0	3
1906-7	3	1	4
1908-9	11	0	11

SOURCE: Compiled from Chicago Board of Education, Fifty-second Annual Report, p. 89, Fifty-third Annual Report, p. 115, Fifty-fifth Annual Report, p. 82.

The Child Labor Law enacted in 1903 forbade the employment of children under fourteen; those between fourteen and sixteen had to procure an age and school certificate approved by the superintendent before they could be employed.[1] The passage of this law resulted in an increased enrollment in schools. Despite this law, many underage Greeks were gainfully

---

[1] Fifty-first Annual Report of the Board of Education Year Ending June 30, 1905 (Chicago), p. 176.

employed, demonstrating the lack of the law's enforcement.

As stated earlier, most Greeks emigrated to America to make money in order to pay off family debts, provide dowries for sisters, and return to Greece with a sufficient amount of money to live comfortably. Consequently, working rather than schooling was the top priority of young boys. The reports of the Immigrants' Protective League describe many accounts of young men engaged in diverse occupations and often exploited.[1] Another factor for nonattendance in Chicago schools was the fact that these boys were alone, without kinship guidance, as Abbott's study indicated.[2] Still, there were a few young men who exerted great effort and sacrifice in order to attend school.[3]

Following World War I, the profile of Greek children attending public schools began to change. As more Greek immigrants arrived and moved into all sections of Chicago, Greek children began to be regularly enrolled in the city's public schools. There were a number of reasons: (1) the fact that Greek communal schools were not conveniently located in all the neighborhoods into which Greek immigrants settled, (2) tuition fees for Greek schools made attendance for some persons prohibitive, (3) the erosion of

---

[1] Many Greek boys were employed in shoeshine parlors. They were hired by "padrones," and to avoid the arm of the truant officer they did not confess less than 17 years of age. For an explanation of the padrone system and the exploitation of young Greek lads see Edward A. Ross, The Old World in the New: The Significance of Past and Present Immigration to the American People (New York: Century Co., 1914), pp. 187-90; and Jones, pp. 191-92. An old-time community leader, Nikitas Nomikos, tells of the hundreds of Greek boys engaged in the building of Chicago's loop elevated system during 1903; the late industrialist John L. Manta cites his personal experiences along with other lads in the building of the steel mills at Gary, Indiana in 1910. Interviews with Nikitas Nomikos, Chicago, 8 July 1967 and John L. Manta, Chicago, 2 October 1967. Also see G. Abbott, Immigrant and Community, p. 39; Immigrants Protective League, Seventh Annual Report for Year Ending January 1, 1916, p. 5. In 1907, 81 percent of the children working were of foreign parentage; a similar ratio was true for girls between 14 and 16. See Chaney, p. 33.

[2] Supra, p. 104.

[3] One example was a Greek lad attending Dore School who swept the classrooms after school in order to support himself. Later while attending McKinley High School he found an evening job with Western Union Telegraph delivering telegrams. Interview with Dimitri Parry, Chicago, 1 July 1971.

Hellenic sentiment along with the acculturative process induced many Greek parents to send their children to public schools, and (4) the increased enforcement of the state's compulsory education law.

By the 1930s, it can be assumed that the majority of Greek children in Chicago were attending public schools. There are, of course, no figures available from the Board of Education pertaining to the ethnic composition of the schools' enrollment, as by the 1930s, interest in ethnicity had diminished considerably. But on the basis of the number of Greeks in Chicago and the number of Greek children actually enrolled in the Greek communal day schools, which perhaps never amounted to more than one thousand pupils for any given year, there is evidence that such was the fact.[1] No inference should be made that Greek children attending the city's public schools had no formal Greek education. As will be seen in the following chapters, the vast majority of Greek children attending public schools also attended afternoon Greek schools or received Greek instruction at home by tutors, not to mention participation in other religio-cultural programs provided by Greek institutions and agencies in Chicago.

Evidence of the educational mobility (or increased schooling of the native-born second generation following World War I is confirmed in a random study made of members in two Chicago Greek parishes and of a Greek professional society during 1965. Interviewing forty-six couples of the first (immigrant) generation and forty-three couples of the second (native-born) generation representing various socioeconomic levels, the researcher was able to show that while formal education beyond the primary level (either Greek or American) was minimum or nonexistent among the first generation surveyed, second generation members increasingly pursued "social class mobility through the educational facilities of higher learning."[2] Educational achievement of generations was ascertained on the basis of formal schooling both in Greek and American educational institutions. Table 30 gives the

---

[1] See figures for Greek school enrollments in chapter 5.

[2] See George A. Kourvetaris, "First and Second Generation Greeks in Chicago: An Inquiry into their Stratification and Mobility Patterns," *International Review of Sociology* 1 (March 1971): 37-47.

percentage of Greek and American schooling of both generations.

TABLE 30

GREEK AND AMERICAN SCHOOLING* OF FIRST AND SECOND
GENERATION GREEK COUPLES IN PERCENTAGES

Type of Schooling	First Generation Couples (N=46)				Second Generation Couples (N=43)			
	Husband		Wife		Husband		Wife	
	Gr. Am. Percentages		Gr. Am.		Gr. Am. Percentages		Gr. Am.	
Some grammar school education .	60	54	76	36	50	2	77	..
Grammar school graduate	21	6	8	..	11	..	..	..
Some high school and high school graduate	..	..	..	..	..	30	..	46
College graduate	..	8	..	..	..	60	..	49
Not ascertained	19	32	16	64	39	8	23	5
Total	100	100	100	100	100	100	100	100

SOURCE: Kourvetaris, p. 42.

* Schooling in both Greek and American educational institutions was cal-
culated in percentages for each spouse separately in both generations.

Looking at table 30 one notes that by and large, first generation couples had
some grammar school education only. By contrast, over 50 percent of the
second generation husbands and almost 50 percent of their wives were college
graduates.

In short, school records and documents, along with available testimony, indicate that Greek children were actively attending the public schools
of Chicago. There is no precise information as to their actual number, since
the public schools did not list pupils according to ethnicity. A comparison
of the Chicago school census of 1908 with the survey of the Immigration Commission made in the same year indicates that less than half of the Greek
children of school age were attending public schools. Only about thirty children were known to be enrolled in the first communal Greek day school that
opened in Chicago during the same year. Accordingly, the majority of Greek

children either were not attending school at all or were gainfully employed.

Greek children who were enrolled in the public schools were generally placed in "retarded" classes, as was the custom of the time with children with insufficient knowledge of English. Most were in the primary grades with heavy attrition after the fifth grade. Very few completed elementary school, and few, indeed, went on to high school. By the 1930s, because of a number of factors, most Greek children were attending public schools. Because by that time children beginning primary grades had a knowledge of English acquired from older siblings or from the broader community, few were placed in "retarded" grades, most finished elementary school and a large number entered high schools, many graduating.

As indicated in this study, the Greek immigrant had a profound loyalty to his homeland and to Hellenic ideals. He was conditioned by his upbringing and the history of his nation to regard Greek culture as inferior to none. Much to his surprise and chagrin he found that in coming to the United States many Americans did not share this view. His consternation increased, when upon entering the public school or enrolling his children therein, he perceived that, in the one place in which he expected Greek culture to be upheld--the schools--the opposite was true. Not only the Greek legacy, but other non-American cultures, with the exception of Anglo-Saxon culture, were not openly appreciated or readily tolerated. The schools appeared to be "destroyers" of culture--they attempted to do away with the indigenous culture of the immigrants and replace it with an "instant" American way of life--an impossible task.[1]

As shown elsewhere in this chapter, the anti-foreign expression of public schools with emphasis on immediate Americanization and the renunciation of Old World loyalties, caused psychological pain among immigrants.

------

[1] The concept, that public schools have been "destroyers" of immigrant cultures is a theme that has been consistently used by Prof. Rudolph Vecoli, Director of the Center for Immigration Studies at the University of Minnesota, in his public remarks on the topic. Cf. his "Education as Detriment," paper presented at the Cross Cultural Educational Conference sponsored by the Archdiocese of Chicago (Roman Catholic) School Board, Westchester, Ill., 12 February 1972; and "Equality of Educational Opportunity: Ethnic Perspectives," paper presented at the University of Illinois at Chicago Circle, 19 May 1972. For an analysis of how public schools of the period under discussion were "destroyers" of immigrant cultures see Fred M. Newman and Donald W. Oliver, "Education and Community," Harvard Educational Review 37 (Winter 1967): 61-105, especially pp. 79-81.

They could not understand why learning the English language and American ways required the abandonment of loyalty to their homeland and ancestral traditions. For Greek immigrants such action was unthinkable. It was tantamount to a betrayal of their ethnic and religious identity, a thing which their own weight of history would not permit.

Testimonies by elderly Greek immigrants who experienced the antiforeign stance of public schools portray their dilemma in confronting this problem. It was an oft-repeated theme among those interviewed for this study. Immigrants in the public schools were perplexed by the schools' strenuous efforts to stamp out their Greek identity. They could not understand this undermining of Greek culture, a culture which they had expected Americans to appreciate and revere as the basis of Western Civilization, as they had been taught. This conduct on the part of the public school system along with the formal and authoritarian nature of the schools which compelled them to conform and adjust to a complex social system which denigrated Hellenic ideals and achievements caused many Greek pupils to become demoralized and contributed, in some cases, to trauma, resulting in those experiencing the latter, to eventually leave the Greek community or to remain only as marginal members.

But the effects of public school attendance were not limited to the children of immigrants. The culture learned at school concerning Americanization was brought home at night.

Foreign-born parents discovered a "Trojan horse" within the home manned by their children who taught them, through the generational conflict characteristic of American society, American ways of conduct which assisted their adjustment to new parental roles to complement those that the younger generation were learning in the schools and in the broader American society.

It was for this reason that Greek immigrant parents persisted in the transmission of the Hellenic heritage to their offspring to counteract the alienating influence of the public school in the area of ethnic identity. It was for these reasons that the various informal and formal educational agencies were established in the Greek community, agencies that contributed to the strong structural cohesiveness of Greek communal life. But perhaps the most pervasive influence on the children of Greek immigrants was the strong commitment their parents had for the transmission of the cultural heritage to

heir American-born children. Typical of this intense commitment is the fol-
owing excerpt:

> When I was very young my father used to read Homer to me. While
> other kids were getting Mother Goose, I was getting Thucydides. The
> Peloponnesian Wars became exceptionally meaningful to me, and I re-
> member how I dreamt of being a Spartan. (Father was from Sparta and
> came to Chicago in 1893.) I also remember many sleepless nights when
> I felt a restless spirit and wondered if strange and mythological gods,
> somehow controlled my destiny. . . . I felt different because I was
> proud that my forefathers were warriors who helped shape the history of
> mankind.[1]

Also indicative of the pervasive impact of the home on ethnic maintenance
on the minds of Greek children growing up in Chicago is the following testimony:

> Father was always telling us about the greatness of Greece and her
> contribution to world culture and civilization. He ran our home like a
> school conducting quizzes at the dinner table asking us questions from
> our Greek lessons on the great men and events of Greek history. We
> enjoyed these sessions as he rewarded us with money. . . . But we
> were dismayed and hurt by the attitude of our teachers in the public
> school who kept telling us that we should forget about Greece and be-
> come good Americans. . . . We wanted to be good Americans but we
> were also very proud to be Greeks. I, for one, looked forward to the
> Greek school which we attended after American school. Here, the
> teacher was always telling us about the glory of Greece and I enjoyed
> my Greek textbook. I marvelled that I was reading about the great men
> of Greece in the Greek language and I dreamed of the day when I would
> go to Greece to visit the land of Plato, Pericles and Alexander the Great.
> When I finally died many years later, I felt that I had come home. . . .
> Hellenic culture has been a lifelong obsession with me and for this I am
> indebted to my father and the Greek school.[2]

In this respect, the role of the public school was significant, in part,
to the external adjustment of Greek immigrants to the dominant American
milieu and in bringing them into the mainstream of American life. However,
there is no evidence that those who attended public schools were brought
into mainstream culture more quickly than those who attended Greek communal
day schools. And while public schools did provide for avenues of acculturation, they were not, in the main, successful in obliterating Greek culture
among pupils of Greek ancestry because of the high priority placed by Greek
immigrants in transmitting the cultural heritage to their children and the

---

[1] C. Orphan, p. 23.

[2] Interview with Theophilus A. Pappas, Chicago, 28 October 1970.

strong structural cohesiveness of the Chicago Greek community with its supportive informal and formal educational agencies.

Evening School

Most Greek immigrants were self-employed and their need for mastery of the English language was not initially imperative. But as they moved up the occupational ladder from push-cart and peddling to grocery stores and restaurants and into other employment, the need for greater proficiency in the world of work induced them to attend evening schools. Learning to speak and write better English would improve business and offer additional opportunities for advancement. They attended evening schools for an average of six to ten months and quit when they felt they had learned enough English to "get by."[1] Very few pursued couses in high school.

For the City of Chicago, general illiteracy was an acute problem. The great body of immigrants between 16 and 25 were past the age of compulsory school attendance in Illinois. Moreover, many Greeks and Italians had emigrated from provinces where the peasants had no direct contact with their country's broad culture; others, like the Poles, Bohemians, Slovaks, and Jews had been subjugated people--often victims of social and political discrimination. From 1899 to 1909, 35 percent of southern and eastern Europeans were illiterate compared to only 2.7 percent among immigrants from northern and western Europe.[2] By 1915, over a million foreign-born in Chicago could not speak English and an estimated 80,000 could not read or write any language.[3]

One of the pioneers in adult education was the Chicago Board of Education. Evening schools were opened to provide elementary English and citizenship training for foreign-born persons and provide literacy programs for native-born adults. Such classes began 8 January 1863, at the Dearborn

---

[1] Nearly all persons interviewed at one time or another attended evening classes in Chicago for this reason. Yet, a United States governmental survey had indicated that only 33.5 percent of Greek employees could speak English. Only the Bulgarians and "Macedonians" had a lower rate. Ross, p. 477.

[2] Chaney, p. 3.

[3] Bertha Lititia Merrill, "Methods of Assimilating Immigrants" (Master's thesis, University of Chicago, 1916), p. 31.

School.[1] At that time, Chicago's total population of 150,000 was served by 17 day schools. The initial class at the Dearborn School enrolled 483 with an average attendance of 280 pupils. This program, interrupted by the Great Fire of 1871, reopened in the fall of 1873. It gained momentum with the influx of "new" immigrants. In 1880, enrollment was 3,344; by 1914 it had increased to 44,846. With the impact of World War I it dropped to 28,500 in 1920.[2]

In the spring of 1915, the superintendent of schools, the Immigrants' Protective League, and the School of Civics and Philanthropy conducted an investigation of English evening classes. The survey revealed that of those 75,580 persons over age 14 who were listed by the 1910 Census as not being able to read and write in any language, only 13,613 (13 percent) of the total non-English speaking group were enrolled in elementary evening schools.[3] Furthermore, practically none of the illiterates were enrolled, possibly because the schools had not exerted special effort to help them.[4] Hence, the city's adult elementary evening program was not reaching these groups.

The high school evening programs were not much different. They were formed in 1869, and existed intermittently until 1910, when Superintendent Young took a radical step toward abolishing the distinction between evening high and elementary school programs. Unification of these two levels of schooling was short-lived. In 1912, they returned as separate entities and were scattered among elementary schools.[5]

---

[1] For an extensive description of the adult education program see William Patterson Wilson, "The History and Development of the Public Adult Education Program in Chicago" (Ph.D. dissertation, University of California, Los Angeles, June 1948).

[2] Ibid., p. 60.

[3] Seventh Annual Report 1916 (Immigrants' Protective League), p. 16.

[4] Ibid.

[5] In 1919 the first evening high school was located at Englewood followed by Schurz in 1924, Crane in 1929; Lakeview, Austin, and Fenger in 1931. For a history of the Chicago evening high school see John Wesley Bell, "The Development of the Public High School in Chicago" (Ph.D. dissertation, University of Chicago, 1939), pp. 52-67.

The classes of the evening high schools were comprised mainly of native Americans seeking to complete their studies and obtain a diploma. The foreign-born, especially the Greeks, were very few in number. Basic reasons cited for nonattendance by non-English speaking or illiterate persons in evening programs were: (1) overtime employment, (2) change from day to night work, (3) fatigue after a day's work, (4) dissatisfaction with school or teacher, (5) teacher unable to communicate in their tongue, (6) discouraged over personal progress, and (7) family or personal illness.[1]

The Immigrants' Protective League urged the Chicago Board of Education to find new ways to meet immigrants' concerns, like holding classes during slack time or near places of employment.[2] The league attempted to hold evening sessions in parts of the city where fewer than one hundred pupil requirement stipulated by the board was possible.[3]

No Greek pupils were mentioned in the 1901 Annual Report of the Board of Education, which listed the birthplace of pupils attending public evening classes.[4] The first listing of Greek immigrants participating in these schools is shown in the 1903 Report, with 356 Greeks cited. Of the 41 nationalities listed, the Greeks ranked ninth--totalling 586 pupils.[5] It suggests that the Greeks, mostly all men, attempted to capitalize on the opportunity to gain some knowledge of English.

From 10 October 1910 to 9 March 1911 there were 10,557 men and 2,158 women--all foreign-born--in night schools. Those nationalities with the largest representatives in the evening elementary schools are shown on table 31. The Greeks ranked eighth out of the large city ethnic population, again showing their concern for some education.

---

[1] Eighth Annual Report, 1917 (Immigrants' Protective League), pp. 10-11.

[2] Seventh Annual Report, 1916 (Immigrants' Protective League), p. 18.

[3] Fourth Annual Report, 1913 (Immigrants' Protective League), p. 22.

[4] Forty-seventh Annual Report Year Ending June 30, 1901 (Chicago Board of Education), p. 140.

[5] Fiftieth Annual Report Year Ending June 30, 1904 (Chicago Board of Education), pp. 103-4.

TABLE 31

NATIONALITIES IN CHICAGO PUBLIC
EVENING ELEMENTARY SCHOOLS
1910-11

NATIONALITY	PUPILS
Russian	2,265
Polish	1,845
German	1,736
Italian	1,675
Swedish	1,314
Bohemian	1,236
Lithuanian	640
Greek	583 *
Hungarian	416

SOURCE: Chaney, pp. 39-40.

* Chaney's figure of 583 for
Greeks does not coincide with the number of Greeks enrolled in 1910 based on
the Annual Reports (Chicago Board of
Education), which show 623 (see table
32). At this time many Greek immigrants attended Americanization classes at Hull House.

Table 32 reveals that during the period for which figures are available, 1902 to 1922, the enrollment of Greek immigrants in adult evening classes reached its peak in the 1907-8 term, when it constituted 4 percent of the
total enrollment. Another high point took place in 1913-14, but it constitutes
only 1.6 percent of the total membership. On the whole, a review of these
years indicates that Greek enrollment in evening schools averaged seventh
largest among ethnic groups. These figures reveal that at no time during this
period did Greek immigrants make up a significant portion of the evening
school enrollment. Nonetheless, when the peak year figure of 817 is compared with the 4,218 Greeks listed in the 1908 Chicago school census, it can
be seen that nearly 20 percent of all Greek immigrants officially residing in

Chicago were attending evening school. This was a high attendance record, one out of five, one of the highest ratios in the city, especially in light of the fact that Greeks who emigrated here had intentions of returning to Greece. By attending these classes they were adjusting to the demands of the American social order as well as enhancing their economic competency.

TABLE 32

ENROLLMENT OF GREEKS IN ADULT EDUCATION CLASSES
CHICAGO PUBLIC SCHOOLS
1902-22

Year	Elementary	High School	Total	% of Total Enrollment
1902-03 . . .	. .	. .	356	2.6
1903-04. . .	. .	. .	586	3.5
1905-06. . .	382	20	402	2.4
1906-07. . .	522	1	523	2.9
1907-08. . .	802	15	817	4.0
1908-09. . .	727	35+	762	3.5
1909-10. . .	541	12	553	. .
1910-11. . .	591	32	623	. .
1912-13. . .	424	12	436	1.5
1913-14. . .	620	24	644	1.6
1921-22. . .	. .	. .	527	2.7

SOURCE: Compiled from data found in Annual Reports (Chicago Board of Education).

+ This figure also includes elementary pupils at Phillips High.

Very few Greek women were enrolled in the evening schools. The 1913-14 Board of Education report indicated 22 women among the 597 Greek immigrants in attendance in the elementary evening program. Of the 24 Greeks enrolled in evening high school, none were women. [1] In contrast, one out of four persons enrolled in evening programs were women. The composition of

---

[1] Sixtieth Annual Report Year Ending June 30, 1914 (Chicago Board of Education), p. 449.

ethnic groups varied, with very few Italian and Greek women, no Spanish, and very few Bulgarian, Turkish, Armenian, or Croatian women. Except for the Italians, the other ethnic groups had few women in the city. By contrast, one-third of all Norwegians and Russian Jews enrolled were women; likewise, three out of every ten Germans enrolled were women.[1]

The Greeks were distributed in practically all of the public schools offering evening classes, as shown on table 33. Understandably, heaviest enrollment was found in the schools close to Greektown--Scammon, Dante,

TABLE 33

DISTRIBUTION OF GREEKS BY SCHOOL IN
ADULT CHICAGO EVENING PROGRAM
1907-8

Burley	1	McAllister	1
Chase	2	Medill Elementary	13
Crane Elementary	31	Phillips Elementary	56
Dante	93	Pullman	52
Englewood	27	Scammon	136
Foster	63	South Chicago Elem.	5
Franklin	22	Tuley Elementary	2
Froebel	2	Waller Elementary	13
Garfield	21	Waller High	1
Hamline	9	Walsh	33
Hammond	1	Washington Elem.	126
Harrison	6	Washington High	1
Jones	69	Wells	9
Lake Grammar	20	Total	815

SOURCE: Compiled from Fifty-fourth Annual Report Year Ending June 30, 1908 (Chicago Board of Education), pp. 243-64.

and Washington Schools--as well as close to employment--Jones and Foster Schools. Greeks were the largest ethnic group at the Scammon School,

[1] Ibid.

second to the Italians at the Jones School, and third largest at the Dante School, where they were outnumbered by the Italian and native American groups.[1] In all three of these schools they comprised a significant part of the enrollment. Growth southward is indicated by attendance at Phillips and Pullman. In 1909, a new Greek community had emerged in Woodlawn, and another community formed later in 1917 in the far south Pullman vicinity. All but four enrollees shown on table 33 were foreign born. The age distribution showed a heavier concentration during the early and mid-twenties as reflected on table 34.

Total enrollment in the five schools shown in table 34 was 3,496, of which 455 were Greek students. This latter figure constituted nearly 56 percent of all Greeks attending evening schools during the 1907-8 school term and was indicative of the importance of residential or employment propinquity. As alluded to previously, for many young Greeks working as waiters, bus boys, and shoeshine boys in the Loop, the downtown location of the adult evening program at Jones School was especially convenient. The other evening school programs at the Dore, Dante, Washington and Crane Schools were very close to their homes in the expanding Greek Delta or to the wholesale market where many of them worked. Hence, these factors help to explain the large number of Greek immigrants in attendance at these school.

Thus, it can be ascertained that with reference to the evening school program sponsored by the City of Chicago, Greek immigrants participated to a considerable extent. Despite their avowed intention to return to their homeland after acquiring material possessions, they took advantage of the opportunity offered by the city to learn the English language. Despite the fact that English was not a prerequisite for Greek immigrants in entering the lower echelons of labor, it did become an important attribute as they progressed up the occupational ladder from push-carts to grocery stores and restaurants, and to employment in American establishments. The knowledge of English then became an important acquisition for economic competency and business opportunities. Such was the consensus of a group of elderly gentlemen who recalled their early immigrant experiences.[2]

---

[1] Fifty-fourth Annual Report Year Ending June 30, 1908 (Chicago Board of Education), pp. 243-64.

[2] Interviews with members of Trikorfa Chapter of the Pan Arcadian Federation of America at a formal meeting in Oak Park, Ill., 5 June 1970.

TABLE 34

AGE OF PUPILS (ACCORDING TO SEX) AT ELEMENTARY EVENING SCHOOLS WHERE LARGE NUMBERS
OF GREEK IMMIGRANTS WERE ENROLLED (1907-8)

School	Greeks	12 – 15yrs.			15 – 18yrs.			18 – 21yrs.			21 – 25yrs.			25 – 30yrs.			Over 30		
		M	F	T	M	F	T	M	F	T	M	F	T	M	F	T	M	F	T
Scammon	136	10	6	16	91	8	99	128	7	135	102	5	107	96	8	104	63	4	67
Dante	93	62	2	64	140	3	143	193	1	194	153	1	154	136	0	136	69	0	69
Jones	69	15	5	20	70	16	86	140	22	162	157	10	167	76	2	78	85	7	92
Washington	126	31	27	58	186	60	246	243	25	268	232	29	261	142	6	148	92	2	94
Crane	31	30	9	39	108	37	145	89	22	111	86	26	112	64	19	83	27	11	38
Total	455	148	49	197	595	124	719	793	77	870	730	71	801	514	35	549	336	24	360

SOURCE: Compiled from Fifty-fourth Annual Report for Year Ending June 30, 1908 (Chicago Board of Education), pp. 240-41.

For the twenty year period from 1902 to 1922 Greek immigrants were
the seventh largest ethnic group participating in the evening program, despite their small total numbers in comparison with other large ethnic groups
in Chicago. In schools which were located close to their places of residence or employment, they constituted a significant majority of students enrolled. In 1907-08, the peak year of their enrollment during the twenty year
period, one out of every five Greeks living in Chicago was attending evening
school, one of the highest ratios of all ethnic groups residing in the city.
Most of those attending these schools were in their early to mid-twenties.
It is quite probable that the many Greek men (very few Greek women attended
evening schools) who took advantage of this opportunity acquired there the
basic knowledge of English which was to serve them well in business in succeeding years. This basic acquisition and their long years in the marketplace
of Chicago accounted for the fact that most Greek immigrant men achieved a
fair command of the English language, which contributed to their success as
entrepreneurs. This was not true of their wives, whose lack of attendance
at these schools and isolation in the home left them with an English language
handicap throughout adulthood.

The Adult Day School

For the adult immigrant no day educational facilities existed up to
1907. Any adult over sixteen who desired to enter the city's public schools
had to obtain permission from the superintendent of schools with the approval
of the Chicago Board of Education. These adult students, for the most part,
were placed in ungraded rooms in elementary and secondary schools that had
low membership.[1] This unsatisfactory procedure forced Superintendent
Edwin C. Cooley to segregate adults in ungraded rooms at Jones School. Because of increased requests, the board finally gave authorization to this plan

---

[1] Merrill, p. 31. With reference to Greek immigrants, 80.5 percent
were able to read their native tongue; as quoted in Ross, p. 314. However,
the average illiteracy rate for Greek immigrants over the entire immigration
period was approximately 25 percent.

[2] Proceedings of the Board of Education, July 3, 1907 to June 17, 1908
(Chicago), p. 341. See also Wilson.

Eventually, the program expanded and occupied the entire fourth floor of the Jones School. An adult education department was formed under direct supervision of William M. Roberts, assistant superintendent in charge of evening schools. Additional ungraded classes opened at the Dore School in Greektown. In 1918 the adult education department was transferred to the Haven School and in 1929 to the Dante School.[1]

All the Americanization programs utilized the regular elementary curriculum. A diploma was granted upon course completion, but time required to finish work varied depending on the learner's efforts and previous formal schooling. Vocational courses eventually were added to the curriculum. For many young Greek men working downtown as busboys, waiters, and shoeshiners the Jones School location was ideal. They found it conducive to attending classes between working hours or prior to beginning their jobs. The Greek ethnic contingent at Jones was among the largest groups enrolled. At the Dore School there were 191 Greeks in the adult program out of nearly 500 students.[2] The large enrollment at Dore was likely due to its location, convenient to the Greek Delta and to the wholesale market on Fulton and Randolph Streets where numerous Greeks were employed.

According to Greek men who attended the Jones School during these years, the "ungraded" program under the sympathetic tutelage of the first assigned teacher, Mrs. Pease, was most effective. One informant stated that "Mrs. Pease liked the Greek boys, because she appreciated our glorious Hellenic background."[3] Another informant remembers Mrs. Pease as "a dedicated teacher who was anxious to help the Greek boys learn English and would spend extra time with them on their lessons."[4] In her 1909 study of the Greeks in Chicago, Grace Abbott writes:

> The testimony of those experienced in teaching immigrants is always favorable to the Greeks. The teacher of the "adult room" of the Jones School,

---

[1] For the historical development of the adult educational program in Chicago see Veronica Phee, "A Study of the Dante Elementary School for Adults" (Master's thesis, DePaul University, 1946).

[2] Greek Star (Chicago), 10 April 1909. This early Greek newspaper exhorted continually its immigrant readers to take advantage of the public school facilities to learn English and the American ways.

[3] Interview with George Pulos, Chicago, 2 April 1968.

[4] Interview with Peter Chamalas, Chicago, 2 April 1968.

which is just outside of the loop in the downtown district, has had 81
Greeks enrolled during the past year out of a total of 252. She says of
all the different nationalities represented in the room, "I think I have
found the Greeks the brightest and quickest to learn." At Hull House
they have been eager and intelligent members of the regular classes and
the men have shown ability in the organization and management of large
clubs and classes for themselves.[1]

From 1929, when the adult day program was transferred to the Dante
School, to the end of World War II, the largest numbers of students enrolled
in the program were from China, Mexico, and Greece; followed by Italy,
Poland, Russia, and Germany.[2] Those immigrants who arrived after the 1924
restrictionist laws had to be blood-relatives of those already in the country.
Hence, few were permitted entrance to America. This fact, for the Greeks,
is reflected in the Dante School enrollment for the years 1929-46 as shown
on table 35.

TABLE 35

ENROLLMENT AT DANTE SCHOOL OF PUPILS
BORN IN GREECE, 1929-46

YEARS	PUPILS	YEARS	PUPILS
1929-30 . .	9	1937-38 . .	12
1930-31 . .	15	1938-39 . .	18
1931-32 . .	13	1939-40 . .	17
1932-33 . .	5	1940-41 . .	8
1933-34 . .	24	1941-42 . .	7
1934-35 . .	22	1942-43 . .	8
1935-36 . .	13	1943-44 . .	1
1936-37 . .	7	1944-45 . .	1
		1945-46 . .	1

SOURCE: Compiled from Phee, pp. 35-51.

A survey conducted in 1946 at the Dante School as to the reasons

---

[1]G. Abbott, "Study of the Greeks," p. 387.

[2]Phee, p. 54.

why adults were attending this school, revealed the following typical responses of the Greek students queried:

Melba Niarchos:

> When I came from Greece I thought that I must learn English. My friends said to me [sic] that the Dante School is the best to learn English.

Aristedis Theodoropoulos:

> I come to the Dante School because I want to learn and speak and write English.

Diana Kekos:

> Why I come to the Dante School? I come to school every day because I wish to learn the English language quickly, and I like to be smart in the English language because on it depends my future life in America.

Bessie Kekos:

> I come to the Dante School to learn English and after I want to go to the High School when I get my diploma.[1]

Classes in the Dante Day Elementary School for Adults were organized in five groups. These groups were arranged homogeneously as possible. Class 1 was the lowest group; Class 2, the next higher group, and on up to Class 5 which was the highest and graduating class. There was, of course, no rigid class grouping and no set promotion time. Like the nongraded programs of today, as soon as a student could do the group work in the next higher class, he was promoted. There was a minimum of group work, and all students worked at their own ability and speed. No one was kept back because of slower members in the group.[2]

For the illiterates and poorly-educated native-born and foreign-born students the curriculum was as follows: English, spelling, arithmetic, reading, and geography. The English class period was used to teach grammar, while oral and written English, a major objective, was stressed in each of the other subjects. The basic objectives for the group were citizenship training and literacy.[3]

---

[1] Ibid., pp. 61-62.

[2] Phee, p. 20.

[3] Ibid.

The Dante School provided extracurricular clubs to assist immigrant students in their adjustment to school and to their new country. One of these organizations was the Greek-American Civics Club formed 13 March 1939. The objectives of the club were cited as ". . . to teach its members to become good American citizens and to be an honor and credit to their newly adopted country, with respect for other nationalities."[1] That such objectives were adopted by the adult Greeks enrolled at Dante School might be indicative of the transition in attitudes that Greek immigrants were experiencing in the 1930s and 1940s. As will be seen in the statistics in the next section of this chapter, Greek immigrants were becoming less adverse to naturalization. The long years in America and the maturation of offspring born in the United States and growing up in the American acculturative milieu, made a return to the homeland more remote. Clearly, some adjustment would have to be found. The solution was hastened by the onset of the Great Depression of the 1930s and the outbreak of World War II, which made a return to the homeland more difficult. These forces made the Greeks opt for American citizenship, although an intense loyalty to the ancestral land continued. They hoped that this loyalty could be transmitted to the native-born generations through the informal and formal agencies of the family, home, church, voluntary associations, and the school.

Americanization Program

From 1891 to 1900 "new immigrants" from Southeastern Europe made up 52.8 percent (3,687,564) of all newcomers in America. Native Americans became more uncomfortable when this alien mass increased between 1901 to 1910 to 71.7 percent (8,795,386) of all incoming people. Furthermore, the 1910 census indicated that foreign-born persons unable to read or speak English comprised 22.8 percent (2,953,011) of the total white immigrant population already in the country.[2] Illiterates were 12.7 percent of this total.

Americans became further apprehensive when data indicated that not only was one immigrant in eight unable to read or speak English, but that few

---

[1] Ibid., pp. 74 and 77.

[2] F. Thompson, p. 9.

of these aliens, as adults, were found in any school.[1] According to many
writers, the new immigrants had political, social, cultural, and language
backgrounds which simply were incompatible with American standards. There
was some doubt whether they could adjust as well as those groups from northwestern Europe.[2] There were patriotic and educational organizations that
felt the newcomers might be led to eventual citizenship by good example and
by giving attention to their problems. In contrast, labor unions and nativist
clubs believed that the newcomers soon would become economic burdens and
political scapegoats. Therefore, they clamored for immigration restriction
policies, literacy tests, and financial restraints for entering aliens.[3]

The need for social action in assisting the immigrants was met, in
part, in the social settlement houses and by caseworkers. The city was for-
tunate in having the world's most famous center, the Hull House. Under the
guidance of Jane Addams and her staff, funds were solicited, buildings rented
and cleaned, teachers hired, and the first Americanization classes and social
activities begun.[4] The courses consisted of English, American history, and
government specifically designed for the foreign-born. Other programs included kindergarten, homemaking, industrial arts, woodshop, and vocational
guidance. Many in attendance were Greeks who resided in that locale.
These programs supplemented the stilted curriculum of the public schools
which had not adapted their content to a changing society. Jane Addams remarked once, "A settlement is a protest against a restricted view of education."[5] Hull House became a pioneer in educational reform, a leader in
attempting to relate education to the realities of urban life.

The first Americanization classes exclusively for Greek immigrants
were organized at Hull House in the following manner:

On the 1st of April the Greeks were invited to Hull House auditorium
where they were addressed by Dr. Solas, [sic] the Greek consul, and

---

[1] Ibid., p. 34.

[2] Hartman, pp. 20-21.

[3] Ibid.

[4] For the panoply of educational services offered at Hull House including Americanization classes see Addams, Twenty Years, pp. 294-310.

[5] Allen F. Davis and Mary Lynn McCree eds., Eighty Years at Hull-
House (Chicago: Quadrangle Books, 1969), p. 90.

other fellow countrymen, friends of the house. They advised them to learn English and to become familiar with American ways. The formation of classes was discussed and the men were invited to come to the house next morning. Later in the evening they sang patriotic songs and danced their dignified historic dances. The response next morning was large and, being vacation for the ordinary classes, the Greek school met at all hours. Some unusual educational methods were evolved, such as the use of the stereopticon and of modified dramatics. Some enthusiastic teachers went so far as to make large-sized primers, substituting railroads for rats and cats.

The school promises to go on indefinitely every morning and afternoon, three evenings a week for classes and two in the gymnasium for games and athletics.[1]

These young men between the ages of fourteen and forty worked on the railroad "gangs," and the substitution of "railroads" for "rats" and "cats" found in primers was understandable. These relevant Hull House classes attracted the young Greeks for a long time.[2] The center's proximity to the heart of the Greek community facilitated attendance. Although Greeks also attended other settlement house, only Hull House had a program geared for the Greeks.[3]

However, these exclusive Greek classes terminated during the 1920s, and the Greeks joined with other ethnics in learning English and Americanization. A later Hull House entry stated:

For many years there have been classes designed especially for teaching English to foreigners. Applicants are graded in groups: English I, II, III, IV. The more advanced of these classes include instruction in grammar and composition and discussion of current events, in addition to drill in spelling, reading and dictation.

Since 1920, the majority of classes have been of a somewhat elementary character--a distinct contrast to those of earlier days of the settlement, when advanced classes in poetry, history and composition were eagerly sought. This change is explained by conditions in the neighborhood, to which large numbers of new immigrants are constantly arriving.

Among the members of evening classes, the following nationalities are now represented: Greek, Italian, Mexican, Spanish, German, French,

---

[1] *Hull House Bulletin* 4 (1 January to 1 May 1901): 15.

[2] It appears that these Americanization classes were offered until the 1920s when they were abandoned due to a lack of attendance. There was a rapid turnover every three to five months. Interview with John Kolias and Constantine Tsatos, Chicago, 15 April 1968.

[3] Ibid.

Macedonian, Armenian, Bulgarian and Scandinavian. All classes meet
twice a week. At intervals of two-three months all English classes are
invited to a party.[1]

A Greek immigrant who arrived in Chicago in 1923 and attended evening Americanization classes at Hull House from 1925 to 1929 recalls that there
were always large numbers of Greeks in attendance.[2] In addition to learning
English and pursuing Americanization programs at Hull House, Greek immigrants also participated in similar programs at the YMCA. This was particularly true prior to World War I when the YMCA conducted an extensive
Americanization program for the immigrants, who made up a large part of
Chicago's labor force. After 1918, the YMCA de-emphasized its programs,
as the public schools offered evening classes where foreign-born students
could study the subjects necessary to qualify for citizenship.[3] It is not
known how many Greek immigrants availed themselves of this opportunity at
the YMCA. The nominal tuition fee probably discouraged some from participating in the program. It seems that mostly Greek professionals, who were
economically more secure than most Greek immigrants, attended the YMCA
programs, as attested to by Peter S. Lambros, the editor of Chicago's Greek
Press, who learned his English and the rudiments of citizenship there.[4]

Although citizenship classes were given as early as 1903 in the
Chicago public schools, historically, it was not until 1918 that a distinct
Americanization program was established.[5] Yet, Chicago was the largest
city in the Middle West and had one of the largest foreign populations in the
nation. Before a systematic program began in 1918, there existed combination
schools, later known as opportunity schools, which offered both elementary

---

[1]Hull House Year Book, 40th ed., 1927-29, p. 6. In all subsequent
editions where such classes are mentioned, the Greeks are listed first. This
indicates perhaps that they continued to constitute the largest ethnic contingent enrolled. It cannot be underestimated that residential propinquity was a
motivating factor for good attendance.

[2]Interview with Constantine Andronis, Chicago, 26 October 1967.

[3]Emmett Dedmon, Great Expectations:One Hundred Years of the YMCA
of Metropolitan Chicago (Chicago: Rand McNally and Co., 1957), p. 274.

[4]Greek Star (Chicago), 23 February 1940.

[5]Hartmann, p. 24.

and secondary level courses. The public school policy stated that when large groups expressed an interest and a teacher could be procured, such requests would be implemented.[1] By 1918, there were twelve opportunity schools, three evening high schools, and twenty elementary schools.

A drop in enrollment occurred when the evening schools merged with smaller schools. At that time, Frances K. Wetmore had taught English to foreign-born back-of-the-yards people via the University of Chicago Settlement House and was induced to have her work sponsored by the Chicago Board of Education. Her flexible program was designed to be convenient for pupils. Her work began in October 1918, with four classes meeting twice a week in one hour sessions. The program grew rapidly and Miss Wetmore became Supervisor of Americanization. By 1923, there were 7,278 enrolled, and classes were held in schools, churches, synagogues, park fieldhouses, clubhouses, branch libraries, trade union headquarters, industrial plants, office buildings, YMCAs and settlement centers.[2]

The majority of the Greeks did not take advantage of these expanded opportunities. More likely, during this period, the factory, railroad, and union rather than the formal school served as assimilating agents. In 1909, a Greek language newspaper told its readers to "become citizens and join labor unions."[3] Many Greeks received their early Americanization and English instruction in their places of employment. A number of Greeks received such instruction while employed by the huge Western Electric Company in the early 1900s.[4] According to one report, these factory classes "emerged as the most successful method of teaching English to immigrant wage earners,

---

[1] Fifty-seventh Annual Report, 1910-1911 (Chicago Board of Education), p. 114.

[2] For the evolvement of the Americanization program in Chicago see Mary Margaret Lovgren, "The Chicago Board of Education Classes in Americanization" (Master's thesis, Chicago Teachers College, 1942); also Katherine Rontos, "The Study of the Development of the Americanization Program of the Chicago Board of Education" (Master's thesis, DePaul University, 1957). See also E. Abbott, Select Documents, pp. 549-56.

[3] Greer, Cobweb Attitudes, p. 5.

[4] Interview with George Damolaris and Angelo Besbekos, Chicago, 15 August 1968.

as public school evening classes . . . failed to bring results expected of them.[1]

It does not appear from the literature that the organized Greek communities sponsored any Americanization courses prior to the 1930s. Apparently, those classes held at Hull House were deemed sufficient. Some attended the public school sessions. In the late 1930s, two Greek parishes --Saint Andrew on the North Side and Saints Constantine and Helen on the South Side--began sponsorship of Americanization classes with the services of a Chicago public school teacher. At Saint Andrew Church, the reason advanced for the establishment of such a program in 1936 was that "the time had come for Greeks to become American citizens," as it was improbable that they would be returning to the homeland.[2] A similar reason was advocated at Saint Constantine Church when it formally established its Americanization program in 1937. It offered an additional rationale for implementing the program by stating that it was only proper for Greeks to become naturalized in order to take advantage of benefits which were becoming available under the New Deal administration of President Franklin D. Roosevelt.[3] These two parishes were viewed by many Greek people as the most "progressive" and "Americanized" of the Chicago Greek churches and were the first to reflect the acculturative influences of the American milieu in their church organizational policies. Classes were held during the day and evenings in both churches, but no records are extant to indicate enrollment. The day classes at Saint Constantine Church were attended primarily by mothers who awaited their children to be dismissed from the parish day school; the evening classes were attended principally by men.[4]

---

[1] William M. Leiserson, Adjusting Immigrants and Industry (New York: Harper & Bros., 1924), p. 260.

[2] Minutes of Saint Andrew Board of Trustees (Chicago), 14 October 1936 (in church office).

[3] Minutes of Saint Constantine School Board (Chicago), 3 April 1937 (in church office). An Americanization class operated there as early as 1929 according to an interview with Stella Petrakis, Chicago, (pastor's wife) 10 October 1967.

[4] Letter from Bessie Spirides, Chicago, (former church secretary at Saint Constantine Church) 4 May 1968.

With the coming of World War II and the resultant sweep of American patriotism throughout the nation, additional Greek parishes undertook Americanization programs and these classes increased considerably. By the war's end in 1945, ten out of the eleven Greek parishes which then comprised the Greek community of Chicago had such programs.[1] Unlike the earlier period, Greek immigrants were now desirous of becoming American citizens. Poverty and two world wars had left scars of insecurity in their homeland which made return seem unlikely.

Upon reviewing data of the early decades of this century and from interviews with Greek immigrants from this period, it can be said that Greek immigrants were curious and anxious to learn some English and something about America. But becoming knowledgeable of English and about American history and customs did not negate their attitude toward avoiding American citizenship. The former was pure education; the latter denied one's fatherland. There was no dire need felt to become legalized citizens, since they were becoming patriotic and loyal to American ideals as well as those cherished in Greece. One successful Greek businessman has stated:

> We were ignorant of the English language and if we were to succeed in business, it was necessary for us to learn English. Besides, we wanted to learn American ways so that we wouldn't be called "greenhorns."[2]

Another expressed the view that

> We were proud of our Greek heritage, but that did not stop us from learning English and the customs of America. We wanted to be good "Americans" even though we planned eventually to return to Greece.[3]

Still another, who became an attorney, remarked:

> In those days, even though we were young boys and hoped to make enough money to retire in Greece, it was necessary to learn English, especially if one wanted to enter a profession. I attended the Auburn Park Elementary School and decided that I wanted to become a teacher. I enrolled at the Normal School when Ella Flagg Young was superintendent; she took a deep interest in foreign students. But I decided that teaching was not for me and I went into law instead and decided that I would stay in America.[4]

---

[1] Ibid.

[2] Interview with George N. Pappas, Chicago, 9 October 1969.

[3] Interview with Thomas Chakinas, River Forest, Ill. 1 October 1969.

[4] Interview with George Porikos, Chicago, 25 August 1967.

Greek immigrants resented any accusation that they were being disloyal to America by not becoming American citizens. They were grateful for the opportunity to be in America and according to an attorney:

We were proud of our adopted country. We worked hard and obeyed the laws of the land and when the war came, we proved our loyalty to America by volunteering to fight in France. Percentage-wise, we supplied more men--some 70,000 for the army--than any other immigrant group in the United States.[1]

That this seemed to be the general view of Chicago's Greek community is borne out by a full-page advertisement placed in a Chicago newspaper by leading Greek immigrants extolling the virtues of Chicago's Greeks. After listing the commercial and social accomplishments of Greek immigrants in Chicago, the article concludes that:

. . . the Greeks of this country, especially of Chicago, furnish the best material for good American citizenship, for their record stands high not only in commercial and social lines, but also in matters of morality and justice. The Greek believes in family and home life and reputation, and as such, is mindful of the honor and reputation of his neighbor. He has no criminal or anarchistic tendencies whatever. A look into the court records will convince one of the truth of this statement. His loyalty and allegiance to his adopted country are beyond question. This statement is proved by the fact that out of 350,000 Hellenic population living in this country, 70,000 served in the American army during the world war.[2]

When the nativist movements got underway around the time of the First World War, Chicago's Greek immigrants resented this "instant Americanization" which asked them to deny their loyalty to Greece as a form of "Prussianism." They saw no conflict in owing allegiance to two lands.[3] Perhaps this is what Dewey meant when speaking about Americanization to the National Education Association. He objected to the forced imposition of American culture on ethnic groups and called for the harmonious blending of all ethnic cultures in America.[4]

---

[1] Interview with Paul Demos, Chicago, 19 July 1970.

[2] Chicago Daily Journal, 31 December 1925.

[3] Interview with Dr. S. D. Soter, Chicago, 12 October 1967.

[4] See Dewey, "Nationalizing Education," pp. 184-85. That this view was shared by others in the native American community is shown by Julius Drachsler, "Cultural Aspects of Immigration," Proceedings of the National Conference of Social Work, 48: 485-92. For a particular point of view on this topic see Roberts, p. 89. For a new interpretation see Carlson, pp. 440-64.

The dichotomy manifested by Greek immigrants in their willingness to participate in Americanization programs but their reluctance to acquire American citizenship can be illustrated by the following statistics. The Greeks ranked sixteenth out of 38 ethnic groups listed in the 1920 Federal Census with reference to size, with a total alien-born population of 175,972. Yet, with reference to participation in the citizenship training program of the public schools in the nation, they ranked ninth during the 1921-22 period with a total number of 5,486 enrolled in Americanization classes across the nation. However, they dropped to twelfth place during the 1922-23 term, when their enrollment dropped.[1]

According to the same census, Illinois had 1,206,951 foreign-born whites of which 1,144,157 were over eighteen. Of the latter, only 14,849, or 1.29 percent, were reported enrolled in Americanization programs. Yet, 3.2 percent of all Greek immigrants in the United States over eighteen were enrolled in Americanization classes. Hence, the national rate of Greeks participating in such programs was more than double the Illinois rate for all immigrants.[2] The Greek rate was one of the highest in the nation.

Despite their willingness to attend Americanization classes, however, they were apprehensive about taking advantage of the ultimate goal of such classes--the acquisition of American citizenship. This can be evidenced in tables 36 and 37, which give comparative figures for the number of Greek immigrants acquiring American citizenship during 1910 and 1920.

It can be readily seen from table 36 that the overwhelming majority of Greek immigrants in Chicago (those from Turkey are included in the table, since the majority were Greeks), did not opt for American citizenship. The reason is probably due to the prevailing strong sentiments for eventually returning to Greece.

---

[1] U.S., Department of Labor, Bureau of Naturalization, Citizenship Training of Adult Immigrants in the United States (Washington, D.C.: Government Printing Office, 1925), p. 7.

[2] Ibid., p. 10.

TABLE 36

CITIZENSHIP OF FOREIGN-BORN GREEKS, MALES 21 YEARS AND OVER
FOR CHICAGO: 1910

Country of Birth	Total	Naturalized	Having 1st papers	Alien	Citizenship not reported
Foreign-born white males, 21 years and over	379,850	190,693	31,585	124,553	33,619
Greece	4,496	619	361	3,054	462
Turkey in Europe . . .	561	45	37	452	27
Turkey in Asia	656	160	79	345	72

SOURCE: Burgess and Newcomb, 1920, p.26.

TABLE 37

CITIZENSHIP OF FOREIGN-BORN GREEKS, BY SEX 21 YEARS AND OVER
FOR CHICAGO: 1920

Country of birth	Total		Total for Each Sex		Naturalized		1st Papers		Aliens		Aliens Not Reported	
	Number	%	Male	Female	Male	Female	Male	Fem.	Male	Female	Male	Female
Foreign-born whites over 21	743,803	100	401,965	341,838	214,854	192,341	93,682	6,000	72,266	122,551	17,163	20,946
Greece	10,690	1.44	8,713	1,977	2,209	554	2,022	29	4,020	1,278	462	116

SOURCE: Burgess and Newcomb, 1920, p. 28.

It can be discerned in table 37 that despite the passage of ten years, Greek immigrants in Chicago, notwithstanding their participation in Americanization programs, were still reluctant to acquire American citizenship. Fewer than 30 percent had done so. Compared to other ethnic groups, the Greeks had one of the highest alien statuses of all immigrant populations in the city. Yet, when compared to the 1920 national percentage of Greek immigrants naturalized, the Chicago rate was almost twice as high. Table 38 shows that according to the 1920 census, only 16.8 percent of Greek immigrants were naturalized.

TABLE 38

PERCENT OF FOREIGN-BORN WHITE POPULATION OF ALL AGES NATURALIZED
1920-1940, RANKED BY COUNTRY OF ORIGIN

Foreign-Born White	Percent Naturalized 1940 1930 1920	Rank According to Percent Naturalized 1940 1930 1920	Rank According to length of Residence (1930)
Greece . .	58.4 44.7 16.8	22 24 23	24*

SOURCE: Brown and Roucek, p. 657.

* Out of 24 countries compared.

A plausible explanation for this phenomenon might lie in the important influence the Hull House Americanization program had on the Greek immigrants. Its immediate physical proximity to the Greek community served as a stimulus for these residents to participate actively in programs which eventually led to their naturalization.

Table 38 reveals that the national rate of naturalization of Greek immigrants nearly tripled ten years later (44.7 percent) and by 1940, 58.4 percent of Greek immigrants had become naturalized. This was brought about by the forces of acculturation and the erosion of Hellenic sentiment during the 1920s and 1930s over political dissension in Greece. Nonetheless, by 1940, the Greeks still ranked only twenty-second, according to percent of all ethnic groups naturalized in the United States.

Reluctance continues among the postwar Greek immigrants to become American citizens as evidenced by the fact that only 3,413 in 1960, and 2,906 in 1970, were naturalized. Yet, as shown on table 6 in chapter 2, 47,708 Greek immigrants arrived in the 1951-60 decade and 85,969 during 1961-70. The number of Greeks naturalized in 1971 was a low figure of 2.4 percent.[1]

Illustrative of the attitude of Greek immigrants in Chicago in not desiring to acquire American citizenship are the remarks made by Jane Addams in a convocation address at the University of Chicago. In her usual perceptive manner based on close contact with the Greeks at Hull House, she described to her audience an incident reflecting the pride of Greeks in their ancestry:

> How far a certain cosmopolitan humanitarianism ignoring national differences is either possible or desirable, it is difficult to say; but certain it is that the old type of patriotism founded upon a common national history and land occupation becomes to many of the immigrants who bring it with them a veritable stumbling block and impediment. Many Greeks whom I know are fairly besotted with a consciousness of their national importance and the achievement of their glorious past. Among them the usual effort to found a new patriotism upon American history is often an absurd undertaking; for instance, on the night of last Thanksgiving Day, I spent some time and zeal in a description of the Pilgrim Fathers, the motives which had driven them across the sea, while the experiences of the Plymouth colony were illustrated by stereopticon slides and little dramatic scenes. The audience of Greeks listened respectfully, altho [sic] I was uneasily conscious of the somewhat feeble attempt to boast of Anglo-Saxon achievement in hardihood and privation to men whose powers of admiration were absorbed in their Greek background of philosophy and beauty. At any rate, after the lecture was over, one of the Greeks said to me quite simply: "I wish I could describe my ancestors to you; they were different from yours." His further remarks were translated by a little Irish boy of eleven, who speaks modern Greek with facility and turns many an honest penny by translating, into the somewhat pert statement: "He says if that is what your ancestors are like, that his could beat them out." It is a good illustration of our faculty for ignoring the past, and of our failure to understand the immigrant estimation of ourselves. This lack of a more cosmopolitan standard, of a consciousness of kind founded upon creative imagination and historical knowledge, is evident in many directions, and cruelly widens the gulf between immigrant fathers and children who are "Americans in process."[2]

Perhaps the spirit of the Greeks could be expressed succinctly in the words of a Greek scholar and lawyer:

> . . . a tendency prevails lately to confuse the word Americanization with

---

[1] *Statistical Abstract of the United States*, 1972, p. 99.

[2] Jane Addams, "Recent Immigration: A Field Neglected by the Scholars," *Educational Review* 29 (March 1905): 253-54.

the word naturalization. There is nothing more erroneous than to consider every naturalized person as Americanized, or to accept . . . that a person not naturalized cannot be Americanized. Naturalization is simply a matter of form, while Americanization refers to a person's heart and soul and mind . . . What has the state or nation to gain from the man who is induced by the petty politician to become a citizen because it pays? . . . Prudence requires us to educate the foreigner and thoroughly Americanize him, if he appreciates Americanism, before admitting him to citizenship . . . we must show to the foreigners by our own example, by acts and deeds . . . in our every-day contact.[1]

Dewey was of the opinion that immigrant children were "too rapidly de-nationalized," thus losing the "positive and conservative value of their own native music, art, and literature." He suggested that the school should attempt to safeguard these attributes and blend them into the American milieu. Unfortunately, Americanization activities too frequently assumed that American culture was complete and the newcomer must learn to adopt it in its entirety. Such an attitude promoted immigration restriction and did not help advance the assimilation of all immigrants who were in America.[3]

World War I brought about a change in attitude regarding the future of Greek immigrants and it was reflected in their institutions. Instead of satisfying themselves with the temporary and makeshift arrangements of the past, they began to think in long range terms about their schools, churches, and organizations. These shifts in attitudes were felt not so much by the local societies as by organizations that were nationwide in character. The latter groups called for a de-emphasis, if not a complete abandonment, of the national aspirations of Greece, replacing it with a philosophy geared to the needs of people who were to be lifetime residents of the United States.[4]

---

[1]Canoutas, pp. 315-16.

[2]See John Dewey, "The School as Social Center," Proceedings of the National Education Association 41 (1902): 374-83.

[3]Although AHEPA sponsored Americanization programs beginning in the the 1920s, earlier Immigration Commission findings such as 1911 show that only 20 percent of United States Greeks had acquired citizenship after five years of residency. This figure contrasted to those immigrants from northwestern Europe who had 80 to 92 percent citizenship. Although the Greeks were part of the newcomer influx, in which percentages were lower than northwestern Europeans, they still had a very low record. Again this reflects a concern to return to the homeland. See Ross, p. 265.

[4]Eleutheros Typos [Free Press] (Chicago), 31 July 1943.

The change in attitude was especially reflected in the rate of naturalization acquired by Greek immigrants. Census statistics bear out the
premise that naturalization was acquired slowly, as indicated in this study.
On a national level, fewer than 5,000 of the 74,975 Greeks twenty-one or
older had acquired citizenship, and only a slightly smaller number had filed
their first papers. After World War I, naturalization proceeded at a more
rapid pace, the 1920 rate almost tripling that of 1910. By 1930, the percentage
more than tripled that of 1920, as shown in table 39.

TABLE 39

NATURALIZATION OF GREEKS IN UNITED STATES 1910-30

Year	Total	Males Naturalized			Females Naturalized		
		Number	%	First papers	Number	%	First papers
1910	74,975	4,946	6.6	4,550	5	..	..
1920	175,972	23,786	16.6	21,080	5,693	17.6	371
1930	174,526	62,649	49.9	22,701	12,825	30.7	2,158

SOURCE: Compiled from Abstract of the Fourteenth Census of the
United States, 1920, pp. 339, 341; and Abstract of the Fifteenth Census of
the United States, 1930, p. 163.

An annual tabulation of Greek aliens admitted to United States citizenship, beginning with 1923, shows that the peak in naturalization was
reached during the 1920s, then it tapered off after that date, and then began
rising again during the 1930s and the first half of the 1940s, rising again in
the late 1950s and 1960s. Decennial figures for 1940 to 1970 indicate naturalization as follows: 1940 (4,378), 1950 (1,667), 1960 (3,413), and 1970 (2,906).[1]

The increase in the naturalization rate of Greek immigrants is indicative of how attitudinal changes of the Greeks occurred with the passage

[1]Figures for 1923 to 1932 are to be found in the U.S. Department of
Labor, Bureau of Naturalization, Annual Reports of Commissioner of Naturalization; those from 1933 through 1936, from the Statistical Abstract; those from
1937 through 1942, from the Annual Report of Immigration and Naturalization;
and those for 1943 through 1970 from the Annual Report of the Immigration and
Naturalization Service.

of time in their new land. It was no longer considered treason to become an American citizen. By no means, however, did American citizenship reduce one's allegiance and devotion to the ancestral homeland. This was epitomized by the masthead carried by the Greek Star newspaper during the 1920s and 1930s:

> He who is a good Greek can be a good American
> and vice versa. The danger does not lie upon a
> man who loves two countries--but upon a man
> who loves none.[1]

In a sense, these later Greek immigrants wanted to capitalize on and retain the best of the cultures of both Greece and America.

In short, it can be ascertained that Greek immigrants residing in Chicago were participants in the Americanization programs sponsored by Hull House, the YMCA, and the city of Chicago. By far, during the early years, the settlement house program was the most attractive for those in the vicinity of Hull House. Later, the Greek churches themselves sponsored Americanization programs in cooperation with the Chicago Board of Education. There is evidence, however, that Greek immigrants also received basic Americanization training at the place of employment, the factory, on the railroad, or at the union. For those who were in business for themselves, Americanization training was received at the adult day and evening programs sponsored by the Chicago public school system in various parts of the city. Others preferred attending YMCA Americanization programs.

While government statistics indicate that Greek immigrants had one of the highest national rates for participating in Americanization and citizenship classes, the Greeks were initially reluctant to accept American citizenship. This was due to their intense loyalty to the homeland, for to the Greek mentality denying one's homeland was tantamount to treason. Consequently, Greek immigrants in Chicago during the first three decades of the present century, and even later, remained one of the city's largest ethnic groups which refused to be naturalized. Their attendance at Americanization activi-

---

[1]This expression typified the belief of Peter S. Lambros, founder and editor of Chicago's most influential Greek paper, the Greek Star, from 1904 to 1945. He was an articulate spokesman of dual citizenship and through his paper campaigned continuously for the naturalization of Greeks. For a summary of his views see his If It's All Greek to You The Greeks Have A Word for It (Chicago: Privately printed, 1946).

ties appears to have been motivated by curiosity to learn more about the United States and to achieve facility in the English language in order to improve their economic opportunities. It was not until the late 1930s, perhaps even after World War II, when erosion of Hellenism set in and the growing realization that with American-born and educated children the opportunity for returning to Greece was diminishing, that they began to acquire citizenship status, voluntarily deciding that they were in the United States permanently. However, with the new arrival of Greek immigrants after World War II, once again there appears to be reluctance to accept American citizenship.

Early Attempts to Influence Public School Policy

The Germans were one of the first ethnic groups that attempted to alter public school practices by influencing school officials to include ethnic languages in the curriculum.[1] In contrast, the Greek immigrants did not take a similar route for many years because they had made their own arrangements for Greek language maintenance and the transmission of their cultural heritage. They had organized three day schools, many afternoon and weekend schools, tutorial services, and other private ventures to serve their needs. Secondly, the Greeks did not have strong political leaders who could serve as emissaries in relating their demands to the broader American community.

With the passage of years and the erosion of Hellenic sentiment over the military dictatorship in Greece in 1935, the immigrants' dreams of returning to their ancestral home weakened. At the same time, the Chicago Greeks became alarmed at the prospect of their offspring becoming alienated from Greek heritage.[2] In 1935, the first formal citywide educational organization was established by the Greek educational leaders. The name of the group, Hellenic Educational League, was chosen deliberately to encourage the coop-

---

[1] The inclusion of German prompted a statement years later from Howard C. Hill of University of Chicago: "Many large schools in American cities have been spending more for teaching German to American children than for teaching English and civics to aliens." See Hill, 612.

[2] For the erosion of Hellenic sentiment among the second generation Greeks see Saloutos, Greeks in the United States, pp. 310-25.

eration of all the Greek parishes in the task of language maintenance.[1]

The league consisted of educational leaders and representatives from every Greek parish in Chicago. A serious effort was made to assess the efficacy of current educational arrangements in meeting community needs and transmitting the cultural legacy to the American-born generation. It noted with dismay that the few communal Greek day schools were no longer attracting large numbers of children of Greek immigrants; the majority were enrolled in the city's public elementary schools. This was not considered catastrophic, as most of these children attended the supplementary afternoon Greek schools or were receiving private Greek instruction in their homes. What disturbed the league most, however, was the situation in the city's public high schools. It was here that Greek youth were weaned away from their Greek heritage; and it was the acculturative influence of the high school that alienated them from their Greek-speaking parents and ancestral milieu.[2] It was on this level that the league decided to take action.

Remembering that the German inhabitants of Chicago had succeeded in bringing about the teaching of German in the city's public schools because of popular demand, the league conceived of a similar venture, even though it realized that the number of Greek residents was quite small compared to the German element. It recalled, nonetheless, that the study of Greek had at one time been part of the curriculum of Chicago schools. It was part of the classics curriculum when the city's first high school, Central, was opened in 1856, and continued to be taught until 1883.[3] The league hoped that it could prevail upon the Chicago Board of Education to restore the study of Greek, not only based upon precedent and the fact that Greek was one of the world's greatest historical and literary languages, but especially because the Greek citizens of Chicago were now demanding it by popular request. The league drafted a petition to this effect and presented it to the Chicago Board of Education for its approval early in 1936.

---

[1]Organizers of the league were Nicholas Cheronis, a physics teacher at Wright Junior College and Paul Demos, a Greek attorney actively involved in the Greek community. Interview with Paul Demos, Chicago, 19 July 1970.

[2]Ibid.

[3]Clark, p. 74.

The petition consisted of a number of key points. In synopsis, they were: (1) that of 2,000 students of Greek descent only a small number had the opportunity to be taught modern Greek; (2) that Greek instruction in the city's high schools would attract both Greek and non-Greek students, especially those who planned to enter the professions of medicine, linguistics, philology, philosophy, and the fine arts; (3) that the study of Greek would enable all students to understand and interpret the teachings of Holy Scripture and the Apostles by reading the original works, as well as reading modern Greek literature; (4) that the teaching of Greek would increase respect for the ideals and traditions of Greek culture that have influenced western civilization; (5) that Greek language skills would enable students to improve their mastery of English, since so many words are derived from Greek; (6) that opportunity would be offered to those students who wish to pursue the study of Greek in greater depth by having advanced classes; (7) that the introduction of Greek would not be a financial burden to the Board of Education, since there were qualified teachers available in the school system; and (8) that the Hellenic Educational League, on behalf of the Greek community of Chicago, authorized and supported the implementation of the plan and urged its adoption by the Board of Education.[1]

The solidarity among Greeks implied in the petition was far from true. With characteristic factionalism, several parishes objected on the grounds that it would threaten Greek school enrollment; that expansion of communal schools would cease if children could learn Greek in public schools without the cost of tuition. The Hellenic Educational League responded to these charges by stating that in the mid-1930s the Greek day and afternoon schools were accommodating a small percentage of the Greek children as compared to earlier decades. Furthermore, by having Greek studies in the public high schools it could compensate for the lack of having a Greek gymnasium (high school) in the city. The Greek day schools could serve as a preparatory level from elementary to secondary levels in advanced Greek studies. A dual objective would be achieved if non-Greek students participated in these studies, because it would serve as an incentive to counteract the growing indifference of Greek parents toward Greek scholarship.

---

[1] The Greek text of the petition is to be found in the Greek Star, (Chicago) 24 January 1936.

The league insisted that an overhaul--a revolution--was needed in the Greek educational structure and a beginning could occur with the high school program of Greek instruction.[1] Much discussion followed in Greek community meetings, along with editorializing in the Greek newspapers. One editorial viewed the adoption of the petition by the board as a definitive step in the restoration of Greek studies, a status that had been lost with the advent of pragmatic education at the turn of the century.[2]

Amidst this controversy, the Chicago Board of Education responded by accepting the petition with the stipulation that a minimum of fifteen students must be enrolled in any program. However, upon the death of Superintendent Bogan in February 1936, the required enrollment was increased to one hundred students by the new superintendent; William Johnson. This action prompted parents from the West Side Greek community of the Assumption to sign an agreement to enroll their children in a Greek language course at Austin High School in the fall term, 1936.

The program began in 1936 with ninety students in three Greek classes at Austin High School on the city's far West Side, where a heavy concentration of Greek immigrants was developing around the Assumption Church. It increased to two hundred students in six classes in 1937. Some of the classes were for advanced students--children of Greek immigrants who had a basic foundation in the Greek language from their homes. The instructor for these classes was George Drossos, a former principal of a Greek communal day school and an ardent exponent of Greek education. The success of the pilot program was a factor in the board of education responding favorably for the approval of Greek studies in other high schools where requested by Greek parents. Amundsen and McKinley on the North Side offered Greek studies late in 1937, as did Englewood High School on the South Side in 1938. The Hellenic Educational League had established as its ultimate goal the introduction of Greek studies in at least ten Chicago high schools. In appreciation of the support of Superintendent Johnson for the introduction of Greek instruction in the Chicago schools, the league sponsored a testimonial dinner in his honor. It was well-attended by the Greek community, and on this

---

[1] Forty Years of Greek Life, pp. 107-8.

[2] Greek Press (Chicago), 30 January 1936.

occasion Johnson was awarded a medallion by the Greek government through its consul general in Chicago.[1]

The program, which was to last for twenty-five years, met with initial success. The Greek community throughout the city responded enthusiastically and saw to it that Greek students of high school age enrolled in these classes. Additional Greek instructors were hired by the public schools to staff the growing number of classes. It has been estimated that thousands of children of Greek immigrants from all parts of the city attended one of the four schools offering Greek instruction.[2] Part of this success, aside from the thrust of the Greek community, stemmed from the authorized permissive transfer plan adopted by the Chicago Board of Education, which allowed students to leave their school districts in order to pursue Greek studies in districts that offered such courses. This permissive transfer was inaugurated to permit flexibility for those Greek families that lived outside such districts. This ruling, however, proved to be the downfall of the Greek instruction program years later. Its initial purpose was supplanted gradually when non-Greek students began enrolling in Greek courses at these high schools in order to avoid attending schools in neighborhoods which were changing from white to black. As the racial issue in the city became more acute, the board of education began deliberating action to curb permissive transfers.

At the same time, there was a diminishing interest in Greek studies among students of Greek descent, chiefly due to student rebellion and growing parental indifference.[3] Despite exhortation from the pulpit in Greek Orthodox churches and in the Greek press, fewer Greek students enrolled in these classes. Many resented being forced to take Greek, complaining that this made them look "clannish" and insular in the eyes of their peers, especially since they were all grouped together in their Greek classes and, in some schools, in the same division or homeroom. Parents succumbed reluc-

---

[1] Interview with Paul Demos, former member of the Hellenic Educational League, Chicago, 19 July 1970.

[2] Interview with George Drossos, Chicago, 17 November 1967.

[3] A similar situation was occurring at the same time in Lowell, Mass. The school board dropped Greek instruction from high schools in spite of the large Greek population in the city. See Ethnikos Kyrix [National Herald] (New York), 16 July 1961.

tantly to the growing acculturative influences of the environment and did not insist upon their children enrolling in Greek classes. Gradually, with the decline of students from Greek homes and the rising number of non-Greek students from racially-changing neighborhoods, the Greek classes assumed a new character. Advanced classes were discontinued and students from Greek homes served as informal tutors for the non-speaking Greek students who had no real interest in learning the language. One former student remarked:

> We knew Greek from home and yet we were placed in the same class with beginners who knew no Greek. It was easy for us to get by while the non-Greek kids were struggling to learn the language, so we goofed off.[1]

This state of affairs no doubt brought displeasure to parents and contributed to the declining enrollment in these classes.

A belated effort by the Greek community under the leadership of the Greek Orthodox Bishop of Chicago in 1960 sought to buttress and retain the program in the high schools, but it met with failure. Despite petitions that exceptions be made for Greek students, Superintendent of Schools Benjamin Willis decreed the end of permissive transfers in 1961, and in due time the Greek instructional program came to an end. As mentioned, the program's failure was compounded by Greek parental indifference, but another contributing factor was opposition from within the school system. Some high school principals and language department chairmen objected to Greek studies because of attrition in other foreign language enrollments.[2] In theory, many Greek parents supported the idea of Greek instruction in high schools, but found it difficult to impose their personal values on their children due to acculturative forces beyond their control.

Nonetheless, for the period of time that the program was operative, there is evidence that it succeeded well in fostering knowledge of Greek, especially among the American-born generations. In the first instance, it helped to reinforce the knowledge of Greek among those coming from homes where Greek was spoken. In the second instance, it provided advanced knowledge of Greek for those who were products of the Greek afternoon

---

[1] Interview with Peter J. Chiaculas, Chicago, 12 June 1970.

[2] Interview with George Drossos, Chicago, 17 November 1967.

schools and introduced those who had not attended Greek schools to the formal study of Greek, ineffective as it may have been in some cases. Finally, for the Greek students, it legitimized and gave status to the study of Greek by its very inclusion in the public school curriculum These factors resulting from such a program in the public schools contributed to the perpetuation of the Greek cultural ethos in Chicago. As one respondent stated, "if it wasn't for the Greek I learned in high school, I would not be familiar with my cultural heritage, and I am glad my parents insisted that I take Greek in school."[1]

Recent Attempts to Influence Public Schools

It is interesting to note that some sixty to seventy years after the peak of immigration in this country, the public schools of Chicago are confronted with a situation similar to that faced at the turn of the century. Today as then, the schools contain large segments of children whose first language is other than English. The largest group is Spanish-speaking, who as of 30 November 1971, numbered 33,509 in the regular elementary schools.[2] They comprised 67 percent of the total "bilingual" students enrolled having English deficiencies in the public schools. Surprisingly, the second largest group (although much smaller numerically than the Spanish group) in the Chicago elementary schools whose mother tongue was other than English were the Greeks, consisting of 1,309 pupils. It must be understood, of course, that this was the number of those who did not speak English. The actual number of children of postwar Greek immigrants enrolled in the city's schools was, as in the case with the Spanish group, considerably larger. In the high schools the Greeks who spoke little or no English were the second largest group, consisting of 339 students, exceeded only by the Polish group of 531 students.[3]

The large number of Greek children with inadequate knowledge of English were enrolled primarily in the public schools of the Ravenswood,

---

[1]Interview with Barbara Stamas, River Forest, Ill., 3 August 1970.

[2]Chicago Public Schools, "A Comprehensive Design for Bilingual Education," (Chicago: Board of Education, 1972), p. 3. (Mimeographed.)

[3]Ibid.

Albany Park, and Belmont-Cragin districts of Chicago's North Side. The postwar Greek immigrant settled in those areas, creating a new "Greektown." Typical of the heavy concentration of Greek-speaking children in public schools of the area is the Budlong Elementary School, immediately across the street from the Saint Demetrios Greek Orthodox Church in the Ravenswood community. Eighty percent of the school enrollment was of Greek stock, of which almost 30 percent had an extremely limited knowledge of English.[1] In contrast to previous years when the Chicago public schools had no official policy for handling such a situation and, consequently, foreign-speaking children were placed in "retarded" classrooms, the school environment was changed to conform to the communication and adjustment needs of students.

Such a change in policy was made possible by the recent resurgence of ethnic identity in American society. In Illinois an ethnic studies section was formed under the auspices of the Office of the Superintendent of Public Instruction. The rationale for this new unit is described, in part, by the state superintendent, Michael J. Bakalis, himself a son of Greek immigrants:

> Despite the fact that the melting pot concept has been largely discredited, our schools persist in their efforts to assimilate the young. An educator, of Italian descent, reflecting his years in school, put it this way: 'We were becoming Americans by learning how to be ashamed of our parents.'
> This is cultural genocide. It has no place in our schools. To depreciate, in the name of Americanization, a student's culture, or his language, or his history is to risk crushing his self-esteem and pride so as to affect his heart and mind for life.
> I believe that schools can help facilitate that movement. We can do so by helping students adapt to the reality of diversity. Ethnic Studies have a place in the classroom for two basic reasons. First, ethnicity in America is important. Ethnicity has always been and is likely to remain one of the most pervasive influences in our politics and culture. Second, America is just a small part of a racially, culturally, and linguistically diverse world, and that world is increasingly shrinking on account of population growth, urbanization, industrialization, and communication. Therefore, our existence on this planet may become utterly intolerable unless we rise to new levels of understanding about the human species. Our objective should be to heighten every student's perception of his place and his relationship to others in the scheme of things.[2]

---

[1] Interview with Becky C. Orphan, Budlong principal, Chicago, 11 February 1972; see also "Chicago Public Schools, Selected School Characteristics 1971-72," p. 13. (Mimeographed.)

[2] Office of the Superintendent of Public Instruction, Rationale of the Ethnic Studies Section, (Springfield, Ill.,: n.d.)

Also, a factor in the policy change was the partial decentralization of American public education, which, in the case of Chicago schools, brought about the establishment of local school advisory councils which encouraged parental input in the selection of local school administrators and in school governance.

In 1971, the Budlong School Advisory Council, composed of many Greek parents, some of them recent immigrants themselves, with some assistance from the local Greek community of Saint Demetrios Church, selected from among qualified candidates a Greek-speaking, bilingual-bicultural person (second generation) as principal of the school, along with other Greek bilingual-bicultural personnel.[1] As a result, the school has developed a congenial atmosphere of bilingual-biculturality. It has signs in Greek and English and parents are made to feel welcome by being spoken to in their native Greek tongue. Similar conditions have developed elsewhere in the area where Greek-speaking principals have been assigned to other public schools with large enrollments of Greek-speaking children.

Interestingly, a generation after the first successful attempt was made to introduce Greek studies in the Chicago public schools through the Hellenic Educational League in the 1930s, a similar attempt developed in the 1970s.[2] However, this time the venture was promoted mostly by second and third generation Greek-Americans who perceived it as part of the current ethnicity movement, and it involved more than just the teaching of Greek in public schools. On 10 December 1971 educators from public and private schools organized the Hellenic Council on Education in order to promote and coordinate the educational concerns of the Greek community of Chicago in light of the new ethnicity. The new professional group was organized to act as the focal point for the convergence of the legitimate concerns of educators of Hellenic extraction with its membership drawn from all levels of education in both teaching and administration. Its program was outlined to include the exchange of information relative to educational problems and opportunities, the development of an awareness of the place of the Greek-American educator within the mainstream of American education, the safeguarding of the educa-

---

[1] Interview with Becky C. Orphan, Chicago, 11 February 1972.

[2] Greek Star (Chicago), 23 December 1971.

tional rights of Greek-American youngsters, and the promotion of its role as the organized voice of the larger Chicago Hellenic community in matters of education.

One of the first projects of the Hellenic Council on Education was to encourage Greek immigrant parents to become involved in the local advisory school councils of the twenty public elementary and four public high schools on the North Side of Chicago, where there was a significant enrollment of Greek children. Letters in Greek and English advocating their participation in these councils were prepared and distributed in these schools with the approval of the school principals. This action was intended to gain more representation of Greek parents on these councils in order to give them a greater voice in policy decisions affecting schools in which their children were enrolled. Prior to this project, with the exception of a few schools, Greek parental representation at these local councils was minimal.

Another project was the development of Greek ethnic studies mini-courses for use in social studies in elementary schools with large numbers of Greek children. The project was conceived as an attempt to provide ethnic and cultural identity for these pupils and was in keeping with recently passed state legislation (Ethnic Studies Bill, H.B. 19H) which required local school districts to develop materials for acquainting school children with ethnic groups that make up the American population.[1] The Greek material was written by educators in the Greek community with the cooperation of the Hellenic Council on Education and submitted to the Department of Curriculum of the Chicago Public Schools. After a hearing for revision in the Greek community the unit was finally approved by the board and sent to the schools for their use.[2] The Greek ethnic studies unit represents one of three programs (the others being Polish and Italian) that have been completed for white ethnic groups among a projected number for other ethnic groups planned by the Division of Social Studies.[3]

---

[1]Letter from Mary E. Grieg, Director, Division of Social Studies, Chicago Public Schools, 5 May 1972.

[2]See "Ethnic Studies Process" (Chicago: Board of Education, 1972), pp. 1-46. (Mimeographed.)

[3]Ibid., and interview with Mary E. Grieg, Director, Division of Social Studies, Chicago Public Schools, 14 February 1972.

Reacting to complaints from parents that their children were unable to communicate with teachers due to language differences in the public schools of the Ravenswood area, the Hellenic Council on Education attempted to rectify the situation by requesting of the board of education the assignment of qualified Greek bilingual teachers to these schools. A letter was dispatched to the general superintendent of schools stating

> . . . that the Greek-speaking community demands that bilingual, bicultural teachers be transferred, assigned and appointed into schools and positions on a seniority basis where Greek-speaking children are in membership . . . and that positions as administrators, supervisors, consultants and ancillary staff as well as paraprofessionals at school, district, area, and central office levels be staffed with bilingual, bicultural personnel to meet the needs of the Greek-speaking community.[1]

A reply from Superintendent Redmond on 2 August 1972 failed to satisfy the council, and prompted the following telegram to be sent to him:

> We have received your letter of August 2 in which you respond to our letter of July 10. We have either not communicated clearly or you have misinterpreted our intent. We have a concern for the staffing of bilingual, bicultural specially-funded programs. However, this concern is peripheral to our major concern of the regular staffing of schools which have concentrations of numbers of non-speaking children other than Spanish.
> Regular staffing from the Department of Personnel is now done with categories of race and bilingual, bicultural Spanish. We are requesting that a directive be sent to the assistant superintendent in charge of personnel to the effect that the category of bilingual, bicultural be extended to categories additional to Spanish. For example, where there are large numbers of Greek-speaking children concentrated in membership at a given school, regular staff appointments and transfers include bilingual, bicultural Greek-speaking teachers. There are many such qualified teachers available for both assignments and transfers to regular positions in these schools.
> We are not deploring that Spanish-speaking children are being served. Rather, we applaud this recognition and effort. We only ask that similar needs of other non-English speaking children be similarly served. Our organization would appreciate receiving a copy of your directive to the assistant superintendent in charge of personnel.[2]

---

[1] Hellenic Council on Education to Superintendent James F. Redmond, 10 July 1972.

[2] Hellenic Council on Education to Dr. James F. Redmond 26 August 1972.

The superintendent replied that:

> . . . the concerns you expressed were taken into consideration under Procedure 2 of the plan adopted by the Board of Education . . . entitled "Plan to Integrate School Facilities and Equalize Per Pupil Costs." It provides that fluency in foreign language where required for communication with children be considered in the assignment of staff. That policy is being implemented and has been considered as it relates specifically to schools with large numbers of Greek speaking children.[1]

This favorable response opened the way for a series of meetings with the assistant superintendent in charge of personnel with representatives from the Hellenic Council for the purpose of implementing its request. As a result of these meetings the Bureau of Teacher Personnel was convinced of the importance of identifying and screening bilingual Greek teachers for possible assignments to the public schools in Chicago containing high levels of Greek speaking pupils. The Hellenic Council provided the bureau with a Greek language examination instrument to be used in the screening. Accordingly, the board of education issued a personnel bulletin announcing that certified teachers in the school system who were bilingual Greek were needed for staffing and could apply for possible assignment to schools with large enrollments of Greek-speaking children. The bulletin read as follows:

"OPPORTUNITIES FOR TEACHERS BI-LINGUAL IN THE GREEK LANGUAGE

"A need exists for teachers bi-lingual in the Greek language who are interested in teaching in schools where there are large concentrations of Greek speaking students.

"The Bureau of Teacher Personnel is seeking to identify bi-lingual Greek teachers for the possible assignment to those schools.

"In addition to meeting the general and specific requirements for a teaching certificate, the teacher must be able to work well with individuals and groups, and to relate effectively to teachers, administrators, other school personnel, and parents. Knowledge and understanding of Greek culture and language is essential and a necessity.

"Interested teachers should write to Mr. Raymond C. Principe, Administrator, Bureau of Teacher Personnel, Room 1001. Applications should reach the above office on or before Monday, April 23, 1973. Letters should indicate Name, Address, Home Phone, Social Security Number, Type of Certificate (i.e., Regular - High School English, or Temporary - Kindergarten-Primary, etc.), and if presently employed by the Board of Education, the name of the school. In a brief paragraph explain how and when you learned to speak Greek."[2]

---

[1] Dr. James F. Redmond to Hellenic Council on Education, 5 September 1972.

[2] Chicago Public Schools, Personnel Bulletin No. 205, "Opportunities

As of 3 May 1973, 187 teachers of Greek descent in the Chicago
public school system had indicated interest to the Bureau of Teacher Personnel in such an assignment.[1]

Finally, the major undertaking of the Hellenic Council on Education,
which unexpectedly brought controversy in the new Greektown area, was its
support of a voluntary program of a Greek bilingual-bicultural program for
the area's public schools. After meeting with officials at the Office of Government Sponsored Programs of the Chicago Board of Education, the council
proposed that schools with large Greek enrollments consider the development
of a bilingual proposal for possible government funding. In the late autumn
of 1972, two elementary schools, Budlong and Lovett, both with Greek-speaking principals, drew up proposals with local input and submitted them to the
board of education for approval, requesting funding under the Bilingual Education Act of 1968 as amended to the Elementary and Secondary Educational
Act of 1965. The board approved the proposals on 30 January 1973. In the
meantime, because federal funding had been cut off as a result of economic
retrenchment in federal educational programs by President Nixon, the proposals had to be rewritten to conform to state guidelines so that they could be
submitted for state funding.

The news that the Budlong School had submitted a proposal for the
teaching of Greek was ill-received by members of the symboulion (board of
trustees) of the Saint Demetrios Church located across the street from the
school. There was fear expressed that the teaching of Greek in the adjacent
public school would adversely affect its parish afternoon Greek school, which
enrolled a large number of pupils attending Budlong.[2] Thus, the same argument which was given by the Greek communal schools in opposing the efforts
of the Hellenic Educational League to introduce Greek in the public schools
in 1936, was raised again. The parish school would not tolerate competition

for Teachers Bi-lingual in the Greek Language," (5 April 1973); see also
Greek Star (Chicago), 5 April 1973.

[1] Telephone conversation with Otho M. Robinson, Assistant Superintendent in charge of Personnel, Chicago Public Schools, 3 May 1973.

[2] Greek Star (Chicago), 19 April 1973.

from public schools in the teaching of Greek!

The Hellenic Council on Education replied that such was not the case The Greek language was not to be taught per se, but only as a means to facilitate the immigrant child's entry into the American mainstream. It claimed that the program was voluntary and "the general thrust of the program is to ground Greek children in their native language--to teach them better Greek and then go on to good English. If a youngster is not grounded in one language, he won't do well in another."[1] It further claimed that

A bilingual program is a tool for learning. As such, its value is judged by the manner in which it achieves its goal, namely, to offer the foreign-born child the best opportunity to succeed with his American education while still retaining his ethnic identity.[2]

The public became aware of the issue and voices of approval and disapproval began to be heard. The Archbishop of the Greek Orthodox Church, in a Chicago meeting called by the Hellenic Council with members of the Saint Demetrios community to resolve the issue on 21 January 1972, endorsed the bilingual proposal, stating that he saw no conflict with existing Greek schools. He felt that " . . . on the contrary, the program will supplement the work of parish schools . . . expanding the knowledge of spoken Greek."[3] The Budlong School Council, principally composed of native-born Greek Americans, denounced the proposal on the grounds that it had not been previously consulted and that children would be used as guinea pigs in an experimental program that would eventually turn the school into a second-rate institution. The argument was that in teaching two languages, less learning would occur, and that the school would become overcrowded with the addition of staff and special rooms required for such a program.

The Budlong Council asserted that the neighborhood always had been able to take care of its own and, therefore, no new programs were needed. Furthermore, "these programs are only for low-income areas. Our area is not such, and it is insulting to so call it."[4] However, Greek-born members

[1] Orthodox Observer (New York), 2 February 1973.

[2] Greek Press (Chicago), 21 April 1973.

[3] Greek Press (Chicago), 2 February 1973.

[4] Greek Star (Chicago), 26 May 1973.

of the school council did not agree, and at an election for new officers a riot almost erupted. A new organization called the "Concerned Parents of Budlong School," composed mainly of foreign-born Greek parents, emerged immediately in support of the program and to combat the opposition. [1]

The Saint Demetrios Board of Trustees rejected the proposal as inimical to its parish school and on the grounds that it would attract more Greek immigrants to its area, thus making it more of a Greek ghetto and thereby causing property values to decrease. It contended that there was no identity "crisis" on the part of Greek children in the parish in attendance at Budlong School, since:

> . . . all Greek immigrant children come from very fine homes with very strong family ties. They understand their culture--they are proud of their Greek heritage. Spending money, even if federal or state money, to teach that which is already known is an absolute waste. [2]

In due time, the Saint Demetrios Greek community was engaged in conflict. Accusations and counter-accusations confused the issues with personalities. The community became polarized. Soon non-Greek civic groups joined the fray. The issue became more complicated with the involvement of neighborhood civic and business associations whose opposition to the bilingual proposal was solicited. Meetings were held with state and city officials to try to resolve the problems and minimize the rampant confusion and confrontation. School officials connected with the issue came under verbal attack. They included the school principal, the state superintendent of public instruction who was accused of violating his own guidelines for bilingual education and whose office would be responsible for funding the program, the associate superintendent of Chicago public schools, also of Greek descent and a member of the Hellenic Council on Education, and several other educators who, as members of the council, supported the concept of Greek bilingual education. [3]

In support of the program were the Concerned Parents of Budlong School, the Greek Orthodox Archdiocese, the Hellenic Council on Education,

---

[1] Greek Press (Chicago), 11 May 1973.

[2] Greek Star (Chicago), 26 May 1973.

[3] Greek Press (Chicago), 20 April 1973; Chicago Tribune, 8 July 1973.

several other Greek professional associations who adopted resolutions en-
dorsing the proposal, and the Greek ethnic press. It seemed that the newly-
arrived Greek immigrants who formed the bulk of the 40,000 Greeks in the
Saint Demetrios community favored the proposal, and this was reflected by
the strong support given to it by the Concerned Parents group, who, as immigrants, mistrusted the local church programs.[1] This was perhaps the case
because the local church was controlled mainly by American-born Greeks
who argued that Greek history and traditions already were taught in the local
church and, therefore, opposed the proposal. As a minority group, fearful
that the community would become an ethnic ghetto and in order to combat the
professional educators and "liberal do-gooders" in the Hellenic Council on
Education, the American-born group marshalled non-Greek community support
and vociferously opposed the project. This confrontation had all the marks
of a social class conflict between foreign-born and native-born Greek Americans, according to one individual at the Chicago Board of Education.[2]

The controversy received national attention in the Greek ethnic press
and considerable coverage in the local metropolitan and neighborhood papers.
The Chicago Greek language newspapers covered the issue thoroughly, and
the Greek Press editorialized in support of the bilingual proposal as follows:

> The gallant efforts of the Hellenic Council on Education to resolve
> the educational concerns and needs of Chicago's Greek community were
> about to be crowned by a well-deserved success when a group of Greek-
> Americans in the Saint Demetrios area voiced opposition.
> Opposition coming from Greeks was the last likelihood one could ex-
> pect. Especially from Greeks associated with Saint Demetrios, the church
> that boasts the largest membership in the city of Chicago, never consid-
> ered seriously to undertake the effort of creating a daily school, while
> other smaller communities like Holy Trinity, Assumption and Saints
> Constantine and Helen maintain a daily school at great sacrifices.
> These churches did not object to the teaching of Greek in public
> school, obviously feeling that . . . Chicago boys and girls of Greek
> descent have a right to be also exposed to a Greek ethnic studies program.
> This newspaper will not care less if teaching of Greek in Chicago pub-
> lic schools will take away some customers from Saint Demetrios. This
> newspaper's primary concern is the educational needs of . . . boys and
> girls of Greek descent who are not served by Saint Demetrios or any other
> Greek Orthodox Community.[3]

---

[1] Chicago Today, 13 December 1973.

[2] Greek Press (Chicago), 28 December 1973.

[3] Greek Press (Chicago), 27 April 1973.

In the midst of all this turmoil, an assessment team went to the Budlong School on behalf of the Illinois Office of the Superintendent of Public Instruction on 19 September 1973. On 1 October 1973 the program was funded by the state in the amount of $86,000, providing bilingual instruction for 142 Greek-speaking pupils in the school.[1] A similar program in the amount of $56,000 for the Lovett School was funded by the state during the summer. Unlike the Budlong proposal, that proposed for Lovett received no opposition from the Holy Trinity Greek community in which the school was located.[2] Both proposals were hailed as the first Greek bilingual-bicultural programs to be government-funded in the United States. Thus, eighty years from the time the first formal Greek community was established in Chicago, a public policy for the teaching of the Greek language and Greek culture was enunciated for the city's schools and supported by public funding. This was indeed a transformation in the public attitude that the original Greek immigrants encountered in Chicago in 1893, when they first laid the tenuous foundations for the perpetuation and survival of their ethnic and religious heritage in the New World.

The controversy did not end, however, with the funding of the program. It continued in school boycotts, threats to have the principal removed, picketing of the area and district superintendent's offices, and continued protests at the Chicago Board of Education meetings. Despite these harassments, the program was implemented and the Hellenic Council on Education proceeded to address its attention to other educational matters--namely the re-establishment of Greek instruction in high schools with large enrollment of Greek students, the adjucation of disputes involving public school teachers of Greek descent and school officials, and involvement with other ethnic professional groups, locally and nationally, in the promotion and development of an improved ethnic studies curriculum under the Ethnic Heritage Studies Act approved by Congress in December 1972. The council is an active participant in the Chicago Consultation on Ethnicity in Education, which sponsored the first statewide conference on ethnic studies in May 1972, for the expansion

---

[1] Greek Star (Chicago), 18 October 1973; Greek Press (Chicago), 19 October 1973; Hellenic Chronicle (Boston), 25 October 1973.

[2] Ibid.

of ethnic studies in the state's school systems.

The aggressive efforts of the Hellenic Council on Education have
made an impact on the educational environment of the Greek community in
Chicago, but it is still too early for a valid assessment. It is, nevertheless,
another example of the changes that have taken place in the struggle of the
Greeks for ethnic survival in the eighty-year period covered by this study.

Summary

It is apparent that until recently, the public schools of Chicago
failed to make accommodation for the children of immigrants. The offspring
of Greek immigrants (along with the children of other immigrants) were ignored
or treated like native-born pupils in the city's schools. No special policy
existed nor were any special provisions made for them to learn English or to
adjust to the formal school structure. Of course, the Chicago schools were
not unique in this respect; a similar pattern prevailed in most all large American cities with perhaps the exception of Cleveland and Los Angeles. In
essence, Chicago public schools were "destroyers" of immigrant cultures,
so great was the need felt by American society to Americanize immigrants and
their descendants in order to rid the nation and the city of a threatening situation. Indeed, contemporary critics have raised serious doubts as to whether
or not the public schools did serve as unifiers of a diverse society and as
significant agencies of socialization.

The role of the public school in Greek adjustment consisted primarily
in bringing the Greeks and their children into the mainstream of American life.
This was not, however, the direct result of the public schools, for most immigrants did not achieve the upward mobility that Greeks, Japanese-Americans,
and eastern European Jews did. The Greeks, along with the others mentioned,
achieved this upward mobility because of the heavy emphasis placed upon
personal achievement by their ethnic culture, and the fact that they were
among the first of the so-called "new immigrants" to achieve middle-class
status. This process was perhaps hastened by informal educational adjustments that took place among the Greek inhabitants of Chicago via business
endeavors, the factory, the church, the playground, and even their limited
participation in politics. Nor is there evidence that children who attended
public schools were brought into mainstream culture more quickly than those
who attended Greek communal day schools. And while public schools did

provide for avenues of acculturation, they did not obliterate Greek culture among pupils of Greek ancestry due to the high priority placed by Greek immigrants in transmitting the cultural heritage and the strong structural cohesiveness of the Greek community with its supportive educational agencies.

The number of Greek children attending public schools in Chicago was never very large in comparison with other ethnic groups. Though it is difficult to gather precise figures, it is projected on the basis of census data that of the nearly 12,000 Greek children born in Chicago by 1930, three-fourths matriculated at Chicago public schools. It is likely that this ratio was greater after 1930.

While Greeks lived in all sections of the city, the heaviest concentration during the early decades of the present century was in the Greek Delta area. Consequently, enrollment of Greek children in the public schools of that area was heavy. Retardation rates for these schools were higher than the city's average because of the students' inadequate knowledge of English. Most completed the primary grades, leaving after completing fifth grade to go to work. It is estimated that large numbers of children of Greek immigrants not accounted for in the public schools were probably gainfully employed, though few bothered with the formalities of procuring a school age certificate required by law. After the 1930s, most Greek children completed elementary school and many entered public high schools. In addition, the vast majority attended supplementary Greek afternoon schools after public school hours or received tutorial instruction at home.

· With reference to evening schools, young Greek adults were avid participants. From 1902 to 1922, the Greeks were the seventh largest ethnic group enrolled in the evening school programs. During the 1907-8 school term, one out of every five Greeks officially residing in Chicago attended evening school--one of the highest ratios of all ethnic groups in the city. The large attendance of Greeks at evening schools is attributed to their desire to learn English for economic competency. Most attended schools from six to ten months, then dropped out when they felt they had learned enough. While they attended evening schools in all parts of the city, the heaviest concentration was in the Greektown area, where residential and employment propinquity made it convenient to attend. The adult day school program also attracted Greek immigrants, because of the daytime hours and schools located close to their place of work.

Chicago's Greek immigrants were also heavy patronizers of Americanization classes. The most successful was the class organized exclusively for Greeks at Hull House. Later, when these classes were abandoned in the mid-1920s, Greeks enrolled in the city's special Americanization program and in those sponsored by several parishes of the Greek community. It seems, however, that many Greeks attended such classes at their places of employment--the factory, the railroad, or at some other place. Government statistics reveal that nationally the Greek immigrants had one of the highest ratios of all ethnic groups participating in Americanization or citizenship training programs. Yet, they were reluctant to acquire American citizenship, and in Chicago both in 1910 and in 1920, the majority did not hold American citizenship. This is explained by the fact that according to the mentality of the Greek immigrant, acquiring American naturalization was tantamount to betrayal of his homeland. This status was especially to be avoided, since they intended to return. Their attendance at citizenship training programs was motivated by the desire to acquire knowledge of their adopted land and to achieve greater facility in English for improving their job opportunities. It was not until after the 1930s, with the erosion of Hellenic sentiment, that they began acquiring American citizenship.

By the mid-1930s the Greek community became alarmed over the fact that its educational arrangements were not reaching Greek youth in the high schools. A city-wide educational association was formed to deal with the matter. The result was the formulation of a petition presented to the Chicago Board of Education requesting that the teaching of Greek be placed in the public high schools where requested by Greek parents. The board responded affirmatively, and in the fall of 1936, Greek instruction was inaugurated at Austin High School, followed later in other city high schools. The program lasted until the early 1960s, when it was abolished because of the lack of enrollment brought about by the growing indifference of parents and acculturation. Its final demise was decreed by the superintendent in order to put an end to the misuse of permissive transferring of students from changing neighborhoods--permissive transfer being one of the features of the program.

More recently, statistics show that the second largest ethnic group in the Chicago public schools whose first language is other than English is the Greeks, a result of postwar Greek immigration. Most of these children along with a larger number of native-born Greek children who are knowledgeable in English, attend schools in the Ravenswood area and other North Side communities where a new Greektown has emerged. Unlike the situation that prevailed in the early days of the present century, today there is a formal policy existing on the part of the Chicago Board of Education for facilitating the educational adjustment of non-English speaking students.

The appearance of a new professional organization of educators of Greek descent in Chicago--the Hellenic Council on Education--is symptomatic of the current ethnicity movement taking place in the United States. Deliberate attempts were undertaken by the organization to accommodate these students by the assignment of Greek-speaking administrators and teaching personnel to schools with large Greek enrollment and the implementation of a Greek ethnic studies program along with the successful promulgation of a bilingual-bicultural Greek program in two public schools. The latter, however, generated a controversy in a segment of the Greek community. These opportunities have been made possible through the cooperation of the Chicago Board of Education with the formal Greek community as represented by the Hellenic Council on Education, which is concerned with educational matters pertaining to the Greek community of Chicago.

The establishment of this new voluntary association of Greek educators represents a new commitment on the part of second and third generation educators of Greek ancestry to the successful adjustment of recently arrived immigrant children in the city's public schools and to the perpetuation and survival of the Greek identity and way of life in the cultural pluralistic society which is America. The next chapter discusses the ways in which the Greek community responded to ethnic needs by the establishment of its own educational institutions.

CHAPTER IV

GREEK RESPONSE TO EDUCATIONAL NEEDS

Early Attempts to Promote Greek Education

The historical content of American education is the story of an immigrant people facing complex adjustments in a new land. In building schools and teaching their young they had to decide on the role of the federal government, the relations between church and school, the nature of the curriculum, the governance of schools, and the groups who would receive schooling. The Greek immigrants to Chicago, though latecomers to the American scene, are part of this historical framework of responding to educational concerns for one's ethnic group.

As shown earlier in the study, the Greeks attempted to graft the social and cultural life of their homeland on a new environment through their family and community life. Above all was the concern for the perpetuation of the Greek language that "gave light to the world." They perceived this concern as a mission to preserve the cultural heritage of their forefathers. The immigrant parent faced an ambivalent struggle of trying to learn English and at the same time attempting to instill in his offspring an appreciation for the Greek language and heritage. His fears were accentuated by harassment by critics who reminded him of his obligation to Americanize and forget his past.

In order to accommodate their needs, the koinotis, or organized church community, accepted the responsibility of offering instruction in the Greek language. Often the parish priest served as the first teacher. Although the first Greek community in Chicago organized in 1892, it was not until 1908 that the first communal day school appeared. The delay apparently was due to agitation over the type of school to establish, the paucity of families, and the inability of persons to cooperate collectively toward a similar goal.

The first community, the Annunciation Church, was in existence from 1892 to 1897, but did not give serious attention to the formation of a school, because the members were non-family men and the parish had no permanent

230

structure. The concern for organizing a communal school appeared in 1897, with the establishment of the Holy Trinity Church in the Greek Delta.[1] From the available community records it cannot be determined whether or not any school existed between 1897 and 1902. A general assembly held by the Holy Trinity koinotis on 27 July 1902 indicated that one of their aims was the erection of a communal school and hospital. The community already had acquired two cemetery sections at Elmwood and Rosehill cemeteries. At the subsequent meeting on 14 December 1902 a fund-raising committee was appointed to embark on the collection of monies for the school and hospital.

After the election of the energetic physician, Gregory A. Papailiou, to the presidency of the koinotis (community) early in 1904, a concerted drive took place to provide for the educational needs of the parish. A mass meeting of community members held in May 1904 discussed the purchase of property to build a larger church and to accommodate a school in order to educate the "many children of the community in the paternal faith and proper Hellenic upbringing."[2]

Realization of this building project was delayed by a dispute over the priest, the Reverend Nectarius Maurokordatos, who was dismissed by the symboulion (board of trustees) with general assembly approval. This dismissal action was not supported unanimously, and a dissident group led by a parish trustee, Demetrios Manousopoulos, brought suit to circuit court in order to retain the priest.[3] The suit was won, but the priest in the meantime had been reassigned to a parish in Berlin, Germany. Hence, the Holy Synod of Greece dispatched a new priest, the Reverend Cyril Georgiadis, in 1903, and by September 1904 he, too, was recalled by the Holy Synod at the request of the president, Gregory Papailiou, and the symboulion.

With the dismissal of a second clergyman in a short period of time the community schism solidified into two divisions. The one faction insisted that the existing board of trustees be replaced with new members.[4] This dis-

---

[1] Forty Years of Greek Life, p. 48.

[2] Greek Star (Chicago), 13 May 1904.

[3] Supra 117. See also Greek Star (Chicago), 9 September 1904, 2 December 1904, and 31 March 1905 for a full coverage of the controversy.

[4] Chicago Chronicle, 27 December 1903.

sident group finally withdrew from Holy Trinity and organized the Mutual Benevolent Society of Family Men. They formed another koinotis, Saint Nicholas Church, just south of the Loop on State Street, with John Stefanos as president of the symboulion and the dismissed priest, Father Georgiadis, as pastor.[1] They organized the first communal school for Greek immigrants of Chicago in rented quarters at Johnson (Peoria) Street in the Greek Delta. A Greek newspaper announced that the hours of instruction were from 10:00 A.M. to 12:00 M, 2:00 to 3:00 P.M., 4:00 to 5:00 P.M., and 7:00 to 9:00 P.M. daily.[2] Nothing is known about the actual operation of the school or the size of enrollment. The parish and school venture was shortlived.[3]

Formation of the School of Hellenism

The following year another voluntary group, the Society of Family Men, announced the opening of a day school with boarding facilities.[4] It is not clear whether this new organization was comprised of members of the Mutual Benevolent Society of Family Men who had parted from Holy Trinity in 1903. It is likely that with the collapse of the Saint Nicholas parish these members returned to Holy Trinity to persist in their mission of establishing a school. Disagreements emerged over the structure of school curriculum. Many wanted the familiar rural type grade school they had in Greece; others preferred Americanization programs; still others, especially the professionals who controlled the parish, wanted a Greek gymnasium, despite the fact that most immigrants lacked formal schooling.

Nonetheless, a private day boarding school was opened in rented quarters located on the southern "shores of Lake Michigan" at 3611 Lake Avenue and called the "Hellenic Educational Institute of Chicago Hellenism."[5]

---

[1] Forty Years of Greek Life, pp. 52-53; Greek Star (Chicago), 8 March 1904.

[2] Greek Star (Chicago), 9 December 1904.

[3] Forty Years of Greek Life, p. 53.

[4] Greek Star (Chicago), 1 December 1905.

[5] Greek Star (Chicago), 19 January 1906.

The school opened its doors on 19 January 1906 with several teachers and with Spyridon Kotakis as principal. He also was a publisher and lawyer and one of the most erudite Greek immigrants in the city.[1] A twelve-man board governed the school. Attending the official opening ceremonies on 28 January 1906 were the Greek consul of Chicago and the editor of the Greek Star. Boarding school tuition was twelve dollars per month. Commuting pupils paid three dollars per month.[2]

The local Greek newspaper promoted the fact that Chicago's Greeks not only founded the first organized Greek community in the United States, but also the first Greek school. Peter Lambros, editor of the Greek Star, spoke of the school as being "the organ that will save our language, and the means by which Greek letters will be taught along with our glorious history." Accordingly, the "Greek school will train children to be Greeks so that they will not be digested in the vastness of America."[3] The school principal mentioned the church and school as being "the two pillars which support our national aspirations . . . and they must become our two anchors if we are to maintain our ethnicity in America and remain Greek and Christian Orthodox . . . we must depend on the church and school."[4]

Much editorializing took place in the Greek press concerning the importance of the church and school in perpetuating the ethnic heritage in America. One such editorial pointed out that even if the Greek immigrants did not intend to return to their homeland, it was essential that they remain Greeks. Furthermore, it was important for those who remained in the United States to have ethnic institutions such as schools, voluntary societies, churches, newspapers, and other similar undertakings established on a larger scale in order to combat the "fanatical efforts of Protestant missionaries" to alienate the Greek from his ancestral patrimony.[5]

----

[1]Greek Star (Chicago), 26 January 1906. A picture of the school is included with the article.

[2]Ibid.

[3]Greek Star (Chicago), 9 February 1906.

[4]Greek Star (Chicago), 16 February 1906.

[5]Greek Star (Chicago), 15 June 1906.

Persuasive oratory and editorials, however, were not sufficient to sustain the first Greek school in Chicago for long. This heralded project collapsed; the Greek newspapers were silent on the reason for the demise. In any event, these efforts gave impetus to the eventual opening of a permanent Greek School in 1908.

Peoples School

Another schooling venture, the Peoples School, was formed in 1907 to provide "certain necessary general and practical subjects of value" to young men with little formal education.[1] Among the intellectual leaders who organized the program was the Reverend Leon Pegeas, who had taught at the Peoples School in Athens. Instruction was held in a free-rent room at Hull House with free tuition. The founders considered the possibility of converting the program to a gymnasium (secondary school), but the lack of basic academic skills among Greek immigrants precluded such a development.

The classes met twice a week--Sunday at 3:00 P.M. and Wednesday at 8:00 P.M. The curriculum consisted of religion, history of the Greek Revolution of 1821, Greek, English, health, rights of citizens and soldiers, and commercial business subjects. Additional courses added later were mathematics, music, geography, cosmography, practical medicine, ancient and medieval Greek history, and political economy.[2] According to testimony, the school operated for several years and reached large numbers of young Greek immigrants.[3]

Phoenix Music School

A surprising development took place in 1906 with the organization of a music school by Greek immigrants interested in a philharmonic orchestra. It was preceded by a voluntary association known as the Phoenix Society, founded by George Gramatikakis, who had performed in European orchestras.

---

[1] Greek Star (Chicago), 25 October 1907.

[2] Ibid.

[3] Interview with James Gallanis, Evanston, Ill., 22 June 1968.

Classes were held in rented quarters in the Greek Delta and were financially subsidized by business and professional men in the community. Shortly thereafter, a Greek Philharmonic Orchestra emerged, and an unknown Italian instructor was replaced in 1907, with Spiro Becatoros, a Greek musician from New York. He "taught music to large numbers of young Greek boys and girls in the community and the program became the foundation of musical talent that developed in the Greek community."[1] Concerts were performed at major Greek religious and social events as well as in the broader American community. The musical group did not long survive. Apparently, the average Greek immigrant did not have enough education to appreciate his homeland's musical literature. He was probably too busy earning a living to be concerned with aesthetic ideals. As contributions dwindled, the music school ceased to function by 1909.

Education at Hull House

Hull House became the educational center for guidance, fellowship, and adjustment of the many Greek immigrants who lived in the Greek Delta. All kinds of helpful services were available--from finding employment to tracing lost immigrant girls. So important was the work of the social workers, especially of Jane Addams, that the young immigrants looked upon Miss Addams as their "mother." When she died, the Greek community mourned; the Greek-owned businesses were closed on the day of her funeral. She was eulogized as the "saint of Halsted Street."[2]

As noted earlier, Hull House sponsored a large and successful Americanization program for these immigrants, and housed several private educational enterprises such as the Peoples School. One of the most effective endeavors was the Greek Educational Association, which was chartered by the State of Illinois on 9 February 1909. A group of young men organized the association in order to provide for the educational, spiritual, and physical development of young Greek immigrants. In Greek the organization became

---

[1] Forty Years of Greek Life, pp. 61-62.

[2] Orthodox Observer, 1 (9 June 1935): 5; Theodore N. Constant, "Greek-American Colonies, Churches, and Schools in the United States," Athene 12 (Spring 1951): 34.

known as the "Hellenic League for the Molding of Young Men" and had hundreds of active members.[1] They sponsored scholarships and athletic activities along with military drill in which young men met regularly at the Hull
House gym for strenuous workouts under the direction of former Greek army
officers.

> It was in connection with a large association of Greek lads that
> Hull House finally lifted its long restriction against military drill. If
> athletic contests are the residuum of warfare first waged against the
> conqueror without and then against the tyrants within the State, the
> modern Greek youth is still in the first stage so far as his inherited
> attitude against the Turk is concerned. Each lad believes that at any
> moment he may be called home to fight this long-time enemy of Greece.
> With such a genuine motive at hand, it seemed mere affection [sic] to
> deny the use of our boys' club building and gymnasium for organized
> drill, although happily it forms but a small part of the activities of the
> Greek Educational Association.[2]

With reference to the athletic program, Jane Addams relates:

> The Greek immigrants form large classes and are eager to reproduce the
> remnants of old methods of wrestling, and other bits of classic lore
> which they still possess, and when one of the Greeks won a medal in a
> wrestling match which represented the championship of the entire city,
> it was quite impossible that he should present it to the Hull House trophy
> chest without a classic phrase which he recited most gravely and charm-
> ingly.[3]

When Theodore Roosevelt visited Hull House in 1911 he was greeted
by young Greek men in full-dress uniform who escorted him through the
premises. The following day a Chicago newspaper described the event and
quoted Roosevelt as saying he "came to Hull House not to teach, but to
learn."[4]

With the approaching Balkan wars, a quasi-military group--the Greek
Volunteers of America--was organized by the Greek Educational Association.
Larger quarters were procured for military preparedness, and in 1912, five
thousand Chicago Greek immigrants volunteered to help Greece "liberate her

---

[1]Forty Years of Greek Life, pp. 23-24.

[2]Addams, Twenty Years, p. 305.

[3]Ibid., pp. 304-5.

[4]Chicago Tribune, 21 and 22 February 1911.

subjugated sons and daughters in Macedonia, Epirus and Thrace."[1] The
first contingent of three hundred men embarked to war, after attending religious ceremonies at Holy Trinity Church, and with an accompaniment of
Greek organizations, band and unfurling banners, departed from Union Sta-
tion.[2] Another three thousand Greek immigrants left later to participate in
the Balkan wars; many remained in Greece, some returned to America with
wives.[3]

The military phase of the Greek Educational Association was only
one aspect of its active program. The gymnastic program was well attended
nightly because the young men, bereft of families, found it friendly and educational. Many became amateur and professional fighters, winning regional
and national championships.[4] Others were persuaded to attend the craft
shops of Hull House, where useful trades became their life's work.[5] And
for many, the efforts of the association served as a catalyst to enter the professions and broader American society.[6]

Numerous patriotic programs associated with the ancestral homeland
were sponsored by the Greek Educational Association, including the annual
Greek Independence Day celebration on 25 March. Another event commemo-
rating Greece's one year participation in World War I was held at the Black-
stone Hotel Theatre, with Samuel Insull, the utility magnate, as chairman of
the evening on 27 June 1918. Celebration of patriotic events have been an
integral part of the Greek community ritual and when the association ceased
to function in the 1920s, the Greek churches assumed the sponsorship of the
annual Greek Independence Day celebration. From the 1930s to the 1950s,

---

[1] Interview with Aristotle Collias, an original member of the group,
24 July 1969.

[2] Chicago Tribune, 10 October 1912, had pictures of event.

[3] Chicago Tribune, 27 September 1913. It is estimated that 42,000
Greek immigrants returned to Greece to fight in the Balkan wars; see Saloutos,
Greeks in the United States, p. 114.

[4] Hull House Yearbook, 1 January 1913, p. 23, 26-27; and 1 January
1927, pp. 9-10.

[5] Interview with Bessie Spirides, Chicago, 18 July 1968.

[6] Interviews with S. N. Soter, Chicago, 12 October 1967, and Ellie
Michalaros, Chicago, 28 November 1967.

elaborate festivities were held at Chicago's Civic Opera House or Medinah Temple. In the 1960s, citywide committees comprised of members from churches, schools, and voluntary associations sponsored the annual Greek Independence Day parade on State Street.

It seems that the association's activities were poorly attended in the 1920s at Hull House. By that time, the bulk of Greek immigrants had married and had acclimated to city life. Nonetheless, the organization played an important role in the educational adjustment of the Greek immigrants in their formative years. Such fellowship counteracted loneliness; skills were learned in order to earn a livelihood; leisure time activities made existence more meaningful, and sharing with those similar in customs and traditions made adaptation and adjustment acceptable.

The Greek immigrants also turned to the Immigrants' Protective League that had offices in Hull House. As a social service agency, it rendered extensive services in facilitating the adjustment of Greek immigrants, including problems such as broken family ties and the red tape intricacies of the non-quota immigration system in the 1920s.[1] Another institution used by the Greeks for assistance was Chicago Commons, located in the Milwaukee and Grand Avenue district and founded by the late Graham Taylor.

Educational Organizations for Greek Women

Despite the Greek tradition of restricting women to the home, one of the first clubs for Greek women in America was organized at Hull House. Some men were induced by Jane Addams to permit their wives to attend gatherings where problems affecting the home and family were discussed. In 1909, a club was organized under the leadership of Miss Neukon, a Hull House resident, with Miss Addams as honorary president. Elected officers were wives of the Greek community's professional men. The group, Philoptochos Society of Greek Women (Friends of the Poor), aimed to provide charity for indigents. Their twice-monthly meetings also involved lessons in English, Americanization, and "European dances."[2] This club became the forerunner of the numerous ladies societies that evolved in later years.

---

[1] The Immigrants' Protective League in 1930, (Chicago), p. 21.

[2] Interview with Voula Javaras, Chicago, 21 March 1970.

One of the most widespread of these latter societies evolved into the Greek Orthodox Ladies Philoptochos Society which was organized in 1924, as part of a national association of Greek women under the aegis of the Greek Orthodox archdiocese. Ostensibly organized for charitable purposes, it espoused educational programs aimed at elevating the educational level of its members and fostered Americanization programs. By the mid-1930s, chapters were established in most Chicago Greek parishes, where they became important agencies in the financial support of Greek parochial schools and other formal educational programs.[1]

Early in the 1920s, unmarried Greek women met at Socrates School to form a cultural society for the promotion of the arts. Despite opposition from conservatives, the Philomusae represented the first attempt of young Greek women to free themselves from male dominance. They succeeded in sponsoring cultural and musical productions in Greek until just prior to World War II, when they began to have programs in the English language. Today the group is known as the Young Ladies' Hellenic Philomusical Society of Chicago and is comprised of third and fourth generation women of Greek ancestry. Their sponsored programs are in English.

A similar organization for unmarried women was founded in 1936, under the name of "Young Ladies Hellenic Society NEA GENEA" for the purpose of perpetuating their Greek cultural legacy. The society, in addition to performing its avowed purpose, continues to support many educational endeavors to promote Greek culture--formally and informally--and financially supports the work of the Greek communal schools.[2]

Other Educational Ventures

Indicative of the rising number of immigrant Greek women graduating from college was the establishment in 1931, of the Greek Women's University Club. While the number was quite small compared to the total female Greek population of Chicago, it was deemed important enough to organize a special unit catering to this group. The club quickly embarked upon a formal program

---

[1] Interview with Stella Petrakis, Chicago, 10 October 1967.

[2] Interview with Demetra Tripodis, Chicago, 2 July 1970.

of promoting higher education among Greek women by scholarship programs and other activity. It, too, concerned itself with the financial support of the city's Greek schools, and announced a long-term drive to build a Greek cultural center in Chicago.[1]

The Knights of Saint Constantine the Great, founded in 1927, professed to preserve and protect the tenets of Greek Orthodoxy. Several schools for religious instruction emerged, but they soon became abortive.[2] Their failure possibly was due to opposition from the Greek church, which claimed jurisdiction over religious education of its communicants.

Another venture, the Orthodox Christian Education Society, proved to be more promising. It was founded in 1930 by a lay religious brotherhood concerned with the religious education of the younger generation.[3] The society also was interested in translating and promoting the writings of Apostolos Makrakis, an outstanding but controversial philosopher-theologian of Greece during the latter part of the nineteenth century. His works were condemned by the Church of Greece.[4]

A printing press was established, and the Makrakis works were translated and distributed to Orthodox faithful and institutions of higher education throughout the country. In addition, the society sponsored several Greek schools which met weekly after public school under the banner of Saint Paul from 1930 to 1948. A prescribed program devised by Makrakis was followed for the study of Greek and religion. Although the church did not sanction these schools, it was there that many second generation Greeks received basic Greek instruction and absorbed Makrakis' influence in religious catechism.[5] Due to small attendance in the late 1940s, the schools closed, but

---

[1] Interview with Theano Rexinis, Chicago, 23 July 1970.

[2] Atlantis (New York), 2 September 1927.

[3] Interview with Constantine Andronis, Chicago, 26 October 1967, last surviving member of the original founders of the society.

[4] See Menas Charitou, Historia tou megalou didaskalou tou Hellenikou geneous kai tis Orthodoxias Apostolou Makrakis [History of the great teacher of the Greek nation and of Orthodoxy, Apostolos Makrakis] 2nd ed. (Chicago: Orthodox Christian Educational Society, 1964), and Constantine Andronis ed. Apostolos Makrakis: An Evaluation of Half a Century (Chicago: Orthodox Christian Educational Society, 1966).

[5] Interview, Nicholas Ellis et. al., Chicago, 29 July 1970.

the society continues today to print religious tracts.

Development of Communal Day Schools

Socrates School

The Holy Trinity community proceeded in earnest to establish a permanent communal day school following the abortive school formed by the dissident Saint Nicholas parish. Two capable priests, Leon Pegeas and Ambrose Mandilaris, arrived on 23 September 1904 from Greece and immediately attempted to heal the parish wounds.[1] Property for the erection of church and school was purchased on 19 March 1906 for forty thousand dollars, of which six thousand dollars was paid the first year. The land, with two houses, was located on Sibley (May) Street between Vernon Park and Polk Streets, just west of the Greek Delta.[2]

Some members considered the cost exhorbitant, and charged the controversial president, Dr. Gregory Papailiou, with not having authority to have made such a purchase. A long court fight ensued, and the purchase of the land was upheld because authorization had been granted at a general assembly meeting of 18 September 1904.[3] Once more conflict arose over the court battle and the forced resignation of the symboulion (board of trustees) and two rival groups emerged--the Progressive and Reform parties. An election held on 20 December 1906 placed the Reform Party in power and named Demetrios Manousopoulos president of the community.

The Greek press hailed the election and urged peace and progress toward the establishment of a school, since much time had been lost due to the political controversies.[4] The press campaigned for the school and emphasized that fears over finances or qualified teachers were not justified. If need be, a private home could be used as the school, and the priests could serve

---

[1] Canoutas, p. 188.

[2] Forty Years of Greek Life, p. 61.

[3] Ibid.

[4] Greek Star (Chicago), 30 December 1906.

as teachers, since they were "well-qualified and besides it was their duty to do so."[1]

Finally, the first permanent Greek day school in America opened on 4 May 1908 and held classes in the two old houses located on the purchased property. There were thirty students, and the first teacher was George Arvanitis, a certified elementary school teacher from Greece.[2] The following month, 26 June 1908 inaugural ceremonies were held, with the Greek Minister to Washington, George Coromilas, present.[3] The school was named Socrates, after the famous ancient Greek philosopher, as was the usual Greek custom. At the outset, there were three primary grades and, initially, no tuition was charged. By 1910, when the Reverend Cyril Georgiadis had assumed principalship of the school, there were over one hundred pupils enrolled in four elementary classes and one Hellenic, or intermediate class.[4] That year it is estimated that about two hundred Greek children were attending the two established full-time day schools--Socrates and Koraes. There were four teachers on the staff by 1916, when the community embarked on a fund-raising drive for larger quarters. The campaign was so successful that within a year, the two old houses were demolished and a new school building was erected at a cost of thirty thousand dollars.

Despite the fact that Socrates School was an organized project of the formal Greek community, it apparently enjoyed complete autonomy. According to the written bylaws of Holy Trinity Church, dated 24 November 1910, article fifty-five specified that the communal school was to have its own board of directors and, as a separate legal entity, was to be responsible for its own

---

[1] Greek Star (Chicago), 22 November 1907. Because of the delay, a group of parents organized the "Peoples School" at Hull House in 1907, as mentioned earlier in this study.

[2] When the Dillingham Commission made its investigation in Chicago in 1908, it found (as indicated in chapter 4), 193 Greek children (and five Turkish children) enrolled in the public schools of Chicago. Also, it found that there were 34 Greek children attending a parochial school (Abstract of Report on Children of Immigrants in School, pp. 66-67). These children are presumably those enrolled at Socrates School.

[3] Greek Star (Chicago), 3 July 1908.

[4] Forty Years of Greek Life, p. 69.

financial affairs.[1] This arrangement seems to have prevailed for several years, although there was always a close connection between the board of trustees of the church and the board of directors of the school. Oftentimes, the same men sat on both boards, and sometimes the parish pastor would serve as chairman of the school board. The school board had a written constitution and policy sheet consisting of forty-nine articles which became operative on 2 October 1917 after the new school building had been completed. In grandiloquent terms, it called for the eventual establishment of a nursery and secondary school--equivalent to a Greek gymnasium; an academy, a college and university, and even a vocational school with branches in Chicago and other parts of Illinois.[2]

Obviously, these long-range objectives were based upon the presumption that the board of directors for the school would be responsible for the total educational program of Chicago's Greek community. But as additional Greek parishes or communities were organized independently of Holy Trinity, each assumed responsibility over its own educational concerns and made its own educational arrangements. This predicament negated the development of a unified educational program among the Greek immigrants and gave rise to the congregational nature of educational arrangements. Realizing that the independent educational board did not enjoy city-wide support, the Holy Trinity symboulion on 23 April 1923 revoked the independent status that had been provided for Socrates School and its board and made it a property of the parish to be governed by a school board to be elected by parish members.[3] Popular control of the school was further diminished by a revision of the parish bylaws pertaining to the school which decreed on 30 June 1933 that the governance of the school was to be vested in the hands of a three-member board appointed by the parish board of trustees, or symboulion.[4]

---

[1] The original 1910 constitution and bylaws are preserved in the archives of Holy Trinity Church.

[2] A copy of this constitution is preserved in the Holy Trinity Church archives.

[3] Forty Years of Greek Life, p. 72.

[4] Ibid.

Up to 1917, the language of instruction at Socrates School was Greek; English was not part of the curriculum. In that year, the school board expressed concern over the fact that Greek children were matriculating at the school without receiving any formal instruction in English for pursuing higher studies at public schools. This concern apparently originated with parents who were beginning to send their children to public schools after their term at Socrates only to find that they were inadequately prepared for studies in English.[1] Consequently, in the fall of 1917, on the occasion of the opening of the new school building, English instruction was added and three English-speaking teachers were added to the staff.[2] But English never became the primary language of instruction; it was used only during the time when formal English was taught.

All other standard subjects, even arithmetic, were taught in Greek. The school was patterned after the typical school in Greece, consisting of six grades--four comprising the primary or elementary grades and the upper two comprising the "Hellenic," or middle, school. Upon graduation from the sixth or last grade, the students advanced to the seventh grade in Chicago public schools. This was more common for boys than for girls; the latter were usually kept home after finishing six years at Socrates School. This is why girls were taught special homemaking skills.[3]

The heavy emphasis on Greek as the primary language of instruction through the years was to be found only at Socrates School. Graduates of the school found themselves "saturated" with Greek, and the effect remained noticeable many years after the students had left school. Graduates were bilingual, and often knew better Greek than English.[4] One graduate of the school, an architect, remarked: "To this day I do all of my mathematical

[1] Minutes of the Socrates School Board (Chicago), 20 March 1917 (in parish archives).

[2] Ibid., 8 September 1917.

[3] Interview with Maria Rifakes, former teacher at Socrates, Chicago, 7 November 1967.

[4] This is the testimony of a number of students of Socrates School who have been interviewed for this study.

calculations in Greek, for we learned how to do arithmetic in Greek, doing it in the Greek way."[1] Another, a municipal court judge, contends that as a result of his experience at Socrates School, "When I have a problem, I think it out in Greek, and then I make the translation into English; invariably, I do much of my thinking in Greek."[2] As a result of such training, several generations of American-born children of Greek descent received an intensive background in Greek. Socrates School became known for its Greek instruction, and attracted the attention of parents from all parts of the city, who sent their children there for the express purpose of learning the Greek language and cultural heritage.

This monolingual approach to ethnic education, with the almost exclusive use of Greek as the chief medium of instruction, remained a distinguishing feature of Socrates School. Down to the present time, despite objections on the part of some communicants, Greek has enjoyed special status. All subject matter, such as social studies, arithmetic, and science, continue to be taught in Greek.[3] In cases where children are deficient in their knowledge of Greek, special tutoring takes place in English, but only until they achieve proficiency in basic Greek. Then they are placed in regular classes with Greek instruction. The study of English remains basically another course subject, reinforced, of course, by the broader milieu from which pupils come. This condition prevails perhaps due to the fact that the school clientele consists of children of recent immigrants. The community of Holy Trinity has become a receiving center for postwar immigrants from Greece, and not unlike earlier immigrants of the turn of the century, they retain an active concern for the promulgation of Greek among their offspring.

Because of the belief that all school age children should be in attendance in the communal day school, Holy Trinity did not establish an afternoon school until 1967, and then only to accommodate the large number of Greek children who could not attend the day school due to limited space. Similarly, because of the prevailing belief that religion is part of the day school's regu-

---

[1] Interview with Chris G. Kalogeras, Chicago, 4 December 1967.

[2] Interview with Judge James Geroulis, Chicago, 25 January 1968.

[3] Interview with Elias K. Polites, principal of Socrates School, Chicago, 20 August 1973.

lar curriculum, there was no need felt to establish a Sunday school such as other Chicago Greek communities had. Religious studies were an integral part of a child's schooling in the parish school. It was not until much later, after the school had left the Greek Delta for a new location, that a Sunday school was organized.

In 1963, the original church and school were razed, along with neighboring Hull House, to make way for the new University of Illinois Circle campus. The Greektown of seventy years came to a virtual end. Actually, by this time most Greek residents had long since left the area. Business establishments catering to the needs of the Greek population were all that remained. Chicago's first _koinotis_, Holy Trinity Church, and first Greek school, Socrates, moved to the northwest side of the city and built a new community complex at 6400 West Diversey Avenue. The community has become, once again, a new mecca for Greek newcomers as well as for native Greek residents. It is now in the process of erecting a new million-dollar school building.

Unfortunately, enrollment statistics for this first Greek day school of Chicago are incomplete. No enrollment figures for the first ten years (1907-17) or for the period 1924-32 are available. According to published reports, the estimated student body for the latter period ranged from a low of 150 to a high of approximately 650 pupils in the 1928-29 term when the school reached its peak enrollment.[1] It was during this period that a monthly school paper was published by the pupils (in Greek), with a city-wide distribution. A variety of activities were sponsored which placed the school in the limelight of the Greek community.

Enrollment dropped during the depression years due perhaps, in part, to the instituting of tuition, thus creating a financial hardship for parents. Another contributing factor was the opening of additional Greek schools in the city, along with the normal attrition to public schools. During this time, pupil enrollment averaged 200 per year, with approximately forty pupils being graduated each year.[2] Interestingly, during the entire span of the school's history, female enrollment always surpassed that of male, reflecting perhaps

---

[1] _Forty Years of Greek Life_, p. 73.

[2] Ibid.

the willingness of parents to send their daughters to the "safety" of the Greek school rather than expose them to the "dangers" of public school.[1] Following World War II, and with the influx of new immigrant Greeks into the area, enrollment increased so that it averaged from 250 to 300 pupils during the 1950s and 1960s.[2]

The student body consisted of not only the newly-arrived immigrant Greek children, but also native-born children of the second and third generations. By the mid-1960s, however, the former surpassed the latter. Table 40 shows the yearly enrollment for this postwar period. The low figures for the 1962-65 period reflect the unstable conditions brought about by the relocation of the school. From 1963 to 1965, the school was located temporarily in quar-

TABLE 40

PUPIL ENROLLMENT AT SOCRATES SCHOOL
FOR PERIOD 1963-73

Year	Enrollment
1963	72
1964	79
1965	80
1966	87
1967	134
1968	176
1969	195
1970	237
1971	232
1972	238
1973	254

Average Annual Enrollment for Period
1963-73: 162

SOURCE: From school records supplied by the principal of Socrates School.

[1] Ibid.

[2] Interview with Elias K. Polites, principal of Socrates School, Chicago, 25 March 1968.

ters at the Holy Archangels-Saint Haralambos Church. From 1965 until the present, it has been housed in temporary quarters on the Diversey property.

As mentioned previously, an afternoon school was established for the first time in 1967 to accommodate the growing number of children who could not be housed in the day school due to the limited facilities of temporary quarters. Enrollment has averaged 200-225 pupils and has been growing steadily. In addition, a seventh grade was added to the day school and an eighth grade is contemplated. Once this takes place, Socrates will become a full-fledged elementary school of eight grades.

Koraes School

The second _koinotis_ to be organized in Chicago, Saints Constantine and Helen Church, also was the second community to have an all-day communal school, starting in the fall 1910. Earlier in this study it was mentioned that the first decade of this century found the Greek community as a battleground over the issues of priests, schools, building locations, and politics. The need to form another parish developed when Greek immigrants established businesses along Sixty-third Street in the Woodlawn area and found that distance made it difficult to be active at Holy Trinity. However, in order to avoid another community rift, the Association of the Greek Community of Chicago (Holy Trinity) urged a united community approach. It prevailed upon the Kosmiton Society--a voluntary group made up of immigrants from Kosma, Greece--to transfer title of its newly-purchased property at 6105 South Michigan Avenue--intended site of a new community--to the association. In turn, the association would build a church and school for Southsiders and eventually follow a similar program for Northsiders.[1] In such a plan, the association would have three churches and schools forming a united Greek community in Chicago. The idea never materialized.

A meeting on 9 February 1908 at Holy Trinity Church left the issue unresolved.[2] When the incumbent Reform Party was defeated in December 1908 it switched loyalties and supplied the needed leadership for an indepen-

---

[1] Canoutas, p. 189.

[2] _Saint Constantine Church, 1909-1959, Golden Anniversary Album_ (Chicago: Norman King Co., 1959), p. 52.

dent Southside Greek community. The group formally organized on 26 February 1909 with Theodore Koumountzis (Charles Cummings) as first president. He was a South Side ice cream manufacturer. The community was named in honor of the Roman emperor, Saint Constantine, founder of the Byzantine Empire, and his mother, Saint Helen.

Agreement was reached with Holy Trinity to transfer title of the Michigan Avenue property to the new parish, which opened its doors in October 1910 with an architectural structure designed to house the school on the first floor and the church on the second level. The school was a six-grade day school from the beginning and was named Adamantios Koraes after the intellectual father of the Greek Revolution of 1821. The principal, Mrs. Spyridoula Kotakis, was a trained teacher and the wife of the editor of the Greek language newspaper, Loxias.

Koraes School was patterned after the provincial primary schools of Greece, as was Socrates School, with the exception that English was taught from the very beginning as a foreign language. Twelve years later, however, parents realized the urgency to restructure the curriculum in order to provide for more English instruction. Accordingly, in 1922, and operative until the mid-1930s, equal time was distributed between Greek and English studies, thus making Koraes School the first Greek bilingual school in Chicago.[1] In 1936 when the seventh and eighth grades were added, the instructional program was divided into two departments that functioned daily with a schedule having English instruction from 9:00 A.M. to 12:00 M, lunch on premises, and Greek instruction from 1:00 to 3:00 P.M. Occasionally these hours were reversed to adapt to the religious or holiday calendar of the Greek community. The adoption of additional instruction in English was necessitated by the fact that the school had become accredited by the Chicago Board of Education, whose graduates would be admitted to public high school without examination.

Unlike the Roman Catholic parochial schools, religion did not permeate the total curriculum, nor were special textbooks used for instruction. Originally, religion was taught as part of the Greek curriculum in Greek by Greek teachers. Later, religion was taught by the priest in catechism for one period a week in the intermediate and upper grades, both in Greek and English.

---

[1] Koraes School Board Minutes (Chicago), 25 July 1922 (church archives).

It also was incorporated with Greek history for three half-hour periods taught by the Greek teachers. During the school year, the children participated in the sacraments of confession and corporate communion, church holidays, and traditions.

English department. The English portion of the curriculum was similar to that of the public schools, consisting of reading, writing, spelling, English, history, geography, and composition; the Greek studies were patterned after programs in Greece, consisting of reading, writing, Greek grammar, spelling, composition, Greek history, geography, and religion.[1] Strong emphasis was placed on language arts and arithmetic, moderate emphasis on social studies, and little on science. There was almost no opportunity for laboratory observation and experimentation because of limited facilities and time allotment. There was a void in areas of visual aids, counseling, and special education services, as well as any standardized testing. However, Koraes School boasted of a respectable library founded by an enterprising principal in 1922, and "composed of the best and chosen Greek and American books suitable for the pupils to read."[2]

Music instruction was limited to learning a few assembly songs without benefit of note reading, taught by the English teacher. Opportunities for dramatics occurred at the annual school festival and occasionally at such times as the birthdays of Washington and Lincoln, which were observed with patriotic skits and songs. A Christmas program also was generally performed.

Most of the teachers of English were not of Greek descent, since ethno-religious preference was not a criterion for selection. Generally, they had degrees from accredited colleges and universities; some were former Chicago public school teachers.[3] All subjects were taught in self-contained classrooms, since departmentalization did not exist.

During the Depression of the 1930s, for the first time kindergarten and woodshop classes were established and financed by the WPA. No tuition

---

[1] Yearbook of the Saint Constantine Church and Koraes School (Chicago, n.p., 1936), p. 97.

[2] Ibid., p. 96.

[3] Ibid.

was charged. Both programs were well-attended, and taught by teachers from within the Greek community. These course additions to the school program were made possible by Spyros Vorres, a WPA organizer, who, as an immigrant boy had studied trades at Hull House and later taught engineering at the Chicago Technical College.[1]

Greek department. With minor deletions, the Greek department was closely patterned after the six grades of Greece, with two additional grades added in 1937. A core curriculum included the Greek language, with particular emphasis on grammar and syntax, as well as conversational skills, Greek classical and modern literature, ancient, Byzantine and modern Greek history, geography of modern Greece, church history, and catechism. The pupils in seventh and eighth grades received instruction in advanced Greek equivalent to the first two years of the Greek gymnasium.

Curriculum guidelines were nonexistent until the education office of the Greek archdiocese was formed in 1931. Often these Greek teachers, graduates of normal schools or gymnasia, had no knowledge of the English language or did not allow conversation in English during the time of Greek instruction; therefore, the pupils had to use the Greek language in order to communicate with the teacher. Of course, discipline problems also arose, but were "handled" with the application of corporal punishment. The teaching techniques used offered little opportunity for shared discussions because of the use of rote memorization and didactic methods.

The pupils received limited instruction in music which usually included the singing of church hymns, patriotic songs, and Greek folk songs often taught by the church cantor, as well as the teachers. Yet, there was an extensive program in elocution and dramatics for all classes. Twice during the school year, at the celebration of Greek Independence Day on 25 March and at the school festival held on graduation or "examination" day at the end of the school year, every pupil participated in a program of singing, reciting poetry, and presentation of plays. Lower grades presented comedy or patriotic skits on the "glory of Greece," while the graduating class performed one of the ancient Greek tragedies. The latter was done with a great

---

[1] Interview with Bessie Spirides, former secretary at Saint Constantine Church (1928-54), Chicago, 18 July 1968.

deal of professionalism, and halls were rented and admission fees charged for these productions. Much time was devoted during the regular class hours for the preparation of these programs. Because of the Greek school tradition that children be "examined" on what they had learned during the school year, it was believed that these were good exercises for learning the Greek language and heritage. At the same time, they brought in needed revenue for the school.

In 1922, the total value of Saint Constantine parish, school, and three surrounding lots was estimated at $100,000.[1] Long-range plans called for the erection of a separate school building in the empty property lots.

Afternoon school. With the arrival of a new pastor, the Reverend Mark E. Petrakis, in 1923, an afternoon Greek school was established for those children who were unable to attend day school due to finances, distance, or other reasons. Classes were held three times a week—Mondays, Wednesdays, and Fridays—from four to six o'clock, following the regular school day. This program, introduced by the pastor, proved to be so popular that it surpassed the day school enrollment from 1929 through the 1950s (see tables 42, 43, and 44). In 1965 the afternoon school was discontinued due to a drastic enrollment drop and was replaced by a Saturday program that was more acceptable to parents. They found it easier to drive their children to school once instead of three times a week; also, the former schedule interfered with after-school activities, such as music lessons and neighborhood play.

Sunday school. One of the first Greek Sunday schools was established at Saint Constantine Church. Taught in Greek, the lower grades had Bible stories and the upper grades had catechism lessons. Incentives were given to youngsters in the form of religious coloring books and pre-colored Bible cards. The Sunday school teachers were the same Greek teachers of the communal day and afternoon schools. In the 1930s, enrollment reached 750 pupils and changes began to take place. The role of the Sunday schools in promoting ethnicity is described later in this chapter.

A fire in April 1926 destroyed the community structure, but the school

---

[1] "Proceedings of the General Assemblies of Saint Constantine Church (Chicago), 26 December 1911 to 25 July 1922," p. 43 (church archives).

continued to function in several rented neighborhood stores. The following year a new basilica-style building was erected on the same site with a school containing seven classrooms, a lunchroom, and an auditorium. In 1937, when the seventh and eighth grades were added to the day school, it received the first formal accreditation from the Chicago Board of Education.[1] Graduates no longer had to take examinations to be admitted into public high schools.

It was during this period that the day and afternoon parish schools, as well as the Sunday school, reached a high level of enrollment and a degree of efficacy in transmitting the cultural legacy. An alumnus of the parish communal educational system, speaking many years later at an educational conference, made the following observation of his experience:

> The Greek Orthodox parish in which I was reared had, since 1910, operated a bilingual day elementary school, whose graduates went straight into the Chicago public schools. For those parents whose children attended the "American" school, an afternoon Greek language school was available. I attended this school on Mondays, Wednesdays, and Fridays from 4:00 P.M. to 6:00 P.M. for six years. I graduated from this school. From native Greek-trained teachers I learned both katharevousa and demotiki types of Greek. The textbooks were imported school books from Greece. The curricular content was literary, historical, religious, and grammatical. From that experience in Greek language study and with a couple of courses in classical Greek . . . , I am now able to converse in modern demotic Greek, read a newspaper, write a letter with the aid of a grammar and dictionary, and read technical materials and Koine Greek with a dictionary. At the doctoral level, I passed a reading translation test in modern Greek. . . .
> I grew up in the shadow of the Greek Orthodox Church and its schools, the Greek language school, the Sunday school, the several youth groups of the church, and several public service Greek-speaking national groups. It is in this church environment that I still live, albeit in another city and state today.[2]

Despite such testimony, the Greek communal school, as typified by Koraes School, was not without its detractors within the Greek community. Much criticism emanated from the cultural conservatives who objected that

---

[1] Henry S. Crane, secretary of the Chicago Board of Examiners, Chicago Public Schools, to Rev. Mark E. Petrakis, 15 March 1938 (church archives).

[2] James Steve Counelis, "Ethnicity: Science, Being, and Educational Opportunity," paper presented at the Annual Meeting of the American Educational Research Association, New Orleans, 26 February 1973, pp. 8-9.

the school, because of its bilingual curriculum, was not emphasizing Greek studies enough; others, presumably assimilationists or absorptionists, complained that pupils were being shortchanged in their English studies and would find adjustment to American life difficult.[1] To these criticisms, the school officials retorted:

> . . . the day school operates under such arrangements [bilingual program], believing that it is fulfilling the purpose for its existence in transmitting the Greek as well as the American spirit, combined together, to the innocent souls of pupils.
> Perhaps, assuredly, [the school] is behind in this respect from the Greek schools of our fatherland, in that it does not develop perfect Greeks, . . . nor perfect Americans. It can proudly boast, however, that it does educate perfect Greek-Americans, worthy of their parents as Greeks and synchronized [adjusted] to their contemporary environment as Americans.[2]

The bilingual program in which Greek and English studies were arranged in two distinct curricular areas and taught by two separate departments--English teachers in the morning and Greek teachers in the afternoon--continued until the mid-1950s, when it was slightly modified. Because of parental pressure for more emphasis on English studies and formal religious instruction, the time allotment and emphasis was shifted. This shift was accomplished by transferring music, religious instruction, and physical education from the morning to the afternoon. This had the effect of increasing English instruction by almost three hours a week and reducing Greek instruction by approximately three hours a week.

The change was brought about by a variety of factors. The usually all-male and generally culturally conservative school board had been reorganized to include the election of parents from the community, including for the first time women, and representation from the school's PTA. This liberalization represented a departure from previous policy which required that only members of the symboulion (board of trustees) could be appointed to the school board. The departure was made possible by the election of several American-born individuals to the board of trustees and represented the emergence of native-born Greek-Americans on the governing councils of the Greek parishes.

---

[1] Interview with Constantine Glynos, former school principal, 1933-46, Oak Lawn, Ill., 10 December 1971.

[2] Yearbook of Saint Constantine Church and Koraes School, p. 98.

With the entry of American-born persons on these councils, concern began to be expressed about the curriculum of the communal school. The concern was reflected in remarks made by parents that the parish school concentrate more on English studies and less on Greek studies, as the child had to be equipped to compete in an American milieu. It was felt that the equal amount of time given to Greek studies was depriving the child of acquiring a comprehensive education to compete with his American counterpart in the public high school.[1] Others objected to the continued emphasis on Greek nationalism and requested that it be curtailed and that the universal aspects of Greek civilization "which are respected by the whole world" be emphasized instead.[2]

These concerns, of course, were indicative of the maturation of the American-born generation which viewed ethnic education from an acculturative point of view. While interested in maintaining the ethnic educational system of the community, it was, nevertheless, more concerned about providing for a better education in English and religious studies. This acculturative stance was reflected in the linguistic change that had taken place in the Greek home. A survey made by Koraes School in May 1955 on language spoken at home by pupils and their parents, revealed that only 22 percent spoke Greek or mostly Greek at home, while 33 percent spoke English or mostly English at home. Forty-five percent spoke Greek and English equally at home (see table 41). This varied from previous years when second generation children spoke Greek almost exclusively in the home. Despite the fact that nearly 70 percent of the student population in the survey was of the second or third generation, the survey reflected the extent of acculturation in the Greek home as represented by the Koraes School sample.

The school board, while agreeing with the need for increasing English studies and de-emphasizing of chauvinism, did not, however, look with favor upon the reduction of the time allotted to Greek studies. Instead, to compensate for the nearly three hours lost in the Greek curriculum by the addition of music, gym, and religion, it extended the school day by a half-

---

[1] Minutes of the Koraes School Board (Chicago), 16 February 1955.

[2] Ibid.

TABLE   41

BACKGROUND AND LANGUAGE USED BY PUPILS OF KORAES SCHOOL
MAY 1955

FACTORS	PERCENTAGE	
Language Usage		
Speak only Greek at home	04.5%	
Speak mostly Greek at home	17.5	(Greek = 22%)
Speak Greek and English equally at home	45.0	
Speak mostly English at home	24.0	
Speak only English at home	09.0	(English = 33%)
National Composition		
Both parents born in Greece	30.8	(one-third second generation)
One parent born in Greece	41.3	(mixed 2nd and 3rd generations)
Both parents born in the United States	27.9	(one-fourth third generation)
Pupils born in Greece	05.2	(postwar refugees)
Pupils born in the United States	94.8	

SOURCE: Archives of Koraes School.

hour. Consequently, the beginning of the school day was changed from
9:00 A.M. to 8:45 A.M. and from 3:00 to 3:15 P.M. The additional two-
and-a-half hours per week gained were added to the Greek department,
thus neutralizing the nearly three hours deduction in its time allotment
caused by the change mentioned previously.[1]

Thus, Koraes School has remained essentially a bilingual-bicultural
school, the only Greek communal day school in Chicago with such a pro-

---

[1]Minutes of the Koraes School Board (Chicago), 16 February 1955.

gram. While English studies are given high priority, so are religious studies. Both are treated as important areas in the training of the Greek-American child. The former is to equip the child for effective American citizenship and the latter is to provide him with fundamental tenets of religious values. In recent times, the study of Greek has been lowered in the priority scale of school objectives. While still valued for its ethnic importance, it is, nonetheless restricted to the learning of the language simply in its linguistic aspects without undue nationalistic overtones.

The Koraes School course of study, as illustrated on the following pages, reflects the bilingual-bicultural nature of the school. The morning hours are devoted to English studies in the areas of language arts, social studies, arithmetic, music, and physical education. These studies resemble those offered in public schools in the city. They constitute the "secular" portion of the Greek school curriculum. Unlike Roman Catholic parochial schools, religion does not permeate these courses. The afternoon hours are designated for study in religion, Greek language, and Greek history. They comprise the "sectarian" portion of the curriculum. The morning hours embrace the language of instruction in English; the afternoon hours are taught entirely in Greek, except religion, which is presented in both Greek and English.

In the first grades religious instruction focuses on simple personalized prayers in both languages; at the beginning of the third grade there are a progression of learnings which include stories from the Old and New Testaments; grades five through eight encompass the study of the history of the early Christian church, Orthodox catechism, development of the Eastern Orthodox church, and readings in the original Koine Greek of the Bible in the eighth grade.

Similarly, Greek instruction begins in the first grade in the demotic dialect and progresses until the sixth grade when a transition is made to the katharevousa, or puristic form. Hence, grades seven and eight include the reading of modern Greek literature in katharevousa. Beginning in grade three, students are introduced to Greek mythology, ancient Greek history, Byzantine era and the Greek Revolution of 1821, and modern Greek history after the revolution. A detailed description of the courses of study at the Koraes Day School follows.

"Syllabus for the study of Greek

"Grade I

A. Oral exercises: Simple conversation about the child's life; a child in his family; occupation of the parents; child's occupation at home; family events of interest; religious feast days; the child among his friends of the same age; the games they play; a child in school; size and other bodily characteristics of the children. Stories and fables. Practical distinction between a complete and an incomplete sentence on the occasion of an incomplete answer by a pupil; analysis of a sentence to words and then to syllables; analysis of syllables to letters and synthesis of letters to syllables; analysis of syllables to letters and synthesis of letters to syllables; persistent attention to the accent of the syllables and correct pronunciation of letters.

B. Reading and writing: Based on a primer; correct reading word by word; regular handwriting. Memorizing and reciting poems.

C. Spelling: Distinction and designation of accents; different ways of writing vowel sounds; spelling of words and sentences in the reader; distinction between comma, period, question mark; accent on omicron and epsilon and on the antepenult.

"Grade II

A. Reading: From a reader; correct reading by sentences; persistent attention to the proper accenting of a sentence. Memorizing and reciting poems.

B. Oral exercises: Analysis of the actions of a pupil throughout a working day or a holiday; analysis of the sentences used into smaller parts; for example, "I washed," "How did you do it? What first? Then second?" etc. A similar analysis of the impressions of a pupil about his family life; occupations of father, mother, grandfather, grandmother, elder and younger brothers and sisters. Teach the pupil to recite in an uninterrupted way the stories of his reader, fables, description of his town, etc.

C. Spelling exercises: Spelling and copying parts from the reader; writing on the chalkboard by heart or from dictation. Spelling and copying of active and passive verbs in the first person indicative; formation of the first person plural; remarks on the accent of verbs.

"Grade III

A. Reading: From reader; correct reading of longer sentences; attention to a natural accentuation of longer phrases. Memorizing and reciting poems.

B. Oral exercises: Analysis of the impressions of a pupil and of his personal observations. Free and continuous recitation of material from the reader.

C. Spelling: Copying of parts of the reader at home; correction at school. Spelling and writing of the material in the oral exercises.

Active and passive verbs in the first person present indicative; classification according to endings; formation of the present tense in all persons; future tense. The usual non-contracted nouns in three declensions; accentuation. Systematic development of the oral exercises.

"Grade IV

A. Reading: From reader; natural and logical reading; review of reader. Reciting poems.

B. Composition exercises: Narration and description concerning the pupil's life at home and in school. Description of simple events from his immediate observation.

C. Systematic teaching of grammar.

"Grade V

A. Reading: As in Grade IV.

B. Composition: Extension of methods in Grade IV.

C. Systematic teaching of grammar.

"Grade VI

A. Reading: As in Grade V.

B. Compositions: With greater frequency.

C. Systematic teaching of grammar with special emphasis on the forms of the "katharevousa," or "puristic," dialect.

"Grades VII and VIII

A. Reading: Books of Greek literature (first year gymnasium text); Prose and poetry of modern Greek literature from an approved collection. Reading and explanation of the simplest prose authors in ancient Greek.

B. Compositions: Memorizing; rhetoricals.

C. Review of the grammar. The most common of the ancient forms of grammar found in the texts; comparison with those of modern Greek. Etymology. Syntax of the simplest forms."

"Syllabus for the study of Greek history

"Grade III

Greek Mythology: Hercules and his labors; Theseus; Alcestis; the expedition of the Argonauts; the Trojan War and its consequences; the story of Odysseus.

"Grade IV

Ancient Greece: Greece before the Persian wars; Sparta, Lycurgus, Solon; Persian wars, Marathon, Thermopylae, Salamis; prosperity of Athens, Pericles, etc., the "Golden Age;" other important cities of Greece, Thebes, Corinth; Peloponnesian War; Epaminondas, Pelopidas; Macedonia, Philip, Chaeronea; Alexander the Great, his successors; Greece occupied by the Romans.

"Grade V

    Byzantine Greece: Greece under the Roman Empire; Christianity, Constantine the Great, religious dissensions; establishment of Constantinople, Hellenization of the Roman Empire in the East; the Greek language and the Christian faith; Justinian, Theodosius, Heraclius; siege of Constantinople by the Arabs; Iconoclasts; Mohammedanism, Mohammed, Arabs, Turks; Bulgarians and Slavs, conversion to Christianity, conversion of Russia; Crusades; the Nicean Empire; Turks against Byzantium, fall of Constantinople, Greece under the Ottoman yoke; the flight of Greek scholars to the West, beginning of the Renaissance in Western Europe.

"Grade VI

    Modern Greece--The Greek Revolution: Political conditions in Europe in the 15th century in relation to Greece (Venice, Russia, Austria); organization, Ecumenical Patriarchate, communal system, Phanariots; education, revolutionary movements; preparation for the Greek Revolution, the Friendly Society; Greek Revolution in detail; the liberation of the Greek Nation.

"Grades VII and VIII

    Modern Greece--to the Present: Review of the Greek Revolution; the organization of the Greek State; the Cretan insurrection against the Turks; the Greco-Turkish wars; the Balkan wars; World War I and the exchange of population between Greece and Turkey following the Asia Minor disaster; Greece in World War II, occupation by the Axis Powers, Liberation; Greece and the Truman Doctrine, defeat of the Communist menace; the Cyprus crisis; modern Greece in world affairs."

"Syllabus for the study of Religion

"Grade I

    Prayers at the beginning and end of school day; emphasis on saying prayers at meals, bedtime, and on rising each day; learning to pray for family members and friends; memorization of simple church prayers; poems and religious hymns from the reader; stories from the life of Christ taught orally by teacher.

"Grade II

    Additional prayers learned for mealtime and other events related to the church calendar; review of learnings from previous grade and stories about the Virgin Mary and Lazarus.

"Grade III

    More extensive prayers connected with the Old Testament teachings; stories from the Old Testament and the creation of the world and man; explanation of religious festivals; the study of geography related to the lands of the Old Testament.

"Grade IV

Greater details of stories in the New Testament, including the Virgin Mary, John the Baptist, the life of Jesus, parables and prayers in the New Testament; the study of geography related to Palestine.

"Grade V

The history of the early church and the life of early Christians; the Church Fathers and the Schism between East and West; the Protestant Reformation; the Orthodox Church under the Turks; the role of monasteries as guardians of national education and religion at the time of the Ottoman Empire; the Church in liberated Greece; other national churches under Eastern Orthodoxy; the Greek Orthodox Church in America; religious prayers, poems, and hymns for church worship; readings and explanations of the original Gospel concerning the life, miracles, and teachings of Jesus Christ.

"Grade VI

Catechism lessons on kinds of religious expressions of other denominations; the Nicene Creed; the Ten Commandments; the seven sacraments in the Orthodox Church; the Sermon on the Mount; the meaning of prayer.

"Grade VII

History of the Orthodox Church from the Great Schism of 1054 to the present time; further study of the New Testament in the original Greek; greater memorization of standard church prayers; the study of church hymns.

"Grade VIII

In depth study of the Greek Orthodox Archdiocese of North and South America and the Ecumenical Patriarchate at Constantinople; readings in the original Greek on the Acts and Epistles of the Apostles; doxology and the introduction to Christian Ethics." [1]

---

[1]

Syllabi of the Koraes School of Saint Constantine Church, 1962-63. Teachers in the Greek department, together with the parish priest and principal, met periodically to revise a course of study that would more effectively meet local needs. These syllabi were based on the curriculum guidelines provided by the department of education of the Greek Orthodox Archdiocese of North and South America. This procedure is typical of the Greek communal schools due to the congregational nature of the Greek communities.

Enrollment statistics. No enrollment data are available for 1910-20 decade for the day school. Attendance figures for both the day and afternoon schools for the period 1921-36 are shown in table 42.

TABLE 42

PUPIL ENROLLMENT AT KORAES DAY AND AFTERNOON
SCHOOLS 1921-36

Year	Day School	Afternoon School
1921	165	. .
1922	175	. .
1923	180	25
1924	185	75
1925	190	90
1926	110 *	100
1927	115	110
1928	120	120
1929	125	130
1930	125	140
1931	130	155
1932	133	150
1933	135	208
1934	140	236
1935	145	225
1936	155	245

Average Annual Enrollment for Period:

Day School   145 pupils

Afternoon School - 144 pupils

SOURCE: Forty Years of Greek Life, p. 86.

* Enrollment decreased because of fire that com-
pletely destroyed church and school building. During
1926-27 term school was conducted in rented quarters.

Twice in the late 1920s and again in the late 1940s, the church-school community experienced a loss in membership, first because of fire and then because of a changing neighborhood. Due to the latter, the koinotis voted at a general assembly in 1946, to move to the South Shore area, where many parishioners had relocated. Property was purchased at the corner of Seventy-fourth Street and Stony Island Avenue and an elaborate Byzantine edifice was erected between 1948 and 1950. The interim period found the

community holding church services at the Grahàm Taylor Chapel of the
Chicago Theological Seminary and the school holding classes in inadequate
and improvised quarters at the Stony Island location pending the construction of a new school building. Table 43 reflects attendance figures for both
the day and afternoon schools for the period 1937-49.

TABLE 43

PUPIL ENROLLMENT AT KORAES DAY AND AFTERNOON
SCHOOLS 1937-49

Year	Day School	Afternoon School
1937	177	289
1938	201	311
1939	223	340
1940	238	377
1941	286	403
1942	301	443
1943	291	466
1944	298	459
1945	282	430
1946	277	390
1947	189	212
1948	113	165
1949	98	160

Average Annual Enrollment for

Period: 1937-49	For Decade: 1937-46
Day School - 229 pupils	Day School - 257 pupils
Afternoon	Afternoon
School - 289 pupils	School - 322 pupils

SOURCE: Compiled from Koraes School records
in church archives.

An internal community controversy over the South Shore location and
the dismissal of the school principal over a theological issue (the principal
was a clergyman) temporarily divided the parish. These issues along with
the makeshift school facilities created a drop in school enrollment as shown
in the 1950-51 figure of only 80 pupils (see table 44). For the decade, up to
1946, when these issues came to the forefront, the enrollment averaged approximately 257 in the day school and 322 in the afternoon school as shown
on table 43. By 1955 the rift between the community factions over the issue

of the principal and relocation had been healed and school facilities had to
be doubled because of increased enrollees.

    In 1965, the parish built a modern, fifteen-room facility with audi-
torium at a cost of $550 thousand. Table 44 gives the enrollment figures for
the period 1950 to 1973.

TABLE 44

PUPIL ENROLLMENT AT KORAES DAY AND AFTERNOON
SCHOOLS 1950-73

Year	Day School	Afternoon School
1950	80	143
1951	94	188
1952	110	198
1953	134	213
1954	151	230
1955	188	241
1956	207	227
1957	231	230
1958	266	202
1959	273	175
1960	298	140
1961	303	92
1962	315	79
1963	323	48
1964	329	35
1965	332	22 *
1966	272	
1967	285	
1968	281	
1969	297	
1970	305	
1971	308	
1972	286	
1973	298	

Average Annual Enrollment for

	Period:	Peak Decades:
Day	(1950-73) - 249 pupils	(1964-73) - 299 pupils
Afternoon	(1950-65) - 154 pupils	(1950-59) - 205 pupils

SOURCE: Compiled from Koraes school records.

* Afternoon school discontinued.

    A comparison of enrollment figures reveals the following information:
during the period from 1921 to 1936 (table 42), the day school, which had been

in existence from 1910, averaged 145 pupils annually; the afternoon school, which was established in 1923, averaged 144 students annually until the end of the 1936-37 school year. This suggests the growing popularity of the afternoon school in comparison with the day school, indicating that approximately half of the pupils enrolled in the parish schools received their total education --English and Greek-- at the day school, while the other half received their English education in the public school and their Greek education in the afternoon school.

Enrollment statistics for the middle period (table 43) indicate that during the 1937-46 decade the average annual enrollment in the afternoon school surpassed that of the day school, 322-257. While day school enrollment did increase from the previous period, the larger figures for the afternoon school can undoubtedly be attributed to the depression years. Parents found it difficult to pay day school tuition and opted for the lower afternoon school tuition.

However, as shown in table 44, this situation was reversed in the following decades. After the parish weathered the internal controversy of 1947-51, which was reflected in the low school enrollment during these years, day school enrollment began to increase, while that of afternoon school, which increased for a short period, began a noticeable decline, resulting in the closing of the afternoon program in 1965. This may be attributed to the growing discontent on the part of children and parents with the afternoon school (as discussed elsewhere) and the new attraction offered by the day school's revised curriculum and new school building. Average enrollment figure for the peak decade (1950-59) in the afternoon school was 205; that for the day school during the last decade (1964-73) was 299.

In summary, the bilingual program of the Koraes School was supported by their board of trustees, school board, PTA, and other auxiliary associations. They believed that it was the finest communal school in the nation and exhorted other koinotites to follow their practice. The implicit faith of the community is testified by the following excerpts which appeared in their various church albums. In 1936, a statement read as follows:

The pupils, besides their educational lessons, are taught music and dancing. At celebrations their voices hum in harmony. Under such circumstances, the school is functioning and the result is not only perpetuating Greek religion, language, and nationalism, but also Americanizing the pupils by the best possible method.

It would be a salvation and a blessing if other cities in America would imitate the Chicago Greek school, and build similar institutions all over the country, so our new generation would be known as perfect Greek-Americans.[1]

In 1959, the parish of Saint Constantine observed its golden jubilee. A large section of its commemorative album was dedicated to the work of the parish school which was in continuous operation for half a century. The album observed:

Today the parish school continues performing its educational services to the community. Our parish youngsters receive bilingual education in the standard English basic core curriculum and in the tenets of the Orthodox Christian faith. Emphasis continues to be made upon the importance of our Hellenic heritage and the Greek language. . . .[2]

That this emphasis continues to be an important objective, reflecting the persistence of ethnic survival, is indicated by the following parish bulletin:

SCHOOL ANNOUNCEMENT FOR 1971-72 TERM

Koraes Elementary School will commence on September 13, 1971, at 8:55 A.M. We will once again endeavor to provide for your children an excellent academic curriculum in both Greek and English with the intent of achieving the following objectives:
1. 'a pursuit of excellence and a desire to always excel.' It will be the purpose and intent of our school staff to instill these Greek ideals into each pupil and to assist him to perform now and in the future at a level comparable to his intellectual capabilities.
2. 'to know thyself.' To develop a sense of personal understanding and self-assurance within each pupil and to add to his growth in the democratic values and behaviors which are the foundations of our American way of life. We will concentrate our efforts to show the modern Greek family's contribution to the United States.
3. 'to become adopted sons of God.' To develop within each pupil the beliefs, attitudes and practices of the Greek Orthodox Church. This year our School will offer a seminar in which we will compare scientific and religious thought. This seminar will be taught by a teacher who holds a B.S. Degree and a Master's in Theology.
4. 'to nurture within each pupil the heritage of his progenitors, namely the Greek language and actions.'
5. 'to develop a sound mind and body.' Physical education remains one of our strong points. With our own personal gymnasium and athletic programs we condition our youth into healthy young boys and girls.[3]

---

[1] Yearbook, Saint Constantine Church and Koraes School, p. 98.

[2] Saint Constantine Church 1909-59: Golden Anniversary, p. 49.

[3] "Saint Constantine Bulletin," 22 August 1971 (Mimeographed.)

Solon School

The name of the first Greek church established in Chicago in 1892, the Annunciation of the Virgin Mary, lingered on in the memory of Greek immigrants from the province of Laconia, even though the church was short-lived. It was used again by them when the third Chicago community was formed in 1910. The Annunciation Church was built in the Byzantine style, typical of most Greek churches, at 1017 North LaSalle Street, to serve the needs of Greek immigrants on the city's North Side. Subsequently, it was designated the cathedral of Greek Orthodoxy in Chicago. With the establishment of this community, the Greek immigrants had parishes and community facilities in three sectors of the city--West, South, and North--and for the next fifteen years they were to serve as focal points of Greek communal life in the city.

Understandably, the new community's first concern was the establishment of a school in the pattern of the two earlier communities. From the very beginning the idea prevailed that it would be a day school, and plans were laid to erect one as soon as it was economically feasible. Unfortunately, many years would pass before this could be accomplished. Aside from financial considerations, the new community was undecided as to where to locate the parish school, due to the increasing movement of Greek immigrants further north and northwest of the church. The problem was resolved finally in 1928, when a day school (named after Solon, the Athenian lawgiver) was organized and established in a specially-designed structure having ten classrooms, gymnasium, and a chapel at 2727 West Winona Avenue. This was in the Ravenswood district on the Northwest Side of Chicago, a considerable distance from the church. This compromise solution was deemed satisfactory, as it anticipated the increasing mobility of parishioners to the Northwest Side, thus providing them with a chapel where church services could be conducted on Sundays for those living in the area.

Unfortunately, due to the onset of the Great Depression of the 1930s, the Solon Day School operated only a few years before being converted into an afternoon school. The action was considered imperative due to the rapid attrition of enrollment from the initial two hundred students enrolled when the school opened.[1] Meanwhile, attendance at church services conducted in the Chapel of Saint Demetrios began to exceed that at the mother church on LaSalle Street, and the focal center of activity shifted to the Ravenswood church. In 1941, the two parishes became known as the "United Communities," and were administered by one symboulion, maintaining one treasury with a joint membership of six thousand people.[2] Under this mutual arrangement, afternoon schools operated at both church centers.

During the post-World War II period, the Saint Demetrios community again became a receiving center for new Greek immigration. A new Greektown, reminiscent of the old Greek Delta, was created in the Lawrence and Western area with Greek shops, restaurants, and centers. By 1970, it was estimated that thirty thousand Greeks lived in the new "Greek Town North."[3] Because of this postwar migration, the Saint Demetrios parish was transformed from a second-third generation Greek community into one in which first generation Greek immigrants predominate. The church, as in the past, became a focal point in Greek social and religious life. The Greek commitment to education was again manifested by the increased enrollment in the community schools. The Solon School inaugurated a daily kindergarten program meeting from 9:00 A.M. to 12:00 M and currently accommodates over two hundred children. The afternoon school, meeting on Mondays, Wednesdays, and Fridays, has over 500 pupils. Two branches, one in the northern suburb of Skokie and another in the North Austin district of Chicago, enroll 75 and 55 respectively. The Sunday school attendance has passed the 1,000 mark and is still growing. The community, which is now the largest Greek koinotis in the nation, is currently assessing the desirability of re-instituting the day school to meet the needs of the enlarged community.[4] Meanwhile, the public schools of Ravenswood and Albany Park have a large enrollment of Greek children, many whose first language is Greek, not unlike the situation which prevailed among Greek

---

[1] Interview with Rev. James Nestor, pastor Saint Demetrios, Chicago, 4 October 1967.

[2] Ibid.

[3] Chicago Tribune, 23 October 1970.

[4] Interview with George Louris, principal, Solon School, Chicago, 21 August 1973.

children in the Chicago public schools during the first two decades of the century. In one of these schools, located across the street from the Saint Demetrios Church, 80 percent of the enrollment is made up of Greek children, of which 30 percent use Greek as their first language.[1] In September 1973 a public-funded bilingual Greek program was inaugurated in this Chicago public school, as described in chapter 4.

Presently, the Solon School operates on an extensive basis, serving the new Greektown of the Saint Demetrios community. While still not a day school, it holds classes daily, including Saturdays, in three different locations, constituting five divisions. Three divisions, meeting at the main school building in the parish complex, consist of: (1) an afternoon school holding classes three times a week from 4:00 to 6:00 P.M. on Mondays, Wednesdays, and Fridays; (2) a Saturday school meeting weekly from 9:00 A.M. to 12:00 M; and (3) a kindergarten that meets daily from 9:00 A.M. to 12:00 M. Two divisions meet at branch locations: (4) the Austin area of Chicago in a rented Catholic high school, and (5) in a rented public school in suburban Skokie. Both branch schools meet from 4:00 to 6:00 P.M. on Tuesdays and Thursdays.

Attendance figures for the last ten years indicate that the school has doubled its enrollment during that period (see table 45), averaging 778 pupils per year, thus making it the largest communal Greek school in the city.

TABLE 45

PUPIL ENROLLMENT AT SOLON SCHOOL FOR PERIOD 1964-73

Year	Enrollment	Year	Enrollment
1964	540	1969	810
1965	590	1970	850
1966	650	1971	909
1967	705	1972	962
1968	755	1973	1010

Average Annual Pupil Enrollment for Period: 778

SOURCE: Interview with George Louris, principal, Solon School, Chicago, 21 August 1973. Enrollment figures for previous years are not available.

[1] Interview with Becky Orphan, principal, Budlong School, Chicago, 17 October, 1970.

Plato School

Of necessity, the early Greek settlers in the Garfield Park and Austin areas on the far West Side, who numbered about fifty families, banded together socially. A closely-knit community relationship existed without the commonly organized koinotis. Primary among their shared problems was the education of their children in the Greek language, religion, culture, customs, and fellowship. As mentioned throughout the study, the Greek immigrants considered the Greek language a necessary link for Greek survival in America --a link for identity and legacy and, indirectly, a weapon in the struggle against alien absorption.

The Greek families who lived in the western part of the city felt they could continue to attend religious services at Holy Trinity, but that it was not practical for the children to have to travel daily to attend Socrates School. Transportation was slow, distances far, and the children were too young.

A felt need for a school on the West Side was discussed at many informal gatherings until 28 November 1924 when the first definite step was taken. Some thirty-five men met at Burn's Hall, 3958 West Madison Street, to formally discuss the problem and inaugurate plans for a school. The minutes of this initial meeting reveal that:

> . . . without one exception, and with one will, all expressed their enthusiastic support of the purpose [organizing a school] and indicated they would donate generously to the cause . . . To the complete surprise of those present, a sum of $8,000 was pledged.[1]

Less than a month later, on 14 December 1924 a board of trustees of twenty-five men was elected with John Koliopoulos as president, thus completing the formation of an organized koinotis. A constitution drawn up the following year lists as one of the major objectives of the newly-organized group "the establishment of a building necessary for their Greek-American education and that of their descendants."[2]

---

[1] Minutes of the meeting of 28 November 1924, Board of Trustees of the Greek Orthodox Church, The Assumption (Chicago), also quoted in the Plato School of The Assumption Greek Orthodox Church Album (Chicago: n.p., 1962), p. 58.

[2] Community Life, 6 (Autumn 1962): 9. (A facsimile of the original parish minutes appears in this official parish monthly publication.)

The newly-organized community wasted no time in confronting its immediate problem, to procure a site for its school. During the month of January 1925 a committee was appointed to investigate possible sites on the West Side. After discounting some vacant property owned by the Chicago Board of Education, it reported on a large piece of property located at Harrison Street and Central Avenue. Its location was considered ideal not only because of the availability of good transportation, but also because of its proximity to the western suburbs and its central location, dividing the North and South sides of the city. Hence, it was accessible to the Greeks located on the city's West Side and western suburbs.[1] The meeting room that day was filled with enthusiasm because permission was granted the committee for the purchase of the site.

It must be borne in mind that the West Siders were still members of the Holy Trinity Church in the Greek Delta, but sought to establish a school of their own on the West Side. But once the formal structure for establishing a school was organized, a desire for a church of their own had already developed. It was then decided to have a committee meet with the board of trustees of Holy Trinity Church to discuss the situation.

The West Side Greek immigrants felt that the future of the Orthodox church was on the West Side, as evidenced by the increased movement of Greeks into the area. Consequently, they sought to convince the Holy Trinity board of trustees to build its new church on the newly-acquired site at Harrison and Central Streets. But because of the concentration of Greeks in the Halsted-Harrison location, Holy Trinity maintained that there was no future on the West Side and that it would build its new church at its present location.[2]

At the next meeting of the board of trustees of the newly-organized West Side community the members realized that it was imperative that they build their own church along with the school and become an independent parish under the Greek Orthodox Archdiocese of North and South America.[3] This

_____

[1]Assumption Church Board of Trustees Meeting (Chicago), 22 January 1925.

[2]Ibid., 23 March 1925

[3]Ibid., 24 April 1925.

was finally achieved on 9 July 1925 when the new community formally adopted
the name, "The Greek-American Community of Chicago and Western Suburbs."
A wooden building was erected promptly on the Harrison and Central site to
serve temporarily as a church and school. The church was named in honor of
the Assumption of the Virgin Mary, and the school became identified with the
name of the Greek philosopher Plato. [1]

Almost a year had passed since the initial meeting of 28 November
1924 when organizers had met to discuss the problem of establishing a Greek
school on the West Side. During this period, all energies were expended
for the establishment of the parish and the erection of a temporary structure
for a church and school. It was on 26 August 1925 that the first mention is
made of a school in the church records. The building was erected. The
parish had procured its charter from the archdiocese and legal recognition
from Cook County. The West Side community was ready to embark upon the
establishment of a school, the primary need which originally drew the group
together.

At this meeting, mention was made of the immediate establishment
of a day school. It would be a true Greek-American school, similar to the
other two--Socrates and Koraes--already established in Chicago. All subject
would be taught in Greek, and the English language would be taught as a
foreign tongue. For those boys and girls not able to attend the day school,
there would be an afternoon school. However, many of the board members
felt that the community was too young and needed greater financial strength
to undertake such a costly project at that time. Instead, a suggestion was
made to have the parish operate an afternoon school only--a supplementary
school that would meet three times a week after public school to teach Greek
only. A committee was appointed to investigate the prevailing conditions in
the community in order to determine what would be the most feasible solution
to the immediate problem. [2]

At the next board meeting in September 1925 the committee reported
that there was an insufficient number of pupils to warrant the establishment
of a day school. Accordingly, an afternoon school was established with six

---

[1] Ibid., 9 July 1925; 17 December 1925.

[2] Ibid., 26 August 1925.

grades patterned after the provincial schools of Greece. A school committee was appointed to administer the school, determine tuition, hire two teachers, and open the school in two weeks.[1] By the end of the school year, sixty-two pupils were enrolled, necessitating the appointment of a third staff member, George Nicolopoulos, who served as teacher-principal. As the mobility of Greeks to the West Side continued, afternoon annex schools were opened at the Harlem and Grand Avenue area and in suburban Cicero.

The community prospered and grew in size to become the largest Greek Orthodox parish in the United States in the 1950s. In 1937, the wooden church and school structure was replaced by a lannon stone Byzantine style edifice, and plans were projected for an adjoining school building. The $112 thousand church was dedicated on 13 October 1937, and the thousands assembled heard on that day:

> We are laying a cornerstone not only to the Temple of God; but also a cornerstone to the temple of good Hellenism and good Americanism. It will be a perpetual testimony to our love for our Church, to the trust and faith of our younger generation; an ever-living monument of the concerted efforts of a wide-awake and conscientious congregation.[2]

The advent of World War II delayed the construction of a building to house the long-desired day school. And it was not until the arrival of an energetic clergyman, the Reverend George Mastrantonis, and the appointment of a special school building committee in 1949, that serious plans were made to establish a day school for the large parish.[3] Finally, in September 1952 the Plato Day School opened its doors in a newly-constructed two-story lannon stone structure that was erected on property adjoining the church at a cost of approximately $375 thousand. The new building contained fourteen classrooms, auditorium, cafeteria, and ancillary rooms, housing grades kindergarten through eight.

Unlike the bilingual program of Koraes School described earlier in this chapter and contrary to the original expectations, Plato School introduced a new concept for Greek communal schools, that of monolingual education in

---

[1] Ibid., 3 September 1925

[2] Plato School Album, p. 59.

[3] Minutes of Board of Trustees, Assumption Church (Chicago), 17 March 1949.

which English was the exclusive language of instruction. Greek was taught as a foreign or second language one period each day. The curriculum was patterned closely to that of public schools and in accordance with the Illinois Curriculum and Course of Study for Elementary Schools.[1]

The goals of the new day communal school were formulated as follows:

1. The ultimate aim of life and education is to know, love, and serve God. The chief purpose of education is to guide children to attain the ultimate aim and the basic objectives of life and education.

2. Plato School endeavors to cultivate the religious values of the Greek Orthodox Church. Through the partaking of the sacramental life of the Greek Orthodox Church on the part of its pupils, and generally through their participation in the life of the religious community which established and sustains it, the Plato School endeavors to cultivate in the souls of its pupils the religious values as experienced by the Orthodox Church. It endeavors to aid the students in attaining a greater understanding of the faith, ethical values and demands, worship life, and practices in general of the Eastern Church.

3. Plato School endeavors to develop democratic ideals. The ideals which the school seeks to develop include a profound respect for the dignity and worth of every human being; a recognition of equality of opportunity for all; and an acceptance of all the implications involved in the ideal of justice for all.

4. Plato School guides children to think, feel and act more effectively. Since education is a process in which a desirable change in behavior is made, Plato School concerns itself with the development of the whole personality in all its mental, physical, spiritual, and moral phases; with helping children to guide their conduct and reach decisions by reason and intelligence rather than blind obedience, habit or prejudice; and with helping children acquire a knowledge of self and an understanding of the consequences of behavior.

5. Plato School deals with all aspects of life. All aspects of life are integrated in an effort to develop young people to be worthy home members, to live in harmony with neighbors, to become abiding citizens, to understand and appreciate our cultural heritage and to develop a wholesome way of life and contribute to the welfare of others and make their own lives happy and good.

6. Plato School is only a part of the child's education. It helps him recognize the necessity of a continuing education, and provides incentive skills and opportunities for such continuance of learning throughout life.

7. Plato aims at self-direction. Initiative and self-direction of the individual child are developed that the child may take the responsibility of developing his fundamental skills and abilities, proficiency in thinking, proper health and safety habits, ability of exploration of environmental factors and forces, and ability and willingness to work.[2]

---

[1] For the extensive history of the school see Klement, "History of Plato School."

[2] Klement, pp. 57-59.

The school did not attempt to teach a thorough comprehension of Greek grammar and syntax, but instead concentrated on conversational Greek, basic reading and writing skills, and some Greek history. New methodology under the influence of governmental projects in foreign languages was employed with a modern language laboratory.

Religious instruction was held once a week by the local parish clergy. It was also taught during the Greek lessons as part of Greek history. In addition, pupils met for weekly prayer services in the church or chapel, and participated in the obligatory sacramental and symbolic life of the church. The extensive religious aspect of the curriculum was endorsed by the parents who often participated with their children in the program.[1]

Primary and intermediate grades had an enriched, self-contained classroom organization. The sixth, seventh, and eighth grades were departmentalized into language arts, social studies, mathematics, and science. Emphasis was both on the language arts and "new" mathematics. Specialists taught music and physical education to all grades. The nearby Columbus Park facilities were used periodically for physical education. As an elective, piano lessons were offered for a fee during school time, either in private or in small groups. Monthly assemblies included skits in Greek and English. There were celebrations for the 1821 Greek Independence and the Week of Greek Letters honoring the patron saints of education. Since 1956, the archdiocese has urged that all Greek day communal schools celebrate the three hierarchs as educational and religious leaders. This is another example of shifting from nationalistic to religious symbolism in the Greek community.

In addition to a central school library with books purchased by the Plato School Board and Plato PTA, there were individual libraries in every classroom. Along with purchased books are hundreds of books from the Chicago public library on a two-year renewable loan basis. Another innovation was the implementation of a testing program for all children, administered by trained personnel. Readiness testing, two I.Q. and three achievement tests per pupil were administered during the eight years. Tests included the California Mental Maturity, California Achievement, the SRA, Stanford Achievement, and Metropolitan Readiness. The report cards reflected those of the Chicago public schools in format.

---

[1] Interview with Dr. Constantine Mihalakis, former principal of Plato School, Chicago, 28 April 1968.

Another new feature for Greek communal schools was the regular guidance and counseling services. Students with special needs were identified and referred to supportive services in Chicago who could guide the children by offering specialized help. Cooperative effort was established with physicians and dentists from the local community who provided health services to the pupils, and an infirmary was established by the school's PTA. All pupils were covered by medical insurance. A school lunch program was provided with hot meals and partially subsidized by the federal food surplus program. Hired help took care of preparing and cleaning up the daily food service operations.

Selection of faculty has been based on educational background and experience with certification approval from the State of Illinois. Religious or national affiliation has never been a criterion for obtaining a teaching position, and the fact that so many of the teachers have been Greek Orthodox is only because they have been the candidates who have applied for such positions.

Faculty members who teach the Greek language, in many cases, have not been educated in Greece. Availability of trained teachers increased with the archdiocesan establishment, in 1945, of a training institution, the Academy of Saint Basil, in New York, where those individuals wishing to teach in communal schools are trained. All teachers of Greek must be certified by the department of education of the archdiocese.

Both the faculties of English and Greek became members of professional organizations and participated in regional and national conferences. Reports were presented to the PTA. Greater involvement in broader educational circles ended an era of isolation that had been the practice of earlier decades in Greek communal schools.

The new day school was under the direction of the Reverend Constantine Volaitis, an American-born priest, and George Topping, a second-generation Greek educator and then Assistant Cook County Superintendent of Schools, who served as consultant and supervisor. Accreditation was received in 1953, when Harold C. Hunt, General Superintendent of Chicago Public Schools, wrote in response to a recommendation received from a committee under the chairmanship of Leo G. Herdeg, district superintendent, who visited Plato School, that:

The Plato School, 601 South Central Avenue, Chicago (operated by the

Greek Orthodox Church) should be added to the Board of Education's list of private elementary schools in Chicago whose eighth grade graduates are admitted to Chicago Public High Schools without examination.[1]

TABLE 46

PUPIL ENROLLMENT AT PLATO ELEMENTARY SCHOOL
1953-73

Year	Enrollment	Year	Enrollment
1953	162	1964	330
1954	154	1965	320
1955	267	1966	380
1956	285	1967	334
1957	311	1968	313
1958	336	1969	243
1959	357	1970	154
1960	341	1971	138
1961	350	1972	148
1962	330	1973	165
1963	311		

Average Annual Pupil Enrollment for
Period: 273

SOURCE: Plato School records.

Current enrollment of Plato day school (table 46) has been drastically reduced because of an abrupt demographic change in the neighborhood and the flight of parishioners to the western suburbs. The afternoon school was discontinued for "safety" reasons and made into a Saturday school, meeting from the morning hours nine to twelve. It has a current enrollment of 142 pupils who are brought by parents or school bus. By comparing the average annual enrollment of the afternoon school (207) during the first twenty-eight years of its existence, 1925-52, (see table 47) with the average annual enrollment of the day school (273) since its establishment twenty-one years ago (see table 46), it can be seen that the day school filled an important need, justifying the vision of its founding fathers. Up until the change in the neighborhood in 1968-69, the day school enrollment was increasing steadily, with more children enrolling in the day school than was ever the case in the afternoon

---

[1]Klement, p. 52.

school. Of course, some consideration must be given to the fact that this enrollment may have been increasing because of the changing environment; Greek parents may have been sending their children to Plato in order to avoid having them attend racially-changing public schools in the area. But this does not seem to have been the case, judging by information gathered. Notwithstanding, the parish has made no decision to leave the area, and a determined effort continues to have children bussed from outlying suburban areas to keep the school from closing. As table 46 shows, there has been a slight upturn in enrollment since 1971.

The current Greek program in the day school is comprised of three qualified Greek instructors who teach Greek daily as a foreign language for thirty minutes in the primary grades, forty minutes in the intermediate, and fifty minutes in the upper grades. The prescribed course of study of the archdiocese, which maintains that classical or puristic Greek is to be taught in the upper grades, is not adhered to. It is considered superfluous, since the purpose of the Greek language school in America is not "to develop Greek scholars, but to promote a speaking knowledge of demotic Greek," which is taught to all the grades.[1] This view of the school principal seems to be shared by the community-at-large.

Indicative of the continuing concern for the ethnic and cultural legacy is reflected in an advertisement shown in figure 2.

Afternoon school. The Plato afternoon program met three times a week for a total of approximately six hours for the benefit of those children attending public schools. As was anticipated, a sharp decrease in afternoon school enrollment occurred when Plato Day School became a reality (table 47). Because of the changing neighborhood and the moving of families, the school was abolished in 1969, and replaced with a three-hour Saturday morning school which enrolls an average of 140 pupils each year. The Saturday program attempted to crowd in 3 hours what was normally taught in the 6-hour afternoon school which met thrice weekly. However, the program proved to be too heavily saturated and parents complained that the course of study was too demanding of the children. Consequently, the program was modified.

---

[1] Interview with Esther Sakellariou, principal, Plato School, Chicago, 2 July 1973.

Figure 2. Plato School recruitment advertisement.[1]

PLATO SCHOOL

of the

Greek Orthodox Church "The Assumption"

601 E. CENTRAL AVE. CHICAGO, ILL.

ANNOUNCEMENT OF REGISTRATION

SCHOOL WILL BEGIN ON THURSDAY, SEPTEMBER 5, 1974, AT 9:00 A.M.

PARENTS: Enroll your children at Plato School for the the coming school year 1974-1975.

FACTS ABOUT PLATO:

1. Established as a full time elementary school in 1952.
2. Fully accredited by the State of Illinois Department of Education and the Boards of Education of Cook County and the City of Chicago.
3. Community-centered, related to the Greek Orthodox Church "The Assumption".
4. A school where great concern is shown to prepare the individual child to take his proper place in a democratic society as a mature and responsible citizen with a sense of pride in his ethnic background, religion, language and cultural heritage.
5. Plato offers a complete course in elementary education in English, from Kindergarten through the Eighth Grade.
6. The excellent curriculum in English provides quality education in small classes with individualized instruction and the children also have the opportunity to learn the Greek language, spoken and written, Greek history and geography, Greek mythology, Religion and all about their glorious Greek heritage.

REGISTRATION: MONDAY, AUGUST 26th — SATURDAY, AUGUST 31st, 1974.

TIME: 9:00 a.m. — 1:00 p.m.

PLATO SCHOOL, Office of the Principal.

BUS SERVICE: A professional Bus Service is available for those desiring it.

TOUR OF THE SCHOOL: So that new parents and students may become acquainted with the physical facilities of Plato School, a tour of the school will be conducted immediately after the Second Divine Liturgy on SUNDAY, AUGUST 25, 1974. The tour will originate from the office of the Prrincipal.

INFORMATION: Call the Church Office: MA 6-3114.

THE PLATO SCHOOL BOARD.

---

[1] Greek Press (Chicago), 16 August 1974.

The program attempts to develop cultural awareness and some working knowledge of the Greek language. Like the day school, Greek is taught as a second language through the medium of English.

TABLE 47

PUPIL ENROLLMENT OF THE PLATO AFTERNOON SCHOOL

Year	Enrollment	Year	Enrollment
1925	62	1942	188
1926	141	1943	183
1927	146	1944	233
1928	180	1945	246
1929	230	1946	264
1930	225	1947	252
1931	235	1948	267
1932	210	1949	243
1933	219	1950	231
1934	220	1951	212
1935	245	1952	110 *
1936	250	1953	69
1937	240	1954	61
1938	265	1955	66
1939	220	1956	69
1940	205	1957	57
1941	191		

Annual Average Pupil Enrollment for Period 1925-52: 207

SOURCE: Klement, p. 42. Enrollment figures from 1958 to 1969, when the afternoon school was disbanded, are not available.

* Day school established.

Sunday school. In 1927, the parish organized a Sunday school in keeping with the movement then taking place for the establishment of formal religious educational programs for Greek children. Due to the swift growth of the community, the Sunday school grew in size, surpassing the enrollment in the day and afternoon schools. By the 1950s, its enrollment increased to 2,200 registered students with an average Sunday attendance of 1,200 to 1,500 students. Accommodating such a large number of children was a severe problem since existing classroom facilities were not adequate. The problem was alleviated with the partitioning of the church basement into classrooms and the construction of a chapel so that separate worship services could be held for these youngsters.

As discussed elsewhere in this chapter, initial instruction in the Sunday school was in the Greek language. But the change to English instruction at the Assumption Sunday school took place earlier than at other Chicago Greek Orthodox Sunday schools, due perhaps to the greater impact of acculturation as reflected in the greater number of American-born individuals in position of parish leadership.

Thus, Plato School and the other educational agencies of this parish, exhibited a monolingual approach, with the utilization of English as the almost exclusive language of instruction, for the purpose of transmitting ethnic and religious heritage. In this respect, it differed from the Socrates School of Holy Trinity Church, which also employed a monolingual approach, but with Greek as the primary language of instruction. Similarly, it differed from the Koraes School of Saint Constantine Church, which employed the bilingual --Greek and English--approach, where both languages were used as instructional media.

Afternoon Schools

Despite conciliatory and persistent efforts exerted by parish communities for the operation of day schools, most Greek immigrant parents sent their children to public schools for various reasons: Greek day schools charged tuition, though nominal; they were few in number and most children had to use public transportation; parents were often dissatisfied with their inadequate facilities and equipment.[1] According to one Greek newspaper, in 1914, the two day schools graduated one child for every five attending public schools.[2]

Since afternoon schools were cheaper to operate and could assist in the mission of Greek language and heritage, they soon outnumbered the day schools. Unlike the day schools, which operated during the day or simultaneously with the public schools and which were usually accredited by public educational agencies, the afternoon schools met after the regular school hours, twice or three times a week, usually between the hours of four and

---

[1] Interview with Helen Poulos, Chicago, 3 September 1968.

[2] Saloniki (Chicago), 4 and 26 December 1914.

six in the late afternoon. They were not accredited schools, and, unlike the
day schools, were not intended to replace the public schools, but to supplement them. They generally conducted classes in rented halls, stores, public
school classrooms, or church basements. Instruction was strictly in Greek
and was concerned with teaching the Greek language, geography, history,
and the Orthodox religion.

Plutarch School

One of the earliest, if not the first afternoon communal Greek school,
was the Plutarch School, chartered by the State of Illinois on 23 June 1917.
The school was organized by the community of Saint Spyridon which was established by Greek immigrants in 1916 in the Pullman district of the city.
Both, a church and school were established to meet the needs of immigrant
families who resided in this far South Side area where the men had found employment at the massive George Pullman Works and other industrial concerns
in the neighborhood. The area was too far removed from the Greek Delta and
other existing Greek communities, and thus necessitated the establishment
of a separate Greek community--the fourth in Chicago at the time.

The school opened with classes held in a rented hall at the Palmer
Park fieldhouse under the direction of George Poulakides, a graduate of the
Tripolis Teachers College in Greece. However, the community encountered
financial difficulties and six months later Plutarch School was closed by the
church symboulion (board of trustees). In 1919, in response to parental requests, the Pericles Hellenic Political Society, a local voluntary association
reopened the school, using its own quarters at 11358 South Front Street.
Eight years later, in June 1927, the community agreed to assume responsibility
for the school again and it was moved to the newly-built church structure of
Saint Spyridon at 11357 South Park Avenue. The church symboulion formed a
committee to govern the school, and a women's voluntary group was formed
to provide financial support.

During 1929, there were fifty-five children enrolled with two instructors who taught reading, writing, history, geography, citizenship, diction,
Greek songs, religious music, dialogues, poetry, and drama--all in Greek.
The Greek teachers who taught in these afternoon schools in most cases had
no fringe benefits (sick days, insurance coverage, pension, or death benefits); therefore, many gave private Greek lessons to augment their income.

After World War II, the afternoon program at Plutarch expanded with a branch in the southern industrial suburb of Harvey, Illinois. The combined current enrollment is approximately 120 pupils.[1]

Saint George School

Another location where Greek children acquired Greek education was at Saint George School, founded in 1923, and housed on the first floor of the church building at 2701 North Sheffield Avenue. It was organized simultaneously with the church, and its charter included a Sunday school, one of the first in the Greek community. The Reverend Daniel Golemis became the pastor and school director. He was a graduate of the Patriarchal Theological Seminary of Constantinople and held a law degree from the University of Athens. In 1927, the parish organized the Saint George Ladies Educational Society with the specific purpose of providing for the financial needs of the school. Table 48 shows enrollment statistics for the 1923-36 period with an average of 123 pupils annually.

TABLE 48

PUPIL ENROLLMENT AT SAINT GEORGE SCHOOL
1923-36

Year	Enrollment
1923	48
1924	97
1925	116
1926	115
1927	125
1928	110
1929	110
1930	142
1931	124
1932	133
1933	139
1934	149
1935	159
1936	157

Average Annual Enrollment for Period: 123

SOURCE: Forty Years of Greek Life, p. 98.

[1] Demos Fotopoulos, Plutarch School principal, 20 May 1972.

The school's constitution, drawn up in 1924, gives a profile of the way most Greek afternoon schools operated. Selected articles reveal the following:

Article   I   Classes will begin on September 14, the Feast of the Holy Cross, the traditional day when schools open in Greece.

Article   II   The enrollment fee is five dollars; tuition two dollars monthly.

Article   III   Students who are unable to pay tuition are to be aided.

Article   IV   The School shall have a minimum of five grades.

Article   V   Pupils must be over seven years of age.

Article XIV   Physical punishment is prohibited.

Article XVII   The Eastern Orthodox religion, Greek letters, and Greek history are to be taught.

Article XIX   Hours will be from 4 to 6 p.m. and 9 to 12 noon on Saturdays.[1]

As shown in table 49, the average yearly enrollment for the last decade (1964-73) has been 145 pupils. This is apparently a one-fifth increase over the average annual enrollment of 123 students during the first fourteen

TABLE 49

PUPIL ENROLLMENT AT SAINT GEORGE SCHOOL 1964-73

Year	Enrollment	Year	Enrollment
1964	107	1969	174
1965	138	1970	155
1966	142	1971	161
1967	140	1972	142
1968	166	1973	130

Annual Average Enrollment for Period: 146

SOURCE: From school records at Saint George Church.

years of the school's existence (1923-36). However, similar to enrollment

---

[1] Forty Years of Greek Life, pp. 98-99.

in other Greek schools in Chicago, majority of the current enrollees are children of recent immigrants.[1]

Saint Andrew School

As Greek immigrants moved northward, they purchased a large
Masonic temple at 5648 North Winthrop Avenue and converted it into a
church and school in 1926, to serve the religious and educational needs of
communicants in the Lakeview and Rodgers Park districts. This new congregation of Saint Andrew in due time became one of the wealthiest Greek communities in Chicago. In 1956, a new church, chapel, community center, and
school complex were constructed off Lake Shore Drive at Sheridan and Holly-
wood Avenue.

The afternoon Greek school was organized in 1926, by the learned
pastor of the parish, the late Reverend Constans H. Demetry, a graduate of
the Patriarchal Theological Seminary of Constantinople and a leading figure
in the Greek Sunday school movement in Chicago at that time. He served as
the first teacher-principal of the school in addition to his religious duties as
pastor. The school was modeled after the six-grade elementary schools in
Greece, as was the case with other Greek afternoon schools.

Following the church pastor as principal of the school was Pantelis
Parpadis, a graduate of the Great National School of Constantinople, who
later became principal of Socrates School. With the cooperation of an energetic school board chairman, Paul Demos, the school entered upon a period
of growth and prosperity. Its program of Greek studies and religious instruction, the latter taught by the Reverend Irenaeus Tsourounakis, who later became Bishop of San Francisco, attracted a large student clientele. During the
first three decades, the average yearly enrollment was approximately 145.[2]
Like other Greek schools, Saint Andrew was aided financially by various voluntary associations in the community. Until 1937, the school's expenses exceeded its income and the church community absorbed the difference.

Growth and dispersion of the Greek population in the area forced the
community to have additional schools. Currently, the school enrolls nearly

---

[1] Interview with Helen Georgopoulos, principal, Saint George School,
Chicago, 8 July 1973.

[2] Forty Years of Greek Life, p. 93.

three hundred children at four locations--Saint Andrew Church and at branch
schools in the Edgebrook section of Chicago and in the northern suburbs of
Evanston and Morton Grove. Most children are transported to school by
vehicles owned by the parish. The language of instruction remains almost
exclusively Greek, with English used for purposes of explanation. The student body is comprised mostly of second and third generation children, with
a sizable number of children from homes of recent immigrants. Enrollment
for 1965-73 (table 50) indicates an average yearly attendance of 243 for the
period, a considerable increase over the 145 average annual attendance of
the school's first three decades.

TABLE 50

PUPIL ENROLLMENT AT SAINT ANDREW SCHOOL, 1965-73

Year	Enrollment	Year	Enrollment
1965	178	1970	270
1966	192	1971	286
1967	185	1972	293
1968	232	1973	298
1969	251		

Average Annual Enrollment for Period: 243

SOURCE: Interview with John Diamantis, principal,
Saint Andrew School, Chicago, 25 April 1973.

Homer School of Saint Nicholas Church

Although the Saint Nicholas community was founded in 1927, as a
branch of Holy Trinity Church to serve the growing Greek area in West Englewood on Chicago's South Side, it became an independent parish in 1931.
Though the new church edifice was completed in 1931, an afternoon Greek
school was established in 1928. For the first twenty years, the pastor, the
Reverend Daniel Gambrilis, directed the school and performed all administrative functions. The school grew slowly, averaging 121 pupils yearly during
the first nine years of its existence (table 51).

In 1945, a nearby Protestant school building was purchased to house
the school's growing population and to serve as a community center. A former
teacher at Socrates School, Nicholas Lamprinidis, a graduate of the Great
National School in Constantinople, was made principal. During the 1940s

and 1950s the neighborhood began to change racially, and parishioners began
relocating in the southwestern suburbs. In due time, branch Greek schools
were established in suburban Evergreen Park and Oak Lawn. Enrollment
dropped at the main school, but picked up somewhat at the branch school.
It is estimated that during this period, enrollment averaged between one
hundred and one hundred fifty annually in the three schools collectively.[1]

TABLE 51

PUPIL ENROLLMENT AT HOMER SCHOOL, 1928-36

Year	Enrollment	Year	Enrollment
1928	45	1933	142
1929	70	1934	158
1930	87	1935	173
1931	114	1936	186
1932	115		

Average Annual Enrollment for Period: 121

SOURCE: Forty Years of Greek Life, p. 101.

By 1965, the community had acquired a new site in Oak Lawn and
recombined all three schools in a modern school building at the new location. A few years later, the church building was erected and the entire community complex was completed at a cost of approximately two million dollars.
Enrollment at the school increased and during the last decade has averaged
175 each year (see table 52).

Most students presently enrolled are from second generation families,
unlike other schools in the city which currently have heavy enrollments of
immigrant children.

---

[1] Fiftieth Anniversary, Reverend Daniel Gambrilis Golden Jubilee
(Chicago, n.p. 1961), p. 29.

TABLE 52

PUPIL ENROLLMENT AT HOMER SCHOOL, 1964-73

Year	Enrollment	Year	Enrollment
1964	83	1969	177
1965	102	1970	203
1966	115	1971	238
1967	138	1972	245
1968	189	1973	261

Average Annual Enrollment for Period: 175

SOURCE: From school records at Saint Nicholas Church.

Saint Basil School

A one-time flourishing community was that of Saint Basil, located just west of the Greek Delta at Ashland and Polk Streets. It was founded by a dissident group in 1927, and from its inception had a successful afternoon school housed in an annex rented hall and later in the church building itself. Average annual enrollment during the first ten years of the school's existence was ninety-eight, as shown in table 53. In the late 1930s, two supplementary

TABLE 53

PUPIL ENROLLMENT AT SAINT BASIL SCHOOL, 1927-36

Year	Enrollment	Year	Enrollment
1927	148	1932	49
1928	120	1933	116
1929	119	1934	112
1930 . , . .	87	1935	93
1931	47	1936	92

Average Annual Enrollment for Period: 98

SOURCE: Forty Years of Greek Life, p. 102.

schools were opened to accommodate Greek families living in outlying areas of the parish. These were located at 3437 Ogden Avenue and at North and California Avenues. The combined enrollment of the three schools averaged approximately 145 yearly until the 1950s.[1] School enrollment and church membership declined thereafter, as communicants began moving away due to the deterioration of the neighborhood. However, the church community still remains at the original site; an urban renewal project and the expansion of the nearby West Side Medical Center are bringing about a revitalization of the neighborhood. Although growth is slow, the community is experiencing a renaissance, with some second and third generation Greek people returning to the area. While no enrollment figures are currently available, it is reported that the school is serving fifty to seventy pupils annually. There is informal talk that a new day school may be established due to the central location of the parish.[2]

Aristotle School

A postwar community was founded in 1951, comprised mostly of new Greek immigrants on the near Northwest Side of Chicago and named Holy Archangels and Saint Haralambos. By 1956, the new koinotis had started the Aristotle School, and a year later relocated several blocks north, at 1357 North California, in a commodious building that was formerly a Jewish house of worship. The community prospered, and with zeal reminiscent of the early Greek immigrants, made great sacrifice for the support of the parish school. The average annual enrollment for the eighteen years the school has been in existence is 149 (see table 54).

However, as in similar instances with other Greek communities located in the inner city, the area has begun to change into a predominantly Spanish-speaking neighborhood. Members of the parish, possibly due also to their rise on the economic scale, have begun moving into the suburbs. In order to keep children in the Greek school, the parish has established a bus service for the pupils. Costs in financing this service and the long distances that are sometimes involved precipitated discussion within the congregation about the relocation of the parish. As of this writing, the board of trustees

---

[1] Interview with the Reverend Joachim Yalouris, pastor of Saint Basil Church, Chicago, 10 January 1969.

[2] Ibid.

has approved the relocation, and property has been purchased in suburban Niles for the erection of a new community.

TABLE 54

PUPIL ENROLLMENT AT ARISTOTLE SCHOOL, 1956-73

Year	Enrollment	Year	Enrollment
1956	43	1965	172
1957	67	1966	187
1958	80	1968	182
1959	123	1969	191
1960	119	1970	190
1961	135	1971	183
1962	158	1972	188
1963	161	1973	196
1964	145		

Annual Average Enrollment for Period: 149

SOURCE: Interview with the Reverend Chrysostom Economakos, pastor of Holy Archangels and Saint Haralambos Church, Chicago, 5 October 1973.

Homer School of Assumption Church

In 1923, Greek immigrants living in the far South Chicago community of Hegewich, mostly employees of the nearby steel mills, established a Greek school to serve their children. Nominally, these immigrants belonged to the Saint Spyridon community in nearby Pullman, which had been organized several years earlier. The need for such a school was felt due to fears of parents for the safety of their children travelling long distances to attend the Plutarch School of Saint Spyridon Church. Accordingly, with the aid of a regional topiko somateion, (voluntary association), the Macriyannis Remueliote Society (Remeli is a province in central Greece), an afternoon Greek school named after the Greek poet, Homer, was opened in rented quarters in February 1924.

As in the case of the Greek immigrants in the Austin area on the far West Side, these immigrants decided that as long as they now maintained a Greek school, they should also establish a church for their religious needs. By Easter 1924 the church had been organized and dedicated to the Assumption of the Virgin Mary, the second church of that name in the city. The following year, the school and church were housed in a modest frame building at 13631 South Brainard Avenue.

The school was organized with only the first four grades of the typical six-grade Greek school, and was from the very beginning until the present day the only Greek school that did not charge tuition.[1] The parish community absorbed all necessary expenses. The priests, sometimes with the assistance of another instructor, were the only teachers. Enrollment during the 1930s and 1940s averaged sixty. In 1936, the frame structure housing the church and school was destroyed by fire and was replaced by a brick edifice consecrated according to the rites of the Greek Orthodox church in September 1937.

The school is governed directly by the symboulion (board of trustees), which handles all fiscal and educational matters. Because enrollment has fallen off through the departure of families to the outlying suburban areas, the school is experiencing a financial crisis, and tuition will be charged for all students during the next school term.[2] The pastor, who has been at the church since 1938, has also been the main teacher of the school since that date. The 1970-71 enrollment was forty-two. Enrollment statistics for earlier years are not available.

In retrospect, Chicago's Greek immigrants organized eleven communities, or koinotites,[3] by 1927, all products of the original first generation immigrants. Another community was organized in 1951, by postwar Greek immigrants, making a total of twelve organized communities. It was in these centers of immigrant Greek culture and aspiration that the Greek immigrant sought to perpetuate his cultural legacy in his offspring. These communities maintained four day schools and ten afternoon schools; some also sponsored Saturday schools. A similar pattern was followed in the surrounding Greek centers of Waukegan, Joliet, Chicago Heights, East Chicago, Hammond, and Gary--all having afternoon schools by the 1920s.

----

[1]Interview with Reverend Basil S. Heniades, pastor, Assumption Church, Chicago, 23 July 1971.

[2]Ibid.

[3]The terms, community, koinotis, and parish are used interchangeably in this study to denote the formal organization of Greeks into functional social units. The term koinotites is the plural form of koinotis.

As the second and third generations of Greek immigrants climbed the socioeconomic scale, an exodus to the suburbs resulted in the establishment of new Greek Orthodox communities. These new centers are located in Glenview (Saints Peter and Paul), DesPlaines (Saint John the Baptist), Elmhurst (Saint Demetrios), Westchester (Holy Apostles), Summit (Holy Cross), Oak Lawn (Saint Nicholas), Olympia Fields (Assumption), and Palos Hills (Saints Constantine and Helen). Interestingly, the suburban communities have embarked on afternoon and/or Saturday schools in modern and well-equipped buildings, and emulate the desire of the original immigrant parents to have their children perpetuate the Orthodox faith and ethnic legacy, even though they now have settled in new, assimilative suburbia.

While some second and third generation Greek-Americans relocating in the suburbs were apathetic about the perpetuation of the Greek ethos, there was sufficient consensus among them to support the establishment of suburban Greek schools. Perhaps typical of this sentiment is the following statement made by a second-generation Greek father of four children who had moved to the northern suburbs:

> I grew up in the old Greektown area. My father was a poor, uneducated immigrant who worked hard to assure his children of a good Greek education by sending us to Socrates School. I don't regret this education, for we learned much about our Greek heritage and religion. I intend to see that my children, too, learn something of their cultural legacy. I don't see why they cannot have the best of two worlds--Greek and American.[1]

As shown by the available enrollment statistics, attendance at the Greek language schools, for the most part, was constant during the early years, decreased somewhat during the depression years, and increased after World War II. This increase took place despite the growing dissatisfaction, on the part of some second-generation parents, with the nationalistic aspects of the curriculum and despite the normal rate of attrition resulting from the inroads made by acculturation in the Greek family. This suggests that, on the whole, the Greek home was favorably disposed to the exposure of its children to some type of Greek ethnic education, whether it took place in the communal language school, the Sunday school, or under private auspices. Indeed, even children without homes were exposed to Greek education. One social worker recalls a Greek educational program at the Chicago Orphan Asylum, located

---

[1] Interview with James A. Koulogeorge, Northbrook, Ill., 15 December 1971.

at 5120 South Parkway. In 1930-31, the asylum housed thirty-three orphaned Greek children who received Greek instruction every Saturday by teachers from the Koraes School. Not only were they taught Greek, but transportation was provided for them to attend Sunday school at Saint Constantine Church and holiday school events, where they would be given gifts by the Mothers Club.[1] This practice is indicative of the strong desire for ethnic education by the Greek community in its attempt to reach all of its children, even those under institutional care.

A word must be said about enrollment statistics of communal language schools. Attempts to gather information were handicapped by the lack of available records. Few afternoon schools kept permanent enrollment figures through the years. Such records that were kept were lost in the fluid situation in which these schools operated. Frequent changes in location, administrators, faculty, and personnel contributed to the sparsity of these records. Consequently, enrollment statistics included in this study were culled from available archival materials found in parish offices, from secondary sources, or from testimony of current school administrators. For some schools, no enrollment figures were available, and attendance information is based on estimates made by the school administrator or parish priest. Nevertheless, it is believed by the writer that the enrollment figures contained in this study represent a composite picture of actual enrollments in these schools. From these, it has been possible to make inferences relative to general attendance patterns.

Private Greek Schools

In addition to the communal language schools, there existed several private schools under the auspices of voluntary associations, parental groups, or individuals. Most were not-for-profit institutions; several were entrepreneurial enterprises. These private schools, for the most part, reached their height from 1920 to 1950, when the rapid spread of the Greek people throughout Chicago made it difficult for children to attend communal schools far from home. Private schools were convenient and flexible, and the instruction was similar to communal schools, including the use of the same textbooks. These

---

[1] Interview with Ione A. DuVal, director, Immigrants' Service League, Chicago, 25 September 1970.

sessions were held closer to the homes of pupils in late afternoon or early evening, and were conducted most often by teachers who also taught at communal schools. Scheduling was arranged so that these teachers could work on alternate days at the private schools.

The informal governance of these schools often was more effective than that of communal schools, which were subject to factionalism in the symboulion, or community. During the 1930s, at least eight private schools had programs and enrollments comparable to communal schools. Shortly after World War II, these private ventures began to disappear, primarily because of an antipathy of the second-generation parents toward afternoon schools that followed public schooling all day and the fact that the communal schools improved and took away some of the business. In the past few years, postwar Greek immigrants have established a Hellenic gymnasium under private auspices--the first Greek school of secondary studies in Chicago. It is called the Hellenic Lyceum and has English and Greek instruction with a current enrollment of sixty. It is located at 3500 West Fullerton Avenue. As a result of the accelerated postwar Greek immigration some fourteen private Greek schools are reported as currently operative in the city. Most are small, averaging twenty-five to forty pupils; a few have nearly one hundred enrolled. All charge tuition and generally follow the instructional program used in the communal schools. Some are accredited by the department of education of the Greek archdiocese.

Tutorial Services

A large number of children received Greek instruction in their homes or neighborhood by private tutors. The tutorial services were a common practice and rather lucrative for the many tutors who also were teachers in the language schools. Possibly, the custom of private tutoring developed from the practice of Greek families having boarders who tutored the children in lieu of paying rent. Many of these boarders had been lawyers, accountants, or in other professions in Greece, or had been graduates of the gymnasium in Greece, as attested to by a number of educated persons interviewed.[1] The early tutors initially were predominantly men. When they entered other

---

[1] Interview with Pantelis Parpadis, Chicago, 13 July 1968; and John Pappadopoulos, Chicago, 15 May 1968, et al.

occupations, they were replaced by women who were gymnasium graduates or products of teacher training institutions in Greece. They charged an average fee of one dollar per child per week.[1] Oftentimes children from the neighborhood would gather at one home and instruction would be two hours, depending on many factors. Basically it was easier to arrange a program to meet family needs through tutors than through communal schools. At the end of the year, "certificates of promotion" or "diplomas" were presented, although these documents were not always honored at the formal communal language schools.

The tutorial arrangement has endured because of its flexibility. Second and third generation Greek families continue to use this practice in the city and suburbs. There are well-trained tutors available from Greece and from the teacher institute sponsored by the Greek archdiocese at Garrison, New York. Accordingly, given the variety and numbers of the educational facilities available, it is a safe assumption that most Greek children in the Chicago metropolitan area have received some Greek instruction either from communal schools, private ventures, or tutors.

Summary

        The Greek experience demonstrates that education may be identi-
fied as the process whereby the culture of a society is transmitted from
generation to generation. Every ethnic group has certain knowledge, skills,
folkways, and mores which it regards as indispensable to its survival. In
order to regularize the transmission of these forms, some sort of an educational system is set up. The informal system carried on in the home, church,
and voluntary groups is not as easily discernable as the formal school system. With the Greek immigrants of Chicago, the formal ethnic school system did not materialize until late in the first decade of this century. The
Greek response to educational needs arose with the development of family
life in the city. Since early communal attempts to establish ethnic schools
proved abortive, family men took matters into their own hands and established
the first Greek school in Chicago in 1904. This action served as a catalyst
for the establishment of the first permanent Greek communal day school in
1908, by the organized koinotis of Chicago, after it had overcome a serious
internal feud.

        Following the establishment of the school, the early Greek com-
munity of Chicago organized a variety of educational institutions catering
to different segments and age levels of the Greek populace. Most of them
were short-lived, but illustrative of the Greek immigrant's commitment to
education. One of the greatest assets to the Greek community in its concern for educational arrangements was Hull House. Through its services to
the nearby Greek community, a number of private educational enterprises
were organized to take care of the needs of the community in two major
areas: adjustment to the urban American milieu for the immigrant and his
wife, and the transmission of the cultural heritage to his children. A viable
Greek organization at Hull House was the Greek Education Association,
formed in 1909, which sponsored a number of educational programs for young
Greek immigrants.

        With the dispersal of Greek immigrants to all parts of the city and
the establishment of new communities or parishes, additional Greek schools
were organized. Not all were day schools; the large expense necessary
to operate such schools made them prohibitive to many communities. As a

result, a supplementary school--the afternoon Greek school--evolved,
meeting several times a week after public school hours. Another type of
ethnic school that evolved was the private Greek school, maintained by
voluntary associations and parental groups, also meeting after public school
hours. In addition, many youngsters received their Greek training at home
by private tutor, especially in areas where Greek schools were not close
at hand. Another form of communal school, the Sunday school, was religious
in nature. But it was ethnically oriented and used the Greek language initially as its medium of instruction. Some parishes also sponsored adult
education classes for the learning of Greek.

The multiplicity and variety of Greek educational institutions in
Chicago made them accessible to Greeks residing throughout the city. Poorly organized, often inadequate and ill-supplied, they served nonetheless to
supplement the informal educational system of the home, church, and voluntary groups, and thus reinforced the transmission of the religio-cultural
heritage of Greek immigrants to their offspring.

It is believed that every Greek child born of immigrant parents was
exposed to one or another of these educational arrangements. The Greek
immigrant's commitment to education and his insistence that his children
learn the Greek language and heritage probably account for the fact that
the vast majority of second generation Greeks had a fluent command of the
Greek language and were cognizant of their Hellenic heritage, despite
alienation and indifference by some. To a great extent, these educational
arrangements have served members of the third generation and now are serving those of the fourth generation.

These educational enterprises were shaped to a great extent by
institutional structures which related them not only to the Greek community,
but to the broader community as well. The most important of these was the
formal church structure (koinotis) with its several agencies--the general
assembly, the board of trustees (symboulion), the school board or committee, and the clergy. Another significant aspect was the role played by the
voluntary associations within the church community, such as the parental
and charitable groups, and those external to it, such as local chapters of
the large national fraternities of AHEPA and GAPA. Of increasing importance
after 1931, was the archdiocesan structure of the Greek Orthodox church in

America, as exemplified by the supreme board of education. Of significance also were the Greek language press and other communications media.

The formal organizations of professional educators also influenced the educational arrangements of Greek immigrants. The efforts of the Greek Teachers League to improve the status of Greek language teachers and to bring about curricular change in Greek schools,and the efforts of the Hellenic Council on Education in the educational adjustment of children of recent Greek immigrants in the public schools indicated the concerns of these agencies. In addition, quasi-governmental bodies, such as the Chicago Board of Education and the Cook County Educational Service Area, as well as the Greek government, assisted the Greek communal schools in accreditation, service, and influence.

The final chapter summarizes the role of the formal and informal educational arrangements existing in Chicago during this century as they relate to the problem of Greek adjustment and integration into American society and reaches a conclusion with reference to ethnic survival.

CHAPTER V

SUMMARY AND CONCLUSION

Immigration is the oldest and most persistent theme in American history and helped to shape the distinctive institutions of the nation. Most important, immigration brought to the United States people of diverse cultural antecedents, who played a central role in the formation of American culture. The demands of the frontier and of labor encouraged unrestricted immigration and the United States became known as the land of the free, the haven for the oppressed subjects of political and religious tyranny, and the land of opportunity for the poor and destitute.

Nativist agitation over newer immigrants manifested itself in the 1830s, in the Know-Nothingism of the 1850s, the APAism of the 1890s, and the Ku Klux Klanism of the 1920s. However, prior to 1882, the vast majority of immigrants came from countries in northwestern Europe, and Americanization took place readily because of similarity of social institutions in the New World. A greater antipathy toward immigrants occurred with the arrival of large numbers from southern and eastern Europe. Before 1885, nine-tenths of the immigrants were from countries of northwestern Europe; by 1905, three-fourths were from countries of southern and eastern Europe.

Few of the later immigrants had the common background of Protestant Christianity which had distinguished the great majority of their predecessors. Most later newcomers were either Roman Catholic, Eastern Orthodox, or Jewish. Similarly, striking contrasts were found in the values, customs, and habits of the old and new immigrants. Moreover, some of the newcomers manifested little intention of making America their permanent home.

Despite the growth of nativism, unrestricted immigration continued unabated and reached over twenty-three million between 1880 and 1920. The question of the survival of Americans as an Anglo-Saxon people became a heated point of discussion, especially after World War I. Attempts were made to suppress nonpublic schools and the teaching of foreign languages

299

in public schools, culminating in the Oregon and Nebraska Supreme Court cases.

Indicative of the nativists' concern was the hastily conceived and inept Americanization program introduced in the nation's public schools and agencies to help eradicate foreign elements. The belief that the newer immigrants were inferior and unassimilable brought Congressional enactments which discriminated against immigrants from southern and eastern Europe and by 1927 the law with a "national origins" provision limited their quota to 150,000 yearly. This statute remained operative until 3 October 1965, when President Lyndon Johnson signed a new immigration reform bill into law, eliminating the discriminatory quota system.

In direct opposition to the Americanization movement was the concept of cultural pluralism. This idea challenged the melting pot theory that immigrants would intermingle and amalgamate into a new American species. It denied the desirability of having an amalgamation of varied groups to form the "new American." It conceived of the United States as a mosaic of nationalities and advocated a system of private ethnic schools in which the old country language and culture were taught. Those in defense of minority cultures argued that true Americanism lay in the conservation and fostering of group differences, not in melting them down.

While the melting pot theory is now in decline and the wrongs of the Americanization program have been acknowledged, agreement to the cultural pluralism theory remains debatable. Lack of agreement, however, has not affected adversely the existence of ethnic and private schools. Chicago's Greek immigrants faced the issues of Americanization and cultural pluralism. Many parents sent their children to public schools and availed themselves of adult evening classes provided by the Chicago Public School System. Others subscribed to a cultural pluralist theory and embarked on the creation of Greek communal schools and other forms of schooling for ethnic survival in the hope that such formal educational agencies would augment the role of the informal agencies—home, voluntary associations, and ethnic press in this task.

As shown in this study, habits and learnings were transmitted over successive generations through inculcation and persistency by group pressure of the Greek community. Greeks showed an acute awareness of their heritage and attempted to preserve and transmit their legacy and language to successive generations within new social patterns. As this transmission took place, they modified their behavior to meet changing circumstances and still retain their subculture. Some Greek immigrants could not bear the stress and strain of two conflicting cultures and disappeared into the expansive American milieu. Others remained cultural conservatives; some worked to bring the immigrant culture into the American mainstream. This study portrays the various positions on the issues of language maintenance and chauvinistic Hellenism that brought about division and conflict within the Greek community.

It has been stated that while attention has been given to the migration and settlement of immigrants in America, the reverse face of the coin—the acculturation-assimilation process—has been neglected until recently. Sociologists have had difficulty in agreeing upon a common definition of this process, despite formal attempts to do so. The definition used in the context of this study has been advanced by Milton Gordon and S. N. Eisenstadt. They hypothesize two kinds of assimilation: cultural assimilation (or simply acculturation), and structural assimilation (or simply assimilation).

Cultural assimilation means the absorption of the cultural patterns of the host society—the internalization of the new cultural standards by immigrants. Structural assimilation, on the other hand, indicates the entrance of the immigrants and their descendants into the social cliques, organizations, institutional activities, and civic life of the receiving society. It is this structural assimilation that leads to the creation of either primary relationships, such as friendship, or secondary relationships, such as earning a living or carrying out political responsibilities. The thesis is that while cultural assimilation (or acculturation), has taken place among immigrants in America, structural assimilation has not been extensive. There evolves, therefore, a basic distinction between what can be described as cultural and structural assimilation.

The implications from these distinctions are that in cultural assimilation the immigrants are assimilated to the degree that they internalize and express major American cultural patterns and values of the host society. In this arrangement they retain certain particularistic traits from the old culture. However, these traits are modified in their transplantation from the old traditional culture to that of the American society. Structural assimilation evolves mainly around the actual participation in the political, educational, occupational, and other aspects of the American social system.

While cultural assimilation (acculturation) has been keenly felt among Greeks in their educational arrangements and community life, structural assimilation (assimilation)--the disappearance of the Greek cultural system--has not taken place. Religion and the family seem to be the two institutions largely responsible for preserving the Greek culture into the second and third generations. In addition, the homeland influence on the social organization of the Chicago Greek community resulted in special ties between the Greek immigrant and the mother country. These ties included customs, ceremonies, values, ideals, kinship, organizations, cultural legacy, and feelings of eclectic ethnic identity. They were influential in the formation of various institutions, social divisions, factions, modes of thought, values, and patterns of social interaction in the New World. Because of their central role as links in the life of Greek-Americans, many cultural patterns associated with religion and family remain distinctly Greek and are more tenaciously conserved than in Greece proper. On the other hand, structural assimilation has occurred in areas such as economic status, education, politics, and formal associations.

Hence, the story of the education of Greeks in Chicago may well stand as an example of the survival of a people and the perpetuation of a culture. It is the story of an ethnic group busily going through the process of adjustment in an alien city, grasping at every opportunity to build a better way of life for return to the homeland, and retaining tenaciously a profound consciousness of their identity and heritage. Preservation of the cultural ethos was not achieved without conflict and devisiveness, nor without the modifying and acculturative impact of the American milieu, and in time, led to the emergence of a new Greek-American subculture in Chicago.

Every ethnic group must be seen against the background of the social order of which it is a part. A review of historical perspectives of the Greek nation and its people does suggest for their transplanted reinforcement of Greek identity and commitment upon arrival in Chicago. Geographic and economic conditions are shown as contributing heavily to the thrust for emigration to the New World. The political development from ancient to modern times illustrates one source of the Greek immigrants' pride in the achievements of their ancestors.

Historically, the strong sense of individualism and identity growing out of a long history and lengthy period of Turkish domination made for
the cohesive and highly structured Greek community in Chicago which nurtured nationalism and identity. The close connection between the religious
life of the Greeks and Hellenism was a bond strongly reflected in their educational aspirations in the New World. Finally, education and schooling--
highlighted in classical and Byzantine times--disappeared during the long
night of Turkish occupation and began a feeble emergence during the modern
period--the period which conditioned the limited schooling of Greek immigrants in America. Insight into the Greek background contributes to an understanding and possible appreciation of why intense feelings for ethnic
survival were exhibited in their adjustment to a new environment. The phenomenon of Greek emigration was presented as a necessary corollary to the
study to show the persistent mobility of Greeks throughout their history.
From the demographic data we learn that in the early years of immigration,
it was a male phenomenon. Furthermore, we learn by reviewing the quantitative data that the Greek stock is smaller in numbers in Chicago than
generally claimed.

The first twenty years of this century were described as the "age
of the immigrant." The presence of a large number of foreign-born excited
much comment over whether or not America's aliens could ever become useful citizens. This influx of immigrants prompted an Americanization movement to teach English and citizenship to them. However, the Greek way of
life, which revolved around its communal institutions, provided a sheltered
enclave for Greeks in which insecurity could be overcome at their own pace.
This was possible since sufficient numbers had emigrated to the city, making it the largest Greek community in the nation with approximately 10 percent of the Greek population. Initially, the group gathered in a Greek
"colony" on the near West Side and established churches, schools, coffeehouses, voluntary associations, and the immigrant press. This self-contained communal life with compatriots served as a decompression chamber
in releasing some of the stresses and strains of an unknown setting. The
social agency of the family and the church were perhaps the most unifying
forces in ethnic survival.

Important, too, from a structural point of view, were the many
voluntary associations which financially supported the educational endeav-

ors of the Greek community. In addition, Greek immigrants were closely associated with the famed Hull House, which tried to preserve their best traditional values and at the same time assist them in adapting to the ways and values of a new culture. Hence, all these institutions were part of a highly supportive structure which promoted the Greek community's efforts for ethnic survival.

As we look back upon the eighty years of educational adjustment of Greek immigrants and their children, some features of the process which contributed to ethnic survival become evident. Public schools in Chicago lacked adequate provisions to accommodate immigrants and their children and judged their performance by American cultural standards of conduct. The schools' formal attempts to bring about the enforced Americanization of immigrants at the expense of their cultural legacy were demeaning to them. They could not understand why learning the English language and American ways required the abandonment of loyalty to their homeland and ancestral traditions. In many instances public school policy had the apparent effect of alienating the Greek child from the immigrant culture and contributed to tension among family members, especially in the area of language maintenance. As a result, some discarded their tradition and became absorbed into American life.

For most Greek students, however, the role of the public school was significant in their external adjustment to the dominant American milieu by providing avenues for acculturation. The existence of the structural cohesiveness of the Greek community and the fact that nearly all Greek children attending public schools were enrolled in supplementary Greek schools and other educational arrangements helped to reinforce the cultural identity that was continuously projected by the informal agencies in the Greek communal system.

Communal day schools, compared to public schools, aimed to perpetuate the legacy and help acculturate children to the mainstream of American society. The adjustment became less abrupt in this friendly atmosphere, which legitimatized the transmission of Greek culture as part of the formal school curriculum. Consequently, products of Greek schools were knowledgeable of their heritage and more apt to be active expositors of Hellenism within the Greek community as well as in the broader American society. Of course, the Greek school did not perform this task alone;

other agencies--the home, church, voluntary associations, communications media, and varied other schooling programs--all focused on the importance of devotion and dedication to cultural maintenance.

Not only did the day schools protect Greek children from heterodox teachings which their parents were in no position to correct or controvert, but they also served to create a bond of unity by bringing the children territorially together in a church-school environment where language, religion, and history were inculcated to the old and new generations. Even though it is likely that these day schools slowed up the process of acculturation, at the same time, they assisted in the transition toward acculturation by easing their adjustment to a different society.

Despite conflicts that arose between the first and second generation products of ethnic schooling over chauvinistic attitudes, there did not seem to result any appreciable alienation between the immigrant generation and the American-born offspring. A recent study of Greek immigrants and their native-born children in New Jersey concluded that the opposite was true--a high level of interaction existed between generations.[1] That there is no unbridgeable gulf between the two generations is due perhaps to the existence of a functioning Greek community which is oriented toward imbuing the second generation with the language and ideals of Greece. As mentioned in the study, few other ethnic groups within the larger American community are so structurally organized.

The dispute over extreme forms of Greek nationalism which the immigrant generation insisted be maintained in the communal schools did not result in complete rejection of Hellenic ideals by the native-born generation. Rather, they maintained that they were Americans of Greek descent with no political allegiance to Greece, but a cultural allegiance to Hellenic ideals that were the basis of Western Civilization and a source of great pride.

With particular reference to the third generation grandchildren of Greek immigrants, it seems that certain ethnic components still have

---

[1] Nicholas Tavuchis, Family and Mobility among Second Generation Greek-Americans (Athens, Greece: National Centre of Social Research, 1972).

important relevance. In another study of selected college age, third generation Greek-Americans in New York City, it was shown that religion provided the context of self-identification and social location for third generation Greek-Americans in accordance with Herberg's hypothesis that grandchildren of immigrants, while rejecting ethnic definitions, are manifesting
the phenomenon of "third generation return" by affirming their identities
along religious lines.[1] That study did not bear out Herberg's explicit assumption that with increased assimilation religious differences have replaced
ethnic differences as a major differentiation of the American population.
Instead it revealed that the college sample considered the ethnic factor inextricably intertwined with the religious factor.[2]

Other studies concur that the descendants of Greek immigrants in
the United States have adapted to the American way of life, but have retained
certain ethnic components; therefore, they have not been totally assimilated.[3] Collectively, these studies, along with the present one, lead us
to presume that the United States Census Bureau may be premature in divorcing the grandchildren of Greek immigrants from the Greek ethnic stock.

It can be inferred from the above that communal schools have been
an important adjunct of the Greek community in keeping alive and insuring
a welded continuity of ethnic identity. Acculturative changes, however,
have occurred and have had an impact upon schooling, as shown in shifts
in philosophy, objectives, governance, personnel, and student population.
A summary of these changes follows.

---

[1]Will Herberg, Protestant, Catholic, Jew, an Essay in American
Religious Sociology (Garden City, N. Y.: Oxford University Press, 1964).

[2]See Alice Scourby, "Third Generation Greek Americans: A Study
in Religious Attitudes" (Ph.D. dissertation, New School for Social Research, 1967).

[3]Cf., Chrysie M. Costantakos, "American Greek Subculture: Processes of Continuity" (Ph.D. dissertation, Columbia University, 1969);
James Patterson, "The Unassimilated Greeks of Denver," Anthropological
Quarterly 43 (October 1970): 243-53; and Evangelos C. Vlachos, The Assimilation of Greeks in the United States with Special Reference to the Greek
Community of Anderson, Indiana (Athens, Greece: National Centre for
Social Research, 1968).

Much has been written by Greek Orthodox educators in the United States on methods of Greek linguistic and religio-cultural education, but little has been accomplished in defining a philosophy of Greek communal schooling. The pressing priorities of financial support and practical administrative operations have absorbed the time and energy of those in a position to solve persistent pedagogical problems.

Because the philosophy and function of Greek communal education has not been clarified, this study shows that there is no standard of judgment to provide a reliable, valid measurement of the effectiveness of these schools. Although there is no general consensus among educators and parents about what the schools should be, it is obvious from their development that Greek communal schools were intimately connected with survival and perpetuation of the Greek way of life. Based on this fact, the Greek communal schools seem to have been pre-eminently successful.[1]

This study points out that learning American ways was not a priority concern for the early Greek immigrants; most had intentions of returning to the homeland. The concept of an American of Greek descent and a shift of concerns toward some facets of Americanization evolved later. The study supports the generalization that Greek education in America has been essentially a process of social adjustment to the American environment and cultural preservation of Hellenic identity. This process encompasses American and Greek aspects. In its adaptation to the New World environment, the goal was to develop a harmonious, integrative, functioning individual and group that would relate to the social pattern of the broader culture on a selective basis. Supportive of its Greek aspect was the tenacious retention of its national legacy and the avoidance of the anomie of assimilation. Stated differently, the process employed in the Greek communal schools--past and present--dealt with ethnic survival, character development, and respectable democratic citizenship.

From the educational tasks mentioned, it is clear that the Greek educator faced some difficult issues throughout the years: (1) how to provide for sufficient cultural identity of his ethnic group without segre-

---

[1] Encyclopaedia Britannica, 1955 ed. , s. v. "Orthodox Eastern Church," by Matthew Spinka.

gating it from the mainstream of American society, (2) inversely, how to integrate Greek lifestyle and values with American culture without losing the distinctive Greek character, (3) how to assist the Greek immigrant and his family to gain resiliency in their restrictive and traditional Greek milieu, (4) inversely, how to imbue ethnic loyalty and survival without hampering the individual's effectiveness in the American environment. By no means have the Greek communal schools solved these problems, but each community has attempted to find solutions in its own way and with varying results.

Since the perpetuation of the Greek language and the survival of Hellenism became prime concerns of Greek immigrants, they, along with community leaders, priests, ethnic press, and voluntary associations joined in the demand that children born of Greek parents learn the language that "gave light to the world." This was a mission that had to be carried out, as well as a heritage that had to be preserved. The missionary zeal shown for the study of the parent language probably explains why so many children learned to speak Greek before learning English prior to World War II. Thus, the Greek language and ethnic identification with Greece became important educational objectives since most Greek immigrants expected to return to the homeland with their families.

For this reason, when Greek schools--day, supplementary afternoon, and Sunday--were established by the church communities, the teaching of Greek and nationalistic aspects of Hellenism were given top priority. They were followed by the teaching of religion which was in many ways inextricably related to the Hellenistic objective, and the teaching of English in the day schools.

As shown in the study, the acculturative forces through the years brought about changes in the hierarchy of school objectives in Greek schools. Indicative of this change was the attempt of the department of education of the Greek Orthodox Archdiocese to clarify the essence of Greek Orthodox education by publishing a Course of Study based on a decision of the Thirteenth Clergy-Laity Congress, meeting in Washington, D. C., in 1956. The study guide pointed out that:

. . . Greek education of the American citizens of Greek descent is not and should not be conceived as an independent and complete educational enterprise. This education is and should be conceived as a special and complementary side of the education that the American society provides by its comprehensive system of education to all citizens of the country.

In accordance with this principle, the Greek school of the Greek community, the educational institutions of the Greek Archdiocese, and generally all the cultural institutions of the organized American Hellenism are centers of a specific education. Their aim is to reinforce and supplement the educational centers and institutions of the country by means of a systematic cultivation and teaching of as many features of the Greek culture as possible.[1]

This passage is ambiguous as to intent, content, and identity of schools --day, afternoon, or once-a-week. Present day schools are definitely an "independent and complete educational enterprise" in which the child receives his elementary schooling, albeit in two languages, in a varying degree, and in two cultures. This does not negate the fact that the child also learns from his informal environment of peers, home, and neighborhood. Nonetheless, the passage represents a departure in the traditional stance of Greek ethnic education. Official recognition was made of the importance of American schooling; Greek schooling was conceived as complementary to American schooling in the education of descendants of Greek immigrants. This view undoubtedly was hastened by the agitation in the 1950s and 1960s among American-born parents (children of the immigrants) who objected to chauvinistic aspects of Greek schooling to which their children were subjected.

A definitive philosophical statement delineating the rationale for the existence of the Greek communal schools was arrived at by the Twentieth Biennial Clergy-Laity Congress of the Greek Orthodox Church, which met in New York in 1970. The statement generated much controversy between the liberal and conservative factions on the language issue due to its association with a resolution affirming English as the chief medium of instruction in the schools of the archdiocese.

In our opinion . . . the necessary prerequisite for the existence of Parochial Schools within our Orthodox Churches must and should always be imparting to our children American education at least equal, if not superior, to that provided by the equivalent Public School System. Additionally, a Parochial School serves its purpose well, when it provides instruction in the spiritual, moral, and cultural values of Greek Orthodox Christianity, our Hellenic Heritage, and in the nearly

---

[1]Philippos D. Emmanuel, Course of Study Prescribed for the Greek-American Elementary Schools (New York: Greek Archdiocese of North and South America, 1958), p. ix.

forgotten qualities of good citizenship, patriotism, and dedication
to the ideals of the American social fabric.

Finally, instruction of Greek as a second language will round
out a wholesome elementary school education, with all the attributes
of a truly private school with strong moralistic and religious undertones.[1]

It is obvious from this statement that one of the early objectives
of the Greek communal schools, that of cultural transmission from one generation to another, has remained virtually unchanged in the nearly seventy
years that Greek schools have existed in Chicago. But there has been a
shift in emphasis, as indicated in chapter 5, and shown in figure 7.

Figure 2. Changes in Objectives of Greek Day Communal Schools
(1908-1973)

Original Objectives	Present Day Objectives
1. Greek language	1. American citizenship
2. Greek cultural heritage	2. Religion
3. Religion	3. Greek cultural heritage
4. American citizenship	4. Greek language

The Greek schools are still interested in the promulgation of ethnic
identity and survival, but not at the expense of Americanism. American
citizenship has replaced the teaching of the Greek language as the highest
priority in the hierarchical scale of objectives. No longer is the Greek
cultural heritage second in priority; it has been replaced by the teaching
of religion. The study of the Greek cultural heritage and Greek language
now rank third and fourth respectively. Thus, while Hellenism is considered important in Greek communal schools, it no longer holds the exalted
position once ascribed to it by the immigrant generation which founded
the schools.

Many forces played a part in the shift of school aims--the erosion
of Hellenic sentiment caused by the continuous political and social upheavals in Greece, the disillusionment within the church in America over

---

[1] Proceedings of the Twentieth Clergy-Laity Congress, p. 27.
See also the Greek Press (Chicago), 19 August 1970.

internal conflict brought about by political turmoils in Greece, the realization that return to the ancestral land most likely would not occur, the subtle
forces of accommodation and acculturation--all these factors influenced
transitional changes in school objectives.

Changes in objectives brought about direct changes in curriculum
by demands made primarily by second and third generation Greek-Americans.
One of the first schools to reflect a shift in curriculum was Plato School,
which was established in 1952. Gradually, other Greek day schools made
curricular changes to parallel public schooling. The study shows how these
schools became monolingual and/or bilingual; all continued to be bicultural,
having both American and Greek studies.

Changes in language priorities have brought about great consternation in some immigrants and conservative Greek leaders. At present, some
day schools have three-and-one half hours of English and two hours of Greek
instruction; others have daily class periods of thirty to fifty minutes for
Greek study. There are parents who would prefer to have Greek language
instruction eliminated and replaced with more instruction in Greek culture
and religion. The efforts of these parents have been abortive due to conservative school boards who fear that further delimiting of Greek will seriously jeopardize the rationale for the existence of parish schools.

Here can be noted the point made by Rossi and Rossi in their study
of denominational schools.[1] Those identified as successful had strong
identification with religion and ethnicity in their effective development,
but prolonged maintenance of communal (parochial) schools ". . . compared
to the public schools, must provide as much or more aid to the emerging
middle classes and at the same time lose some of their ethnic stamp."[2]
They noted that during the past decades denominational schools have held
higher educational standards and a corresponding decline in foreign language
instruction. This description is applicable to the Greek communal schools.
The fact that the second generation, with all its acculturative modifications,
is now in control of these schools would give substance to these changes.

---

[1]Rossi and Rossi, pp. 171-99.

[2]Ibid., p. 173.

Furthermore, the emergence of Greek immigrants and their offspring into the middle class and a shift in emphasis from language to religious instruction supports the thesis of the religious evolvement of American ethnic groups presented by Glazer and Moynihan.[1]

Parallel to the transition in school objectives and curriculum has been the change in form and function of Greek schools. Changes have taken place in the areas of governance and administration, finance, personnel, and pupil composition.

Despite the early objections of community intellectuals over the church's role in education, no other institution provided the necessary sustained leadership to direct the schools. Not only did the churches assume control, but the clergy played an increasingly important role in the educational functions of the koinotis (community). Invariably, the priests were the first teachers or principals of the Greek schools, although many obstacles were set up by the anti-clericalist members of the governing councils to curtail clerical powers. From time to time, disagreements on the nature and control of these schools created sharp division among communicants and resulted in the dismissal of priests and schisms within the parishes.

In the early immigration period, the school governing councils were comprised mostly of professional men and learned individuals in the Greek community. These members, cognizant of their superior education, did not hesitate to impose their beliefs in school governance. Negative attitudes towards clericalism had been acquired in Greece, where the elitists had a low opinion of priests and did not accept their role in controlling education. The resultant feuds and court cases seriously undermined the ability of the early Greeks to work collectively for the good of the community.

Nonetheless, with the change in the composition of church boards of trustees and school boards, along with conciliatory efforts by clergy, the church began to exercise exclusive control over schools. This does not imply, however, that lay control ceased in school governance. The nature of the Greek community and mentality is heavily rooted in shared and democratic rights of lay people and is guaranteed by the archdiocesan

---

[1]Glazer and Moynihan, pp. 310-15.

constitutional bylaws. The position of the clergy in school governance was
enhanced further with the establishment of a Greek Orthodox Theological
Seminary in the United States in 1937. A new conflict arose because of the
acculturative impact inherent in the education of American-trained priests
and American-born parishioners vis-a-vis the ethnic conservatism of foreign-
born trustees and members. In fact, opposition to school changes and governance continues at the present time. The transition of the school boards
through the years under discussion can be conceived as shown in figure 8.

Figure 3. Changes in School Board Composition

1908-1930	Comprised of professional men and intellectual male leaders elected by the Greek community.
1930-1950	Businessmen and intellectuals appointed or elected by the Greek community.
1950-1973	Business people and parents (men and women) appointed or elected by Greek community.

The role of the administrator also changed in the last seventy
years. In the early days, the principal, or director, was the parish priest,
who often had limited training in pedagogy. When anti-clericalists had
their way, a lay person was hired to teach and serve as headmaster. He
usually was a "learned" man; occasionally, the administrator only had a
gymnasium (secondary) education. Having a full-time principal to fulfill
a specific job was unknown.

After World War I, a change began taking place with the influx of
families with children and the arrival of professionally-trained Greek teachers. Parents demanded qualified teaching staff and administrators to super-
vise both the Greek and English departments of the day schools. And for
greater efficiency some schools had full-time secretarial assistance.

Following World War II parental demands brought about the hiring
of some qualified American-educated administrators whose backgrounds of
supervision and administration helped to bring about shifts in school objectives that second generation parents desired. Therefore, the English
curriculum of these day schools became similar to the American public
school models. Usually the principal of the day school was also the

person in charge of the late afternoon programs. The transitional pattern of administration of the Greek communal schools can be summarized as shown in figure 9.

Figure 4. Changes in School Administrators of Greek Schools

1908-1920	Priest or lay headteacher; non-professional and Greek-born; no role definition for administrator; part-time.
1920-1950	Lay teacher-administrator; Greek-born and Greek trained; emergence of role of principal; some office help.
1950-1973	Full-time administrator; usually American-born and trained; professional concept of role of administrator; full-time office help.

From their inception, the Greek communal schools have been maintained and financed almost exclusively by the Greek community. Until 1920, fees, if any, were nominal; the cost differences were absorbed by voluntary associations, especially the topika somateia (ancestral hometown societies). The voluntary groups sponsored picnics, dances, and lectures to aid the operation of these schools. These events were well-attended, probably because they were the main social functions in the early Greek community life in Chicago. It can be stated that without the assistance of the voluntary associations, the schools would have been in a precarious situation at that time.

The financially independent position that communal schools enjoyed was curtailed after World War I. Rising costs and diminishing assistance from voluntary associations made it necessary for church communities to assist in subsidizing schools. The Great Depression of the 1930s created additional fiscal problems. Large organizations like AHEPA and GAPA, as well as the Philoptochos (Friends of the Poor Society), and Mothers Clubs conducted ongoing fund-raising programs to supplement the school treasury.

After World War II, school board records show a continuation of financial problems. Tuition rates increased yearly, and by 1973, they ranged from $350 to $500 annually per child, with a graduated decrease for additional children from the same household. This increased tuition pays for a negligible portion of the total school operating expenses. Transportation fees for school buses are not included in the tuition, but are additional fees that must be paid by parents or subsidized by the church community.

Since 1954, in an attempt to help alleviate the heavy financial burden faced by church communities, the Greek Orthodox Archdiocese has been subsidizing communal day schools on an annual basis. These subsidies have increased from an average of $1,000 in that year to $5,000, and sometimes more, in 1973. The amount varies with the size of the school, but this token contribution from the archdiocese has not solved the problem of financing these schools. Parishes have had to increase their own subsidies, and their associated voluntary organizations have had to embark upon varied fund-raising events on a continuous basis in order to maintain the parish school. The emergence of an archdiocesan subsidy program has raised questions concerning the traditional congregational control of communal schools, and is not unlike that of the encroachment faced by public schools with the advent of federal aid to education. Figure 10 shows the shift in the financial support of Greek communal schools.

Figure 5. Changes in the Financial Support of Greek Schools

1908-1920	Monies from topika somateia; fund-raising events such as picnics, dances, lectures, bazaars; tuition; schools fiscally independent; extensive autonomy.
1920-1950	Tuition grants and funds from AHEPA and GAPA; fund-raising events by Philoptochos and Mothers Club; church subsidy; fiscally dependent upon boards of trustees; less autonomy.
1950-1973	Increase in tuition; increase in local church subsidy; Greek Orthodox Archdiocese subsidy; governmental aid; limited fiscal autonomy.

The role of the teacher commanded respect and status in the Greek community, a carry-over from values held in Greece. There was no teacher shortage, because enough persons were available with general education or with degrees in law, theology, and journalism that gave them teaching potential.

Students of the 1910-20 decade recall the teachers as "good, but stern disciplinarians."[1] A growing demand for professionally-trained staff occurred after World War I (as mentioned in chapter 5). Teachers were recruited from the two most prestigious teacher institutions in the Greek-speaking world--the Arsakeion School in Athens and the Great National School in Constantinople. Others were recruited from the Greek normal schools, and some were hired with only a gymnasium background. Several were graduates of the University of Athens but with no special preparation in education.

During this period, English instruction was introduced, which meant the hiring of additional teachers who were educated in American institutions. Some of the non-Greek teachers came from the Chicago public schools and remained until retirement. Their professional experiences over many decades in Greek communal schools are recalled with nostalgia and as "exciting times," despite low salaries, poor equipment, and lack of professional standards.[2] These teachers often were the only formal "links" that the Greek child had with the broader American society, and consequently were highly respected by both pupils and parents.[3]

With the exception of those from the public schools, teachers in the English and Greek departments were noncertified. However, after World War II, the Greek schools embarked upon an accelerated program of instructional improvement to meet the growing demands of parents, as shown in the previous chapter. Retiring English teachers were replaced with younger college graduates who had difficulties obtaining assignments in public schools, because of oversupply. The new staff became certified by the State Office of Public Instruction. In the Greek departments, many of the "old and tried" teachers remained. They had become acculturated and American-

---

[1]Interviews with Gus Spirakes, Chicago, 7 February 1968; and Tom Macropoulos, Chicago, 6 October 1968.

[2]Interviews with Henrietta Block, Chicago, 3 April 1968; and Helen Weble, Chicago, 31 July 1968; letter from Catherine Kennedy, Phoenix (Arizona), 24 May 1969.

[3]Interview with C. J. Glynos, school inspector, Second Archdiocesan District, Greek Orthodox Archdiocese, and former day school principal, Oak Lawn, Illinois, 10 December 1971.

ized, and identified more readily with the pupils than teachers from Greece who began arriving as part of the provisions of the Displaced Persons Act of 1948. Schools were also becoming increasingly staffed with Greek teachers from the Academy of Saint Basil in New York, an institution established by the archdiocese in 1945 specifically for the preparation of Greek teachers in communal schools.

For many decades the salary schedules of teachers in the English and Greek departments were exceedingly low compared to public schools, despite similar qualifications for English instruction. The rationale for these low salaries was the assumption that they were part-time teachers and subject to part-time income. This analogy was deceptive, because in some day schools they performed a full day's service crammed into three or three-and-one-half hours. In many ways, in the opinion of this writer, their work was more arduous, having to concentrate so much activity in a short span of time.

No uniform salary scale existed, and each teacher negotiated with the administrator, based on seniority of employment. Only since the mid-1950s, have there been improved and more uniform salaries, fringe benefits, and better working conditions. Figure 11 indicates changes in personnel policies.

Figure 6. Changes in Personnel Policies in Greek Schools

1908-1920	Foreign-born and trained; limited formal educational experience; nationalistically oriented; low salary; no fringe benefits.
1920-1950	Both foreign and American-born and trained; mixture of certified and non-certified personnel; mostly Greek-oriented; low and/or part-time salary; minimal or no fringe benefits.
1950-1973	Mostly American-born and educated in United States; minimum of B.A. degree and certification approved by the State of Illinois; American-oriented; improved salaries and fringe benefits; all-day employment.

Pupils enrolled in Greek communal day schools in the early years of the twentieth century consisted of either the immigrants from Greece or their children. However, due to economic stringencies, most Greek children attended public schools, as shown in chapter 4, even though parents preferred to have them enroll in Greek schools. However, those who attended public schools were enrolled in supplementary Greek schools or received private tutoring at home. During the interwar period (1918-41), the school's clientele became the American-born children of the early immigrants. Another shift was evidenced after World War II, with an increase of Greek-born children resulting from renewed postwar immigration from Greece.

Close support between the school and home minimized discipline and other school problems. One instructor stated that "it was always a pleasure to teach Greek children, they were so bright and attentive and there was never any problem in getting lessons across to them."[1] Another faculty member said, "Greek children have an exceedingly high esteem and love for education. Their willingness to learn and respect shown for the teacher made teaching in the Greek school much more enjoyable than teaching in the public schools".[2] Similar views were expressed by officials of public high schools who were familiar with Greek students from nonpublic schools. A public school official from Austin High School recalls that "our most proficient students, especially in languages and mathematics, were those who came to us from Plato Greek School."[3] These comments are corroborated by official reports of accrediting committees who have evaluated these schools, as shown in chapter 5.

Greek school educators have attributed the pupils' level of achievement to the fact that they concentrate on the basic or essential learnings-- the three R's. In their opinion the stress on basic skills and knowledge of the Greek language aids students in English grammar and reading and explains their academic competency.[4] Further investigation would be most

[1]Unsolicited letter from Isabel Hazlitt, retired English teacher of Greek school, San Diego, California, 7 December 1969.

[2]Interview with Elizabeth Oettershagen, Chicago, 23 September 1969.

[3]Interview with Raymond Lussenhop, former assistant principal, Austin High School, Chicago, 9 August 1970.

[4]Interviews with C. Glynos, E. Polites, G. Louris, J. Paziotopoulos, C. Mihalakis, E. Sakellariou on dates indicated supra.

helpful in finding out the occupational and educational achievements of
students from Greek communal schools.

Unfortunately, practically no reliable research has been conducted
on the effectiveness of Greek schools. However, several long-term Greek
school officials noted, after a cursory longitudinal study of graduates over
the past half-century, that they were more likely to become leaders in the
Greek community than those Greek-American children who attended public
or other non-Greek schools.[1] In reviewing names of members of symboulia
(church boards of trustees) and active voluntary associations, the vast
majority that provided leadership were people who had spent their formative
years in the Greek ethnic schools. An observation of the newer Greek communities in Chicago's suburbs provides additional insight. Persons who
took the lead in organizing these new communities and ministering to the
religious, ethnic, and social needs of church members were former communal
day school pupils. It can be inferred that while these students were not more
religious or altruistic than the children who attended public schools, they
were more aware of their heritage and participated with greater regularity in
ethnic activities and the sacramental life of the church. Research studies
made on other nonpublic schools have indicated similar findings.[2]

It can also be inferred from this study that Greek communal schools
served as important vehicles in helping Greek children adjust to the American
milieu. In the homogeneous and comforting "kinship" atmosphere of these
schools many youngsters acquired a self-concept of who they were, where
they came from, and what their status could be in American society. Figure 12 depicts the changes in the student population of Greek communal
schools during this century.

---

[1] George Drossos and Pantelis Parpadis, "The Role of our Greek
Schools in Perpetuating Hellenism," paper presented at Greek Teachers
Conference, 20 March 1968. (Text in Greek.)

[2] Cf., Fichter; Donald A. Erickson, "Differential Effects of Public
and Sectarian Schooling on the Religiousness of the Child" (Ph.D. dissertation, University of Chicago, 1962); Gerhard Lenski, The Religious Factor:
A Sociological Study of Religion's Impact on Politics, Economics, and
Family (Garden City, N. Y.: Doubleday & Co., 1961); Andrew M. Greeley
and Peter H. Rossi, "Correlates of Parochial School Attendance," School
Review 72 (Spring 1964): 52-73, and their Education of Catholic Americans.

Figure 7. Changes in Pupil Population in Greek Schools

1908-1920   Immigrant generation; children of labor-
              ers and peddlers; Greek language spo-
              ken exclusively at home; proud of
              ethnic identity; vast majority male.

1920-1950   Admixture of foreign and American-
              born; children of blue and white
              collar workers; offspring of business-
              men; mostly Greek spoken at home;
              ambivalent responses toward ethnic
              identification; girls and boys in
              schools.

1950-1973   Grandchildren of early immigrants;
              parents in businesses or professions;
              mostly English spoken at home; ac-
              ceptance of ethnic identity within
              American milieu; increase of Greek-born
              children based on new influx of Greek
              immigration in some schools.

In short, this study shows that the Greek communal school faced overt and subtle changes in the past seventy years. It supports the contention that most Greek immigrants in Chicago wanted their own ethnic schools. Perhaps the most basic change in Greek ethnic day schools is a shift from the concept of a communal (parochial) school to that of a church-related private school.

An elitist concept is emerging, unofficially, which suggests that the progressive Greek day schools should seek to educate promising students who will provide future ethnic leadership. It is premised on the idea that it takes vast sums of money to maintain and operate these schools, while for demographic and economic reasons, they have been unable to reach all the children in the Greek community. Furthermore, the escalating tuition makes it difficult for children of poor families to attend ethnic schools. This criterion of elitist selectivity of students is far removed from the prototype communal school of a half-century ago! It suggests a continuation of the Greek commitment to ethnic survival. Indicative, perhaps, of the application of this commitment on a wider scale is the idea of social deviancy.

What, then, can be happening to the Greek communal schools of Chicago? Will the decline of Greek language instruction contribute to their eventual demise, as was the case in some Roman Catholic schools where

the et, :c aspect was diminished? The possibility is there! However,
another phenomenon is emerging, unlike Roman Catholic denominationalism.
As mentioned elsewhere, the Greek form is cohesive, exclusive, restrictive
--moreso than most other ethnic groups. Evidence indicates that improved,
affluent economic status, persistent religious ties to Orthodoxy, and an
awareness of cultural identification with a long historical tradition combine
to produce a "deviant" Greek culture in Chicago.

It has been suggested that an affluent urban society in this century
has a "mass culture."

Since a culture is a common and standardized set of ways of thinking
and believing, a mass culture is one in which most people think and
behave alike. They share a maximum of goods and services. They
have the same amusements. They read and view the same newspapers
and TV programs. They eat the same food and wear the same clothing.
Goods are manufactured for a mass market. Popular taste and popular
fashion are undifferentiated. The image of a mass culture is conveyed
by the thought of millions of families sitting before television and
watching Jackie Gleason. Some people sit in five hundred dollar
chairs and divans in their penthouse apartments, while others sit on
soiled and rancid overstuffed sofas in ghetto slums. They all participate in the mass culture.[1]

The mass culture is a secondary level relationship in which most Americans
participate. But on the primary level of relationship--the more intimate
level that involves family, relatives, friends--many Americans belong to
subcultural groups, whether ethnic, religious, social, or economic. Sometimes these subgroups are referred to as "deviant" cultural groups.

In the United States there are "deviant" cultural groups that are
transitional and moving into the mass culture, such as the southern Appal-
achian white or black, Spanish-speaking Americans, and some eastern and
southern Europeans. Often they are erroneously labelled "culturally deprived,"
or "socially disadvantaged," until they acculturate with the mass culture.
These groups operate in some kind of tradition--literary, religious, ethnic,
aesthetic--and their productivity and lifestyle are determined by this tradition.

The tendency in contemporary society is to be assimilated by the
mass culture at the expense of losing subcultural identification. A dichotomy appears, with transitional social groups seeking assimilation and the

[1] Robert J. Havighurst, "The Acculturation Process," in Anderson
and Kolesnik, pp. 2-3.

so-called "elitist" groups cherishing identities and seeking to escape the
mass culture which they think threatens to engulf them. Therefore, the
lower cultural groups strive to move upward while the higher cultural groups
and those with group morale (ethnic or religious) strive to keep above the
mass culture. In both cases, education is the major instrument for achieving these goals. The traditional role of public schools has been to acculturate its students to the reigning mass culture as well as to acculturate certain select groups into "deviant" cultures which supposedly are better than
the mass culture. The latter function also has been that of private schools
and some parochial schools. In other words, for some people, education is
a way of joining the American society; for others, it is a way of escaping the
regimentation and standardization of American society.

Such a "deviant" approach can well describe the Greeks in Chicago.
In chapter 3 mention was made of the astute business acumen and mercantile ability of the Greeks, as well as their being one of the first of the "new"
immigrants to reach middle-class economic status. As others have observed,
the Greeks along with the Jews, "were quicker to develop effective community
organizations than were other immigrants who had not previously faced the
problem of adapting as minority groups."[1] Despite their individualism and
factionalism, they succeeded in the mission of transmitting the cultural
legacy by way of the family, voluntary associations, church, school, and
communications media.

Naturally, the acculturative influences are apparent in the daily life-
styles of Greek-Americans. Nonetheless, the retention and expansion of
cultural activities and schooling arrangements indicate a renewed determination to perpetuate their ethnic tradition without necessarily using the Greek
language to achieve the classic heritage. However, new problems are aris-
ing as to approaches for Greek ethnic survival. Greek nationalism is favored
by the more recent Greek immigrants, while the American-born generation
favors preservation of religious and cultural legacies. Perhaps, like the
Greeks of the Byzantine period, they are oppressed by the weight of their
own history; the continuity of their culture is too strong for alteration.

----

[1] Rosen, pp. 47-60.

Employing the technical language of Gordon, Greek immigrants of Chicago went through a cultural assimilation (acculturation), which involved the process of the immigrant group learning the manners and style of a new society--hence, adjustment. Structural assimilation (assimilation), in which members of immigrant groups related to members of other groups, particularly on the intimate levels of family formation and friendship, without regard to ethnic differences, did not occur to any great extent. The Greeks of Chicago have maintained particularistic modes of group cohesion, while also comfortably accommodating to the achievement standards of the larger American society. This "best of two worlds" adaptation may well be the distinguishing mark of Greek-American ethnicity.

ΤΕΛΟΣ ΚΑΙ ΤΩ ΘΕΩ ΔΟΞΑ!

SELECTED BIBLIOGRAPHY

Books

Abbott, Edith, and Breckinridge, Sophonisba P. Truancy and Non-Attendance in the Chicago Schools. Chicago: University of Chicago Press, 1917.

Abbott, Grace. The Immigrant and the Community. New York: Century Company, 1917.

Addams, Jane. Twenty Years at Hull-House. New York: Macmillan Company, 1910; Signet Classics, 1961.

Allen, Harold B. Come Over into Macedonia: The Story of a Ten-Year Adventure in Uplifting a War-Torn People. New Brunswick, N. J.: Rutgers University Press, 1943.

Allesios, Allison B. The Greek Immigrant and His Reading. Chicago: American Library Association, 1926.

Anderson, Ernest V., and Kolesnik, Walter B. Education and Acculturation in Modern Urban Society. Detroit: University of Detroit Press, 1965.

Antonakaki, Kalliniki Dendrinou. Greek Education. New York: Bureau of Publications, Teachers College, Columbia University, 1955.

Ayres, Leonard P. Laggards in our Schools. New York: Russell Sage Foundation, 1909.

Bailyn, Bernard. Education in the Forming of American Society. New York: Random House; Vintage Books, 1960.

Baird, Henry M. Modern Greece: A Narrative of a Residence and Travels in that Country. New York: Harper and Brothers, 1856.

Baynes, Norman H., and Moss, H. St. L. B. Byzantium: An Introduction to East Roman Civilization. Oxford: At the Clarendon Press, 1948.

Belelis, Lazarus. O Kapodistrias os idritis laikis paideias en Helladi (Capodistrias as founder of popular education in Greece). Athens: John N. Sederis, 1908.

324

Benz, Ernst. The Eastern Orthodox Church: Its Thought and Life. New York: Doubleday and Company, 1963.

Bierstadt, Edward Hale. Aspects of Americanization. Cincinnati: Robert M. McBride and Company, 1922.

Billington, Ray Allen. The Protestant Crusade 1800-1860: A Study of the Origins of American Nativism. New York: Macmillan Company, 1938.

Booras, Harris J. Hellenic Independence and America's Contribution to the Cause. Rutland, Vt.: Tuttle Company, 1934.

Bratsiotis, Panagiotis. The Greek Orthodox Church. Translated by Joseph Blenkinsopp. South Bend, Ind.: University of Notre Dame Press, 1968.

Brickman, William W. Guide to Research in Educational History. New York: New York University Bookstore, 1949.

Brown, Francis J., and Roucek, Joseph S. One America: The History, Contributions, and Present Problems of Our Racial and National Minorities. Rev. ed. New York: Prentice-Hall, 1945.

Burgess, Ernest W., and Newcomb, Charles. Census Data of the City of Chicago, 1920. Chicago: University of Chicago Press, 1931.

_____. Census Data of the City of Chicago, 1930. Chicago: University of Chicago Press, 1933.

Burgess, Thomas. Greeks in America: An Account of their Coming, Progress, Customs, Living, and Aspirations. Boston: Sherman, French and Company, 1913.

Butts, R. Freeman, and Cremin, Lawrence A. A History of Education in American Culture. New York: Henry Holt and Company, 1959.

Byron, Robert. The Byzantine Achievement: An Historical Perspective A. D. 330-1453. New York: Alfred A. Knopf, 1929.

Callimahos, Demetrios. To Hellenikon ideologikon kinima en tais enomenais politeias (The Greek ideological movement in the United States). New York: National Herald Press, 1927.

Campbell, Roald F.; Cunningham, Luvern L.; and McPhee, Roderick F. The Organization and Control of American Schools. Columbus, Ohio: Charles E. Merrill Books, 1965.

Canoutas, Seraphim G. Hellenism in America or the History of the Greeks in America. New York: Cosmos Publishers, 1918.

Chaconas, Stephen George. Adamantios Korais: A Study in Greek Nationalism.
    New York: Columbia University Press, 1942.

Chassiotis, G. L'Instruction publique chez les Grecs depuis la prise de
    Constantinople par les Turcs, jusqu'a nos jours. Paris: Ernest
    Leroux, 1881.

Clark, Hannah B. The Public Schools of Chicago. Chicago: University of
    Chicago Press, 1897.

Cline, Myrtle A. American Attitude Toward the Greek War of Independence
    1821-1828. Atlanta, Georgia: Higgins-McArthur Company, 1930.

Cline, Rodney. Builders of Louisiana Education. Baton Rouge: Louisiana State
    University Press, 1963.

Commager, Henry Steele, ed. Immigration and American History. Minneapolis:
    University of Minnesota Press, 1961.

Counts, George S. School and Society in Chicago. New York: Harcourt, Brace
    and Company, 1928.

Cremin, Lawrence A. The American Common School: An Historic Conception.
    New York: Bureau of Publications, Teachers College, Columbia
    University, 1951.

_____. The Transformation of the Schools: Progressivism in American
    Education, 1876-1957. New York: Alfred A. Knopf; Vintage Books, 1961.

Cubberley, Ellwood P. Changing Conceptions of Education. Boston: Houghton
    Mifflin Company, 1909.

Dakin, Douglas. The Greek Struggle for Independence 1821-1833. Berkeley:
    University of California Press, 1973.

_____. The Unification of Greece, 1770-1923. New York: St. Martin's
    Press, 1972.

Davis, Allen F., and McCree, Mary Lynn, eds. Eighty Years at Hull-House.
    Chicago: Quadrangle Books, 1969.

Davis, Philip. Immigration and Americanization. Boston: Ginn and Company,
    1920.

Demetry, Constans H. Catechism of the Eastern Orthodox Church with Most
    Essential Differences of Other Principal Churches Scripturally Criticized.
    Detroit: Eagle Printing Company, 1929.

Diehl, Charles. Byzantium: Greatness and Decline. Translated by Naomi Walford. New Brunswick, N. J.: Rutgers University Press, 1957.

Drachsler, Julius. Democracy and Assimilation: The Blending of Immigrant Heritages in America. New York: Macmillan Company, 1920.

Dumond, Dwight Lowell. America in Our Time, 1896-1946. New York: Henry Holt and Company, 1947.

Duncan, Hannibal G. Immigration and Assimilation. New York: D. C. Heath and Company, 1933.

Durant, Will. The Story of Civilization. Vol. 2: The Life of Greece. New York: Simon and Schuster, 1939.

Economidou, Mary S. E Hellenes tis Amerikis opos tous eida (The Greeks in America as I saw them). New York: D. C. Divry, 1916.

Economos, Christos P. Koraes os ethnikos paidagogos (Koraes as national educator). Athens: John N. Sederis, 1904.

Edwards, Newton, and Richey, Herman G. The School in the American Social Order. 2nd ed. rev. Boston: Houghton Mifflin Company, 1963.

Eisenstadt, S. N. The Absorption of Immigrants. Glencoe, Ill., The Free Press, 1955.

Fairchild, Henry Pratt. Greek Immigration to the United States. New Haven: Yale University Press, 1911.

Felton, Cornelius C. Greece, Ancient and Modern. 2 vols. Boston: Ticknor and Fields, 1867.

Ferriman, Duckett Z. Home Life in Hellas: Greece and the Greeks. London: Mills and Bonn, 1910.

Fichter, Joseph H. Parochial School: A Sociological Study. South Bend, Ind.: Notre Dame University Press, 1958.

Finlay, George. History of Greece 146 A.D.-1864 A. D. 7 vols. Oxford: Clarendon Press, 1877.

Fishman, Joshua A. Language Loyalty in the United States. The Hague: Mouton and Company, 1966.

Freeman, Kenneth J. Schools of Hellas: An Essay on the Practice and Theory of Ancient Greek Education from 600 to 300 B. C. London: Macmillan Company, Ltd., 1907.

Friedl, Enestine. Vasilika: A Village in Modern Greece. New York: Holt, Rinehart and Winston, 1962.

Garnett, Lucy M. J. Greece of the Hellenes. New York: Charles Scribner's Sons, 1914.

Gavin, Frank. Some Aspects of Contemporary Greek Orthodox Thought. Milwaukee: Morehouse Publishing Company, 1923.

Geanakoplos, Deno John. Byzantine East and Latin West: Two Worlds of Christendom in Middle Ages and Renaissance. New York: Harper and Row, 1966.

_____. Greek Scholars in Venice: Studies in the Dissemination of Greek Learning from Byzantium to Western Europe. Cambridge: Harvard University Press, 1962.

Ginger, Ray. Altgeld's America, 1890-1905: The Lincoln Ideal Versus Changing Realities. New York: Funk and Wagnalls Company, 1958; reprint ed., Chicago: Quadrangle Paperbacks, 1965.

Glazer, Nathan and Moynihan, Daniel Patrick. Beyond the Melting Pot. Cambridge: Massachusetts Institute of Technology Press, 1964.

Goldman, Eric. Rendezvous with Destiny: A History of Modern American Reform. New York: Alfred A. Knopf, 1952; Vintage Books, 1956.

Gordon, Milton. Assimilation in American Life: The Role of Race, Religion, and National Origins. New York: Oxford University Press, 1964.

Gottschalk, Louis. Understanding History. New York: Alfred A. Knopf, 1963.

Grant, Madison. The Passing of the Great Race in America. New York: Charles Scribner's Sons, 1916.

Greeley, Andrew M. Why Can't They Be Like Us? America's White Ethnic Groups. New York: E. P. Dutton and Company, 1971.

Greeley, Andrew M., and Rossi, Peter H. The Education of Catholic Americans. Chicago: Aldine Press, 1966.

Greer, Colin. The Great School Legend: A Revisionist Interpretation of American Public Education. New York: Basic Books, 1972.

Handlin, Oscar. The American People in the Twentieth Century. Cambridge: Harvard University Press, 1954.

Handlin, Oscar. Boston's Immigrants 1790-1865: A Study in Acculturation. Cambridge: Harvard University Press, 1941.

_____. Immigration as a Factor in American History. Englewood Cliffs, N. J.: Prentice-Hall, 1959.

_____. Race and Nationality in American Life. Boston: Little, Brown and Company, 1950; Garden City, N. Y.: Doubleday Anchor Books, 1957.

_____. The Uprooted: The Epic of the Great Migrations that Made the American People. New York: Grosset and Dunlap Publishers, 1951.

Hartmann, Edward George. The Movement to Americanize the Immigrant. New York: Columbia University Press, 1948.

Hauser, Philip M., and Kitagawa, Evelyn M. Local Community Fact Book for Chicago 1950. Chicago: University of Chicago, 1953.

Herrick, Mary J. The Chicago Schools: A Social and Political History. Beverly Hills, Calif.: Sage Publications, 1971.

Herskovits, M. J. Acculturation: The Study of Culture Contact. Gloucester, Mass.: P. Smith, 1958.

Higham, John. Strangers in the Land: Patterns of American Nativism 1860-1925. New Brunswick, N. J.: Rutgers University Press, 1955.

Hofstadter, Richard. The Age of Reform: From Bryan to F. D. R. New York: Random House; Vintage Books, 1955.

Howe, Samuel G. An Historical Sketch of the Greek Revolution. New York: White, Gallaher and White, 1828.

Hull-House Maps and Papers. New York: Thomas Y. Crowell and Company, 1895.

Jaeger, Werner. Paideia: The Ideals of Greek Culture. 3 vols. 2nd ed. Translated by Gilbert Highet. New York: Oxford University Press, 1960.

Jarde, A. The Formation of the Greek People. New York: Alfred A. Knopf, 1926.

Jencks, Christopher. Inequality: A Reassessment of the Effect of Family and Schooling in America. New York: Basic Books, 1972.

Jeter, Helen R. Trends of Population in the Region of Chicago. Chicago: University of Chicago Press, 1927.

Jones, Maldwyn Allen. American Immigration. Chicago: University of
Chicago Press, 1960.

Kallen, Horace M. Cultural Pluralism and the American Idea. Philadelphia:
University of Pennsylvania Press, 1956.

_____. Culture and Democracy in the United States. New York: Boni
and Liveright, 1924.

Kitagawa, Evelyn M., and Taeuber, Karl E. Local Community Fact Book:
Chicago Metropolitan Area, 1960. Chicago: University of Chicago
Press, 1963.

Kotakis, Spyridon A. E Hellenes en Ameriki (The Greeks in America). Chicago:
Privately printed, 1906.

Kraus, Michael. Immigration, The American Mosaic. Princeton, N. J.:
D. V. Van Nostrand Company, 1966.

Lacey, Thomas James. A Study in Social Heredity as Illustrated by the Greek
People. New York: Edwin S. Gorham, 1916.

_____. A Study of the Eastern Orthodox Church. 2nd rev. ed. New York:
Edwin S. Gorham, 1912.

Lannie, Vincent P. Public Money and Parochial Education. Cleveland: Press
of Case Western Reserve University, 1968.

Larabee, Stephen A. Hellas Observed: The American Experience of Greece
1775-1865. New York: New York University Press, 1952.

Lawson, John Cuthbert. Modern Greek Folklore and Ancient Greek Religion:
A Study in Survivals. New York: University Books, 1964.

Leber, George J. The History of the Order of AHEPA, 1922-1972. Washington,
D. C.: Published by the Fraternity, 1972.

Lenski, Gerhard. The Religious Factor: A Sociological Study of Religion's
Impact on Politics, Economics, and Family. Garden City, N. Y.:
Doubleday and Company, 1961.

Linn, James Weber. Jane Addams: A Biography. New York: D. Appleton-
Century Company, 1935.

McManis, John T. Ella Flagg Young and a Half Century of Chicago Schools.
Chicago: A. C. McClurg, 1916.

Magaris, Theano P. Chroniko tou Halsted street (Chronicle of Halsted street). Athens: G. Phexis, 1962.

Malafouris, M. Hellenes tis Amerikis 1528-1948 (Greeks of America 1528-1948). New York: Isaac Goldman Company, 1947.

Marrou, H. I. A History of Education in Antiquity. Translated by George Lamb. New York: Sheed and Ward, 1956; New American Library, Mentor Books, 1956.

Marshall, Grace E. Eternal Greece. Rochester, N. Y.: DuBois Press, 1938.

Mears, Eliot Grinnell. Greece Today: The Aftermath of the Refugee Impact. Stanford, Calif.: Stanford University Press, 1929.

Megas, George A. Greek Calendar Customs. Athens: Press and Information Department, Prime Minister's Office, 1958.

Meyendorff, John. The Orthodox Church: Its Past and Its Role in the World Today. New York: Random House; Pantheon Books, 1962.

Meyer, Adolphe E. An Educational History of the American People. New York: McGraw-Hill Book Company, 1957.

Miller, Herbert Adolphus. The School and the Immigrant. Cleveland: Survey Committee of the Cleveland Foundation, 1916.

Miller, William. Greek Life in Town and Country. London: G. Newnes, 1905.

Murray, John C. The Role of the Independent School in American Democracy. Milwaukee: Marquette University Press, 1956.

Myers, Edward D. Education in the Perspective of History. New York: Harper and Brothers, 1960.

Novak, Michael. The Rise of the Unmeltable Ethnics. New York: Macmillan Company, 1971.

Oaks, Dallin A., ed. The Wall Between Church and State. Chicago: University of Chicago Press, 1963.

Panagopoulos, E. P. New Smyrna: An Eighteenth Century Greek Odyssey. Gainesville, Fla.: University of Florida Press, 1966.

Paparrigopoulos, Constantine. Epitomos historia tou Hellenikou ethnous (Abridged history of the Greek nation). 2 vols. Athens: Demetrios Demetrakos Publishing House, 1952.

Park, Robert E. The Immigrant Press and Its Control. New York: Harper and Brothers, 1922.

Park, Robert E., and Burgess, E. W. The City. Chicago: University of Chicago Press, 1925.

Park, Robert E., and Miller, Herbert A. Old World Traits Transplanted. New York: Harper and Brothers, 1921.

Pierce, Bessie L. History of Chicago. 3 vols. New York: Alfred A. Knopf, 1937-57.

Polyzoides, Germanos. Ekkliastiki historia (Ecclesiastical history). New York D. C. Divry Press, 1939.

Raizis, Marios B., and Papas, Alexander. Greek Revolution and the American Muse. Thessaloniki, Greece: Institute for Balkan Studies, 1972.

Roberts, Peter. The New Immigration: A Study of the Industrial and Social Life of Southeastern Europeans in America. New York: Macmillan Company, 1912.

Robinson, David M. America in Greece: A Traditional Policy. New York: Anatolia Press, 1948.

Rodd, Rennell. The Customs and Lore of Modern Greece. London: David Scott, 1892.

Rose, F. A.; Fry, C. L.; and Sibley, E. The Near East and American Philanthro New York: Columbia University, 1929.

Ross, Edward A. The Old World in the New: The Significance of Past and Present Immigration to the American People. New York: Century Company, 1914.

Runciman, Steven. The Great Church in Captivity. Cambridge, England: University Press, 1968.

Ryan, Mary Perkins. Are Parochial Schools the Answer? New York: Holt, Rinehart and Winston, 1964.

St. Clair, William. That Greece Might Still Be Free: the Philhellenes in the War of Independence. New York: Oxford University Press, 1972.

Sanders, Irwin T. Rainbow in the Rock: The People of Rural Greece. Cambridg Harvard University Press, 1962.

Sarres, Peter J. Historia ton Hellinon en Ameriki (History of the Greeks in America). New York: Anatolia Press, 1941.

Saloutos, Theodore. The Greeks in the United States. Cambridge: Harvard University Press, 1964.

_____. They Remember America: The Story of the Repatriated Greek-Americans. Berkeley and Los Angeles: University of California Press, 1956.

Silberman, Charles E. Crisis in the Classroom: The Remaking of American Education. New York: Random House; Vintage Books, 1970.

Sophocles, S. M. A History of Greece. Thessaloniki, Greece: Institute for Balkan Studies, 1961.

Spencer, Terrence. Fair Greece Sad Relic. London: Weidenfeld and Nicolson, 1954.

Spurlock, Clark. Education and the Supreme Court. Urbana: University of Illinois Press, 1955.

Stead, William T. If Christ Came to Chicago. London: Review of Reviews, 1894.

Stephanides, Basil K. Ecclesiastiki historia (Ecclesiastical history). Athens: Astir, 1948.

Stonequist, Everett V. A Study in Personality and Culture Conflict. New York: Russel and Russel, 1961.

Tavuchis, Nicholas. Family and Mobility among Second Generation Greek-Americans. Athens: National Centre for Social Research, 1972.

Thompson, Ariadne. The Octagonal Heart. Indianapolis, Ind.: Bobbs-Merrill Company, 1956.

Thompson, Frank V. Schooling of the Immigrant. New York: Harper and Brothers, 1920.

Vacalopoulos, Apostolos E. Origins of the Greek Nation, 1204-1461. New Brunswick, N. J.: Rutgers University Press, 1970.

Vardoulakis, Mary. Gold in the Streets. New York: Dodd, Mead and Company, 1945.

Vasiliev, A. A. History of the Byzantine Empire 324-1453. Madison: University of Wisconsin Press, 1952.

Vlachos, Evangelos C. The Assimilation of Greeks in the United States with Special Reference to the Greek Community of Anderson, Indiana. Athens: National Centre for Social Research, 1968.

Walton, Clyde C., ed. An Illinois Reader. DeKalb, Ill.: Northern Illinois University Press, 1970.

Ware, Caroline F., ed. The Cultural Approach to History. New York: Columbia University Press, 1940.

Ware, Timothy. Eustratios Argenti: A Study of the Greek Church under Turkish Rule. Oxford: Clarendon, Press, 1964.

_____. The Orthodox Church. Baltimore: Penguin Books, 1963.

Warner, W. Lloyd, and Hunt, Paul S. The Status System of a Modern Community. Yankee City Series, vol. 2. New Haven: Yale University Press, 1942.

Warner, W. Lloyd, and Srole, Leo. The Social Systems of American Ethnic Groups. Yankee City Series, vol. 3. New Haven: Yale University Press, 1945.

Wendt, Lloyd, and Kogan, Herman. Bosses in Lusty Chicago. Bloomington, Ind.: Indiana University Press, 1967.

Wirth, Louis. The Ghetto. Chicago: University of Chicago Press, Phoenix Books, 1956.

Woodhouse, C. M. The Greek War of Independence in its Historical Setting. London: Hutchinson's University Library, 1952.

_____. A Short History of Modern Greece. New York: Frederick A. Praeger Publishers, 1968.

Xenides, J. P. The Greeks in America. New York: George H. Doran Company, 1922.

Young, Ella Flagg. Isolation in the School. Chicago: University of Chicago Press, 1901.

Young, Kenneth. The Greek Passion: A Study in People and Politics. London: J. M. Dent and Sons, 1969.

Ziogas, Elias K. O Hellenismos tis Amerikis avtos o agnostos (Hellenism in America: the unknown factor). New York: n. p., 1958.

Zoustis, Basil T. O en Ameriki Hellenismos kai e drasis avtou (The Greeks in America and their activity). New York: D. C. Divry, 1954.

Articles

Abbott, Grace. "A Study of the Greeks in Chicago." American Journal of Sociology 15 (November 1909): 379-93.

Addams, Jane. "Recent Immigration: A Field Neglected by the Scholars." Educational Review 29 (March 1905): 253-54.

Balk, Helen H. "Economic Contributions of the Greeks to the United States." Economic Geography 19 (1943): 273.

Bardis, Panos. "Main Features of the Greek Family During the Early Twentieth Century." Alpha Kappa Deltan 26 (1956): 17-21.

"Blueprint for Greek-American Education." Athene 24 (Summer 1963): 93-95.

Botsas, E. N. "Emigration and Capital Formation: The Case of Greece." Balkan Studies 10 (1969): 127-34.

Broom, Leonard, and Kitsuse, John. "The Validation of Acculturation: A Condition to Ethnic Assimilation." American Anthropologist 57 (February 1955): 44-48.

Calvert, Walter D. "When Parochial Schools Failed." Christian Century 74 (13 November 1957): 1349-50.

Campisi, Paul J. "Ethnic Family Patterns: The Italian Family in the United States." American Journal of Sociology 53 (January 1948): 443-46.

Carlson, Robert A. "Americanization as an Early Twentieth Century Adult Education Movement." History of Education Quarterly 10 (Winter 1970): 440-64.

Chaconas, Stephen G. "The Jefferson-Korais Correspondence." Journal of Modern History 14 (March 1942): 64-70.

Coleman, James S. "Social and Cultural Integration and Educational Policy." In Rethinking Urban Education, pp. 125-32. Edited by Herbert J. Walberg and Andrew T. Kopan. San Francisco: Jossey-Bass Publishers, 1972.

Constant, Theodore N. "Greek-American Colonies, Churches, and Schools in the United States." Athene 12 (Spring 1951): 33-36.

Constant, Theodore N. "Racial Prejudice and the Greek Stock in the United States." Athene 5 (1944): 8-11.

Counelis, James Steve, and Kopan, Andrew T. "Chicago--Bastion of Orthodoxy: The Story of Saints Constantine and Helen." Athene 16 (Summer 1955): 17-31.

Cremin, Lawrence A. "The Progressive Movement in American Education: A Perspective." Harvard Educational Review 27 (Fall 1957): 251-70.

Danielides, Demosthenes. E neoelleniki koinonia kai oikonomia (Modern Greek society and economy). Athens: G. Samaropoulos, 1934.

Davidson, Thomas. "The Present Condition of Greece." International Review 6 (June 1879): 597-615.

Doukas, K. A. "Agrarian Reform in Greece." American Journal of Economics and Sociology 5 (1945): 79-92.

Doukas, Kimon A. "The Story of AHEPA." Athene 11 (Summer 1950): 39-43.

Earle, Edward M. "American Interest in the Greek Cause, 1821-1827." American Historical Review 33 (October 1927): 44-63.

Erickson, Donald A. "On the Role of Non-public Schools." School Review 69 (Autumn 1961): 348-49.

_____. "The Plain People vs. the Common Schools." Saturday Review, 19 November 1966, pp. 85-87ff.

"The First Conference of Greek Women at Boston." Orthodox Observer 1 (September 1935): 3-4.

Francis, E. K. "The Nature of the Ethnic Group." American Journal of Sociology 52 (1946-47): 393-400.

Glazer, Nathan. "The Integration of American Immigrants." Law and Contemporary Problems 21 (Spring 1956): 256-83.

Graves, Wallace. "Public Secondary Education in Greece." The High School Journal 45 (May 1962): 329-34.

Greer, Colin. "Public Schools and the Myth of the Melting Pot." Saturday Review, 15 November 1969, pp. 84-86ff.

Hansen, Marcus Lee. "The History of American Immigration as a Field of Research." American Historical Review 24 (May 1926-27): 609-42.

Havighurst, Robert J. "The Acculturation Process." In Education and Acculturation in Modern Urban Society, pp. 1-15. Edited by Ernest V. Anderson and Walter B. Kolesnik. Detroit: University of Detroit Press, 1965.

Hill, Howard C. "The Americanization Movement." American Journal of Sociology 24 (May 1919): 609-42.

Johannis, Philipos. "Public Instruction in Modern Greece." American Journal of Education 12 (1862): 571-72.

Kazamias, Andreas M. "The Style of Educational Change in Greece." Phi Delta Kappan 43 (November 1961): 69-74.

Kopan, Andrew T. "Melting Pot: Myth or Reality." In Cultural Pluralism, pp. 37-55. Edited by Edgar G. Epps. Berkeley, Calif.: McCutchan Publishing Corporation, 1974.

Kourvetaris, George A. "First and Second Generation Greeks in Chicago: An Inquiry in their Stratification and Mobility Patterns." International Review of Sociology 1 (March 1971): 37-47.

Lauquier, Capanidou. "Culture Change Among Three Generations of Greeks." American Catholic Sociological Review 22 (1961): 224.

Lazerson, Marvin. "Revisionism and American Educational History." Harvard Educational Review 43 (May 1973): 269-83.

McCaul, Robert L. "Dewey's Chicago." School Review 47 (Summer 1959): 258-80.

Mercer, Blaine E. "Some Notes on the Concepts of Education and Socialization." Journal of Teacher Education 4 (December 1953): 269-80.

Michalaros, Demetrios. "1960: Jane Addams Centennial." Athene 21 (Autumn 1960): 3.

Murdock, George P. "The Cross-Cultural Survey." American Sociological Review 5 (June 1940): 361-70.

Newman, Fred M., and Oliver, Donald W. "Education and Community." Harvard Educational Review 37 (Winter 1967): 61-105.

Orphan, Constantine D. "Goodbye Greektown." Inland the Magazine of the Middle West, Spring 1963, pp. 20-23.

Papanikolas, Helen Zeese. "Toil and Rage in a New Land: The Greek Immigrants in Utah." Utah Historical Quarterly 38 (Spring 1970): 100-203.

Papantoniou, Demetrios. "Tha epizesi e glossa mas edo eis tin Ameriki?" (Will our language survive in America?) Orthodox Observer 1 (9 December 1934): 6-7.

Pappas, Christos. "To ergo ton scholeion mas." (The task of our schools). Orthodox Observer 1 (31 March 1935): 7-8.

Parker, Franklin. "A Golden Age in American Education: Chicago in the 1890's." School and Society 89 (25 March 1961): 146ff.

Perros, George P. "Officers of Greek Descent in the Union Navy, 1861-1865." Athene 24 (Autumn 1963): 12-14ff.

"Perspective of Greece: An Atlantic Supplement." Atlantic 195 (1955): 97-168.

Psathas, George. "Ethnicity, Social Class, and Adolescent Independence from Parental Control." American Sociological Review 22 (1957): 415-23.

Psomiades, H. J. "The Economic and Social Transformation of Modern Greece." Journal of International Affairs 19 (1965): 194-205.

Rice, Joseph M. "The Public Schools of Chicago and St. Paul." Forum 15 (March-August 1893): 200-215.

Rosen, Bernard C. "Race, Ethnicity and the Achievement Syndrome." American Sociological Review 24 (February 1959): 47-60.

Rossi, Peter H., and Rossi, Alice S. "Background Consequences of Parochial School Education." Harvard Educational Review 27 (Summer 1957): 171-99.

_____. "The Historical Roots of Parochial Schools in America." In Social Foundations of Education, pp. 310-313. Edited by Jonathan C. McLendon New York: Macmillan Company, 1966.

Sanders, Irwin T. "Greek Society in Transition." Balkan Studies 8 (1967): 317-32.

Schlesinger, Arthur M., Sr. "The Significance of Immigration in American History." American Journal of Sociology 27 (July 1921): 71-85.

Smith, Timothy L. "Immigrant Social Aspirations and American Education, 1880-1930." American Quarterly, Fall 1969, p. 523.

_____. "New Approaches to the History of Immigration in Twentieth Century America." American Historical Review 71 (October 1966): 1265-79.

Smith, Timothy L. "The Progressive Movement in American Education, 1880-1900." Harvard Educational Review 31 (Spring 1961): 168-93.

Stycos, J. Mayonne. "Community Cohesion Among the Greeks of Bridgetown." In Minority Problems, pp. 253-58. Edited by Arnold M. and Caroline B. Rose. New York: Harper and Row, 1964.

Theotokas, George. "Some Reflections on the Psychology of the Modern Greek." Link 1 (1938): 66-70.

Thomas, Alan M., Jr. "American Education and the Immigrant." Teachers College Record 55 (1953-54): 253-67.

Thompson, Maurice S. "Notes in Social and Economic Conditions in Greece." Sociological Review 6 (July 1913): 213-21.

Toennies, Ferdinand. "Gemeinschaft and Gesellschaft." In Theories of Society, 2: 191-201. Edited by Talcott Parsons et al. New York: Free Press of Glencoe, 1961.

Treudley, Mary Bosworth. "Formal Organization and the Americanization Process with Special Reference to the Greeks of Boston." American Sociological Review 14 (February 1949): 44-53.

Valaoras, Vasilios G. "The Stand of Science and Education in Greece." Hellenic Review 2 (November 1960): 16.

Walker, Natalie. "Chicago Housing Conditions. X Greek and Italians in the Neighborhood of Hull House." American Journal of Sociology 21 (November 1915): 286.

Weber, Max. "Ethnic Groups." In Theories of Society, 2: 305-8. Edited by Talcott Parsons et al. New York: Free Press of Glencoe, 1961.

Wheeler, Benjamin I. "The Modern Greek as a Fighting Man." North American Review 164 (April 1897): 609-16.

Wirth, Louis. "The Problem of Minority Groups." In Theories of Society, 2: 309-14. Edited by Talcott Parsons et al. New York: Free Press of Glencoe, 1961.

Wish, Harvey. "Governor Altgeld Pardons the Anarchists." Journal of the Illinois Historical Society 31 (December 1938): 162-72.

_____. "The Pullman Strike: A Study in Industrial Warfare." Journal of the Illinois State Historical Society 32 (September 1939): 288-312.

Xydis, Stephen G. "Diplomatic Relations between the United States and Greece, 1868-1878." Balkan Studies 5 (1964): 47-62.

Young, Pauline V. "Social Problems in the Education of the Immigrant Child." American Sociological Review 1 (June 1936): 419-29.

Proceedings, Reports, Yearbooks, and Bulletins

Board of Education. Proceedings of the Board of Education. Chicago: Board of Education, 1906-10; 1914-15.

_____. Annual Report of the Superintendent of Schools. Chicago: Board of Education, 1859-60; 1869-70; 1879-80; 1900-1901; 1903-5; 1907-9; 1910-11; 1912-17.

Dewey, John. "Nationalizing Education." Addresses and Proceedings of the National Education Association 54 (1916): 184-85.

_____. "The School as a Social Center." Proceedings of the National Education Association 41 (1902): 374-83.

Erickson, Donald A., and Greeley, Andrew M. "Non-Public Schools and Metropolitanism." Metropolitanism: Its Challenges to Education, in Sixty-seventh Yearbook of the National Society for the Study of Education, pt. 1. Chicago: University of Chicago Press, 1968.

Greek Orthodox Archdiocese of North and South America. Official Minutes of the Proceedings of the National Youth Conference of the Greek Orthodox Church in America. Chicago: n.p., 1951.

_____. Proceedings of the Tenth Clergy-Laity Congress. New York: Greek Orthodox Archdiocese, 1950.

_____. Proceedings of the Eleventh Clergy-Laity Congress. New York: Greek Orthodox Archdiocese, 1952.

_____. Proceedings of the Sixteenth Biennial Clergy-Laity Congress. New York: Greek Orthodox Archdiocese, 1962.

_____. Proceedings of the Twentieth Biennial Clergy-Laity Congress. New York: Greek Orthodox Archdiocese, 1970.

_____. Yearbooks. New York: Greek Orthodox Archdiocese, 1955; 1958; 1962-68; 1970-72.

341

Hull House. Hull-House Bulletin (later changed to Yearbook). Chicago:
Hull-House, 1901-4; 1906-7; 1912-13; 1915-16; 1920-21; 1926-29;
1930-31.

Immigrants' Protective League. Annual Report. Chicago: The League,
1909-12; 1913; 1915-17; 1930.

Johnston, Shepherd. "Historical Sketches of the Public School System of
Chicago." Twenty-fifth Annual Report of the Chicago Board of
Education for the Year Ending July 31, 1879. Chicago: Clark and
Edwards, 1880.

Orthodox Christian Education Commission. Bulletin of Orthodox Christian
Education. Nyack, N. Y.: The Commission, January 1957; Winter
1961.

Report of the Educational Commission of the City of Chicago. Chicago:
University of Chicago Press, 1900.

Setton, Kenneth. "The Byzantine Background of the Italian Renaissance."
Proceedings of the American Philosophical Society 100 (February 1956):
1-78.

Yearbook of the Saint Constantine Church and Koraes School. Chicago:
n. p., 1936.

Public Documents

Annals of Congress, 1789-1824. Washington, D. C.: Government Printing
Office, 1834-1856. Vols. 40, 41.

Kingdom of Greece. Ephemeris tis kyberniseos tou basileiou tis Hellados
(Government newspaper of the kingdom of Greece). No. 182
(24 October 1964).

U. S. Congress. House. Hearings Before the President's Commission on
Immigration and Naturalization. 82d Cong., 2d sess., 1952.

_____. Senate. Abstracts of the Reports of the Immigration Commission.
S. Doc. 747, 61st Cong., 3rd sess., 1911, vols. 1, 2.

_____. Senate. Reports of the Immigration Commission. S. Doc. 749,
61st Cong., 3rd sess., 1911. The Children of Immigrants in Schools,
vol. 2.

U. S. Department of Commerce. Bureau of the Census. Abstract of the Twelfth Census of the United States 1900.

_____. Abstract of the Fourteenth Census of the United States 1920.

_____. Abstract of the Fifteenth Census of the United States 1930.

_____. Abstract of the Sixteenth Census of the United States 1940.

_____. Decennial Censuses from 1890 through 1970.

_____. Historical Statistics of the United States: Colonial Times to 1957. Washington, D. C.: Government Printing Office, 1961.

_____. Immigrants and Their Children, 1920, by Niles Carpenter. Census Monograph Series. Washington, D. C.: Government Printing Office, 1927.

_____. Immigrants and Their Children, 1850-1950, by E. P. Hutchinson. Census Monograph Series. Washington, D. C.: Government Printing Office, 1956.

_____. Nativity and Parentage of the White Population 1940.

_____. Special Reports, 1950: Population, vol. 4.

_____. Statistical Abstract of the United States, 1965; 1971.

_____. United States Summary, General Social and Economic Characteristics, Final Report PC (1)-C1. Washington, D. C.: Government Printing Office, 1972.

U. S. Department of Justice. Immigration and Naturalization Service. Annual Reports of the Commissioner of Naturalization, 1918; 1923-32; 1944; 1952; 1960.

U. S. Department of Labor. Bureau of Immigration. Annual Report of the Commissioner-General of Immigration, 1910; 1920.

_____. Bureau of Naturalization. Citizenship Training of Adult Immigrants in the United States. Washington, D. C.: Government Printing Office, 1925.

U. S. Office of Education. Education in Italy and Greece. Washington, D. C.: Government Printing Office, 1883.

U. S. Office of Education. Report of the Commissioner of Education for the Year 1896-97. "Education in Greece," by Daniel Quinn, vol. 1. Washington, D. C.: Government Printing Office, 1898.

U. S. Department of State. Papers Relating to the Foreign Relations of the United States, vols. 1, 3. Washington, D. C.: Government Printing Office, 1861-.

Newspapers

American Hellenic Review (Chicago), 20 June; 21 November 1925.

American Hellenic World (Chicago), 28 March 1925; 2, 30 April 1927; 13 July 1928.

Atlantis (New York), 12 July; 17 December 1908; 14 January 1909; 2 September 1927.

Chicago Chronicle, 27 December 1903.

Chicago Daily Journal, 22 April 1924; 31 December 1925; 31 December 1926.

Chicago Daily News, 22 April 1924; 25 March 1926; 29 May 1959; 26 August 1970.

Chicago Herald, 10 May 1887.

Chicago Herald and Examiner, 5, 6 November 1927; 2 May 1939.

Chicago Record, 13 December 1899.

Chicago Sun-Times, 14 July 1951.

Chicago Today, 13 December 1973.

Chicago Tribune, 20, 26 April 1893; 7 April 1895; 15, 16, 18, 21 February 1897; 21, 22 February 1911; 10 October 1912; 27 September 1913; 16 November 1969; 5 July; 23 October 1970; 13 January 1971; 8 July 1973.

Eleutheros Typos (Chicago), 31 July 1943.

Ethnikos Kyrix (New York), 16 July 1961.

Greek Press (Chicago), 18 December 1929 through 5 July 1974.

Greek Star (Chicago), 8 March 1904 through 11 July 1974.

Hellenic Chronicle (Boston), 24 February; 7 December 1972; 25 October 1973.

Hellenic Free Press (Chicago), 15 March 1961.

Kathemerini (Chicago), 18 April 1929; 2, 6 April 1931.

Loxias (Chicago), 12 February; 21 May; 4 June; 15 October 1910; 4 March 1911.

New York Times, 14 August 1921; 2 July; 14 August 1930; 1 September 1957.

Proodos (Chicago), 5, 12 October 1932.

Saloniki (Chicago), 14 February 1914 through 9 August 1930.

Saloniki Greek Press (Chicago), 12 December 1931.

Virginia Gazette (Williamsburg), 29 September; 6 October 1768.

Albums, Guides, and Pamphlets

E semasia tou Hellenikou scholeiou. (The significance of the Greek school).
   New York: Greek Orthodox Archdiocese of North and South America,
   n. d.

Emmanuel, Philippos D.   Course of Study Prescribed for the Greek-American
   Elementary Schools. New York: Greek Orthodox Archdiocese, 1958.

Fiftieth Anniversary, Reverend Daniel Gambrilis, Golden Jubilee, Chicago,
   n. p., 1961.

For Better Teaching: Teacher Training Manual for Orthodox Church Schools.
   Nyack, N. Y.: Orthodox Christian Education Commission, 1959.

Forty Years of Greek Life in Chicago, 1897-1937. Chicago: Aristotle
   Damianos, 1937.

"An Outline of the Aims and Program of Archdiocesan Education." New York:
   Greek Orthodox Archdiocese of North and South America, n. d.

Plato School of the Assumption Greek Orthodox Church Album. Chicago:
   n. p., 1962.

A Program of Adult Education in the Greek Orthodox Church. New York: Greek
   Orthodox Archdiocese, Department of Laity, 1967.

Saint Constantine Church 1909-1959, Golden Anniversary Album. Chicago: Norman King Company, 1959.

Thirty-fifth Anniversary Album of the Assumption Church. Chicago: Community Life, 1960.

Whitman, Cedric H. The Vitality of the Greek Language and Its Importance Today. New York: Greek Orthodox Archdiocese, 1954.

Unpublished Materials

Theses and Dissertations

Allswang, John M. "The Political Behavior of Chicago's Ethnic Groups, 1918-1932." Ph.D. dissertation, University of Pittsburgh, 1967.

Beck, John M. "Chicago Newspapers and the Public Schools, 1890-1920." Ph.D. dissertation, University of Chicago, 1953.

Beeson, Kenneth H., Jr. "New Smyrna Colony." Master's thesis, University of Florida, 1959.

Bell, John Wesley. "The Development of the Public High School in Chicago." Ph.D. dissertation, University of Chicago, 1939.

Eikos, Constance. "Greek Institutions in Chicago." Master's thesis, Roosevelt University, 1966.

Campisi, Paul J. "A Scale for the Measurement of Acculturation." Ph.D. dissertation, University of Chicago, 1947.

Chaney, Florence J. "The Social and Educational Protection of the Immigrant Girl in Chicago." Master's thesis, University of Chicago, 1912.

Chock, Phyllis Pease. "Greek-American Ethnicity." Ph.D. dissertation, University of Chicago, 1969.

Constantacoulos, George K. "Economic Development of Greece in the Post War Setting." Ph.D. dissertation, Columbia University, 1963.

Corovilles, Theodora I. "The Church School Movement of the Hellenic Eastern Orthodox Church in America." Master's thesis, McCormick Theological Seminary, 1933.

Costantakos, Chrysie M. "American Greek Subculture: Processes of Continuity." Ph.D. dissertation, Columbia University, 1969.

Coutsoumaris, George. "Possibilities of Economic Development in Greek Agriculture." Ph.D. dissertation, University of Chicago, 1953.

Cressey, Paul F. "The Succession of Cultural Groups in the City of Chicago." Ph. D. dissertation, University of Chicago, 1930.

DeBoer, Peter P. "A History of the Early Compulsory School Attendance Legislation in the State of Illinois." Ph.D. dissertation, University of Chicago, 1967.

Erickson, Donald A. "Differential Effects of Public and Sectarian Schooling on the Religiousness of the Child." Ph.D. dissertation, University of Chicago, 1962.

Farquhar, Robin H. "Public School Administrators' Perceptions of Nonpublic School Effects on Public Schools." Ph.D. dissertation, University of Chicago, 1967.

Halley, Helen. "A Historical Functional Approach to the Study of the Greek Community of Tarpon Springs." Ph.D. dissertation, Columbia University, 1953.

Hill, Peter Jensen. "The Economic Impact of Immigration into the United States." Ph.D. dissertation, University of Chicago, 1970.

Klement, Andrew. "The History of the Development of Plato School of the Greek Orthodox Church of the Assumption." Master's thesis, DePaul University, 1961.

Lovgren, Mary Margaret. "The Chicago Board of Education Classes in Americanization." Master's thesis, Chicago Teachers College, 1942.

Merrill, Bertha Lititia. "Methods of Assimilating Immigrants." Master's thesis, University of Chicago, 1916.

Mistaras, Evangeline. "A Study of First and Second Generation Greek Out-Marriages in Chicago." Master's thesis, University of Chicago, 1950.

Natsoulas, Theodore. "Samuel Gridley Howe: An American Philhellene." Master's thesis, University of Chicago, 1966.

Phee, Veronica. "A Study of the Dante Elementary School for Adults." Master's thesis, DePaul University, 1946.

Rontos, Katherine. "The Study of the Development of the Americanization Program of the Chicago Board of Education." Master's thesis, DePaul University, 1957.

Scourby, Alice. "Third Generation Greek Americans: A Study in Religious
Attitudes." Ph.D. dissertation, New School for Social Research,
1967.

Seaman, Paul D. "Modern Greek and American English in Contact: A Socio-
linguistic Investigation of Greek-American Bilingualism in Chicago."
Ph.D. dissertation, Indiana University, 1965.

Theodoratus, Robert James. "The Influence of the Homeland on the Social
Organization of a Greek Community in America." Ph.D. dissertation,
University of Washington, 1961.

Thurner, Arthur W. "The Impact of Ethnic Groups on the Democratic Party in
Chicago 1920-1928." Ph.D. dissertation, University of Chicago, 1966.

Tostberg, Robert E. "Educational Ferment in Chicago, 1883-1904." Ph.D.
dissertation, University of Wisconsin, 1961.

Weinberger, Helen. "A Study of the Assimilation of Foreign-born Greeks in
Cincinnati, Ohio." Master's thesis, University of Cincinnati, 1942.

Wilson, William Patterson. "The History and Development of the Public Adult
Education Program in Chicago." Ph.D. dissertation, University of
California, 1948.

Wirth, Louis. "The Ghetto: A Study in Isolation." Ph.D. dissertation,
University of Chicago, 1926.

Wish, Harvey. "The Administration of Governor John Peter Altgeld of Illinois,
1893-1897." Ph.D. dissertation, Northwestern University, 1936.

Yeracaris, Constantine A. "A Study of the Voluntary Associations of the
Greek Immigrants of Chicago from 1890 to 1948, with Special Emphasis
on World War II and Post War Period." Master's thesis, University
of Chicago, 1950.

Minutes

Assumption Greek Orthodox Church (Chicago). Minutes of Meetings of the
Board of Trustees, 1924; 1925-29; 1937; 1949-58.

Holy Trinity Greek Orthodox Church (Chicago). Minutes of Socrates School
Board, 1917-26; 1935-46; 1955-62.

Saint Andrew Greek Orthodox Church (Chicago). Minutes of Meetings of the
Board of Trustees, 1935-39.

Saints Constantine and Helen Greek Orthodox Church (Chicago). Proceedings of the General Assemblies, 1911-20; 1921-27.

_____. Minutes of Meetings of the Board of Trustees, 1913-33; 1945-49.

_____. Minutes of Koraes School Board, 1919-23; 1933-42; 1951-59; 1961-66.

Saint Demetrios Greek Orthodox Church (Chicago). Minutes of Meetings of the Board of Trustees, 1927-29.

Saint George Greek Orthodox Church (Chicago). Minutes of Meetings of the Board of Trustees, 1923-27.

Interviews

Andronis, Constantine. Chicago. Interview, 26 October 1967.

Angelopoulos, Aris. Chicago. Interview, 23 April 1973.

Argoe, Kostis T. Chicago. Interview, 21 July 1971.

Beeson, Kenneth H., Jr. Saint Augustine, Florida. Interview, 23 July 1968.

Besbekos, Angelo. Chicago. Interview, 15 August 1968.

Bishop Timothy (Haloftis). Chicago. Interview, 30 January 1972.

Block, Henrietta. Chicago. Interview, 3 April 1968.

Chakinis, Thomas. River Forest, Illinois. Interview, 23 May 1968; 1 October 1969.

Chamalas, Peter. Chicago. Interview, 2 April 1968.

Chiaculas, Peter J. Chicago. Interview, 12 June 1970.

Christoplis, Bessie. Chicago. Interview, 5 May 1968.

Chunis, Frances. Chicago. Interview, 8 November 1971.

Collias, Aristotle. Chicago. Interview, 24 July 1969; 25 February 1971.

Damolaris, George. Chicago. Interview, 21 May 1968; 15 August 1968.

Demos, Paul. Chicago. Interview, 19 July 1970.

Diamantis, John. Chicago. Interview, 25 April 1973.

Drossos, George. Chicago. Interview, 17 November 1967.

Economakos, Chrysostom, Reverend. Chicago. Interview, 5 October 1973.

Eliakopoulos, Elizabeth. Chicago. Interview, 19 February 1971.

Ellis, Nicholas. Chicago. Interview, 29 July 1970.

Gallanis, James. Evanston, Illinois. Interview, 22 June 1968.

Georgopoulos, Helen. Chicago. Interview, 8 July 1973.

Geroulis, James. Chicago. Interview, 25 January 1968.

Glynos, Constantine J. Oak Lawn, Illinois. Interview, 10 December 1971.

Grieg, Mary E. Chicago. Interview, 14 February 1972.

Haniades, Basil, Reverend. Chicago. Interview, 23 July 1971.

Javaras, Voula. Chicago. Interview, 21 March 1970.

Kalogeras, Chris G. Chicago. Interview, 4 December 1967.

Kolias, John. Chicago. Interview, 15 April 1968.

Kollias, Gus. Chicago. Interview, 12 October 1970.

Koulogeorge, James A. Northbrook, Illinois. Interview, 15 December 1971.

Lembesis, Demetra. Chicago. Interview, 28 September 1967.

Louris, George. Chicago. Interview, 21 August 1973.

Lussenhop, Raymond. Chicago. Interview, 9 August 1970.

Macropoulos, Tom. Chicago. Interview, 6 October 1968.

Manta, John L. Chicago. Interview, 2 October 1967.

Mehos, Katherine. Chicago. Interview, 5 May 1968.

Michalaros, Ellie. Chicago. Interview, 28 November 1967.

Mihalakis, Constantine. Chicago. Interview, 28 April 1968.

Nestor, James, Reverend. Chicago. Interview, 4 October 1967.

Nomikos, Nikitas. Chicago. Interview, 8 July 1967.

Oettershagen, Elizabeth. Chicago. Interview, 23 September 1969.

Orfanos, Catherine. Chicago. Interview, 3 August 1969.

Orphan, Becky C. Chicago. Interview, 17 October 1970; 11 February 1972.

Orphanos, Pericles. Chicago. Interview, 21 May 1968; 7 September 1968.

Papoulias, Constantine. Chicago. Interview, 10 September 1969.

Pappadopoulos, John. Chicago. Interview, 15 May 1968.

Pappas, George N. Chicago. Interview, 9 October 1969.

Pappas, John T. Chicago. Interview, 21 August 1968.

Pappas, Theophilus A. Chicago. Interview, 28 October 1970.

Parpadis, Pantelis. Chicago. Interview, 13 July 1971.

Parry, Dimitri. Chicago. Interview, 1 July 1971.

Paziotopoulos, James A. Chicago. Interview, 8 March 1968.

Petrakis, Stella. Chicago. Interview, 10 October 1967; 12 February 1968.

Philippidis, Nicholas. Chicago. Interview, 3 June 1973.

Polites, Elias K. Chicago. Interview, 25 March 1968; 14 November 1970; 20 August 1973.

Porikos, George. Chicago. Interview, 25 August 1967.

Poulos, Alexandra. Chicago. Interview, 19 September 1969.

Poulos, Helen. Chicago. Interview, 3 September 1968.

Pulos, George. Chicago. Interview, 2 April 1968.

Rexinis, Theano. Chicago. Interview, 23 July 1970.

Rifakes, Maria. Chicago. Interview, 7 November 1967.

Robinson, Otho M. Chicago. Interview, 3 May 1973.

Roussos, George, Reverend. New York City. Interview, 17 March 1972.

Russis, William J. Chicago. Interview, 31 July 1971.

Sakellariou, Esther. Chicago. Interview, 2 July 1973.

Soter, S. D. Chicago. Interview, 12 October 1967.

Spirakes, Gus. Chicago. Interview, 2 May 1970.

Spirides, Bessie. Chicago. Interview, 18 July 1968.

Stamas, Barbara. River Forest, Illinois. Interview, 3 August 1970.

Thalassinos, Theodore, Reverend. Oak Park, Illinois. Interview, 4 October 1969.

Trikorfa, Pan Arcadian Federation of America. Oak Park, Illinois. Interviews with select members at meeting, 5 June 1970.

Tripodis, Demetra. Chicago. Interview, 2 July 1970.

Tsatos, Constantine. Chicago. Interview, 15 April 1968.

Valone, Katherine. Oak Lawn, Illinois. Interview, 14 September 1971.

Vrame, Charlotte. Chicago. Interview, 26 July 1969.

Weble, Helen. Chicago. Interview, 31 July 1968.

Yalouris, Joachim, Reverend. Chicago. Interview, 10 January 1969.